THE VALUE SPHERE

The Corporate Executives' Handbook for
Creating and Retaining Shareholder Wealth

4th Edition

THE VALUE SPHERE

The Corporate Executives' Handbook for
Creating and Retaining Shareholder Wealth

4th Edition

John Boquist
Indiana University of Bloomington, USA

Todd Milbourn
Washington University in St Louis, USA

Anjan Thakor
Washington University in St Louis, USA

World Scientific

NEW JERSEY · LONDON · SINGAPORE · BEIJING · SHANGHAI · HONG KONG · TAIPEI · CHENNAI

Published by

World Scientific Publishing Co. Pte. Ltd.

5 Toh Tuck Link, Singapore 596224

USA office: 27 Warren Street, Suite 401-402, Hackensack, NJ 07601

UK office: 57 Shelton Street, Covent Garden, London WC2H 9HE

Library of Congress Cataloging-in-Publication Data
Boquist, John A.
 The value sphere : the corporate executive, handbook for creating and retaining
shareholder wealth / John A. Boquist, Todd T. Milbourn, Anjan V. Thakor. -- 4th ed.
  p. cm.
 Includes bibliographical references and index.
 ISBN-13 978-981-4277-96-9
 ISBN-10 981-4277-96-7
 1. Industrial management. 2. Corporations--Finance. 3. Corporations--Valuation.
I. Title. II. Milbour, Todd T. III. Thakor, Anjan V.
 HD31 .B6195 2010

2009499347

British Library Cataloguing-in-Publication Data
A catalogue record for this book is available from the British Library.

First published 2010
Reprinted 2011

Typeset by Stallion Press
Email: enquiries@stallionpress.com

Printed in Singapore by World Scientific Printers.

CONTENTS

ACKNOWLEDGMENTS

This book is the outcome of many years of research, teaching, and consulting. The people whose insights contributed to the development of the ideas in this book are far too numerous to mention. Our own research and that of others have been the genesis of these ideas.

Our experiences in working with corporations such as Whirlpool, RR Donnelley, Diebold, Ingersoll-Rand, Borg-Warner Automotive, Heineken, Reuters, Anheuser-Busch, Eli Lilly, Procter & Gamble, Rolls-Royce, and others have helped to shape and refine the ideas. The constant probing by participants in our executive education programs and our MBA and Ph.D. students also deserves mention.

We are very grateful to Kathy Frye whose tireless efforts in typing the initial manuscript and giving us her feedback on improving it as we progressed were extremely valuable. It would have been difficult to produce this book without Kathy's contribution. We would also like to thank Marianne Inman for her hard work in producing the second and third editions of this book, and Christine Hatina for all of her efforts with the third edition.

OVERVIEW

In Chapter 1, Jerry begins to first think about opening his own lemonade business. This causes him to learn about how firms create a distinctive competitive advantage through strategy. He is also introduced to the key concept of the Value Sphere.

Jerry begins his corporate journey in Chapter 2 by opening his first store. He also decides to learn about finance by attending a course at the local university.

The business soon takes off and in Chapter 3, Jerry takes the firm public through an IPO (Initial Public Offering).

As he quickly realizes, the game changes when one taps the public financial markets. Chapter 4 discusses the problems that arise when a firm like Jerry's relies on external financing and how these can be addressed.

In Chapters 5 and 6, Jerry begins to learn how shareholder value can evaporate owing to poor decisions and how this can disrupt the management of the Value Sphere. To minimize potential evaporation of value, the conceptualization of the business strategy and its execution must be right.

As the business grows, Jerry is faced with a variety of new risks. Chapter 7 discusses the relationship between risk and value.

The issue of capturing the risk of a business in a meaningful way is addressed in Chapter 8. There, Jerry learns how risk affects the cost of capital employed in the business.

Chapter 9 presents the criteria Jerry should use to decide which projects should receive this "costly" capital. Jerry then worries about how to judge the actual performance of projects after they are undertaken.

In Chapter 10, he is given a detailed exposure to Economic Profit (or Economic Value Added). This is a popular performance measure.

Chapter 11 presents a summary of the variety of performance measures that firms use, and examines their relative merits.

The measurement system Jerry chooses to employ, based on this comparison, is presented in Chapter 12.

With the right set of performance criteria in place to judge both new and old projects, Jerry sets out in Chapter 13 to design a world-class system for allocating capital resources.

Building on this, Chapter 14 adds to the process a new way to think about capital investments in high-risk, high-payoff projects. This is using a real-options approach to project valuation.

Jerry now has a very sophisticated resource allocation system, but is unsure about his employees' skills in using the system. In Chapter 15, Jerry introduces a managerial training course to provide his managers with the necessary skills to run the new resource allocation system successfully.

Jerry tackles a new set of investment problems in the next four chapters. In Chapter 16, Jerry wonders whether there is an efficient way to use a portfolio approach to project selection. That is, an approach whereby all investment proposals are viewed as a portfolio, rather than viewing each project as a tub on its own bottom.

In Chapter 17, Jerry decides to investigate the pros and cons of the company initiating a dividend payment. He considers doing this as part of a synchronized Value Sphere.

The issue of optimal capital structure is taken up in Chapter 18, as Jerry wonders if the company has so much debt that it might be in financial peril.

Jerry gives further shape to his ambition in Chapter 19 as he proceeds to acquire another firm. This makes him confront issues such as firm valuation and post-acquisition integration.

This acquisition generates a flood of new ideas and also forces Jerry in Chapter 20 to think about how resource allocation tools could be applied to non-traditional projects like investments in marketing and managerial training.

In Chapter 21, Jerry develops a framework for seamlessly integrating the newly acquired company into his own. In the process, he develops a systematic approach to post-acquisition integration.

With the passage of the Sarbanes-Oxley Act in 2002, Jerry wrestles with corporate governance in Chapter 22 and wonders about the wisdom of having taken the company public.

The design of an effective executive compensation at Jerry's is discussed in Chapter 23. Jerry is interested in both the theory of executive compensation as well as its practice.

The issues of how to manage in tough times and how to remain innovative are taken up in Chapter 24. The key success principles and tensions are examined.

As we close in Chapter 25, Jerry brings all the concepts of organizational culture, resource-allocation systems, and compensation systems together under one strategic vision. He has created a lasting enterprise with a well-synchronized Value Sphere.

ABOUT THE AUTHORS

John A. Boquist is the Edward E. Edwards Professor of Finance in the Kelley School of Business at Indiana University. His areas of expertise include corporation finance, financial strategy and analysis, and banking and investments. John was the Project Director of a USAID grant to help managers and faculty members from Poland, Hungary, and the Czech Republic make the transition from a command economy to a market economy. He is an experienced teacher, researcher, consultant, and administrator. John has been a regular visiting faculty member at INSEAD since 1991. In 1994 John was recognized by *Business Week* magazine as one of the top 12 business school professors.

John is the co-author of a casebook and numerous research articles and papers. He is a frequent participant in national professional meetings as a paper presenter, as a paper discussant, and as a session chair. John also serves as a consultant in the areas of corporate finance, financial policy and strategy, public utility regulation, and litigation testimony.

John Boquist holds an undergraduate degree in Industrial Engineering from General Motors Institute and a MSc and PhD from Purdue University.

Todd T. Milbourn is a Professor of Finance and Finance Area Coordinator at the Olin Business School at Washington University in St. Louis. His research and teaching interests are generally centered on corporate finance topics, but he focuses his research primarily on issues of managerial compensation design, performance measurement, and capital budgeting schemes. He has published widely in various financial and managerial journals that span these topics. Todd has also consulted and lectured on advanced corporate finance issues for a variety of organizations, including several Fortune 500 and London-FTSE 100 companies, as well as several global investment banks and consultancy firms. Todd received his PhD in Finance at Indiana and holds a Bachelor of Arts degree from Augustana College, Illinois, where he majored in economics, mathematics, and finance. He has earned several school-wide awards for excellence in teaching at both Indiana University and Washington

University. Before joining the Olin School, Todd spent three years on the finance faculty of the London Business School and one year at the University of Chicago's Graduate School of Business.

Anjan V. Thakor received his PhD in Finance from Northwestern University. He has helped a broad range of organizations, including numerous Fortune 500 firms, navigate the complexities of financing, capital investment, and performance evaluation for strategic decision making. He has built a world-class reputation in corporate finance and banking as a researcher, consultant, and teacher. Anjan is the John E. Simon Professor of Finance and Senior Associate Dean at the Olin Business School at Washington University in St. Louis, where he designs and teaches courses in the PhD and MBA programs, as well as in executive education programs. He was previously the Edward J. Frey Professor of Banking and Finance and Chairperson of the Finance Area at the University of Michigan Business School. He has also served on the faculties of Indiana University, Northwestern University and UCLA. Anjan has served on the Nominating Committee for the Nobel Prize in Economics since 1993. A prolific author with over 100 publications to his credit, Anjan's other books include *Contemporary Financial Intermediation* (Dryden, 1995), and *Becoming a Better Value Creator: How to Improve Your Company's Bottom Line ... And Your Own* (Jossey-Bass, June 2000). Anjan Thakor has served as President of the Financial Intermediation Research Society (FIRS), managing editor for the *Journal of Financial Intermediation* and associate editor of several other financial journals.

Advance Praise for The Value Sphere

"*The Value Sphere* book was a revelation to me. The value concepts presented are so essential to business success I have asked my entire management team to read, study, and implement the lessons of the *Value Sphere*."

Bill Hunt, Chairman,
Former President and Chief Executive Officer
Arvin Industries, Inc.

"An important read for all companies, particularly for those in the Internet space. Successful companies better learn how to create value, and quickly, if they want to survive. This book provides the road map to show you how."

Jim Ritchie,
President and Chief Executive Officer
Transportation.com

"John, Todd and Anjan spin an engaging tale that actually makes the application of advanced value creation concepts interesting. Good job!"

Harry Burritt,
VP, Corporate Planning and Development
Whirlpool Corporation

"In *The Value Sphere: Secrets of Creating & Retaining Shareholder Wealth*, Professors Boquist, Milbourn and Thakor provide a conversational and leisurely, albeit comprehensive, sojourn through the world of corporate financial management. Accessibility is not achieved, however, at the sacrifice of content: All the obligatory topics are covered intuitively, along with more nuanced issues such as quality and real options. Practical problems are plumbed using the essential tools of finance in order to demonstrate the power of financial economics, and the delivery is what one would expect from master expositors. Boquist and Thakor are among the leading teachers of finance to executive audiences, and Milbourn, the junior partner of the team, is a gifted teacher in his own right. It shows! This book will serve well those coming anew at the bewildering finance issues that routinely confront a corporate board or a CFO."

Stuart Greenbaum,
Former Dean, Olin School of Business,
Washington University

"Superb … Supreme confidence and very, very solid in his subject matter. Excellent pace, energy and crisp in his teaching approach. Very talented person, very good teacher. The Value Sphere is a great book (I managed to get up to Chapter 12 during this course and it is a very well discussed account of basic finance and shareholder value concepts). I am confident the rest of this book will be as enlightening as the first 12 chapters. Recommended reading for every finance professional."

Participant in University of Michigan Business School
Executive Education Program: Corporate Financial Management, Hong Kong

"I am very impressed with the topics and writing. It seems to easily incorporate and summarize all of the concepts we have learned in the MBA program. It is very interesting reading indeed. I look forward to reading the rest of the book. I plan to recommend the book to my colleagues as Agilent Technologies when I begin my post-MBA career in July!"

S. Scott Smaistria, CPA, CMA, MBA

Directions for Risk-Strategist Demo

1. Insert Risk-Strategist Demo CD.
2. Using Microsoft Excel, open the Risk-Strategist Demo file.
3. Click, "Enable Macros."
4. To start the Risk-Strategist Demo, click on "File" and then "New" from the menu.

INTRODUCTION

On Wednesday, October 1, 1997, the Minnesota Timberwolves, a team from the National Basketball Association, announced that they had signed basketball player Kevin Garnett to a six-year contract extension worth $125 million. At the time, this was reported to be the richest package in professional sports.

Kevin Garnett was 21-years old then, and two years out of high school. In August 1997, he turned down a six-year, $103.5 million offer from the Timberwolves. The deal he accepted exceeded by $32 million the price owner Glen Taylor paid for the entire franchise in 1995.

At the press conference where the announcement was made, Garnett explained his decision to accept the new offer and his earlier decision to reject the previous offer by proclaiming, "It was never a money issue."

Well, this book is different. It is unabashedly about money. In fact, it is all about money. How to make it, and once it's made, how to prevent its senseless evaporation.

We will introduce you to a fellow named Jerry and then go along with him on his quest to grow a business from scratch into a large company. On the way, we will learn about the basic concepts of value creation, value evaporation and value retention, as well as the key concepts in finance and strategy.

We will also see the many ways in which corporations waste their wealth by misallocating their capital and other resources. Our focus will be on designing resource allocation systems that help to minimize the waste and maximize value retention. We believe that there is something of value in this for all those who want to learn how companies really create wealth in society and also for those who work in corporations where they are constantly frustrated by the enormous frictions created by needless conflict, turf battles, and systems that give rise to perverse incentives. In short, this is a book for everybody interested in business.

The book, organized as a novel, follows the growth of a hypothetical company from inception to maturity. We hope you enjoy this "novel" approach to finance and strategy.

Let's meet Jerry, our aspiring businessman, shall we?

Chapter 1

THE FIRM AND THE VALUE SPHERE: HOW DO WE MAXIMIZE THE CREATION AND RETENTION OF VALUE?

1. The Individual and the Firm

We are routinely inundated with news about exciting new growth companies and stellar mature firms that are earning astronomical returns on their investments. Perhaps the most celebrated picker of such firms is Warren Buffett, CEO of Berkshire Hathaway. *Money* magazine, in its August 2002 issue, reported,

> "But Buffett's strategy of buying and holding big growth stocks with strong franchises has paid off handsomely, with a compound annual return of 24%."

Many believe that one of the secrets of America's economic success is the environment it provides companies to flourish. Indeed, economic growth and national and individual prosperity are commonly viewed as being synonymous with the growth of companies, both mature and new.

But why are firms so important for economic growth?

That is actually a pretty deep question. So, let us step back and first ask: *What is a firm? Why do we need firms?*

Why we may need firms should become apparent when we answer this first question.

1.1. Jerry's lemonade stand

To think about this, suppose we have a fellow named Jerry who wants to go into business selling lemonade. He has got all sorts of dreams about his business growing into a national network of lemonade stands and related products with the name "Jerry's Lemonade, Inc." Sort of like Starbuck's Coffee.

But before Jerry invests a lot of his time and money in opening this firm, he must ask himself: "Why should anybody buy my lemonade?" After all, it is not that difficult to imagine potential customers buying lemons and sugar from the grocery store, and going home and making their own lemonade. What can Jerry do for them?

If Jerry is a shrewd businessman, he will realize that his proposed firm is nothing more than an *intermediary* between the grocery store that sells lemons and sugar — which is itself an intermediary between the farmers who grow lemons and buyers like Jerry — and consumers of lemonade. Sort of like your local bank intermediating between borrowers and savers, accepting deposits at 5% interest and lending the same money out at 10%.

Thus, the answer for Jerry is simple. His firm has a reason to exist if he can *add value* for the *customer* beyond what the customer can do on his/her own.

How can Jerry's firm add value?

- By producing a glass of lemonade at a lower cost than the customer can.

Jerry now begins to think about how his firm can produce lemonade cheaper than an individual customer can. This is easy, thinks Jerry, I will buy lemons in large quantities directly from lemon growers rather than grocery stores, and get volume discounts.

Of course, what Jerry must also realize is that the customer's definition of cost includes not just the cost of the materials — lemons, sugar, ice, water, etc — that go into the lemonade, but also the cost of labor. Going to the store, buying lemons and sugar, and then making fresh lemonade at home takes time and effort. By offering the convenience of ready-made lemonade, the customer's time and effort could be spent more enjoyably on other things.

So, if Jerry can buy lemonade-making equipment and train people to make large quantities of fresh lemonade fast, he can reduce the labor that goes into making each glass of lemonade.

Jerry has now discovered *two* ways to make cheaper lemonade — buy inputs in bulk at volume discounts and train people to mass-produce the output at a lower labor cost per unit.

But is there any other way to add value?

- By producing a *better* glass of lemonade than the customer can himself/herself.

That is simple enough, thinks Jerry, but what is better? I suppose it means better quality, but how do I know what that is?

Little does Jerry realize what a profound question he has just asked. In the teachings of W. Edwards Deming about total quality management (TQM), there are many definitions of quality.[1]

In practice, many firms use *manufacturing defects* as an operational measure of quality. For example, Motorola is famous for its "Six Sigma" quality initiatives. In plain English, this means that the manufacturing goal is no more than 3.4 defects per one million opportunities. Variants of this initiative have since been adopted by various firms, including General Electric and Whirlpool.

Should Jerry use this definition of quality to determine how to make a better glass of lemonade? Perhaps he should hear a story before he decides.

RJR Nabisco, the maker of Oreo cookies, was very concerned about the number of broken cookies in each box. After all, such defects indicated shoddy workmanship. People might think Oreo cookies were of low quality. So, the company spent millions of dollars on a comprehensive quality improvement program to reduce the number of broken cookies in each box. And they succeeded in fixing the "problem."

Did it help? Not really. Sales did not change much, and neither was Nabisco able to charge a higher price.

What went wrong?

The answer is that Nabisco misdiagnosed the problem. They adopted an *engineering* definition of quality. This definition says that quality is consistency or absence of variation. Thus, quality is the pursuit of ever smaller numbers of "defects" or smaller tolerances.

But what is the only definition of quality that matters?

By now, Jerry has caught on. "It is obvious," he says, "the only thing that matters is what the customer defines as quality."

This is known as *user-based quality*. It is a *subjective* definition of quality, and it says that the sole legitimate judge of quality is the customer. In the case of Oreo cookies, Nabisco ultimately discovered that its customers did not care about the broken cookies. It was how the cookies tasted to them that mattered most. In fact, many parents liked to eat *just* the broken cookies and leave the whole ones for their kids. After all, there are no calories in broken cookies, are there?

So, why do not more firms rely on user-based quality in their TQM programs?

Because it is hard! Engineering-based definitions of quality are easy to quantify and set targets for. Human nature is such that it is easier for people to focus their attention on measurable and quantifiable things. On the other hand, operationalizing user-based quality requires a deep understanding of the customer. In particular, it calls for understanding *how* the customer makes purchase decisions.

---

[1] W. Edwards Deming, *The New Economics*, MIT Press, Cambridge, MA 02139, November 1993.

But Jerry is not daunted by such challenges. He realizes that understanding his customers is the key to his future success. He is going to have to think about how to do this. And while he is at it, he is also going to have to understand how the different parts of his future organization are going to work together in a harmonious process to create value. For this, he is going to have to understand the concepts of value creation and organizational process maps.

2. Organizational Process Maps and Value Creation

An *organizational process map* is a pictorially descriptive summary of the manner in which value is created by an organization, and the *value-added* roles played by different agents.

Every organization should have one. Few have really good ones.

A good organizational process map should help the organization to:

- clearly link its strategy to the various activities that add value, so as to define the role of each activity in adding value through execution of the strategy;
- communicate to its employees the danger in people optimizing their piece of the value-added chain at the expense of the entire value-added chain and
- quickly pinpoint activities that have, over time, become peripheral to the value-added chain, and should be candidates for divestiture.

An overall organizational process map for any firm would look like Fig. 1.1.

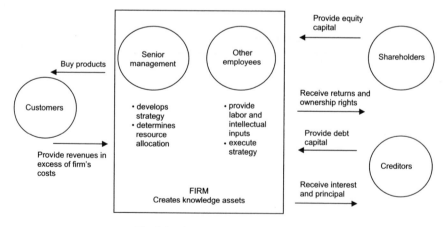

Fig. 1.1.   An organizational process map.

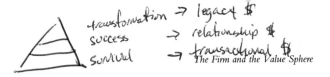

Of course, an operationally useful process map would be loaded with far more detail than this.

What our aspiring business tycoon, Jerry, has to understand is that any firm is merely an intermediary between its customers on the one hand and the providers of capital (financiers) on the other.

Financiers will not provide debt and equity capital unless they expect to earn a return on that capital that is at least as great as that which they can earn elsewhere if they took the same risk. *(and earned the same meaning)*

Not all financiers are the same, of course. Jerry's Lemonade has to promise a higher expected return to its shareholders than to its creditors (banks and bondholders) because the shareholders bear more risk; creditors have priority over shareholders in receiving payment from the firm. But the point is that shareholders will not provide Jerry with equity capital unless they are promised an expected rate of return commensurate with the risk they are taking. The same holds true for the creditors.

So Jerry has to work backwards, in a sense. He must first figure out how much it is going to cost him to produce the volume of lemonade he wants to sell. This requires estimating all of his operating costs, including materials and labor. He must then figure out how much capital he will need to invest, and how much of it will come from outside shareholders (equity) and how much from creditors (debt).

Once he has a handle on all his costs and his capital outlay, Jerry can calculate the revenues he will need to generate to ensure that his shareholders and creditors receive the returns they are expecting. Capital has a cost too.

Since Jerry also knows the number of glasses of lemonade he hoped to sell when he began this exercise, he now knows the price he must charge for each glass of lemonade so that he can earn the desired revenue.

If Jerry provides good products and services, his customers may be willing to pay this price.

But what if they are not? After all, this is a brutally competitive world, and people watch every penny they spend. It is not easy to charge customers what you would like, especially when the market is served by many able competitors.

This is where Jerry must open his organizational process map, and look carefully at each value-added activity and what it costs:

- Can some of these activities be cut out or reorganized? (Process rationalization).
- Can we make more lemonade with fewer people? (Labor rationalization).
- Can we outsource some of the things we planned to do in-house? (Asset rationalization).

Jerry has only two (not mutually exclusive) choices. He can either bring his costs down so that the price at which customers are willing to buy his lemonade is high enough to generate a revenue sufficient to yield his financiers their desired returns. Or he can figure out a way to get customers to pay a higher price. Jerry learns that this is what corporate strategy is all about.

3. Strategy and the Unending Quest for Value Creation

If he is going to start a new company, Jerry realizes that it will be his responsibility to develop the right strategy for the company.

What would the "right" strategy do for the company?

Jerry has an instinctive feel for this. He knows that cost efficiency is the "price of admission," a necessary condition for being competitive in business.

But it is ultimately a dead-end street. If customers are not willing to pay much for your lemonade because every mall and little shopping center in town has a store that sells lemonade that customers like at least as much, then Jerry will never be able to cut his costs enough!

The key, Jerry knows, is to come up with a way to make customers believe that his lemonade is better than everybody else's. Jerry's mind wanders off to the story of how Howard Schultz created Starbucks.

As recently as 1987, coffee had the status of a "pure commodity" in the United States. Simply put, this means that price was the main dimension along which the major sellers competed with each other. And these sellers had a core belief that price was all their customers cared about.

Maxwell House, owned by General Mills; Folgers, owned by Procter & Gamble; and Nescafé, owned by Nestlé; accounted for 90% of the US coffee market, and were engaged in a vigorous competitive battle.

However, the overall market for coffee was in a downslide. As Americans drank less coffee, sales of all three major brands kept shrinking. Eager to prevent further erosions of their sales volumes, the major players poured millions of dollars into advertising.

They even introduced premium brands, including whole-bean coffee, in an attempt to improve margins.

All of these activities were tangible manifestations of a *common strategy* employed by the three major competitors. The strategy was simple. Provide the cheapest possible coffee to the customer in as many grocery stores as possible, and use as much advertising as affordable to attract the customer's attention.

The strategy was predicated on the basic assumptions that: the target customer base was the entire grocery-buying public, the way to differentiate one product from the other was on the basis of national brands and price, and that the customer wanted mass-produced, long-shelf-life ground coffee at the lowest possible price even if the coffee was mediocre.

Did the strategy work?

No. The whole coffee industry was declining by 1988. United States coffee consumption had dropped to 1.67 cups per day, down from a peak of 3.1. General Foods lost $40 million that year on its domestic coffee business. And Procter & Gamble, even though it was winning the market-share wars, was faced with vanishing profit margins.

Enter Howard Schultz.[2] He was a buyer for Starbucks Coffee Co., a seller of whole-bean coffees in Seattle. On a trip to Italy, Howard saw the enormous social appeal of roadside cafes selling high-quality latte, espresso, and cappuccino. The aroma of these coffees would waft through the streets and attract throngs of people for whom these cafes were a focal point of social interaction.

After unsuccessful attempts to get his bosses back home to support his idea for opening similar cafes in Seattle, he decided to go it alone. He served Starbucks' coffee at his first cafe, opened in 1986 in Seattle.

By 1987, Schultz had bought out his former bosses and put the Starbucks name on three cafes.

By 1994, Starbucks, then national in scope, had a market value of over $1 billion and in 2005, the market capitalization reached $18 billion. Much of this growth came at the expense of the major players who were plying coffee as a commodity.

Starbucks, on the other hand, was earning handsome margins. People were paying more than $2 for a cup of coffee. The assumption that coffee was a commodity and that price is all that mattered to the customer had been proven to be spectacularly wrong.

What enabled Starbucks to create value where others had failed?

The answer, Jerry realizes now, lies in *strategy*. Schultz's strategy was the complete opposite of that of Procter & Gamble, General Foods, and Nestlé. His strategy was based on the assumption that people would pay the price if the coffee was viewed as so different from — and superior to — what customers could buy in the grocery stores that he *would not even have to compete* with grocery-store coffee. And he also did not view his customer base as the entire grocery-store public.

He had a different customer base in mind. His customers, at least initially, were the upwardly-mobile professionals, many of whom had been to Europe and enjoyed the fine coffees over there. They would pay, he reasoned, if he could deliver the

---

[2]For further details on the Schultz story, see Adrian J. Slywotzky, *Value Migration*, Harvard Business School Press, Boston, MA, 1996.

"total experience" of fine coffee. This strategy completely changed the rules of the game. Starbucks has now evolved into a "community," offering wireless Internet access and music downloading in some locations.

Jerry knows he must come up with a similar strategy if he wants to create *real* value. But what defines a good strategy?

A distinguished expert on strategy once said, not entirely facetiously, "A good strategy is one that works!" If one looks at the numerous *ex post* accounts of successful corporate strategies in books on the subject, it is hard to argue with this statement. In hindsight, it is easy to have 20-20 vision.

But Jerry wanted something more. After studying numerous successful strategies, from Avon in the 1960s and 1970s to Disney in the late 1980s to Starbucks in the 1990s, he concluded that a good strategy must satisfy the following five conditions:

- It must be simple, so that everybody in the organization can understand it, relate to it, and internalize their role in executing it. As a product of the television age, Jerry thought that a good strategy must have a "two-minute" sound bite that captures its essence. That way employees would not have to refer to a manual every time they wanted to know what the company's strategy was.
- It must clearly define what the company will do and what it will *not* do. There are far too many flowery (and very wordy) statements of corporate strategy that are conspicuously silent about what they commit the corporation to *not* do. They are not worth much. The goal of a good strategy must be to guide corporate resource allocation. As a wise observer once said, "Having a strategy means being able to say no to good ideas."
- It must be closely tied to the way capital and other resources are allocated in the business.
- It must be clearly tied to the key *value drivers* in the business.
- It must differ enough from our competitors' strategies to give us a distinctive competitive advantage.

For Howard Schultz and Starbucks, the key value driver was the superior quality of the coffee as perceived by the customer and the whole coffee experience.

For Walt Disney & Co., the value driver was the firm's creative output, as reflected in the films it made.

The value drivers differ from firm to firm. But the fact remains that strategy must be anchored by these drivers. Figure 1.2 illustrates this point.

So, Jerry's strategy must reflect his knowledge of what the customer is really buying when he orders a glass of lemonade at Jerry's Lemonade, Inc. This knowledge is essential to crafting a value-creating strategy.

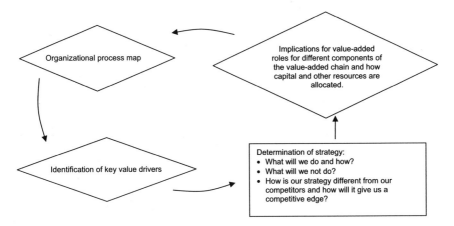

Fig. 1.2. Linking value drivers to strategy.

4. Executing the Strategy: Resource Allocation

Once Jerry comes up with the right strategy, he must worry about executing it. Execution of the strategy means a number of things for Jerry. For example, he must decide:

- where to locate his stores;
- what production process and associated equipment to use;
- what customer segments to attract with advertising;
- how to price his lemonade and
- the number of stores, the size of each store, and common interior design to use.

A large part of Jerry's strategy execution is going to boil down to the *magnitude* of the resources Jerry will commit to the business, and *where these resources will* be allocated.

A smart financial analyst once said, "When I want to understand a company's strategy, I do not read what the CEO says. I look at where the *capital* is being allocated."

It is fairly obvious that the decisions Jerry makes about capital allocation will influence how much value his business will create.

Between 1987 and 1991, Wal–Mart invested huge amounts of capital in expanding its business by opening many new stores. The company had a *negative* cash flow in each of those years because it was investing more cash than the business was generating. This was achieved by borrowing additional amounts from banks and raising more money from the shareholders.

The key was that Wal-Mart was investing all this capital at a rate of return that was about twice that available in similar-risk businesses. The consequence was a *five-fold* increase in Wal-Mart's shareholder value over this short time period.

What made all of this possible?

There were basically two reasons for this phenomenal value creation. First, Wal-Mart recognized that the key value driver in its business was how fast it turned over its inventory.[3] That is, how high its asset productivity was. Simply put, Wal-Mart recognized that the faster it moved products through the value chain from its suppliers to its customers, the more money it would make with less invested in inventory relative to sales, even if this meant sacrificing a bit of its profit margin.

There is an important lesson for Jerry here in executing strategy. Do not get hung up over profit margins. It is not that there is anything wrong with high margins. But sometimes you can create more wealth by lowering your profit margin and increasing the rate at which you move your product inventory through the value chain.

Second, Wal-Mart explicitly tied its competitive growth strategy to this value driver. The whole business design of the company was focused on maximizing asset productivity, with major contributions from information technology and logistics. Moreover, this business design also involved expanding the number of stores to further exploit scale economies that would facilitate an increase in the rate at which the company could turn over its inventory assets. Thus, capital was allocated to opening new stores and warehouses to stock these inventories.

There is another lesson for Jerry here. Once you have identified a value driver that is pivotal to the success of the business, invest as much capital as you can to exploit that value driver. Stop investing more only when the marginal return on investing that capital equals its marginal cost.

If Jerry faces a cost of capital of say 10% and the return on investing this capital in opening a new lemonade store is 15%, it would be unwise for Jerry to get timid and decide not to open the new store.

5. Executing the Strategy: Value Evaporation, Value Retention, and the Value Sphere

What may be less obvious to Jerry is that the capital allocation system he designs to execute his company's strategy should also have another goal: minimizing *Value Evaporation* and maximizing *value retention*.

---

[3]The two key asset items on Wal-Mart's balance sheet were its stores and its inventory. Wal-Mart, which owns most of its stores, was rapidly expanding its number of stores during this time.

By Value Evaporation we mean the literally countless ways in which a company's value creation is diminished due to poor decisions in *executing* the strategy. Thus, strategy creates value but some of it evaporates due to poor execution and other organizational frictions. What remains is value retention. Given a strategy, our goal should be to maximize value retention.

To understand Value Evaporation, we start with the assumption that the strategy is right and, therefore, value creating. Thus, if there is any loss in value due to a poor strategy, it is *not* part of Value Evaporation. Here are a few examples of Value Evaporation.

- Consider the following conversation between two managers in a company:

"You know, I have this equipment I'd like to purchase, but I have exhausted my annual capital budget," says the first manager.

"That's why God invented leasing," replies the second.

Managers in many companies routinely circumvent the rigors of their internal capital budgeting processes by pouring millions of dollars into leasing equipment. They mistakenly think that leasing is somehow fundamentally different from investing capital. Unfortunately for the shareholders, leasing ties up debt capacity just like borrowing the money would. If buying the equipment was a bad idea, it is very likely that leasing is too.

- Here is another fascinating conversation:

"You know, it looks like we won't be able to invest in this project after all. Management says that the return is not high enough to justify the investment, given all the other projects that are competing for funds," says one manager.

"Perhaps not. But if you tell me how high a return management wants, I could rerun the numbers to see if we can get there," responds the other.

How many companies invest huge amounts of capital in projects that never yield the rates of return they promised? Every company we know has a hurdle rate for project acceptance — the minimum acceptable rate of return on the project — that is at or *above* the cost of the company's capital. It is the only thing that makes sense.

Common sense says that if you only invest in projects with expected rates of return above your cost of capital, on average the company should earn a rate of return on its assets that exceeds its cost of capital. But what do the facts say? Hundreds of large publicly-held firms routinely *fail* to earn enough on their assets to cover all of their costs, including the cost of capital. For example, in 1993, stellar firms like Procter & Gamble, BellSouth Corporation, Mobil Corporation, and DuPont fell in this category.

Why does this happen? Is it because these firms did not have good strategies? No. A good strategy is necessary to create value. But it is not sufficient. It cannot prevent the evaporation of value.

Think of a tropical village that is perpetually short of water. So, the villagers come up with a strategy. It involves digging a big hole in the ground to create a reservoir of water from natural rain. The strategy works. The reservoir fills up. But the villagers forgot how mercilessly hot the tropical sun can be. The reservoir did not last very long. Evaporation returned its water to the atmosphere.

For the villagers, what matters is not just how much water was there in the reservoir initially, but how much is *retained* after evaporation. The same is true for any organization. Its goal is to come up with a strategy that maximizes *value creation*. But it must then <u>follow up</u> with *performance metrics*, a *resource allocation system* and an *organization culture* that minimize Value Evaporation, and maximize *value retention*. This is shown pictorially in the **Value Sphere** in Fig. 1.3. Moreover, the Value Sphere must be synchronized, i.e., each of its elements must be attended to and made consistent with each other.

All this is quite a bit for Jerry to think about. The issues are getting more complex as the plot thickens. The question is: What gives rise to Value Evaporation and how do we minimize it?

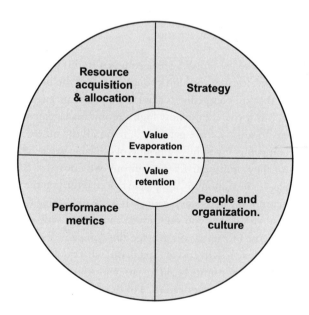

Fig. 1.3.   The Value Sphere.

The rest of this book is devoted to answering this question. Our goal is nothing less than making Jerry's Lemonade, Inc. the next Starbucks.

The basic theme that guides the remaining chapters is that as the global marketplace becomes even more fiercely competitive, we believe the concept of the Value Sphere will become a core element of an integrated approach to improving competitiveness. We will show Jerry how he can go about developing the Value Sphere for his company. The different elements of the Value Sphere must be synchronized with each other. The resource allocation system must ensure that resources are allocated in a way that executes the strategy. The performance metrics must incent people to behave in a way that furthers the execution of the strategy and minimizes Value Evaporation. And the organization culture must help maximize value retention. In each chapter we will highlight the element of the Value Sphere that is the subject of that chapter.

Main Lessons

- The only definition of quality that matters is the customer's.
- Once we understand how the customer defines quality, an organizational process map should be used to identify the value creation chain and the critical value drivers in the business.
- A clearly-enunciated corporate strategy must be simple and tied explicitly to the critical value drivers.
- The key to creating value and maximizing its retention is to create a Value Sphere that harmoniously balances strategy, resource allocation, performance metrics, and organization culture.

End-of-Chapter Exercises

1. How does your company define quality? How was this definition arrived at? What evidence do you have that this is how your customers define quality?
2. How do your competitors define quality? How different is your definition of quality?
3. Is it an advantage or a disadvantage for you if you and your competitors define quality in exactly the same way?
4. Do you have an organizational process map?
5. What is your company's strategy? Does it meet the five conditions identified in this chapter?
6. What are the key value drivers in your business?

 7. What exactly is the link between these value drivers and your strategy?
 8. Can you list the five most significant ways in which value is being evaporated in your company?
 9. Do you know how to stop this Value Evaporation?
10. Examine the different parts of the Value Sphere for your company. Are they synchronized?

Practice Problems

1. What is the Value Sphere and why is it important?
2. What are the consequences of a Value Sphere that is not synchronized?
3. What are the requirements of a good strategy?
4. What is a value driver and what is its importance in the formulation of strategy?
5. What is Value Evaporation?

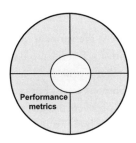

Chapter 2

TIME FOR ACTION: JERRY SAYS HELLO TO FINANCE AND TAKES THE PLUNGE

1. Getting Started

Jerry has decided that he has spent enough time thinking through the issues of the Value Sphere strategy, and the positioning of his new firm. It is time for action.

Nothing ventured, nothing gained, thinks Jerry. So, to solidify his emotional commitment to his fledgling business, Jerry quits his job at the post office. His wife, Sallie, has a steady job in the admissions office at the local university that pays $30,000 a year plus benefits. Since they have no kids, they could probably get by with a little extra frugality.

Sallie senses the excitement Jerry has for his new project. She had never before seen him so alive. All that he could talk about was this new product concept. Fresh squeezed lemon, ice and the usual amount of sugar would all go into the lemonade. But the product differentiation would be a bit of cracked white pepper and salt added to the "basic" lemonade.

There would be variations available in an array of colors, where different fruit flavorings would be blended in to provide just a hint of raspberry, blackberry, pineapple, apple or strawberry. However, lemon would remain the dominant flavor. To entice the kids to his shop, each variation would be named after a popular cartoon character. He planned to amend the characters' names just enough to keep an overzealous copyright attorney at bay. Thus far, his "short list" included Rockin' Raspberry Road Runnur and Pineapple Pluto-nium.

"Have you thought about what kind of a firm this is going to be, Jerry?" asked Sallie as they began dinner one evening.

"Actually, yes," Jerry responded. "I ran into Bob Butterfield the other day — you know, my old buddy from high school. Wouldn't you know he got his Ph.D. in finance a few years ago and joined the business school at the university. Well, of course, we got to talking about my plan. He suggested that it is probably best to start as a sole proprietorship."

A *sole proprietorship* is a business owned by one person. It is the simplest and least regulated form of organization. Its owner keeps all the profits. But he also has *unlimited liability* for business debts. This means that if Jerry takes a bank loan and fails to repay it, the bank can not only take possession of his business assets, but can look beyond them to Jerry's personal assets for repayment. Moreover, there is no difference between personal and business income, so all of Jerry's business income will be taxed as personal income.

Jerry is taking a big risk. But, what else could he have done?

He could have decided to form a *partnership*. This would involve teaming up with one or more other owners. There are two versions of partnership. In a *general partnership*, all the partners share in the gains or losses, and *all* have unlimited liability for all the debts incurred by the partnership. In a *limited partnership*, one or more *general partners* assume unlimited liability. However, there are also limited partners who do not actively participate in the business and who enjoy *limited liability*. This means that creditors cannot touch their personal assets in collecting debts incurred by the partnership.

A third option for Jerry is to form a *corporation*. This is a legal entity that is distinct from its owners. In fact, a corporation enjoys many of the rights and duties of a real person. It can borrow money, own assets, negotiate contracts, own another corporation or partnership, and hire and fire people. Moreover, its owners can enjoy limited liability.

One of the biggest disadvantages of a corporation is double taxation. The income earned by the corporation is taxed at the corporate income tax rate, and then the dividends paid out to shareholders are taxed separately at the personal income tax rate. Another alternative organizational form is a limited liability corporation (or LLC), which provides the limited personal liability and the pass-through taxation of partnerships or S corporations.

2. Where will the Money Come From?

"Jerry, have you thought of a location for the store?" Sallie asked, as Jerry ate dinner.

"Sure. I'm thinking about leasing the store at the mall that has been vacant ever since the travel agency moved out," said Jerry.

"That's a good site. But won't the lease be expensive?" Sallie wondered.

Jerry replied, "Yes, it is expensive. Plus we need to buy the equipment and hire someone to work in the store. We don't have the money for all that, but I'm going to our bank tomorrow to see if they can give us a loan."

Jerry met with the loan officer the next day. After listening to Jerry's vision, the loan officer gave him a list of things that he would need before the bank could process a loan. Among them was a business plan that contained financial projections and ratios. Also included was the bank's standard (boiler plate) loan contract for small business loans, so that Jerry would understand what kinds of restrictions (covenants) the bank would ask for and what his liability was.

Jerry was feeling a bit lost now. "Heck, all I want to do is sell lemonade. Why do I have to know all this financial stuff?" he muttered to himself.

Somewhat dejectedly, he told Sallie about his meeting and what he needed to do. Sallie thought awhile and said, "Why don't you talk to Bob again?"

"You're right," said Jerry, "let me call him."

Jerry's meeting with Bob was very helpful. Bob explained that *loan covenants* were nothing more than a list of conditions the bank would specify. Things that Jerry's Lemonade would have to do and things they could not do. Most of these were expressed in financial terms, but the key for Jerry would be to understand what he would have to do in his business to ensure that the bank's conditions were met.

"This is important, Jerry," emphasized Bob, "because if you violate any of these conditions, the bank could call back the entire loan. And remember what I said about your personal assets being at risk in a sole proprietorship. You could lose your home!"

"This is a tall order, Bob. I don't know that much about finance," mumbled Jerry.

Bob thought for a moment and then said with a smile, "Jerry, why don't you sit in on the corporate finance course I'm offering this semester? It starts next week and we're going to talk about a lot of things you need to know."

"Hmm. That may not be a bad idea. I'll do it," beamed Jerry.

So began Jerry's journey into the world of business finance.

3. What Jerry Learned

In a couple of months, not only did Jerry have the bank loan, but also a working knowledge of basic financial concepts.

Jerry learned that corporate finance was all about answering two key questions: (i) how had the past strategies worked out for the firms owners? and (ii) which strategic course of action seems best for the same owners? Addressing these questions involved analyzing basic accounting statements, deriving and interpreting operational and financial ratios, estimating a firm's or investment project's cash flows and understanding the time value of money. All of the concepts were at the heart of key performance metrics that are part of a well-balanced Value Sphere. Below is a summary of the notes and observations Jerry made for himself from Bob's lectures.

Analyzing Basic Accounting Statements

A firm can be thought of as a collection of assets that are financed by various liabilities and owners' equity. That is, suppliers, bankers, bondholders, and shareholders provide cash or extend credit to the firm for the purchase of assets like production materials, manufacturing equipment, buildings, and property. Seen this way, assets are what the firm owns and liabilities are what the firm owes. An accountant portrays this in a *balance sheet*. A simple example of a balance sheet is given in Fig. 2.1.

Of course, a firm is *more* than simply a collection of assets. How it puts these physical assets to work determines the stream of cash flows that it will produce.[4] And the *value* of the firm is what investors would be willing to pay today for the right to claim this stream of future cash flows. Although the balance sheet tells us what investments have been made by the firm, it says little about the future cash flows that *will* be produced down the road, and hence little about value.

To get some idea of cash flows, we need to turn to the income statement. Figure 2.2 contains an example of an *operating* income statement; that is, it is exclusive of any *financing* expenses associated with *how* the assets were purchased.

Assets	Liabilities and equity
Current assets	Current liabilities
Cash	Accounts payable
Inventory	Other payables
Accounts receivable	Bank debt
Fixed assets	Long-term debt
Plant	Shareholders' equity
Property	
Equipment	

Fig. 2.1.   A simple accounting view of the firm.

---

[4]See Chapter 1, as well as Oliver Hart's *Firm, Contracts and Financial Structures*, Oxford University Press, New York, 1995.

Sales revenue

   — Cost of goods sold (COGS)

   — Selling, general, and administrative (SG&A) expenses

     = Earnings before interest, taxes, depreciation, and amortization (EBITDA)

   — Depreciation expense and goodwill amortization

     = Earnings before interest and taxes (EBIT)

          OR

     Net operating profit (NOP)

   — Cash taxes on operating profit

     = Net operating profit after-tax (NOPAT)

Fig. 2.2. A simple operating income statement.

There are many basic inputs needed to arrive at the rather general definitions of Fig 2.2.

In order, these are defined as:

- **Sales revenue** = Number of units sold × Price per unit
- **COGS** = {(Material cost per unit + Labor cost per unit + Other production costs per unit) × Number of units} + Fixed production costs
- **SG&A expense** = Selling costs + Overhead costs + Administrative expenses
- **Depreciation expense** = Yearly depreciation expense on the fixed assets held by a firm or attributable to a specific project (many times reported as part of COGS)
- **Cash taxes on operating profits** = Cash taxes in current period, that would have been paid on operating profit if the firm had no interest expenses on debt.[5]

With these inputs, Fig. 2.2 shows that:

- **EBITDA** = Sales revenue — COGS — SG&A expenses
- **EBIT or NOP = EBITDA — Depreciation — Goodwill amortization**
- **NOPAT = NOP or EBIT — Cash taxes on operating profit**
  = NOP[1 − T] where T = tax rate

---

[5]The fact that interest paid out by a firm to service its outstanding debt obligations is a tax-deductible business expense is introduced in Chapter 8.

While most of these terms are fairly straightforward, goodwill amortization, and depreciation need further explanation. Goodwill amortization arises in acquisitions. It is simply that portion of the difference between the purchase price and the revised book value (often called "fair market value") of the acquired firm that is treated as an expense in a given year, although the newly-adopted accounting rules (SFAS142, which became effective January 2002) stipulate that goodwill is to be *no longer* treated this way for financial reporting purposes. That is, companies are no longer to treat goodwill amortization as an annual expense in the company's income statement, and goodwill will impact earnings only if it is considered "impaired" and has to be written down. *Goodwill impairment* is supposed to be a "one-time" devaluation of goodwill on the balance sheet and a change against earnings if the company thinks the goodwill on the balance sheet exceeds the economic value of the asset. For example, AOL Time Warner recorded a goodwill impairment of $93 billion in 2004 to recognize the current value of the merged enterprise. Talk about Value Evaporation! To the extend that the amortization of purchased goodwill (along with other Section 197 intangibles) is deductible for *tax* purposes over a 15-year period, one should still treat it just like depreciation and deduct it as shown above. Generally speaking, depreciation reflects an estimate of the cost of an asset used up in the production process. Since fixed assets have a useful economic life exceeding one year, by subtracting yearly depreciation charges from profits each year, the original purchase price of the asset is spread out over the years of its productive life.

Two points are noteworthy. First, depreciation is really a non-cash item since the true cash is the purchase price paid when the asset was acquired. However, this initial purchase price is not tax deductible (as are other expenses, such as the cost of materials). What the tax authorities do allow is that a fraction of the purchase price can be treated as a tax-deductible expense every year. The fraction for each year, called depreciation, when multiplied by the number of years over which the initial price must be spread out, is equal to the initial purchase price. Being able to treat depreciation like a tax-deductible expense creates a cash benefit. This benefit is called a *depreciation tax shield*. We will come back to it when we define a firm's cash flow.

Second, every type of asset has its own *depreciation schedule*. This schedule tells us how to depreciate the asset and over how many years. The tax laws for depreciation vary by country and by whether the asset is a building, property, or equipment.

For instance, buildings are depreciated uniformly over 39.5 years. We therefore say buildings are depreciated *straight-line to zero* over 39.5 years. A building costing $79,000 would, according to this schedule, generate a $2,000 depreciation charge against pre-tax profits each year for 39.5 years.

Properties, such as land, are not depreciable at all.

Year	3 Year	5 Year	7 Year	10 Year	15 Year	20 Year
1	33.33%	20.00%	14.29%	10.00%	5.000%	3.750%
2	44.45%	32.00%	24.49%	18.00%	9.500%	7.219%
3	14.81%	19.20%	17.49%	14.40%	8.550%	6.677%
4	7.41%	11.52%	12.49%	11.52%	7.700%	6.177%
5		11.52%	8.93%	9.22%	6.930%	5.713%
6		5.76%	8.92%	7.37%	6.230%	5.285%
7			8.93%	6.55%	5.900%	4.888%
8			4.46%	6.55%	5.910%	4.522%
9				6.56%	5.900%	4.462%
10				6.55%	5.900%	4.461%
11				3.28%	5.910%	4.462%
12					5.900%	4.461%
13					5.910%	4.462%
14					5.900%	4.461%
15					5.910%	4.462%
16					2.950%	4.461%
17						4.462%
18						4.461%
19						4.462%
20						4.461%
21						2.23%

Fig. 2.3. MACRS table for the depreciation of equipment.

And lastly, equipment can fall into one of six depreciation categories, depending on its economic life. The tax code specifies which types of assets fall into each economic life classification. The appropriate schedule in the United States is given by the *Modified Accelerated Cost Recovery System* (*MACRS*) which is contained in Fig. 2.3.

For example, a piece of computer equipment costing $3,000 would fall into the 5-year MACRS category. Hence, over the six years[6] following its purchase, the

---

[6]Even though the equipment is in the five-year depreciation class, it is assumed that it is purchased halfway through the first year. Thus, a sixth depreciation charge is needed to fully depreciate the equipment.

firm could take depreciation charges of:

- $3,000 × 20.00% = $600 in Year 1
- $3,000 × 32.00% = $960 in Year 2
- $3,000 × 19.20% = $576 in Year 3
- $3,000 × 11.52% = $345.60 in Year 4
- $3,000 × 11.52% = $345.60 in Year 5
- $3,000 × 5.76% = $172.80 in Year 6

Observe that charges are higher in the early years and that the sum of the six yearly depreciation charges equals the original cost of the computer. Thus, the cost of an investment in equipment is written off in an accelerated fashion against profits during its accounting life, producing tax shield benefits in each of those years.

The accounting or "book" value of the asset should reflect this depreciation as it occurs. Hence, we calculate the *net book value* of the computer over its full accounting life as:

- $3,000 in Year 0 (i.e., when the computer is purchased)
- $2,400 at the end of Year 1
- $1,440 at the end of Year 2
- $864 at the end of Year 3
- $518.40 at the end of Year
- $172.80 at the end of Year 5
- $0 at the end of Year 6

Our accountants tell us that the computer has zero book value at the end of Year 6. But remember this is a backward-looking number. Book value at any time, after all, is based solely on historical cost and the accumulated depreciation charges. In reality, book value may have little to do with what the asset is worth in the market. However, let us not worry about this now. It is often assumed that the accounting valuation of the asset is consistent with the economic valuation of the asset. That is, we assume that accounting depreciation coincides with economic depreciation.

We are now ready to revisit the balance sheet presented in Fig. 2.1. Recall that a balance sheet simply reflects the value of assets on one side and the value of liabilities and equity on the other, all at *one point in time*. But these values change over time as assets are depreciated and new assets are added. Therefore, for valuation and performance assessment purposes, we should periodically revise our estimates of the assets employed in the firm. We also want to keep track of assets employed by the firm which are not classified as "fixed."

The total value of a firm's "assets-at-work" at any time is defined as its *Net Assets*. This is the sum of the *Net Fixed Assets* and the *Net Working Capital* held by the firm at that time.[7] These are defined as:

- **Net assets** = Net fixed assets + Net working capital
- **Net fixed assets** = Gross fixed assets (i.e., original cost) — Accumulated depreciation
- **Net working capital** = Current assets — Non-interest bearing current liabilities (NIBCLs).

Net fixed assets represent the value of the firm's fixed assets (i.e., plant, property, and equipment) and net working capital represents the value of the firm's operating capital (i.e., cash, inventories, and accounts receivable, less items such as accounts payable[8]) which are expected to be cash items within the year. We are now ready to prepare a balance sheet and operating income statement. Figures 2.4 and 2.5 show what these would be like for a fictitious company called MJM Incorporated.

Now using Figs. 2.4 and 2.5, we can calculate the following for MJM:

- **2004 Net fixed assets** = 85,000 − 20,000 = $65,000
- **2005 Net fixed assets** = 100,000 − 35,000 = $65,000
- **2004 Net working capital** = 30,000 − 20,000 = $10,000
- **2005 Net working capital** = 45,000 − 25,000 = $20,000

We now use the above information to derive:

- **2004 Net assets** = $65,000 + $10,000 = $75,000
- **2005 Net assets** = $65,000 + $20,000 = $85,000

However, has MJM put its capital to work wisely? Is the income stream generated in 2005 worth the investment in assets?

Operating and Financial Ratios

To answer these questions, we can turn to ratio analysis. Commonly used ratios in financial analysis fall in four categories: margin ratios, asset ratios, leverage ratios, and financial return ratios.

---

[7]Observe that in practice, net assets may be referred to as invested capital, capital employed or even capital at work. These are all names for the same thing.

[8]Interest-bearing current liabilities (IBCLs), such as short-term bank debt and commercial paper, are not subtracted from the firm's current assets. The economic logic behind this rule of subtracting only *non-interest-bearing* current liabilities is that we need to offset a portion of our current assets with the current liabilities which are associated with the *operations* of the business, and not the *financing* of the business. This distinction between operating and financing decisions will be clarified in Chapters 9 and 10.

	2004	**2005**
Assets		
Cash	$5,000	$5,000
Accounts receivable	15,000	25,000
Inventory	10,000	15,000
Current assets	**30,000**	**45,000**
Gross fixed assets	85,000	100,000
Accumulated depreciation	20,000	35,000
Net fixed assets	**65,000**	**65,000**
Total assets	**$95,000**	**$110,000**
Liabilities and equity		
NIBCLs (Accounts payable)	**$20,000**	**$25,000**
Bank debt	**15,000**	**20,000**
Long-term debt	**10,000**	**10,000**
Shareholders' equity	**50,000**	**55,000**
Total liabilities and equity	**$95,000**	**$110,000**

Fig. 2.4. MJM incorporated balance sheet.

(1) Margin ratios: These ratios assess a firm's or project's ability to cover its operating costs. Included are:

$$\textbf{Gross margin} = \frac{\text{Sales revenue} - \text{Cost of goods sold}}{\text{Sales Revenue}}$$

Gross margin reveals the percentage of sales revenue remaining after material and labor costs are accounted for.

$$\textbf{Operating margin} = \frac{\text{Net operating profit}}{\text{Sales revenue}}$$

which determines the percentage of sales revenue remaining after all operating expenses are deducted. In some situations, operating margin is defined more

	2005
Sales revenue	$150,000
Cost of goods sold	60,000
Selling, general, and administrative expense	30,000
Depreciation	15,000
Net operating profit (NOP) or EBIT	**45,000**
Operating taxes at 40%	18,000
Net operating profit after-tax (NOPAT)	**$27,000**

Fig. 2.5. MJM incorporated operating income statement.

generally as:

$$= \frac{\text{Sales revenue} - \text{Cost of goods sold} - \text{SG\&A expenses} - \text{Depreciation}}{\text{Sales revenues}}$$

or

$$= \text{Gross margin} - \frac{\text{SG\&A expenses}}{\text{Sales revenue}} - \frac{\text{Depreciation}}{\text{Sales revenues}}$$

Both gross margin and operating margin help us understand one component of the operating efficiency of the firm by answering the question: What is left of the revenue pie after subtracting the operating costs of production?

How does MJM stack up along these margin ratios? Using the data from Figs. 2.3 and 2.4 we see that

- **Gross margin** $= \dfrac{150{,}000 - 60{,}000}{150{,}000} = \dfrac{90{,}000}{150{,}000} = 60\%$

- **Operating margin** $= \dfrac{45{,}000}{150{,}000} = 30\%$

(2) **Asset ratios:** Another aspect of efficiency has to do with how efficiently the firm uses its assets. Since net assets include both net working capital and net fixed assets, there are ratios to measure asset efficiency that correspond to both current and fixed assets. The first two ratios relate to the current assets component of net working capital, which includes the sum of accounts receivable and Inventory. The first of these ratios reflects on the firm's ability to collect on the credit it extends to customers. It is given by:

- **Days sales outstanding** $= \dfrac{\text{Accounts receivable} \times 365}{\text{Sales revenue}}$

This ratio tells us how many days of sales the firm has on which it still needs to collect money from its customers. The second ratio measures how fast the firm turns over its inventory:

- **Inventory turnover** $= \dfrac{\text{COGS}}{\text{Inventory}}$

Finally, the next ratio relates to a firm's efficiency in deploying its net fixed assets and is given by:

- **Net asset turnover ratio** $= \dfrac{\text{Sales revenue}}{\text{Net assets}}$

This ratio reflects how many dollars of revenue are generated per $1 of assets. Everything else held constant, the higher this ratio the better. Let us now see how MJM has fared on these ratios in 2005:

- **Days sales outstanding** $= \dfrac{20,000 \times 365}{150,000} = 48.67$ days

- **Inventory turnover** $= \dfrac{60,000}{12,500} = 4.8\%$

Observe that we have used the *average* levels of accounts receivable and inventory for 2004 and 2005. The idea is that the assets the firm ties up to generate sales revenue are a weighted average of those with which it begins the year and those with which it ends the year.[9] Similarly, we use average net assets to obtain:

- **Net asset turnover** $= \dfrac{15,000}{80,000} = 1.875$

(3) **Leverage ratios:** Ratios in this category reflect a firm's ability to meet its debt service obligations. They often show up in bank loan covenants. They supposedly measure the firm's ability to avoid financial crises. One of these ratios is given by:

- **Times interest earned (or interest cover)** $= \dfrac{\text{EBIT} + \text{depreciation}}{\text{Interest expense}}$

A creditor would be interested in this ratio because it reveals how many times over the firm's cash operating profits could cover its yearly interest expense. Loan covenants typically require the borrower to retain an interest cover of at least 2 over the life of the loan.

---

[9]Some financial analysts calculate ratios using beginning-of-period asset values for the period, in particular, this is often done when forecasting performance.

Suppose that MJM faced a 10% interest rate on all its debt — bank loans and bonds. Its interest expense for 2005 would have been 10% of $30,000, assuming year-end values of debt as the basis. Thus, MJM has:

- **Debt/Equity ratio** $= \dfrac{\text{Long-term debt}}{\text{Book equity}} = \dfrac{\$30,000}{\$55,000}$
  $= 0.545$ in 2005

This means MJM is using 54.5 cents in debt for every dollar in equity.

- **Times interest earned** $= \dfrac{45,000 + 15,000}{3,000} = 20$

The Times Interest Earned ratio of 20 is a more than comfortable level of interest coverage. MJM is generating enough pre-tax operating income to cover its debt interest expense 20 times over! Note that all items in these leverage ratios are for 2005.

(4) **Financial return ratios:** Our last pair of ratios relates to the overall profitability of the firm. The first is the accountant's measure of the rate of return earned by the firm's shareholders as a percentage of the firm's sales revenue:

Return on sales (Net profit margin) $= \dfrac{\text{Net income for year}}{\text{Sales revenue for year}}$

where net income is given by:

- **Net income** $= (\text{EBIT} - \text{Interest on debt})(1 - \text{Tax rate})$

Based on net income, we can also calculate the return shareholders earn on the book value of their equity investment.

- **Return on equity (ROE)** $= \dfrac{\text{Net income}}{\text{Book equity}}$

where we will use average (over 2004 and 2005) book equity.

Net income is a useful piece of information because it is what our shareholders earned during the year, according to the income statement. But it is not the cash flow generated by the business for its owners since it excludes investments in net assets and includes non-cash items like depreciation.

To calculate these two ratios for MJM, we must first calculate:

- **Net income** $= (\$45,000 - \$3,000)(1 - 0.4) = \$25,200$

Now we have

- **Return on sales** $= \dfrac{\$25,200}{\$150,000} = 0.168$ or 16.8%

- **ROE** $= \dfrac{\$25,200}{\$52,500} = 0.48$ or 48%

where $\$52,500$ is the average of $\$50,000$ (2004 equity) and $\$55,000$ (2005 equity).

(5) The DuPont formula: In the 1960s, DuPont came up with a formula that links ROE to its components, as follows:

$$\text{Return on equity} = \text{Return on sales} \times \text{Net asset turnover}$$
$$\times [1 + \text{debt/equity ratio}]$$

This way we can see how the overall performance of a company is driven by how effectively it manages profit margins, how productively it manages assets, and how well it manages its capital structure.

Estimating Cash Flows

Our next task is to use our definitions of operating profits and net asset values to arrive at an estimate of the cash flows of a business. We are particularly interested in cash flow because value derives from cash, not accounting profits.

We want to focus on the cash flows that come from the operations of the business, before debt interest is paid, but after taxes are paid and investments in capital are made. This is called the free cash flow of a business:

- **Free cash flow (FCF)** for the year = NOPAT for the year
  $$\qquad\qquad\qquad - \text{increase in net assets during the year}$$

where *Increase in Net Assets* represents the change in the value of net assets over the year. It is defined as:

- **Increase in net assets** = Additions to net working capital during the year
  $$+ \text{Additions to net fixed assets (New fixed asset}$$
  $$\text{investment} - \text{Depreciation) during the year.}$$

This suggests three ways to express FCF that are all identical to the FCF formula above:

- **FCF for the year** = NOPAT − increases in net working capital

  − increase in net fixed assets

  = NOPAT + depreciation − investment in property plant and equipment (or capital expenditure)

  − increase in net working capital

  = Net income + depreciation − capital expenditure

  − increase in net working capital + debt interest

  × (1−tax rate).

Any of the free cash flow formulae can be applied to both historical and forecasted data. When used for forecasting, particular attention must be paid to the timing of cash flow as well as the inflationary assumptions used. Remember that in computing FCF we do not subtract interest expenses. We should think about FCF as representing the cash available to pay both the debtholders and shareholders. FCF is sometimes also called the *Operating Free Cash Flow* or *All-Equity Free Cash Flow*.[10]

We can take our definition of FCF a step further to arrive at what's called the *Equity Free Cash Flow*. That is, we can calculate the shareholders' share of the FCF pool by subtracting the cash needed to service the outstanding debt. Debt service payments include both the interest expense incurred on the outstanding principal of the debt, plus any scheduled repayments of the principal itself. Thus, we have:

- **Equity FCF** = FCF − after-tax interest expense during the year

  − debt principal repayments during the year

The equity FCF is often called the *Flows to Equity*. It simply tells us the amount of cash remaining for the owners of the business after all other stakeholders (including the tax authorities) have had their claims satisfied. See the diagram below.

Now for MJM Incorporated, let us calculate its 2005 operating free cash flow first. All we need is MJM's NOPAT and the change in its net asset base. The former is given directly by Fig 2.4 as:

- **NOPAT** = $27,000

---

[10]The term all-equity FCF captures the idea that our definition of free cash flow is on a pre-financing basis and would be identical to the free cash flows associated with a firm which has no debt outstanding, i.e., an all-equity firm.

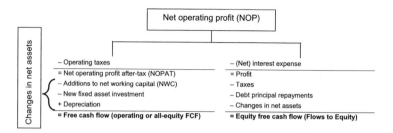

Fig. 2.6.   Cash flow definitions.

However, to calculate the change in the asset base, we need to collect a few items first.

From Fig. 2.6, we see that we need three items: addition to net working capital, new fixed asset investment and yearly depreciation. We calculate each of these next.

Addition to net working capital is given by the difference between the net working capital at the end of 2005 and the net working capital at the end of 2004. Thus, using the figures derived above:

- **Addition to net working capital during 2005** = $20,000 − $10,000
$$= \$10,000$$

New fixed asset investment can be calculated by observing the change in the gross fixed asset account in Fig. 2.4. That is:

- **New fixed asset investment** = $100,000 − $85,000 = $15,000

Lastly, depreciation expense for 2005 is taken from Fig 2.5 and is:

- **Depreciation** = $15,000

Then, as per Fig. 2.6:

- **Operating free cash flow** = $27,000 − $10,000 − $15,000 + $15,000
$$= \$17,000$$

We could have also calculated operating free cash flow more directly as

- **Operating free cash flow** = NOPAT − increase in net assets
$$= \$27,000 - (\$85,000 - \$75,000) = \$17,000$$

This way of looking at a firm's free cash flow shows us that increases in a firm's net assets represent a drain on the free cash flow generated by after-tax operating profits. This does not mean that investing more in net assets is bad. It is a good idea as long as these investments generate sufficiently high returns. But a firm that increases its net assets by investing in projects that return less than the cost of the additional capital allows *value to evaporate*.

For example, Harnischfeger Industries, a maker of machinery for the mining and paper industries, found its cash flow — and hence value — evaporating in the early 1990s, partly due to substantial increases in its accounts receivable each year.[11]

Harnischfeger Industries was also in the business of training naval personnel in the use of command and control centers. And while the business was profitable in terms of margins, the government was often late in paying its bills. Thus, a large fraction of the substantial sales revenue the company generated was tied up in accounts receivable.

Increases in accounts receivable directly increase the net asset base of a firm. Moreover, increases in net assets *reduce* operating free cash flow, and ultimately value. Harnischfeger subsequently dropped this business. However, this example of increased asset usage that leads to Value Evaporation is captured nicely in the following quote[12] by their executive vice president for finance and administration, Francis M. Corby, Jr., as he reflected on the firm's performance in 1993:

> The top line was growing [sales revenue], the bottom line was growing [net income], but the stock price was going nowhere.

Value is a function of *cash*, not profits. Firms that pay too much attention to the income statement, while disregarding the assets employed to generate it, risk Value Evaporation! Wayne Wren, CFO of Allwaste Environmental Services, Inc., once said[13] "If you give me enough capital, and that capital is free, I can assure you that I'll increase income."

Now returning to our example, let us calculate the equity free cash flow for MJM. Using the information already in hand, equity free cash flow can be calculated as follows:

Net operating profit	$45,000
− Interest expense	−3,000
= Profit	42,000
− Taxes at 40%	−16,800

---

[11] See Irwin Ross, "The Stern Stewart Performance 1000," *Journal of Applied Corporate Finance*, Winter 1998, pp. 116–128.

[12] Ibid. Unfortunately the company filed for bankruptcy protection in 1999.

[13] See Irwin Ross, "The Stern Stewart Performance 1000," *Journal of Applied Corporate Finance*, Winter 1997, pp. 115–128.

= Net income	25,200
− Debt principal repayments[14]	+ 5,000
− Changes in net assets	−10,000
Equity free cash flow	**$20,200**

Observe that the equity free cash flow is greater than the operating free cash flow. This may seem strange at first blush, but it is because of the additional funds brought into the firm through the increase in bank borrowing. The increase of $5,000 outweighs the after-tax interest expense of $1,800.[15]

Observe that all we have done so far is analyzed history. Our calculations do not tell us much about firm value. To calculate value, we need to estimate cash flows that will occur in the future. This goes beyond looking at historical data. However, historical accounting data, while not directly relevant for determining value, may help us forecast future cash flows. The idea is that the past may be useful to predict the future.

Of course, when we estimate future cash flows, we are talking about cash flows that occur at *different points in time.* We also need to make these different cash flows similar to each other on the time dimension, so we can add them all up to arrive at value.

The Time Value of Money

A key concept in finance is the *time value of money.* Simply put, a claim to receive $1 one year from today is worth less than $1 today. Why?

First, inflation erodes value. $1 today buys more than it will a year later from now because inflation will drive up prices.

Second, the $1 today is *certain,* whereas the $1 in one year may be *uncertain or risky.* If there is any chance that the party from whom you received the "claim to $1 in one year" would not pay up, the value of this claim is reduced.

Lastly, there is an *opportunity cost* associated with money. If you have to wait to receive your money, you lose the opportunity to do something else with it. That is, value will evaporate if the forgone opportunity is worth more than the chosen one. For example, you could have put the $1 in a bank account and earned interest on it even if inflation were zero.

---

[14]Notice that MJM's total debt has risen from 2004 to 2005 due to an increase in bank debt. Therefore, the entry into the "Debt Principal Repayment" is actually negative. Thus *the deduction of a negative number* leads to a positive adjustment.

[15]After-tax interest expense is calculated as Interest × (1 − tax rate) = $3,000 × (1 − 0.4) = $1,800.

Understanding basic time-value-of-money concepts will prove indispensable when we tackle more advanced topics such as capital budgeting, lease-versus-buy decisions, weighted average cost of capital and firm valuation. In this section, we will begin with a discussion of *future value* and *present value* in the single-period case. We will then move to the multiperiod case and conclude with some special cases for valuing *perpetuities and annuities*.

One-Period Case: Let us begin with an example. Suppose you wish to sell your car and run an advertisement in the local paper to solicit buyers. You have used the car sparingly and decided it was time to remove it from your driveway. By the next morning, you have made two appointments to show the car.

The first respondent to the ad arrives at your house, examines the car, and offers you $5,000 for it. Before you react to the offer, the other potential buyer arrives.

She looks at the car, listens to the motor, checks under the chassis and says, "I'll take it! In fact, I'll give you $5,500 for it. But, I will give you the money in one year." You believe her credit is very good and that there is no chance of her reneging on the deal. You look to the first customer inquisitively, who immediately responds, "My offer stands."

What should you do? $5,500 is clearly more money than $5,000. But who wants to wait a year?

You think for a moment, scribble down some numbers and finally smile. You approach the first bidder and say, "Sorry, but I am going with the $5,500 offer."

Why did you do this?

You knew that if you took the first offer, you would receive $5,000 today. This would give you the *opportunity* to immediately deposit the $5,000 in your bank to earn 8% interest for the year. In one year's time, you would get back your $5,000 in principal, plus the yearly interest of $8\% \times \$5,000 = \$400$, giving you $5,400 in total.[16] We can express this by saying the *future value* (FV) of $5,000 in one year's time earning 8% interest is:

$$FV = \$5,000 + (8\% \times \$5,000) = \$5,000 \times (1 + 8\%) = \$5,000 \times (1.08) = \$5,400$$

Since this is less than what the woman will pay you in one year's time, you decide to go with $5,500 paid-in-one-year offer.

You could have come to the same conclusion by employing the present value concept. That is, you could have asked, "What is the present value of $5,500 to be received in one year's time?" or alternatively, "How much do I have to deposit in

---

[16]For simplicity, we are assuming taxes are not due on the interest income.

the bank today at 8% interest to be able to withdraw $5,500 in one year's time?" That is:

$$PV = \frac{\$5,500}{1.08} = \$5,092.59$$

By comparing the $5,000 cash today offer to the PV of the second offer of $5,092.59, you would have reached the same conclusion.

This simple example gives us the general formula for calculating the present value of a cash flow to be received in one period (denoted CF_1) of:

$$PV = \frac{CF_1}{1+r}$$

where r is the discount (or interest) rate. Moreover, since we are in a one-period world, we can also denote CF_1 as FV and express the relationship between PV and FV in a one-period setting as:

$$FV = PV \times (1 + r)$$

This basic concept now allows us to easily handle the case when cash flows are received across several years. We refer to this as the multiperiod case.

Multiperiod case: To extend the time value of money concept to multiple periods, we must first begin by introducing the concept of *compounding*. Again, let us consider an example. Suppose you wish to deposit $100 in the bank today to earn 10% interest each and every year (otherwise known as per annum).

As we learned above, in one year's time this investment will be worth:

$$FV = \$100 + (10\% \times \$100) = \$100 \times (1 + 10\%) = \$100 \times (1.10) = \$110.$$

Of this $110, $100 is your original deposit (the principal) and $10 is the interest earned on that principal.

What would happen if you left *all* your money in the bank for another year?

A year later you will have:

$$FV = \$110 + (10\% \times \$110) = \$110 \times (1 + 10\%) = \$110 \times (1.10) = \$121$$

Again, you retain your original principal of $100 as well as the interest you had already earned in the first year of $10. But this year, your deposit grew by $11, not $10. Why?

Compound interest! Not only does your original investment of $100 earn 10% interest to give you an additional $10, but now your first year's worth of interest of $10 earns 10% interest as well to give you an additional $1. That is, in the second year you earn 10% on the full $110 available at the end of the first year. This is the beauty of compound interest, or "interest on interest."

However, you could have figured this out at the very beginning by asking, "What will $100 be worth in two years at a rate of interest of 10%?" Your answer would be:

$$FV = \{\$100 \times (1.10)\} \times (1.10) = \$100 \times (1.10)^2$$

For an investment of PV, which earns a rate of interest of r for T periods, we have:

$$FV = PV \times (1 + r)^T$$

Again we can manipulate the relationship between future and present values to answer a different question: "How much is $121 two years from now worth today, using a 10% rate of interest?" The answer is:

$$PV = \frac{\$121}{(1/10)^2} = \$100$$

We can therefore derive the present value (PV) of a cash flow (CF) for a discount rate of r, T periods hence as:

$$PV = \frac{CF}{(1 + r)^T}$$

The multiperiod present value formula above will be useful in a capital budgeting context later. We conclude below with some special cases for calculating present values.

Discounting Multiple Cash Flows (Special Cases): Let us begin by considering one more example which includes *multiple cash flows across multiple periods*. Suppose you had a money-making machine that produced $250 for each of the next three years. If your discount rate was 10%, what is the present value of these three cash flows?

To answer this question, we can use our multiperiod present value formula three times since we receive $250 in one year, another $250 in two years, and the last $250 in three years. The total present value is then the sum of:

1. $PV = \dfrac{\$250}{(1.10)^1} = \$227.27$

2. $PV = \dfrac{\$250}{(1.10)^2} = \$206.61$

3. $PV = \dfrac{\$250}{(1.10)^3} = \$187.83$

which is \$621.71 in total. Observe that we can simply add these three values up because they are all expressed in terms of dollars today (i.e., they are each in present value form).

That was easy enough. But what if we had a money-making machine that gave us \$250 a year for the next 30 years?

We could apply the same methodology, but it certainly becomes tedious. Worse yet, what if this money-making machine produced \$250 per year each year, *forever?*[17] We could obviously use some help here.

The latter case of receiving the same dollar amount every year forever is called a *perpetuity*. Luckily we have a very simple formula for calculating the present value of a perpetuity. It is given by the solution to discounting every year's cash flow (which is the same every year and denoted by CF) and summing them up from now until eternity. We can express this algebraically as:

$$PV = \frac{CF}{(1+r)^1} + \frac{CF}{(1+r)^2} + \frac{CF}{(1+r)^3} + \ldots \text{until infinity}$$

$$PV = \frac{CF}{r}$$

This last formula is known as the *perpetuity* formula. For our example, we could calculate the present value of receiving \$250 a year forever at a discount rate of 10% as:

$$PV = \frac{\$250}{0.1} = \$2{,}500$$

Finally, how do we compute the present value of a cash flow *annuity*. An *annuity* is a stream of identical cash flows for a finite (i.e., less than infinity!) number of years. To arrive at the formula, let us return to our example above when we received \$250 a year for only three years. How do we obtain the present value of these cash flows?

If we were to write out all the cash flows, we would have:

$$PV = \frac{\$250}{(1.1)^1} + \frac{\$250}{(1.1)^2} + \frac{\$250}{(1.1)^3}$$

This can also be written as:

$$PV = \$250 \times \left[\frac{1}{(1.1)} + \frac{1}{(1.1)^2} + \frac{1}{(1.1)^3} \right]$$

and simplified to:

$$PV = \$250 \times \left[\frac{1}{0.1} - \frac{1}{0.1 \times (1.1)^3} \right] = \$250 \times 2.4869 = \$621.71$$

---

[17]Such an investment is not all that unusual. For example, the UK government issues consol bonds that pay a stated interest amount forever.

This is exactly the answer we obtained previously when we summed up the present values of each yearly payment.

In general, the present value of a cash flow (CF) to be received for T periods when the discount rate is *r* is:

$$PV = \frac{CF}{r} - \frac{CF}{r(1+r)^T}$$

or

PV of an annuity for T periods = PV of a perpetuity − PV of the perpetuity
you do not have after T periods

Looking at this formula, a key insight emerges: the present value of an annuity for T periods is the PV of a perpetuity minus the PV of the perpetuity you *do not* have after T periods.[18]

4. Jerry's Concluding Thoughts

As Jerry reflected on what he had learned about the basics of finance, he also realized that there was much that Bob had not yet covered. For example, how does one come up with these estimates of future cash flows that determine value? Where do discount rates come from? And how will the decisions he will make for maximizing value creation and its retention in his lemonade company reflect cash flows and the discount rate? Answers to these questions will have to wait until later chapters.

Main Lessons

- Accounting ratios drawn from historical accounting statements can help us analyze and control our firm.
- Value is derived from cash, not accounting profits.
- Estimates of cash flows depend on profits, captured by the income statement, as well as assets employed, captured by the balance sheet.
- Value Evaporation occurs when firms use excessive asset levels to generate profits.
- There is a time value to money — a dollar today is worth more than a dollar tomorrow.
- Financial metrics help us measure value creation and thus help us monitor our value retention, so that we can determine whether our Value Sphere is synchronized.

[18]In Table 2.1, we include standard tables that display the present value, future value, and present value of an annuity, respectively, for $1.

Table 2.1.

Present value of $1 to be received after t years

Number of years	Interest rate per year														
	1%	2%	3%	4%	5%	6%	7%	8%	9%	10%	11%	12%	13%	14%	15%
1	0.990	0.980	0.971	0.962	0.952	0.943	0.935	0.926	0.917	0.909	0.901	0.893	0.885	0.877	0.870
2	0.980	0.961	0.943	0.925	0.907	0.890	0.873	0.857	0.842	0.826	0.812	0.797	0.783	0.769	0.756
3	0.971	0.942	0.915	0.889	0.864	0.840	0.816	0.794	0.772	0.751	0.731	0.712	0.693	0.675	0.658
4	0.961	0.924	0.888	0.855	0.823	0.792	0.763	0.735	0.708	0.683	0.659	0.636	0.613	0.592	0.572
5	0.951	0.906	0.863	0.822	0.784	0.747	0.713	0.681	0.650	0.621	0.593	0.567	0.543	0.519	0.497
6	0.942	0.888	0.837	0.790	0.746	0.705	0.666	0.630	0.596	0.564	0.535	0.507	0.480	0.456	0.432
7	0.933	0.871	0.813	0.760	0.711	0.665	0.623	0.583	0.547	0.513	0.482	0.452	0.425	0.400	0.376
8	0.923	0.853	0.789	0.731	0.677	0.627	0.582	0.540	0.502	0.467	0.434	0.404	0.376	0.351	0.327
9	0.914	0.837	0.766	0.703	0.645	0.592	0.544	0.500	0.460	0.424	0.391	0.361	0.333	0.308	0.284
10	0.905	0.820	0.744	0.676	0.614	0.558	0.508	0.463	0.422	0.386	0.352	0.322	0.295	0.270	0.247
11	0.896	0.804	0.722	0.650	0.585	0.527	0.475	0.429	0.388	0.350	0.317	0.287	0.261	0.237	0.215
12	0.887	0.788	0.701	0.625	0.557	0.497	0.444	0.397	0.356	0.319	0.286	0.257	0.231	0.208	0.187
13	0.879	0.773	0.681	0.601	0.530	0.469	0.415	0.368	0.326	0.290	0.258	0.229	0.204	0.182	0.163
14	0.870	0.758	0.661	0.577	0.505	0.442	0.388	0.340	0.299	0.263	0.232	0.205	0.181	0.160	0.141
15	0.861	0.743	0.642	0.555	0.481	0.417	0.362	0.315	0.275	0.239	0.209	0.183	0.160	0.140	0.123
16	0.853	0.728	0.623	0.534	0.458	0.394	0.339	0.292	0.252	0.218	0.188	0.163	0.141	0.123	0.107
17	0.844	0.714	0.605	0.513	0.436	0.371	0.317	0.270	0.231	0.198	0.170	0.146	0.125	0.108	0.093
18	0.836	0.700	0.587	0.494	0.416	0.350	0.296	0.250	0.212	0.180	0.153	0.130	0.111	0.095	0.081
19	0.828	0.686	0.570	0.475	0.396	0.331	0.277	0.232	0.194	0.164	0.138	0.116	0.098	0.083	0.070
20	0.820	0.673	0.554	0.456	0.377	0.312	0.258	0.215	0.178	0.149	0.124	0.104	0.087	0.073	0.061

Table 2.1. *(Continued)*

Future value of $1 after t years

Interest rate per year

Number of Years	1%	2%	3%	4%	5%	6%	7%	8%	9%	10%	11%	12%	13%	14%	15%
1	1.010	1.020	1.030	1.040	1.050	1.060	1.070	1.080	1.090	1.100	1.110	1.120	1.130	1.140	1.150
2	1.020	1.040	1.061	1.082	1.103	1.124	1.145	1.166	1.188	1.210	1.232	1.254	1.277	1.300	1.323
3	1.030	1.061	1.093	1.125	1.158	1.191	1.225	1.260	1.295	1.331	1.368	1.405	1.443	1.482	1.521
4	1.041	1.082	1.126	1.170	1.216	1.262	1.311	1.360	1.412	1.464	1.518	1.574	1.630	1.689	1.749
5	1.051	1.104	1.159	1.217	1.276	1.338	1.403	1.469	1.539	1.611	1.685	1.762	1.842	1.925	2.011
6	1.062	1.126	1.194	1.265	1.340	1.419	1.501	1.587	1.677	1.772	1.870	1.974	2.082	2.195	2.313
7	1.072	1.149	1.230	1.316	1.407	1.504	1.606	1.714	1.828	1.949	2.076	2.211	2.353	2.502	2.660
8	1.083	1.172	1.267	1.369	1.477	1.594	1.718	1.851	1.993	2.144	2.305	2.476	2.658	2.853	3.059
9	1.094	1.195	1.305	1.423	1.551	1.689	1.838	1.999	2.172	2.358	2.558	2.773	3.004	3.252	3.518
10	1.105	1.219	1.344	1.480	1.629	1.791	1.967	2.159	2.367	2.594	2.839	3.106	3.395	3.707	4.046
11	1.116	1.243	1.384	1.539	1.710	1.898	2.105	2.332	2.580	2.853	3.152	3.479	3.836	4.226	4.652
12	1.127	1.268	1.426	1.601	1.796	2.012	2.252	2.518	2.813	3.138	3.498	3.896	4.335	4.818	5.350
13	1.138	1.294	1.469	1.665	1.886	2.133	2.410	2.720	3.066	3.452	3.883	4.363	4.898	5.492	6.153
14	1.149	1.319	1.513	1.732	1.980	2.261	2.579	2.937	3.342	3.797	4.310	4.887	5.535	6.261	7.076
15	1.161	1.346	1.558	1.801	2.079	2.397	2.759	3.172	3.642	4.177	4.785	5.474	6.254	7.138	8.137
16	1.173	1.373	1.605	1.873	2.183	2.540	2.952	3.426	3.970	4.595	5.311	6.130	7.067	8.137	9.358
17	1.184	1.400	1.653	1.948	2.292	2.693	3.159	3.700	4.328	5.054	5.895	6.866	7.986	9.276	10.761
18	1.196	1.428	1.702	2.026	2.407	2.854	3.380	3.996	4.717	5.560	6.544	7.690	9.024	10.575	12.375
19	1.208	1.457	1.754	2.107	2.527	3.026	3.617	4.316	5.142	6.116	7.263	8.613	10.197	12.056	14.232
20	1.220	1.486	1.806	2.191	2.653	3.207	3.870	4.661	5.604	6.727	8.062	9.646	11.523	13.743	16.367

Table 2.1. (*Continued*)

Present value of $1 per year for each of t years (annuity)

Number of Years	Interest rate per year														
	1%	2%	3%	4%	5%	6%	7%	8%	9%	10%	11%	12%	13%	14%	15%
1	0.990	0.980	0.971	0.962	0.952	0.943	0.935	0.926	0.917	0.909	0.901	0.893	0.885	0.877	0.870
2	1.970	1.942	1.913	1.886	1.859	1.833	1.808	1.783	1.759	1.736	1.713	1.690	1.668	1.647	1.626
3	2.941	2.884	2.829	2.775	2.723	2.673	2.624	2.577	2.531	2.487	2.444	2.402	2.361	2.322	2.283
4	3.902	3.808	3.717	3.630	3.546	3.465	3.387	3.312	3.240	3.170	3.102	3.037	2.974	2.914	2.855
5	4.853	4.713	4.580	4.452	4.329	4.212	4.100	3.993	3.890	3.791	3.696	3.605	3.517	3.433	3.352
6	5.795	5.601	5.417	5.242	5.076	4.917	4.767	4.623	4.486	4.355	4.231	4.111	3.998	3.889	3.784
7	6.728	6.472	6.230	6.002	5.786	5.582	5.389	5.206	5.033	4.868	4.712	4.564	4.423	4.288	4.160
8	7.652	7.325	7.020	6.733	6.463	6.210	5.971	5.747	5.535	5.335	5.146	4.968	4.799	4.639	4.487
9	8.566	8.162	7.786	7.435	7.108	6.802	6.515	6.247	5.995	5.759	5.537	5.328	5.132	4.946	4.772
10	9.471	8.983	8.530	8.111	7.722	7.360	7.024	6.710	6.418	6.145	5.889	5.650	5.426	5.216	5.019
11	10.368	9.787	9.253	8.760	8.306	7.887	7.499	7.139	6.805	6.495	6.207	5.938	5.687	5.453	5.234
12	11.255	10.575	9.954	9.385	8.863	8.384	7.943	7.536	7.161	6.814	6.492	6.194	5.918	5.660	5.421
13	12.134	11.348	10.635	9.986	9.394	8.853	8.358	7.904	7.487	7.103	6.750	6.424	6.122	5.842	5.583
14	13.004	12.106	11.296	10.563	9.899	9.295	8.745	8.244	7.786	7.367	6.982	6.628	6.302	6.002	5.724
15	13.865	12.849	11.938	11.118	10.380	9.712	9.108	8.559	8.061	7.606	7.191	6.811	6.462	6.142	5.847
16	14.718	13.578	12.561	11.652	10.838	10.106	9.447	8.851	8.313	7.824	7.379	6.974	6.604	6.265	5.954
17	15.562	14.292	13.166	12.166	11.274	10.477	9.763	9.122	8.544	8.022	7.549	7.120	6.729	6.373	6.047
18	16.398	14.992	13.754	12.659	11.690	10.828	10.059	9.372	8.756	8.201	7.702	7.250	6.840	6.467	6.128
19	17.226	15.678	14.324	13.134	12.085	11.158	10.336	9.604	8.950	8.365	7.839	7.366	6.938	6.550	6.198
20	18.046	16.351	14.877	13.590	12.462	11.470	10.594	9.818	9.129	8.514	7.963	7.469	7.025	6.623	6.259

End-of-Chapter Exercises

1. For a division of your company, calculate both your gross margin and your operating margin. How do they compare? What does the difference between the two imply about your operating efficiency? Can you relate the differences in margins to the differences in corporate strategy you identified in Chapter 1?
2. Pick one of your competitors and calculate the same ratios as above. How does your company compare? If differences exist, to what do you attribute them?
3. Calculate the components of return on equity (ROE) as given by the DuPont formula for both your company and your competitor. Does your answer to Question 2 shed light on any differences in the financial performance? Again, relate your answer to possible differences in corporate strategy?
4. Estimate your division's operating free cash flow for the last two years. What was the growth rate you achieved over the past year? Was this growth rate consistent with the strategy.

Practice Problems

1. The Michigan Electronics Co. has the following data:

Income statement year: 2005 ($ thousands)	
Sales	$2,000
Cost of goods sold (including depreciation)	$1,600
SG&A	$200
Operating profit	$200
Interest on debt	$50
Pre-tax income	$150
Taxes (@ 40%)	$60
Net income	$90

Balance sheets ($ thousands)		
	2004	2005
Total current assets	$450	$500
Net fixed assets	$1,200	$1,300
Total net assets	$1,650	$1,800
Payables	$150	$175
Short-term bank debt	$50	$75
Current portion of long-term debt	$150	$125
Total current liabilities	$350	$375
Long-term debt	$1,000	$1,000
Shareholders' equity	$300	$425
Total liabilities and equity	$1,650	$1,800

Calculate Michigan Electronics' free cash flow (FCF) for 2002.

2. Consider the following data for the Wolverine Student Supplies Co.

Income statement year: 2005 ($ thousands)	
Net sales	$150.00
Cost of goods sold (excluding depreciation)	$90.00
Depreciation	$4.00
SG&A Expenses	$36.00
Operating profit (EBIT)	$20.00
Interest	$12.00
Pre-tax income	$8.00
Taxes (@ 40%)	$3.20
Net income	$4.80
Dividends	$2.80
Addition to retained earnings	$2.00

Balance sheets		
	2004	2005
Cash	$25.00	$22.00
Accounts receivables and inventories	$70.00	$75.00
Total current assets	$95.00	$97.00
Net PP&E	$40.00	$50.00
Total net assets	$135.00	$147.00
Accounts payable	$45.00	$60.00
Short-term bank debt	$25.00	$20.00
Total current liabilities	$70.00	$80.00
Long-term debt	$30.00	$30.00
Common stock and paid-in-surplus	$20.00	$20.00
Retained earnings	$15.00	$17.00
Total liabilities and shareholders, equity	$135.00	$147.00

(a) What is Wolverine's operating free cash flow (FCF) for 2005?
(b) Prepare a sources and uses of funds analysis for Wolverine for 2005 to calculate the change in its cash balance from 2004 to 2005 and verify this against the actual change in cash from its 2004 and 2005 balance sheets.

Addendum to Chapter 2

In this addendum we explain in greater detail what free cash flow (FCF) *is* and what it is *not*. In our opinion, FCF is one of the two central concepts in financial valuation, the other being the cost of capital (which will be covered in Chapter 8). Yet, in our experience it is a concept that is often not properly understood. In this addendum, the issues we deal with are:

- What is the difference between FCF and the addition to the firm's cash balance by the end of the year?
- What is the relationship between FCF and sources and uses of funds?
- Does a firm's capital structure — the amount of debt it has — impact its FCF?

We will examine these issues, we will work with a numerical example.

Numerical Example:

JUMPSHOOTER COMPANY Income statement 2005; $ millions	
Net sales	$1,509
Cost of goods sold (COGS)	650
Sales, general and administrative (SG&A)	100
Depreciation	65
EBIT (Earnings before interest and taxes)	$694
Interest on debt	70
Pre-tax income	$624
Taxes (@ 34%)	$212
Net income	$412

Dividends
$103

Additions to Retained
Earnings $309

Balance sheets	$ millions	
	2004	2005
Cash	$104	$160
Accounts receivables	$455	$688
Inventories	$553	$555
Total current assets	$1,112	$1,403
Net PP&E (Property plant & equipment)	$1,644	$1,709
Total net assets	$2,756	$3,112
Accounts payable	$428	$389
Total current liabilities	$428	$389
Long-term dept	$408	$454
Common stock and paid-in surplus	$600	$640
Retained earnings	$1,320	$1,629
Total net assets	$2,756	$3,112

Analysis

Increase in net fixed assets (NFA) during 2005

$= \$1{,}709 - \$1{,}644 = \$65$

Net working capital (NWC) at the end of 2005

$= \$1{,}403$ million (Working capital)

$-\$389$ million (Accounts payable)

$\$1{,}014$ million

NWC end 2004 $= \$1{,}112 - \$428 = \$684$

Increase in NWC during 2005 $= \$1{,}014 - \$684 = \$330$ million

ANALYSIS: SOURCES AND USES OF FUNDS

2005 Sources and uses	$millions
Cash Beginning 2005	$104
Sources by cash	
Operations	
Net income	$412
Depreciation	$65
Working capital	
Nothing	$0
Long-term financing	
Increase in common stock	$40
Increase in long-term debt	$46
Total sources	$563
Uses of cash	
Working capital	
Increase in accounts receivable	$233
Increase in inventory	$2
Decrease in accounts payable	$39
Long-term financing	
Fixed assets acquisitions	$130
(increase in net fixed assets = $65 + Depreciation = $65)	
Dividends paid	$103
Total uses	$507

- Net addition to cash = $563 − $507 = $56 million
- Ending cash = Beginning cash + net addition to cash

$$= \$104 + \$56 = \$160 \text{ million}$$

- *Free cash flow*

$$\text{FCF} = \text{NOPAT} - \text{increase in NFA} - \text{increase in NWC}$$
$$= \text{EBIT}(1 - T) - \text{increase in NFA} - \text{increase in NWC}$$
$$= \$694[1 - 0.34] - \$65 - \$330 = \$63 \text{ million}$$

Notes:

- FCF is NOT the addition to the firm's cash from the start to the end of the year.
- FCF considers profit *above* the interest expense line, whereas net addition to cash is *after* payment of interest and dividends. Thus, the amount of debt on the balance sheet has NO impact on FCF.

- In computing net addition to cash via a sources and uses of funds analysis, we do NOT consider changes in cash while computing increase in NWC, because that *would* be double counting.

  - However, we *do* consider increase in cash as an increase in NWC while computing FCF because, if more cash is needed to operate the business (i.e., we are not just accumulating excess liquidity), then this *is* a drain on FCF.

  - Note that the debt interest tax shield (cash saved on taxes due to tax deductibility of debt interest) is not part of FCF (it is BELOW NOPAT in the income statement) because this tax shield is reflected in the weighted average cost of capital (WACC) that we use to discount FCF with.

- WHAT THEN IS THE RELATIONSHIP BETWEEN FCF AND ADDITION TO CASH?

  - Let us look at this pictorially…. (**T** stands for tax rate)

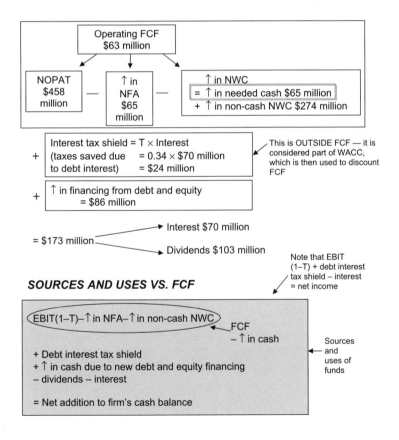

- If the firm accumulates excess cash (i.e., say $5 out of the $65 increase in cash is excess) and not needed for business purposes, then

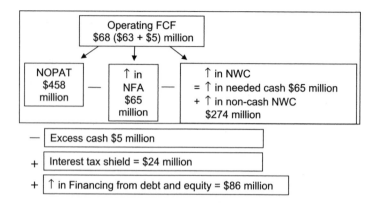

- If you are building up excess liquidity for strategic reasons, then this increase in cash related to excess liquidity is NOT a drain on FCF.

Chapter 3

BUSINESS GROWTH, EXTERNAL FINANCING, AND IPOs: JERRY IS INTRODUCED TO THE "ONE FOR ME, NONE FOR YOU" SLOGAN

1. Jerry's Start

Jerry opened his first lemonade store and discovered the joys and frustrations of becoming an entrepreneur. The lemonade recipe, calling for cracked white pepper and salt, was adapted from an old family concoction his grandmother served during the hot summer months. It used less water than the usual lemonade. In fact, the main ingredients were freshly squeezed lemon juice and ice. Jerry's grandmother used little sugar in her recipe since she preferred the tart, tangy taste of fresh lemons.

After serving his initial customers, however, Jerry got his first lesson in customer satisfaction. The customers disliked his grandmother's recipe! They thought it was too tart.

2. Perfecting the Business

Jerry was perplexed by this reaction. He was forced, however, to recall his earlier lesson on *user-based quality* (see Chapter 1) and realized that ultimately the only thing that mattered was what the customer wanted. In order to do some market research, he enlisted five of his friends, who were among the first customers, to act as a customer panel to advise him of the types of products to offer.

Based on their feedback, Jerry revised his menu to include original lemonade, along with flavored lemonade, hot tea, and shaved ice versions of both tea and lemonade. All would be offered unsweetened, sweetened with sugar or artificial sweetener. Jerry would also offer snacks of cookies, muffins, and the like, all purchased from a local bakery.

Jerry realized, however, that a key component of the business plan was to perfect the shaved ice versions of tea and lemonade. The shaved ice required a machine that uniformly processed a block of ice into a mass of tiny ice crystals that could be placed in a cup to accept the lemonade or tea flavor. Jerry first investigated the machine used to make snow cones, a popular crushed ice product that is offered in many flavors and served in a paper cone-shaped cup. The ice was too coarse and grainy for Jerry's taste. After rejecting the snow cone ice machines, Jerry discovered that few alternatives existed. He would have to develop his own machine. He enlisted an engineer friend of his to help him design and develop a suitable shaved ice machine.

Jerry paid the engineer an hourly wage and had him sign a legal agreement that Jerry would own the rights to any machine that was developed. Two months later, Jerry had a version of the machine that worked. The machine design was a variant of a rotary blade concept with precise positioning of the block of ice to be shaved. The shaved ice easily absorbed the tea and lemon flavors, resulting in very rich flavors of the final product. This attribute was critical to Jerry's strategy of offering excellent products at premium prices since no competitor could match it.

Jerry hired a local attorney to investigate the possible patents for his machine. After confirmation that no similar designs existed, he instructed the attorney to file for patents on the machine. The attorney also suggested to Jerry that he incorporate the business, especially in light of the patented machines. With a corporation Jerry would achieve limited personal liability, should the lemonade business fail.

When all this was done, Jerry invited the customer panel to taste the shaved ice tea and lemonade produced with the machine. They were impressed. Jerry sensed he had a hit!

3. The Business Grows

Jerry and Sallie decided that the best thing to do was to have a grand re-opening to introduce the new menu with the tea and lemon shaved-ice products they could now make with the new machine. The grand re-opening was announced in the newspapers and on the radio. Jerry spent over $6000 to launch the new menu and inform potential customers of his location.

Fortunately, the advertising expenditures paid off. There was a traffic jam at the mall, and the cash register was busy all day. The shaved ice tea and lemon flavors were a hit and the original lemonade also sold well with the increased customer traffic. The receipts for the grand re-opening day totaled $15,000.

Income statement

Sales revenue	$1,800,000
Cost of goods sold	$1,000,000
Gross profit margin	$800,000
SG&A	$300,000
Depreciation	$150,000
Net operating profit	$350,000
Interest expense	$80,000
Profit before taxes	$270,000
Taxes at 40%	$108,000
Profit after taxes	**$162,000**

Balance sheet

Assets		Liabilities and equity	
Cash	$120,000	Accounts payable	$380,000
Accounts receivable	$60,000	Taxes payable	—
Inventory	$450,000	Accrued liabilities	—
Current assets	$630,000	Current liabilities	$380,000
Gross fixed assets	$1,700,000	Bank debt	$800,000
Accumulated depreciation	$150,000	Public debt	—
Net fixed assets	$1,550,000	Shareholders' equity	$1,000,000
Total assets	$2,180,000	**Total liabilities and equity**	$2,180,000

Fig. 3.1.   First year financial statements.

The success of the grand re-opening was sustained in the following months, erasing the early losses of the business. The first year's financial statements are shown in Fig. 3.1. Jerry was pleased to see that first-year profits were $162,000. As sole shareholders of the incorporated business, he and Sallie paid the entire profit to themselves as a dividend.

Jerry's success was drawing the attention of competitors who wanted to franchise the concept or buy the business. Competitors were particularly interested in Jerry's patented shaved ice machine, which offered a product advantage in absorbing flavors.

Jerry contacted Bob Butterfield to show him the financials and possible expansion plans for the business.

"Wow," Bob exclaimed, "these financial statements are great. Your business is really humming, Jerry."

"I know," said Jerry, "but I think I should expand the business to capture the market before competitors move in with a similar concept."

"But don't you have a patent on the shaved ice machine?" Bob interjected.

"Yes, but the competition could potentially develop a similar machine, or substitute a different kind of ice. As you know, Bob, these guys are pretty sharp. Especially Mickey, who owns a majority of the national flavored drinks business. I've met him once, and don't like him. He wanted to buy our patents, but I refused," responded Jerry.

Jerry took Bob's advice and opened two more locations locally. He recruited and trained the employees to staff the two new locations. Although the business was relatively easy to learn, Jerry had to instruct the new employees on the proper use of the shaved ice machine, the recipes used to create the unique tea and lemon flavors, the required dress and demeanor demanded for the job, and the crucial elements of customer service that were necessary for success.

At Bob's insistence, he produced a training manual on how to operate the business. Periodically, Jerry would update the "Bible," the term used to affectionately describe the training manual. In the end, Jerry completely codified the operating procedures that were necessary for success in operating his business.

Six months into the second year of operations, the interim results were as shown in Fig. 3.2. The two new locations were now as profitable as the initial site. Jerry now began to consider expanding to other cities. Once again, he sought Bob's advice.

4. Expansion Plans

"Bob, if I want to expand, what should I worry about?" Jerry asked, as he pushed the interim financial results toward him.

Bob responded, "Financial capital is a constraint, although you just don't see it at this stage. Remember our discussion of financial ratios? Let me add to that with a new concept — sustainable growth.

"The sustainable growth rate calculation is very important for a growing business like yours because it tells you how fast you can grow sales and assets *without issuing new equity to finance the growth*. The reason why you should be interested in this is that, as a privately-held company, you don't have access to public equity markets. If expanding your business requires new equity — perhaps because you don't want to take on more debt — it would have to probably come from your own money. However, you may not want to risk any more of your own wealth in the business." Bob showed Jerry the following.

Income statement

Sales revenue	$1,400,000
Cost of Goods Sold	$800,000
Gross profit margin	$600,000
SG&A	$250,000
Depreciation	$75,000
Net operating profit	$270,000
Interest expense	$47,000
Profit before taxes	$228,000
Taxes at 40%	$91,200
Profit after taxes or net income or earnings	**$136,800**

Balance sheet

Assets		Liabilities and equity	
Cash	$95,800	Accounts payable	$496,000
Accounts receivable	$75,000	Taxes payable	—
Inventory	$527,000	Accrued liabilities	—
Current assets	$697,800	Current liabilities	$496,000
Gross fixed assets	$2,100,000	Bank debt	$940,000
Accumulated depreciation	$225,000	Public debt	—
Net fixed assets	$1,875,000	Shareholders' equity	$1,136,800
		Total liabilities	
Total assets	$2,572,800	**and equity**	$2,572,800

Fig. 3.2.   Second year financial statements — First 6 months.

This sustainable growth rate, G*, is given by:

$$G^* = E \times R \times A \times L$$

where

G* = Sustainable growth rate in sales

E = Earnings retention rate (also equal to 1 minus the dividend payout ratio)

R = Return on sales (net income/sales revenue)

A = Asset turnover ratio (sales revenue/assets)

L = Leverage ratio (assets/beginning equity).

He also remarked that there is an alternative formulation of G^*:

$$G^* = E \times ROE$$

where
ROE $=$ Return on equity
ROE $= R \times A \times L$.

The last formulation of ROE is known as the DuPont formula, which expresses return on equity as equal to the multiplication of return on sales, assets turnover, and leverage ratios. (We saw this in Chapter 2.)

"For your company, the calculation yields a sustainable growth rate of about 27%. Since I need annual rates for these ratios, I have assumed the 6 month's sales will be one-half of the yearly results. As I recall, the business is not very seasonal on a half-year basis." Bob then showed Jerry his calculations:

$$E = (1.0 - 0) = 1.00$$
$$R = 136,800/1,4000,000 = 9.77\%$$
$$A = ((1,400,000) \times 2)/2,572,800 = 1.09$$
$$L = 2,572,800/1,000,000 = 2.57$$
$$G^* = 27.4\%$$

"Note that the ROE is 27.4% and I have assumed all of the earnings are retained in the business. In other words, no dividends are paid, which is usually the case for a fast-growing start-up company like yours. I don't think it makes much sense for you to pay a dividend right now, given your growth opportunities. If you do pay a dividend, the sustainable growth rate will be lower. In fact, if all the earnings are paid as dividends the sustainable growth rate drops to zero. Sometime in the future we should talk about a dividend policy for the company. For now, the zero-dividend policy is fine.

"Given that your plans call for an expansion that will add five locations to the current three, you expect to grow sales at approximately a 167% rate, assuming the new locations perform as the existing ones do.

"This planned growth in sales is well in excess of the self-sustainable growth rate. Something has to give. I'd suggest you prepare for an *initial public offering* (IPO) of shares and sell common stock to the public. That may be the best way for you to get enough capital to expand as rapidly as you want to in order to beat the competition."

"Wait a second, Bob," Jerry interrupted. "I was able to open two new locations without requiring additional capital."

"That is true, Jerry. But you also greatly expanded your debt through increased use of lease financing. When you signed your name to the leases on the two new locations, it was as if you had signed your name to a series of debt payments at the bank. Your annual operating lease obligation is now $60,000. Using the widely accepted standard of eight times annual lease payments to determine the equivalent debt and asset investment, I have recast your balance sheet in Fig. 3.3. Note that on an adjusted book value basis, your debt is half again as much as shown on the original balance sheet. Most financial analysts capitalize operating leases as I have done and include them as debt on the balance sheet you have been greatly increasing the leverage ratio to finance your initial growth. Given the expansion plans you have outlined, I see no alternative that is better than an issue of stock. This will distribute some of your ownership position to others through the IPO."

"Won't that dilute my ownership position?"

"Yes it will, Jerry. However, most entrepreneurs think it is better to own a smaller percentage of a big pie than 100% of a small pie. It is the inevitable consequence of needing financing to fuel the high growth that your strategy is producing. In fact, external financing will allow you to relax the constraint imposed on you by sustainable growth, which is very limiting. At the end of the day, you are interested in good growth, which is all growth at rates of return exceeding your cost of capital, not just growth you can finance internally. Judicious use of

Balance sheet

Assets		Liabilities and equity	
Cash	$95,800	Accounts payable	$496,000
Accounts receivable	$75,000	Taxes payable	—
Inventory	$527,000	Accrued liabilities	—
Current assets	$697,800	Current liabilities	$496,000
		Capitalized	
Leased assets	$480,000	lease liabilities	$480,000
Gross fixed assets	$2,100,000	Bank debt	$940,000
Accumulated depreciation	$225,000	Public debt	—
Net fixed assets	$1,875,000	Shareholders' equity	$1,136,800
		Total liabilities	
Total assets	$3,052,800	**and equity**	$3,052,800

Fig. 3.3.   Recast balance sheet.

external financing to earn higher rates of return is part of a well-synchronized Value Sphere."

Jerry reflected on what Bob had said and asked, "What do you mean by good growth? I thought growth was always good."

Bob shook his head and responded, "No, Jerry. There are two types of growth — good growth and bad growth. Good growth occurs when the return on net assets exceeds the cost of capital. When this happens, every incremental dollar invested creates more value. Bad growth occurs when the return on net assets falls short of the cost of capital. In this case, every dollar invested destroys value."

Jerry looked surprised, "You mean there are firms out there that actually destroy value knowingly?"

Bob nodded, "May seem surprising, but between 1965 and 1981, both the earnings and book value per share *more than doubled* for the Dow Jones Industrial Average while the ratio of market value to book value *declined more than 60%* and P/E ratios also fell. This could only happen if these firms engaged in bad growth. It is different for us. This IPO is going to help us engage in good growth."

"Well, if that's the way it is, how do I get started on this IPO thing, Bob?"

"I suggest you contact Butler and Jones. It's a regional investment banking house in this area that I believe would serve you well," said Bob.

5. The IPO Process

Jerry met with Alex Butler, a founding partner of Butler and Jones, to discuss a potential IPO for his business. What impressed Jerry the most were the questions Alex asked. It seemed as though he wanted to know everything about the business — its history, its strategy, the financials, future plans, background of senior management, the competition, and so on. Mr. Butler was particularly interested in the patent protection on the shaved ice machine. He explained to Jerry that this was all part of the "due diligence" process that his firm must undertake when assessing the prospects for new clients in need of financing.[19]

Alex Butler also explained to Jerry how the IPO process worked from start to finish. This is shown in Fig. 3.4.

A critically important part of an IPO is determining the share price for the stock offering. If the price is too high, the issue might fail. Or even if it succeeds, there might be a significant post-issue price decline that exposes the firm and the

---

[19]In Chapter 19, we will revisit the due diligence process in connection with a merger valuation.

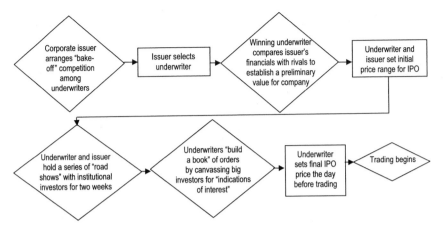

Fig. 3.4.   Anatomy of an IPO.
Source: Wall street Journal, April 16, 1999.

investment banker to the risk of being sued by unhappy investors. If it is too low, the company will sell the shares for less than they are worth and thus suffer more dilution than necessary.

Although there are many ways to value a firm in an IPO, the investment bankers always check the reasonableness of their share pricing by using data from comparable companies. On average, however, it appears that IPOs are underpriced, so that investors who can buy the IPO at the initial price can earn abnormally high returns if they sell off their shares by the end of the day on which they buy the IPO.[20]

Jerry was struck by an article appearing in the July 7, 1998 *Wall Street Journal*. The headline read, "Broadcast.com Soars $3\frac{1}{2}$ Times From IPO Price." Of particular interest was the following paragraph:

> Shares of Broadcast.com Inc., an unprofitable provider of audio and video programming over the Internet, on Friday posted the largest first-day gain of any sizable initial public offering this decade. Shares of the Dallas company, the latest high-tech wonder to dazzle investors and raise questions about the sky-high valuations of many Internet start-ups, rocketed from their offering price of $18 to close NASDAQ Stock Market trading at

---

[20]For desirable IPOs, demand for the new shares may exceed supply at the offering price. In this case, only the best customers of the investment bank will receive an allocation of the new shares. After the Internet boom, when this practice was rampant, the large gains earned by the boomed bank customers was viewed as unfair. Now the SEC requires a chance for all investors to participate in IPOs.

$62.75, a gain of 294% from the offering price. The stock actually opened for trading at $68."[21]

This IPO, managed by Morgan, Dean and Smith, had a huge demand for shares from institutional as well as individual investors. Jerry noted that the IPO underpricing phenomenon was not limited to issues from smaller, less known, investment bankers such as Butler and Jones. To Jerry, the evidence seemed to indicate that the valuation models employed by the investment bankers to set the price were seriously flawed. He needed to find out more.[22]

How does the pricing for the IPO stack up against the comparable data for similar firms that are publicly traded? Through the use of multiples of net income, EBIT, cash flow, etc., the banker can gauge the share price of the IPO relative to comparable, publicly-traded firms. For this reason, Butler and Jones prepared a pro-forma forecasted year-end income statement for Jerry's lemonade in Fig. 3.5.

$$\text{Equity cash flow} = \text{Earnings} + \text{Depreciation} - \text{Reinvestment}$$
$$= \$273 + \$151,740 - \$1251$$
$$= \$424,074.$$

The comparable analysis performed by Butler and Jones, based on the numbers in Fig. 3.5, is shown in Fig. 3.6. It indicates a total share value of over $8.9 million

Sales revenue	$2,800,000
Cost of goods sold and SG&A	$2,100,000
Earnings before interest, taxes, depreciation, and amortization (EBITDA)	$700,000
Depreciation	$151,748
(EBIT) Earnings before interest and taxes or net operating profit interest	$548,252
	$92,290
Profit before taxes	$455,962
Taxes at 40%	$182,385
Earnings (net income)	**$273,577**

Fig. 3.5.   Forecasted year 2 income statement.

---

[21] The record for the largest first-day percentage price increase belongs, however, to a little company in New York, called Globe.com, that went public in November 1998. It opened with an IPO price of $9 a share. The price of the very first trade was $90 a share, a whopping 900% increase!

[22] The Addendum describes the scientific evidence on IPOs and the theories that explain why IPOs are underpriced. In fact, subsequent IPOs of some Internet stocks have eclipsed Broadcast.com's first-day gain.

	Price/ Earnings	Price/ Sales	Price/ EBIT	Price/ EBITDA	Price/ Cash flow
Boise Flavored Drinks, Inc.	22.5	2.3	13.1	11.4	14.9
Bender Toys Corp.	30.3	1.8	17.6	15.3	20.0
Smith and Price, Inc.	21.7	1.9	12.6	10.9	14.3
John and Sam Pizza	18.9	1.5	11.0	9.5	12.5
Davidson Manufacturing	34.2	2.1	19.8	17.3	22.6
Instant Data Corp.	19.9	2.4	11.5	10.0	13.1
Average	24.6	2.0	14.3	12.4	16.2
Implied value of Jerry's equity (millions)	$6.73	$5.60	$7.84	$8.68	$6.87
Average of valuations	$7.140				
25% Premium for growth final value (millions)	$1.785 $8.925				
Value per share (1 million shares)	$8.930				

Fig. 3.6.   Comparable analysis by Butler and Jones.

would be appropriate for Jerry's company. Note that Butler and James performed all of their comparable ratio analysis an equity price basis. Alternatively they could have conducted their analyses of the sales, EBIT, and EBITDA ratios on a firm valuation basis. This procedure recognizes that these ratios are calculated on date *before* the subtraction of interest. Thus, the entire enterprise, financed by both debt and equity, is being evaluated. Under such enterprise valuation, value of the debt must be subtracted from the result to arrive at the value of the equity. Most investment banks would employ this enterprise valuation technique to account for different leverage ratios of the comparable firm sample. However, regardless of the methodology used, comparable analysis generally indicates a range of valuations at best.

Fortunately the comparable analysis confirmed the results of the investment banker's more sophisticated discounted cash flow valuation model which suggested an equity valuation of between $8 million and $9.5 million. Financial projections of the expansion plans, which called for the outright purchase of the property supporting five locations, indicated a need of $5 million. Butler and Jones decided that an IPO price of $7.75 per share and an issue of 666,667 shares were appropriate. Butler and Jones would underwrite the stock issue with a *firm commitment* contract under which they would buy 666,667 shares from Jerry at $7.50 each, and issue them at $7.75 each. These 666,667 shares would raise the $5 million that Jerry needed.

The service provided by Butler and Jones came at a price. The investment banker asked for a 6% fee ($300,000) and intended to market the shares at $7.75 each after buying them from Jerry at $7.50. If all went according to plan, Butler and Jones stood to make $466,667 in total (the $300,000 fee plus the $166,667 on the firm commitment underwriting) or nearly 10% of the $5 million raised by Jerry.

The banker does, however, bear some risk that the issue will fail to attract the anticipated market at the issue price. But under the firm-commitment contract, Butler and Jones must pay Jerry $5 million for the issue regardless of the state of the market at the time of issuance. Alternatively, Jerry could have a *best efforts* contract with the bank, but in that case he would not be guaranteed to raise the full $5 million needed to implement his plans.

Federal law, the Securities and Exchange Commission, state law, and various other statutes all had to be satisfied before the IPO could take place. The entire process took two months and a lot of Jerry's time. Moreover, Jerry and Sallie now owned only one-third of the company since they retained 333,333 shares of the original million shares. The rest were owned by the various investors who bought the IPO.

6. The IPO

The IPO was a success. Jerry was impressed with the way Butler and Jones handled the issue. The stock was listed over-the-counter (OTC), also known as the NASDAQ (National Association of Securities Dealers Automatic Quotation) market, and the price per share immediately rose to $13 per share on the first trade. In fact, Jerry wondered if the IPO price could have been set higher so that the company could have raised the $5 million without as many shares being issued and with less dilution of his ownership position.

On the IPO date, Jerry asked Alex Butler, "Alex, why didn't we set the share price higher?" "Because," Alex responded, "if we had been too aggressive in our initial pricing of the stock issue, the market response may have been less enthusiastic. You don't want that to happen. There is a sort of cascading effect in IPOs. Because the issuer is relatively unknown, investors wait to see what other, ostensibly more informed, investors do before deciding whether to buy shares. By pricing the IPO low, we can ensure that we can attract the initial set of investors to buy, so that we can get the right cascade going. As a new name to the market, you want to develop a good reputation to help with future financings as you continue to grow the business. Moreover, Jerry, as you know, we are supporting the price by doing post-IPO price stabilization. This involves our standing ready to buy back shares from investors if the price begins to fall back to the IPO price. We are committed to continue to support the price for about two weeks."

The arguments made some sense to Jerry. But it made him wonder if there was a potential conflict of interest between the company and the investment banker. The company wanted as high a price as possible, whereas the investment banker wanted a price at which it could sell the issue without having to work too hard. At least he had the comfort of having a successful issue. His business had come a long way and now he had a company that was listed on the NASDAQ. He decided to share the news with his friend, Bob Butterfield.

"Bob," Jerry exclaimed, "I now have a company whose stock trades on the NASDAQ with the symbol 'TART.' The company and I have arrived."

"That's great," Bob responded, "your ownership position is now liquid. The daily stock price also gives you an automatic scorecard on how well you are doing. In fact, the market will judge you every single day. There is, of course, a downside. You now have to manage the business under some scrutiny. The new shareholders may second-guess your decisions, and knowledge of this possibility may change your decisions. You should probably ask Butler and Jones to identify who bought large blocks of the IPO, since you may want to consult with them before making major decisions. They will be most interested in how you are managing your Value Sphere. In a very real sense, these new block shareholders will become your partners in the business."

"OK," said Jerry, "but you know, even though Butler and Jones did a great job, I'm not sure we couldn't have priced the IPO higher. We closed on the first day at $15 per share. By pricing the IPO to net us $7.50, we left $5 million on the table."

"You're right," replied Bob, "it is a bit of a problem. And you know, the ordinary investor out there didn't have much of a chance to get a piece of your IPO to profit from the underpricing. I'm sure Butler and Jones gave it to their best customers. Some of my colleagues call it the 'One for me, none for you' phenomenon. But take heart, all the investments banks do this."[23]

Jerry sighed. The heck with it. He still had a great company. He was justifiably proud of the achievements of the company and its current position. Bob had reminded him, however, that the task would not get any easier. He must now invest

---

[23] The Google IPO attacked this problem by employing a Dutch auction method, whereby the IPO was more widely available to potential investors. This method is described in the addendum to this chapter. Note, however, that even in this case there is evidence of underpricing.

the $5 million wisely and be able to communicate the company's strategies to the new investors who had just purchased the stock.

Main Lessons

- High growth is often not sustainable without additional equity financing. This additional equity financing could either come from the initial owners of the business, or if they wish to go public, then from an initial public offering (IPO) of stock. Going public, however, means loss of some ownership and control for the entrepreneur. Despite this, external financing is often an essential part of a company's Value Sphere.
- IPOs are typically underpriced.
- Once the firm is public, decision making within the firm may be irrevocably altered, and the beliefs of investors about how the firm should be run could significantly affect how it is actually run.

End-of-Chapter Exercises

1. Calculate the sustainable growth rate for your company. How does the rate compare to the planned rate of growth? What managerial actions are needed to align the sustainable growth with the planned growth?
2. When did your firm and others in your industry first go public? What was the share price reaction to the IPOs? What do these price reactions teach you about market expectations and growth strategies?
3. If you do not view external equity financing as a constraint on your growth, what is the most appropriate way to think about your sustainable growth rate?

Practice Problems

1. Calculate the ROE and G* for the ABC company:

   Return on sales = 5%
   Asset turnover = 1.5 times
   Leverage ratio = 2
   Dividend payout ratio = 0.4.

2. If the ABC company plans to grow at a 20% rate in the future, what would you recommend as a plan of action to the Chief Financial Officer?
3. Why is Jerry uncomfortable to sell shares to the public? Are such concerns rational?
4. Often retailers that operate in shopping malls report low leverage ratios. Why would they do this? What changes would you make?

5. What problems do you see in using comparable analysis to value companies? What are the benefits?
6. What are the different theories for why IPO's are underpriced? Critically assess the strengths and weaknesses of each theory.
7. Do you believe Dutch auctions can eliminate all IPO underpricing? Why or why not?

Addendum

1. IPOs are Underpriced

The IPO market has generated many research studies, particularly those aimed at explaining why IPOs are persistently underpriced on average, yielding an average return of 16% on the first day of issue.[24] Clearly the firms issuing the securities would like to capture some of this gain through higher initial prices. Of course, the danger is that too high a price may discourage investors and the company will not raise the funds needed for investments or restructuring. These two conflicting forces play a role in the IPO models that have been developed.

This addendum will explore three of these models: the information heterogeneity model of why new issues are underpriced, the cascades model explaining how potential investors in an IPO can learn from the purchasing decisions of earlier investors, and the litigation risk/reputation model of underpricing.

2. Why New Issues are Underpriced: Information Heterogeneity

Kevin Rock has proposed an interesting explanation for the underpricing of IPOs.[25] The key to his explanation is that there is a group of investors with limited wealth who are "informed" about the future prospects of the firm raising capital through the IPO; i.e., their information is better than that of other (uninformed) investors, the firm issuing the securities, and its underwriter.

Rock offers two justifications for why informed investors have better information than the issuing firm and its investment banker:

1. All relevant information about the issuing company is disclosed in the prospectus.

---

[24]For evidence of the IPO underpricing phenomenon, see Jay R. Ritter, "Initial Public Offerings," *Contemporary Finance Digest*, Spring 1998, pp. 5–30.

[25]Kevin Rock, "Why New Issues are Underpriced," *Journal of Financial Economics*, 15(1986), pp. 187–212.

2. All the individuals in the market, including competitors and other bankers, collectively know more than the issuer and his investment banker.

Informed investors bid for the issue when the offering price is below the true value, creating the possibility of oversubscription. Likewise, if the true value is below the offering price, the informed investors withdraw and there is the prospect of an excess supply of the new shares. Given the potential for excess demand or excess supply, there is no guarantee that an order for the new shares will be filled. Rather, each investor will be allocated shares in an oversubscribed issue in a random fashion.

With the "all or nothing" participation of the informed investors, an uninformed investor views the probability of receiving an allocation of an overpriced issue as being greater than the probability of receiving an allocation of an underpriced issue. Thus, if issues are correctly priced *on average*, the uninformed investors always buy too much when shares are overpriced and too little when they are underpriced, thereby losing money on average. To compensate for this bias, the issuer must price the shares at a discount to attract the uninformed investors to the offering. And the discount must be just enough to compensate uninformed investors for their informational disadvantage relative to the informed investors. The informed investors still earn more profit than the uninformed. But in effect, the "relative losses" of the uninformed investors are absorbed by the issuing firm, so they at least break even.

3. Cascades and the IPO Market

Ivo Welch has proposed a cascades explanation for the underpricing of IPOs.[26] His explanation also implies that IPOs will fail or succeed rapidly. Furthermore, Welch demonstrates that it is possible for underpriced offerings to fail and overpriced ones to succeed.

The basic idea is that subscription to an IPO takes place in stages. This means later investors can learn from the earlier investors. Initial sales success implies that the early investors had a favorable view of the new shares, giving impetus to later investors to invest. With sufficiently strong initial demand, the information conveyed by the initial subscribers may be so strong that later investors may prefer to disregard their *own* information and subscribe to the issue. This is what Welch calls the "cascade effect," and it can guarantee success if initial investors can be enticed to buy.

By the same token, if initial investors abstain, later investors may stay away as well, even if their own information is favorable. The issue then fails. Thus, there

---

[26]Ivo Welch, "Sequential Sales, Learning and Cascades," *Journal of Finance*, June 1992, pp. 695–732.

are both negative and positive cascades. Underpricing an IPO is a way to influence early investors to subscribe and increase the probability of success (positive cascade). In the case of the Broadcast.com IPO discussed earlier in this chapter, there was a huge positive cascade.

4. Litigation Risk, Reputation, and Underpricing

Patricia Hughes and Anjan Thakor theoretically showed that there are plausible circumstances in which it is optimal for the investment banker *and* the issuer to underprice because of litigation risk and/or reputational concerns.[27]

The basic idea is that investors can sue the underwriting investment bank and the issuer for misrepresentation if the after-market price falls below the IPO price *and* the post-issue operating financial performance of the firm is below expectations. Such litigation is costly, not only for the obvious legal reasons, but also because it can damage the investment bank's reputation as well as that of the issuer. Underpricing is designed to reduce the probability of an after-market price decline and hence diminish litigation and reputational risks. After all, it is difficult for investors to sue if they make money on a deal. What is interesting is that the extent of these risks — and thus the extent of underpricing — depends on the reputation of the price setter prior to the issue. The better this reputation, the lower these risks. Since investment bankers can be expected to have better reputations than issuers for pricing issues "correctly," an important prediction of the model is that there will be *more* underpricing if the issuer sells stock directly without using an investment banker than if a banker is used. Thus, Jerry probably underpriced less using Alex Butler than he would have if he had tried directly selling to the public on his own.

5. The IPO as a Branding Event

In the 1990s, IPO underpricing appeared to have been used to gain media publicity for young companies that saw such publicity generating benefits for their future product or service sales.[28] The Internet IPOs seem to be a good example. Unlike the previous hot IPO sectors like Biotech, where start-up companies tried to raise all the capital they needed, many Internet companies seem to view

---

[27] Patricia Huges and Anjan V. Thakor, "Litigation Risk, Intermediation and the Underpricing of Initial Public Offerings," *Review of Financial Studies* 5-4, 1992, pp. 709–742.

[28] In fact, many Internet IPOs quickly follow up a successful IPO with another round of financing.

the amount of money raised as no more important than being the center of a media buzz.

For example, in the summer of 1998, Broadcast.com told its bankers it would rather stick with an offering price of $18 a share, even though it was apparent it could get a higher price. The *Wall Street Journal*, January 19, 1999, reported,

> We could have had $35 a share," says Chief Executive Todd Wagner. But Broadcast.com 'viewed the IPO as a branding event'. A soaring first-day stock "was a way to launch our name."
>
> It worked for Globe.com as well. Its spectacular opening won a mention in publications as far afield from Wall Street as Sports Illustrated and helped the company attract dozens of advertisers. "We're not one of the random Internet companies any more," exults Mr. Paternot.
>
> Adds the chairman, Mr. Egan: "If I left a few million dollars on the table, so what? The IPO is about getting investment money, but in the case of the Internet, it's also a case of getting a public persona. We wanted to make sure we had a home run, not a double."

6. Flipping, Spinning, and Recent IPO Developments

IPO underpricing has been viewed by many people as a way for investment banks underwriting IPOs to curry favor with preferred clients or potential clients. It is difficult for retail investors to buy shares in an IPO. Only those customers who have special relationships with either the underwriter or the retail brokerage houses that receive allotments of shares in the IPO are able to purchase the IPO. By underpricing the IPO, the underwriter is able to "reward" these customers who can turn around and sell their shares at handsome profits. The act of buying shares in an IPO and selling them immediately in the after-market (typically on the first day of trading) is called "flipping," whereas the practice of giving IPO shares to favored or potential clients in hopes of winning future business is called "spinning." The SEC has frowned on this practice, particularly if it is seen as a tie-in sales for future bank services, and has forced banks to allocate some IPO shares to all investors.

Recently, on-line trading has begun to be used as a mechanism to achieve two objectives: (i) permit more retail investors to purchase shares in IPOs and (ii) reduce IPO underpricing.

For example, Wilt Capital Corp. is a firm that specializes in online IPOs. It allocates limited shares of other firms' deals to its own customers on a first-come, first-served basis at the price set by the underwriter. This addresses the goal of broadening retail investors' participation. But it does little to alleviate underpricing.

Hambrecht & Quist LLC goes a step further. It has started a new company that has started selling IPOs over the Internet. The company uses a "Dutch auction" process both to set the offering price and to distribute stock to individual investors.

The plan, called Open IPO, works as follows. Prior to the IPO, potential investors submit bids for the number of shares they would like to buy and at what price.[29] After a few weeks of accepting bids, the IPO offering price is set at the highest price at which all the shares can be sold. Those bidding above the offering price get all of the shares they requested at the offering price. Those bidding at the offering price get a fraction of their orders filled. And those bidding below the offering price get nothing. This is the procedure the major investment banks used in the Google IPO.

The plan has some restrictions. No more than 10% of the shares to a single bidder. And Hambrecht has the right to limit the purchases of anyone who wants to buy more than 1% of the shares.

Before opening the bidding, Hambrecht sets an expected price range for the stock. This is intended to give investors an idea of what the stock might be worth. Hambrecht has promoted this scheme by ridiculing the current system of IPO distribution as the underwriter telling the lay retail investor, "One for me, none for you."

7. IPOs, Capital Market Development, and the Average Age of Firms Going Public

IPOs are facilitated by growing investor participation in the public capital market since this provides greater liquidity and potentially higher prices.[30] Given the significantly higher levels of investor participation in recent years, it is not surprising that IPOs have become more popular. Moreover, as a result of this greater popularity, the average age of firms going public has declined from 40 years in 1960 to about 5 years in 2000.[31]

---

[29]They can submit bids as long as they have a brokerage account through W.R. Hambrecht or one of the five small brokerages that have agreed to participate in the process. See Lisa Bransten and Nick Wingfield, "Hambrecht Goes Online for IPOs," *Wall Street Journal*, February 8, 1999.

[30]It has been shown that greater investor participation leads to potentially higher stock prices. See Arnoud Boot, Radhakrishnan Gopalan and Anjan Thakor, "The Entrepreneur's Choice Between Private and Public Ownership," *Journal of Finance* 61-2, April 2006, pp. 803–8836.

[31]See Jason Fink, Kristin Fink, Gustavo Grullon and James Weston, "IPO Vintage and the Rise of Idiosyncratic Risk", working paper, Rice University, November, 2004.

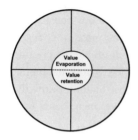

Chapter 4

JERRY SAYS HELLO TO HIS NEW SHAREHOLDERS: AGENCY COSTS AND CORPORATE GOVERNANCE

1. The Growing Clout of External Investors

Jerry's need for capital to finance his growing lemonade business means he must get acquainted with new stakeholders — the shareholders who just purchased the $5 million of shares in the IPO. This means talking and listening to them. Particularly the big investors who purchased blocks of shares and the bankers and analysts who seem keenly interested in the future of his business.

After having lunch with Bob Butterfield, he understands that being questioned by the company's debt and equity financiers is part of the process of running a publicly-held firm. Bob explained what was happening — Jerry was spending his time reassuring external financiers that the agency costs arising from debt and equity financing were not going to be a problem in his business. Understanding *agency costs* was essential to truly understanding the sources of Value Evaporation and the interplay between the different components of the Value Sphere.

2. The Essence of Agency Costs

An agency problem arises whenever one party to a contract can take actions that can exploit the other party. For example, an employee may shirk in the work he does for an employer. Or a borrower may put a bank loan to a riskier use than the bank expected. The waste arising from such exploitation and the attempts to limit it is called an *agency cost*. There are agency costs associated with both debt and equity financing.

Jerry's first encounter with agency costs was when he got excited about the prospects for expanding his lemonade business near US army bases. An investor who bought $500,000 of the IPO called Jerry to tell him of a great business opportunity to open lemonade stores near US army bases. Serving this "captive" market of US personnel stationed at these bases could be highly profitable. This venture could also serve as a model of selling in other settings, such as colleges and hospitals. This potential had attracted this investor to buy many shares of Jerry's IPO.

Jerry liked this idea so much he went directly to his banker. Unfortunately, the banker did not share Jerry's enthusiasm. In his mind, it was just too risky to expand when the lemonade business was just getting underway.

He also reminded Jerry about the protective covenants in his bank loan contract. The bank loan was expressly limited to the purchase of assets listed in the agreement. To make matters worse, the depreciation on the additional assets that would be acquired in the expansion would surely reduce earnings in the short term to levels that did not comply with the covenants.

Jerry interjected, "This is a great idea. One that we must act on quickly before others grab it. Don't forget there is lots of money to be made selling to the armed forces personnel. Can't we just change the loan agreement?"

"Look Jerry, I am your friend and your advisor," replied the banker. "I want to see you succeed. But think of the bank's position. If you succeed, you can easily pay off the bank and keep the remaining money for the shareholders. If you fail, given your status as a company with limited liability, you file for bankruptcy protection and the bank is left holding the bag. That is why it is my job to *monitor* your behavior and protect the bank. We insisted on the protective covenants to protect our investment and to make sure you don't do something reckless with our money. I am sorry, Jerry, but I will not alter the loan covenants to let you expand to military bases."

Jerry related this conversation angrily to Bob. Bob chuckled and said, "Welcome to the *agency costs of debt*! What you have to realize is that the banker's interests differ from yours and those of the other shareholders. The bank's potential return is limited to the interest and principal payments you agreed to in the debt contract. In contrast, the shareholders' potential gain is unlimited. Once the bank is paid back, shareholders get to keep all that is left. That's why we refer to shareholders as residual owners. Given this status as *residual owners*, coupled with limited liability if the business fails, there is a great incentive to invest in high-payoff but risky endeavors. If they succeed, the shareholders win big. If they lose, the shareholders walk away. It's as if the shareholders flip a coin and tell the creditors, 'Heads we win, tails you lose.' The costs this imposes on the bank are part of the agency costs of debt."

"Wait a minute, Bob. I'm not that kind of guy. I always pay my debts," Jerry protested.

"I know that, Jerry," Bob responded. "However, you are new at this lemonade business. You have no track record. The bank doesn't really know how you will respond if the business falters. The only thing they can be sure of is the loan contract you signed. That's why they insisted on those protective covenants, on questioning you periodically, and on audited financial statements. These are all *agency costs* associated with monitoring your behavior to protect the bank's interests. It's not that they don't personally trust you, Jerry. It's just that years of experience have conditioned them to be cautious with borrowers. This is why the true "cost" of debt financing is higher than the stated interest cost. The costs this imposes on the bank are part of the agency costs of debt."

As Bob and Jerry continued their lunch, Jerry related an incident that had occurred between him and another large shareholder. Jerry had an idea to expand the business to include California. He thought he should travel there to check out the idea, potential sites, etc. on a first-hand basis. He had been working hard, especially with the growth of the business, the IPO, and the many conversations with bankers and investors. And he had never been to California. He and Sallie could sure use a break. It would be a nice vacation. He had heard how businessmen creatively linked business travel with personal vacations. An ideal combination trip. It would not be a bad idea to also invite the operations manager and his wife.

His operations manager literally ate, drank, slept, and dreamt lemons. He knew everything there was to know about lemons. Jerry thought it would be a nice gesture of recognition if he and his wife got a "free" trip to California. The two of them could quickly assess business opportunities. If there were any lemonade stores there, they could do some competitive benchmarking.

Jerry had mentioned the California expansion idea and the trip to a large IPO investor. His reaction surprised Jerry. In a rather nasty tone, he said, "Jerry, this trip is a dumb idea. I didn't invest millions of dollars of my hard-earned money in our business so you and your employees can cavort around the country. I invested in the lemon store business, not a travel agency! And who's going to run the business when the two of you are gone? If you want my advice, don't go!"

Jerry asked Bob why the investor would be so upset about the trip.

Bob replied, "Welcome to the *agency costs of equity!* There are agency costs associated with equity, just as there are with debt. What you have to realize is that *external* shareholders view the situation differently from you, an *internal* shareholder and an employee of the business. There is now a separation of ownership by the investors and control by the managers."

"But all of us are shareholders," Jerry responded. "Don't we have the same interests?"

"Well, both of you are very interested in the financial returns earned from the lemonade business. In that regard, both of you are interested in maximizing the value of the business. On the other hand, as a shareholder and an employee, you care about more than just the value of the business. You are also concerned about the leisure time you have away from the business. And, you are legitimately concerned about providing positive incentives to your employees. You think they need rewards, such as the trip, to keep them motivated. External shareholders need to be convinced that corporate expenditures on leisure, incentives, and the like are absolutely necessary. Otherwise they view these as coming out of their own pocket. Nothing more than value evaporation that hurts their rate of return."

Jerry thought for a moment and then said, "First it's the banker, then shareholders. Everybody thinks we are going to steal their money."

"I sympathize with you," Bob interjected, "but these conflicts occur in all businesses. Agency costs of debt and equity are not unique to your business. Creditors will insist on protective covenants in their loan agreements, will monitor behavior, and will require periodic reporting to measure compliance. External equityholders will seek representations on the board of directors to monitor behavior and performance. If large investors get upset with your actions, they may use their significant shareholdings to seek a change in the company's management. In fact, this has happened in numerous large corporations, such as General Motors, Eastman Kodak, and Disney. All that creditors and external equityholders are doing is protecting their positions. In the end, it helps value retention. You shouldn't take it personally."

3. Bob Gets a Job Offer

"Bob, I've had some time to think about this and I'd like you to join the company. We've grown a lot. I now realize that being a public company requires someone to be in charge of finance. Someone to communicate with the bankers, shareholders, accountants, and lawyers. I've always admired your financial knowledge and wisdom, and I'd like you to be my Chief Financial Officer (CFO). As CFO, you'll have free reign over all matters of finance. You'll also be in charge of our real estate activities and information technology. These two areas are really growing as we expand the number of our locations. What do you say, Bob?"

"I am flattered," Bob said. "You have a very good business here and the growth potential looks outstanding. That's what I find attractive about joining the company as CFO. It would also be great to have the chance to apply what I've been teaching, researching, and consulting about over the years. But I also like my present job. It's hard to give up a tenured faculty position, you know. Let's talk some more."

After numerous discussions about Bob's compensation and persuasion by Jerry, Bob accepted the offer.

4. What Really Counts

After lunch, Bob and Jerry set out to discuss how they should assess the success of their lemonade business. Bob knew that it was really important for Jerry to understand how the financial market keeps score when evaluating a business. To begin the discussion, Bob introduced the notion of a balanced scorecard. This concept, first articulated by Kaplan and Norton,[32] is described below.

4.1. *The balanced scorecard*

The essence of the balanced scorecard is that business performance should be judged from a multidimensional perspective. Goals and measures are identified for four perspectives linked with basic questions:

- Financial: "How do we look to shareholders?"
- Customer: "How do customers see us?"
- Internal Business: "What must we excel at?"
- Innovation and Learning: "Can we continue to improve and create value?"

The key is to find measures in all four areas that typically span the company's agenda. This is related to the performance metrics segment of the Value Sphere. Moreover, the innovation and learning perspective is related to the resource allocation process and people and organization culture segments of the Value Sphere. Thus, there are some similarities between the spirit of the balanced scorecard and the Value Sphere. After some discussion, Bob and Jerry came up with the balanced scorecard for their business shown in Fig. 4.1.

These measures would be used across the company and many at each location. By comparing measures at each location, Jerry and Bob thought they could identify the best performers in each area and then be in a position to share best practices with all of the other locations. The inherent continuous improvement in this process should yield superior performance. Many companies have adopted the balanced

---

[32]Robert S. Kaplan and David P. Norton, "The Balanced Scorecard — Measures that Drive Performance," *Harvard Business Review*, January–February 1992, pp. 71–79.

Financial perspective goals	Measures
1. Survive	• Cash flow and income
2. Succeed	• Increased sales at each location
	• Increased market share in each locality
3. Prosper	• Increasing stock price
Customer perspective goals	**Measures**
1. New products	• Percent of sales from new products introduced in the last 2 years
2. Responsiveness/Time	• Percent of customer orders filled in less than 3 minutes
	• Process tie from order to customer delivery
3. Quality of service	• Customer satisfaction rating
4. Cost	• Customer survey ranking
	• Percentage comparison with average costs at McDonald's, Wendy's, and Starbucks
Internal business perspective goals	**Measures**
1. Productivity	• Location's sales per employee on payroll
2. Quality service	• Customer survey of employee behavior
	• Performance on random corporate inspection of each location
3. Cycle time	• Number of steps and time of each from order to customer delivery
4. Cost	• Unit cost per item
	• Labor cost as a percent of COGS
	• Customer survey of product value
5. Control	• Number of hours to issue weekly and monthly reports to each location
Innovation and learning perspective goals	**Measures**
1. Employee training	• Average number of hours of training for each employee per year
2. Business processes	• Number of business process improvements in past year
3. New products	• Cycle time to develop new products
	• Number of product ideas each month vs. number implemented
	• Number of new locations each year

Fig. 4.1. Balanced scorecard.

scorecard idea. Examples are Whirlpool and Ingersoll-Rand. In fact, most companies incorporate performance measures other than financial ones.

Although the balanced scorecard is helpful to encourage improvements and to assess business performance, a significant problem remains. What happens, for example, if the decision to be taken is at different ends of the spectrum along two or more dimensions? An investment may be highly innovative, resulting in a high proportion of future sales coming from the new product. But what if the project also promises to earn less than the cost of capital? Since such conflict among the dimensions is unavoidable, there needs to be an overarching goal, one that supersedes all others. Shareholder value maximization is that overarching goal.

Jerry interrupts the discussion by asking, "Why is shareholder value maximization a goal that supersedes the interest of other stakeholders like customers, employees, and the rest?"

Bob responded, "In part because shareholders have the highest control rights vested in them. And they must have the highest control rights because they have the lowest-priority financial claims. Think of the income statement we produce to monitor performance each month. The prices we charge customers are included in the revenues earned and are related to expenditures on quality improvements. Suppliers are represented in the cost of goods sold and the general and administrative expenses. Employees show up in the salaries and wages paid. In fact, the community is represented by the well-being of all participants in the company's affairs — customers, suppliers, employees, shareholders, bankers, and competitors. The government is represented in the amount of taxes paid. What goes to the shareholders is what is left over after all these parties are paid off.

"When viewed from the income statement point of view, it is clear then that shareholders are the residual owners. If shareholders did not have the highest control rights, there would be nothing left for them. If we adopt the right approach to maximizing shareholder value, we will also make decisions that maximize the interests of those above them in the income statement."

Jerry protested, "But couldn't the business cut employee wages, marketing expenditures or R&D spending in order to report higher profits this quarter?"

"Yes, that may be true, Jerry. But shareholder value is, by definition, a long-term concept, driven by corporate strategy. You know that sacrificing long-term profits for short-term gains is a pact with the devil. When the financial markets learn that you have made short-sighted decisions and jeopardized the long-run profitability of the company, they will lower the value of your shares. My advice, Jerry, is to run the lemonade business for long-run performance. That is the way to insure financial success and balance the interests of all people connected to the business."

"Are there any other reasons to believe that shareholder value maximization should be the overarching goal of my lemonade business?" Jerry asked.

"For sure," Bob responded. "Remember our discussion of the lukewarm response to your California trip? Well, that is why the maximization of shareholder value creation and retention needs to be at the top of our agenda. If you do not provide value, and external shareholders are disappointed, they will launch a bid to take over the company and run it as they see fit. Since shareholders have the highest *control rights* attached to their stock, they can wrest control of the company from the managers. They would then change the direction and strategy of the company to improve shareholder value."

"This is all fine, Bob. But do you have any concrete examples that I can relate to?"

"Sure, Jerry." Bob proceeded to give Jerry three case studies that he had used in class.

5. Coca-Cola

Coca-Cola has been one of the most spectacular creators of shareholder value in the last two decades. Roberto Giozueta was revered as an outstanding CEO of a major corporation in the United States, and the Coke brand name has long been the envy of not only the beverage industry but many others. During Goizueta's 16-year tenure as Coke CEO, the company's market value grew 34-fold from $4.3 billion to $148 billion.[33]

All that changed when Giozueta died in the fall of 1997 and was replaced by Douglas Ivester. Return on shareholders' equity was 56.5% in 1997. But it fell to 42% in 1998 and then to 35% in 1999. The company's market value at the end of 1999 was no different from what it was when Ivester took over. Net income, which was $4.1 billion in 1997, fell to about $3.2 billion by 1999. The stock price performance during Ivester's tenure lagged the S&P 500. Hardly the performance anyone expected from a man who once said, "I know how all the levers work, and I could generate so much cash I could make everybody's head spin."

Eventually, major investors and the Board of Directors of Coca-Cola lost confidence in Ivester. At a meeting in Chicago, directors Warren Buffett (representing Berkshire Hathaway which owned 8.1% of Coca-Cola) and Herbert Allen (who owned about 0.4%) met with Ivester and asked him to consider stepping down. Ivester complied.

What were the reasons for Ivester's ouster? At one level, the answer is obvious. He failed to deliver shareholder value at the level that his predecessor had. Investor expectations at Coca-Cola were very high due to past performance. Even if the company had done better than it did under Ivester, it may not have been enough to satisfy major shareholders.

---

[33]The discussion here is based in part on Betsy Morris and Patricia Sellers, "What Happened at Coke," *Fortune*, January 10, 2000, pp. 114–116.

But we should look deeper. What were the *reasons* why shareholder value was not created?

The reasons fell in three categories. First, Ivestor did not put enough emphasis on perceptions. He was a CEO who took pride in emphasizing substance over style. But to a brand-driven company like Coke, perceptions are supremely important. An example of failures brought about by inadequate attention to perceptions included the pursuit of an inflexible and aggressive acquisition strategy in Europe in the face of anti-big-American-business backlash. This cost Coke the Orangina and Cadbury Schweppes business in most of Europe as well as investigations into alleged anti-competitive practices in Austria, Italy and elsewhere. Another example is his treatment of the crisis created by Belgian school children getting sick after drinking Coke that had bad carbon dioxide. While Ivester viewed it as a minor health hazard, it ended up being a publicity disaster.

Second, Ivester seemed to pay inadequate attention to marketing. By demanding rigorous financial justification for proposed market expenditures, he seemed to have implicitly sent the message that he wanted his troops to concentrate on "sure-thing" marketing campaigns instead of risky but potentially high-impact campaigns. The issue here was not that financially justifying marketing campaigns is a bad thing. On the contrary, rather, the point is that the metrics that were being used to judge marketing outlays were inappropriate.

Finally, he alienated the powerful bottling companies who controlled 90% of Coke's business. In part, he did this by raising concentrate prices. He added to his woes by making comments about developing vending machines that would charge higher prices when the weather was warmer.

The most important lesson to be learned from this case is that before you can create shareholder value, you have to understand the *key value drivers* in your business. Only by optimally managing these value drivers consistently can you hope to develop the right corporate strategy and succeed. For Coke, important value drivers were managing perceptions of the brand, devoting appropriate resources to marketing, and managing the company's relationships with its bottlers. The second important lesson is that a flawed management system — one that has poor metrics or misguided resource allocation processes — often leads to Value Evaporation.

6. Ceridian Corporation

Ceridian Corporation, which split off from Control Data Corporation (CDC), is also a testament to the shareholder value imperative. In 1992, after a decade of very poor performance, CDC was dramatically restructured into two new companies: Control Data Systems and Ceridian Corporation.

Lawrence Perlman, Chairman and CEO of Ceridian, outlined his view of share-holder activism in a published article.[34] He stated that shareholder activism is a positive development because:

> It makes it very clear to those who lead public companies that those companies are not their private preserve and that their primary task is, in a responsible manner, to build shareholder value. Only with that orientation can the responsibilities corporations owe to customers, employees, and their communities be met.[35]

In the case of Ceridian, institutional investors own about 75% of the company's stock, and the 10 largest holders own over 50%. Such percentages are not unusual for a public company.

The history of Ceridian's business certainly helped shape Mr. Perlman's views on shareholder activism and corporate governance. In the 1980s, CDC lost 90% of its shareholder value. Its financial performance ranked near the bottom. Investors were very critical of the firm's performance and its apparent disregard for shareholders.

To turn the company around, in particular to improve clarity of strategy and the shareholder-value focus of the organization culture, it was split in two. This meant the birth of a new company — Ceridian — and a new business portfolio in employee services and information management. To inform the large shareholders of Ceridian's new opportunities and strategies, Mr. Perlman called a meeting with them and the Board of Directors to discuss major issues facing the new company. Since the investors own the company and the directors run it, he felt it was important for them to talk to each other as the company got started as a new entity and began establishing its own performance record. This dialog set the stage for future meetings to insure shareholder value did not evaporate at Ceridian the way it did at its predecessor, CDC. Thus, in this case, managing the CDC Value Sphere was so complex that there were gains to refocusing by creating two different businesses, each with its own unique Value Sphere challenges.

7. Daimler-Benz

Shareholder activism, coupled with management resolve to create shareholder value, is no longer a concern just for Anglo-Saxon firms. In fact, Daimler-Benz, the

---

[34]Lawrence Perlman, "A Perspective on the New Shareholder Activism," *Journal of Applied Corporate Finance*, Vol. 6, No. 2 (Summer 1993).
[35]Lawrence Perlman, "A Perspective on the New Shareholder Activism," *Journal of Applied Corporate Finance*, Vol. 6, No. 2 (Summer 1993).

German industrial giant, had been undergoing its own shareholder value revolution even prior to the merger with Chrysler that created Daimler-Chrysler.

The company first broke ranks with the established German industrial companies by listing its stock on the New York Stock Exchange in 1993. This meant that, under SEC rules, the company would have to report financial performance under US accounting standards.

The results were startlingly different under the US accounting system. The German system, which subordinates the informational needs of shareholders to the secrecy needs of management and bankers, permits companies more latitude that may disguise true financial performance. A major difference in the accounting systems is that provisions for future losses or expenses are allowed to a much greater extent in the German system, through the creation of "hidden reserves." These reserves make it possible to conceal information about poor economic earnings in lean times and thus smooth reported profits through time.

The other factor that has sustained such practices is that German firms have traditionally relied on domestic financing sources, and the pressures of corporate governance have simply not been as intense in Europe as in the United States. In addition, family holdings also help to insulate most German firms from takeovers. But this traditional reliance on banks and other domestic sources of capital was being challenged by the country's need to finance the consolidation with East Germany. This called for more diversified funding sources.

Daimler-Benz's decision to list its shares on the NYSE was motivated by the desire to diversify its sources of capital in order to optimize the resource allocation component of the Value Sphere. With that listing, the company had to be more responsive to the corporate governance dictate to earn rates of return higher than the cost of capital in order to create shareholder value. Among other things, these changes involved equipping employees with the decision-making tools needed to maximize shareholder value and to make the organization culture more shareholder-value conscious. In the case of Daimler-Benz, major corporate changes have been made to accommodate this.

The company has sold off major pieces of business operations, closed plants, reshuffled top management, and embarked on a major shift in strategy, culminating in the $30 billion merger with Chrysler Corporation to form Daimler-Chrysler. The chairman, Juergen Schrempp, reaffirmed his commitment to creating shareholder value.[36]

> Another important Schrempp move was to try to drive home the new and strange concept of shareholder value, something that was countercultural on a continent where social consciousness ruled.

---

[36]Jay Palmer, "Shake-up Artist," *Barron's*, March 23, 1998, pp. 35–40.

Daimler had arranged for its stock to be traded on the NYSE in November 1993 and, as part of that move, has been reporting its results according to generally accepted accounting principles ever since. Still, even if the company's accounts were no longer quite as mysteriously opaque as most German financials, Daimler's top executives were not in the habit of putting shareholders first. To sell the idea of shareholder value, Schrempp started calling colleagues at random and asking them for Daimler's current stock price. At first, he says, 'seven didn't know and three were wrong. Nowadays they can tell me. I was bitterly attacked, but I think I have sold the idea that only a profitable company can be a socially responsible company.'

The issue of whether the merger with Chrysler under Schrempp's leadership was a shareholder-value-maximizing move is quite another matter altogether, and one we will return to in a later chapter.

Main Lessons

- Both debt and equity financing have agency costs associated with them.
- As a result of agency costs, investors insist on monitoring the behavior of the company's managers and influencing their actions to minimize Value Evaporation and enhance value retention.
- Shareholder value maximization should be the overarching goal of the corporation.
- A balanced scorecard *may* help assess the performance of a company in a manner consistent with long-run shareholder value performance.
- The Coke, Ceridian, and Daimler-Benz cases illustrate the importance of managing the Value Sphere to the benefit of shareholders.

End-of-Chapter Exercises

1. How does your company communicate with its shareholders? Who are the major shareholders of your company? Are there "special efforts" taken to keep major owners informed about the company? Are the major shareholders becoming active, i.e., making managerial proposals directly to the company?
2. What is your company's Mission Statement? Does it, or any other similarly-visible statement, include shareholder value creation as a goal?

3. What covenants and restrictions are included in your firm's debt obligations? Could they affect future strategic actions of the company? How easily can the restrictions be removed?
4. How does your company assess operational performance? Are there elements of the balanced scorecard in place? How would you change the assessment?
5. How does your company balance the short term and the long term to optimize the Value Sphere in the best interests of the shareholders?
6. Gather some of the key employees in your company and ask them to write an imaginary newspaper article about your company 5 years into the future. The headline should be "Company XYZ (your company name) experiences 90% decline in market value over the past 5 years." Ask these employees to write the article to focus on the agency problems that led to this situation. Then ask them to assess how realistic this threat is and what they can do to deal with it.

Practice Problems

1. What are agency costs? Why do they occur?
2. What are the agency costs of equity? How would you attempt to minimize them? Can you relate the mechanisms you are proposing to those observed in practice? (*Hint:* Focus on executive compensation.)
3. What are the agency costs of debt? How would you attempt to minimize them? Can you relate the mechanisms you are proposing to those observed in practice?

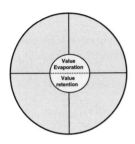

Chapter 5

WHY FIRMS FAIL TO MAXIMIZE SHAREHOLDER VALUE: HOW VALUE EVAPORATES

1. How Does Value Evaporate?

Jerry was impressed by the three cases Bob had given him. The message that stuck with Jerry was that none of the companies got back to a shareholder focus without a major shakeup; a new management team at Coke, the creation of a separate Ceridian business unit out of CDC, and a fundamental, and continuing, restructuring of Daimler.

As Jerry returned the cases to Bob, who had now moved into his new CFO office, he remarked, "These case studies are amazing. How is it that such well-known companies fail to maximize shareholder value? Do you think we could end up making the same mistakes?"

"Well, Jerry, there are things you can do right now to minimize Value Evaporation at our company. Why don't you take a look at the following (Fig. 5.1) that summarizes the three cases you read. The systematic patterns that emerge are instructive."

Providing competitive shareholder returns often requires investing in employee training and development to equip employees with the appropriate decision making and leadership tools and also changing the organization culture to make it more shareholder-value focused.

81

COCA-COLA

• Focus on customer satisfaction and employee morale is not enough: shareholders must also be taken care of. Shareholders have to be included in any definition of "excellence."
• Earning a return that is greater than the cost of capital is what keeps shareholder happy. This can only be done by optimizing the value drivers.
• If returns are inadequate, management changes will be made to ensure shareholders are rewarded for their investment. The Board of Directors will ultimately replace poorly performing managers.
• New management has the obligation to recalibrate the company's strategy to add value if the existing strategy is not doing so.
• Fundamental change is usually needed to resurrect a company that has been performing poorly. And this is not easy.[37]

CERIDIAN CORPORATION

• It is often better to split a large organization into smaller, more sharply-focused enterprises in order to improve the clarity of strategy and the shareholder-value focus of the organization culture.
• It is important to keep large institutional investors informed about company strategies and operations.
• As residual owners, shareholders have the most at risk in corporations because they have the lowest-priority financial claim. They must therefore have the highest control rights. Taking care of shareholder interests is not incompatible with satisfying customers, employees, communities, and others who have a higher-priority claim on income.
• To protect their claims, shareholders, particularly institutions, have become more active in the affairs of the companies they own.

DAIMLER

• Layers of ownership structures and significant cross-holding of shares by families, banks, or other companies work to create a system of inside owners which is common for German companies.
• The system of inside-ownership makes hostile takeovers very difficult to succeed. This can hurt shareholders.
• Even with an inside-ownership system, poor performance requires that changes be made, particularly if the firm wants access to global equity capital and lists its shares internationally.
• A strong global brand name does not insulate you from the need to provide competitive shareholder returns.

Fig. 5.1.   Summary of Coca-Cola, Ceridian, and Daimler Cases.

---

[37]As noted by Robert Quinn in his book, *Deep Change: Discovering the Leader Within*, Jossey-Bass Publishers, San Francisco, 1998, there are many who prefer slow death to deep change.

2. Generalizing from the Case Studies

Jerry studied the table and remarked, "These companies all thought they could dictate success in their markets; that strong brand names, or technical pioneering, or protected capital markets made them immune to pressures from their shareholders. As time went on, more and more value evaporated until something major needed to be done to stop the evaporation and improve value retention. It appears to me that management just got too complacent, started rationalizing their actions, and inefficiently responded to competitive challenges. The Value Sphere was not synchronized for these companies. I agree with you, Bob. We needto insure that this sort of thing does not happen here. What can we do?"

"Before we can identify a prescription, we must understand Value Evaporation some more," Bob suggested. "Look at the following (Fig. 5.2) which is another table showed my students listing the various ways companies have allowed value to evaporate."

As Jerry finished studying the table, Bob remarked: "It seems as if there are countless ways in firms' evaporate value. However, we can generalize based on the Value Sphere." He then pulled out a white paper on Value Evaporation to discuss with Jerry.

3. Value Evaporation and the Value Sphere: White Paper

The concept of Value Evaporation is part of the Value Sphere (see Fig. 5.3). The Value Sphere asserts that all value creation springs from four aspects of an organization's design: its strategy, its resource allocation system, its performance metrics, and its people and organization culture.

While the total amount of value creation potential of the organization depends on these four aspects, the *actual* amount of value creation enjoyed by the organization is typically far less. The reason is that part of the value creation potential is dissipated due to a key phenomenon called *Value Evaporation*.

Value Evaporation refers to systematic patterns of behavior within organizations that cause value to evaporate. Any organization that employs people suffers from Value Evaporation; the task is to minimize Value Evaporation, not eliminate it. Basically, Value Evaporation stems from systematic errors of omission and commission in decisions that result in the value enjoyed by the shareholders — which we refer to as value retention — being less than the total value creation potential of the organization. Thus value retention = value creation potential−Value Evaporation.

Cause of Value Evaporation	Company situation
1. Not sharing technical standards with others in industry	Apple computer retained complete control over the Macintosh standards. By contrast, IBM adopted an open-architecture approach, so its PC was cloned by many producers, leading to market share dominance of the IBM standard.
2. Too slow from R&D to product commercialization	Philips Electronics NV, the Netherlands company, has a long and rich history of new product research and development. For example, they "invented" the VCR. Unfortunately, due to a flawed internal management system, they were lax in commercializing the concept and conceded the market to Japanese companies such as Panasonic.
3. Permitting loss of market share to competitors with innovative product ideas	The major US television networks, ABC, CBS, and NBC stood by while cable TV companies, independent producers, and satellite companies eroded their markets. So product ideas: failure much market share has been conceded that the networks now have a major problem in regaining their share of TV viewers.
4. Failure to invest in supply chain and distribution	The failure of Sears and others to innovate the supply chain allowed Wal-Mart to revolutionize the mundane business of discount retailing by reengineering the supply and distribution chains within the industry. Consequently, Wal-Mart took considerable market share from Sears and small competitors.
5. Overinvestment in assets	In the 1980s, the oil industry greatly over invested in oil exploration, which was a failure of the resource allocation process within oil companies. The conventional wisdom was that oil prices would keep rising beyond $40 per barrel. The stock market disagreed, leading to the observation that it was cheaper to drill for oil on Wall Street than in Texas. Ultimately, the market view prevailed and oil companies added value by announcing decreases in exploration spending.
6. Poor definition of market	The major coffee producers such as Procter & Gamble and Nestlé defined the coffee market too narrowly, until the 1980s. They failed to notice Starbucks was redefining the US coffee market with a more European approach. Before long, Starbucks grew beyond the west coast and emerged as a national leader.

Fig. 5.2.   Mismanaging the Value Sphere: How value evaporates.

Cause of Value Evaporation	Company situation
7. Artificially increasing sales make the accounting numbers look good at the end of the quarter ("Trade loading")	Some companies take advantage of the accounting cycle by aggressively shipping product before the end of the quarter or the year. Such actions were motivated by poor management systems that included performance metrics driven by "Trade loading" rather than shareholder value. For example, management system prior to its leveraged buyout, RJR-Nabisco would force its products through the distribution chain in order to book sales revenue in the current year. While such a practice might help current accounting profits, it had a perverse effect on product quality because old, stale products wound up in the distribution chain. Booking profits, which really did not affect cash flow, consequently harmed product quality strategies.
8. Overpaying for merger partners	Much value can be evaporated by overpaying for a merger partner. Such overpayment is often the consequence of flawed financial valuation emanating from a weak resource allocation process. An example is the Quaker Oats acquisition of Snapple. While it may have made strategic sense to add Snapple to Quaker's existing Gatorade business, the potential value added is not independent of the price paid for the acquisition. As Quaker unfortunately discovered, the potential synergies with Snapple did not materialize and billions of shareholder value disappeared through the Snapple acquisition and subsequent divestiture. Many managers lost their jobs in the process.
9. Use of corporate funds for personal pleasures	Sometimes personal expenditures find their way into corporate for personal pleasures: accounts, thereby evaporating value. For example, for many years, failure of people and Don Dixon ran Vernon Savings & Loan as his personal fiefdom, organization culture running many lavish and questionable expenditures through the company. Travel, art collections, contributions, and the like found their way into the corporate accounts. Unfortunately, such expenditures can continue for a long period of time. Value is enhanced by the departure of such executives.
10. Lack of fresh strategic perspective from outside the industry	The problem of being a dominant, successful firm in an industry is that managerial hubris can take over. A case in point is IBM, which used to control over 70% of

Fig. 5.2. (*Continued*)

Cause of Value Evaporation	Company situation
	the mainframe computing market. Such dominance can be taken as a given and there is a reluctance to take a fresh perspective. DEC used this reluctance on the part of IBM to make huge inroads into IBM's business through the introduction of midrange computers. Unfortunately, DEC suffered the same fate when personal computers and computing network servers cut into their market.
11. Belief in the "quick fix" of cost cutting	Many firms sacrifice long-term value because they want short-term numbers to look good. Such "slash and burn" tactics may be appropriate at companies with significant corporate flab. But their indiscriminate use can be disastrous, e.g., "Chainsaw" Al Dunlap's failure at Sunbeam.
12. Focus on accounting numbers instead of value	A management performance evaluation system that focuses unduly on accounting numbers can also lead to value problems. A bad management example is Cendant, which was ordered by the SEC to restate its system accounts. "Manufacturing" accounting earnings instead of products and services cost this company billions. Another example is Oracle which lost significant market value in 1990 when it was revealed that it had aggressively (and erroneously) recognized some trial sales as actual sales. Many of the corporate governance scandals that led to the enaction of the Sarbanes-Oxley Act in 2002 involved accounting statement irregularities.
13. Fraudulent manipulation of investors	Sometimes, there is Value Evaporation because of fraud. A notable case is that of BreX mining, which doctored geological data to mislead people. Investors flocked to the stock in light of the promising discovery, only to be scalped when the analysis was shown to be a sham.
14. Inaction while competitors change the business design	Toyota changed the business design in the auto industry and gained considerable market share at the expense of the big three US auto manufacturers. Toyota engaged their suppliers in a cooperative effort to manage inventory levels and product quality. As a result, Toyota cars achieved much higher quality and were produced with less investment in inventories.

Fig. 5.2.   (*Continued*)

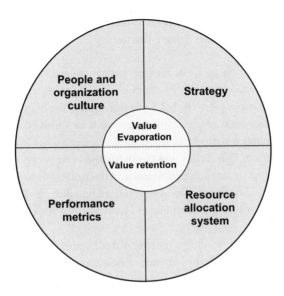

Fig. 5.3.   The Value Sphere.

Value evaporation occurs due to four basic reasons:

1. The decision maker does *not* know the strategy;
2. The decision maker is in a *bad* management system;
3. The decision maker does *not* have the tools to decide, manage, and lead and
4. The decision maker does *not* feel like an owner.

That is, the literally thousands of ways in which value evaporates in organizations can be classified into these four high-level groups.

It is important to note that Value Evaporation is *not* the value lost due to honest, unavoidable mistakes. Examples would be previously-made decisions that now look bad because of an unexpected recession or war. Value Evaporation is also *not* the value lost due to the unfavorable realization of an uncertainty, such as lightning or flood or say credit drying up due to a bank run. Basically, Value Evaporation refers to the value lost in a situation in which the decision made could have been improved by improving on one or more of the four basic reasons mentioned previously: the strategy; the management system; the tools for deciding, managing and leading; and the sense of ownership.

By reducing Value Evaporation, an organization can substantially increase the shareholder value it creates, without changing its strategy, operating environment, or people.

4. The Solution to the Value Evaporation Problem: Making Employees into Smart Owners

Jerry wanted to get Bob to focus on the specific issues of his company, "Well, Bob, as you know we have over 20 stores now, and managerial delegation is the norm. We train our people well, but I am not totally sure they always act in the shareholders' best interests. At your insistence, we have added an internal audit staff to monitor compliance with good accounting practice and to correct accounting problems that surface. The accounting group has also been very good at developing systems that allow us to measure performance at the stores, control cash collections, optimize disbursements, and the like. Do you think the internal audit staff is enough to ensure the store managers and employees act in the best interests of the company and its shareholders?"

Bob looked out the window, thought for a moment, and said, "While our internal auditors are essential, they are not sufficient to solve the Value Evaporation problem. All of the firms on my list that suffered significant Value Evaporation had employed internal auditors. Many of the audit teams at the companies were quite good, particularly at detecting outright fraud. However, fraud is the issue only in a very few Value Evaporation cases. This means there needs to be more than a good internal audit staff to stop Value Evaporation."

Jerry was getting a bit irritated now, "If the internal audit group won't stop Value Evaporation, what will?"

Bob sensed Jerry's slight irritation and said, "Well, Jerry, the four categories of Value Evaporation I referred to earlier provide a useful framework to think about how one can address Value Evaporation. Here's the framework as a diagram".

With that Bob showed Jerry Fig. 5.4.

Bob continued, "So you see Jerry, the first thing we need to do is to clearly communicate our strategy and corporate focus to our employees. Make sure they know where we, and the company, are headed."

Jerry nodded, "Ok. So they will make resource allocation decisions in a way that is consistent with our strategy. That is a communication issue. I am sure you will handle it. What next?"

"Well," said Bob, "It may be more than just a communication issue, but we also need to take a careful look at our internal management process — resource allocation, performance metrics, information systems, delegation in decision making, etc. We need to make sure these are facilitating the execution of our strategy and not impeding it."

Jerry mused, "Hmm... that sounds like a tall order. Not something I could expect tomorrow, eh?"

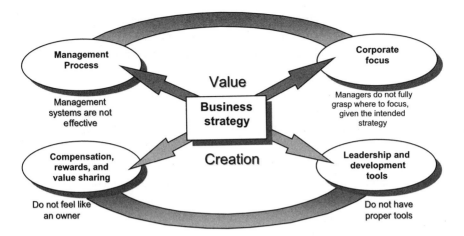

Fig. 5.4.   The framework to assess the causes of Value Evaporation.

"Exactly," agreed Bob, "that is something we will have to address over the next few months. But I will talk to some folks and get the ball rolling. The third issue is to see if our employees have the necessary tools to make the right decisions and that we are attending to their leadership development."

Jerry smiled, "I did not realize we were not doing that, Bob. But I suppose Barb Sidwell can handle that."

Bob nodded. Barb was the VP of human resources. And a good executive. If he could have a brief meeting with her, he was sure he could get her to attend to the leadership and development tools issues he had in mind.

"Now comes the hardest part, Jerry," continued Bob.

"And what is that?" asked Jerry, looking at his watch. He was expecting this meeting to wind down soon.

Bob sensed Jerry's impatience and said, "Well, Jerry, we need to align the interests of the managers and employees with those of the shareholders. The easiest way to do this would be to make all the managers and employees shareholders. If we do that, then we will increase the odds that they will take actions with the shareholders' interests at heart."

Jerry looked disturbed, "Wait a minute, Bob. I didn't put in all the hard work of nursing this company along just to give it away to some youngster just completing our training program. I've already got big shareholders breathing down my neck as a result of the IPO. Now you want me to give away shares to all the managers and employees. At least the IPO investors paid for their shares."

Bob, slightly taken aback by Jerry's annoyance, interjected, "Wait a second, Jerry. Let me explain. I never said we should give shares to the managers and employees. Rather, I said we should *make* them shareholders, including having them buy stock. Let me outline some alternatives:

1. Establish an ESOP (Employee Stock Ownership Plan) that serves as a pension for the managers and employees. The pension invests in our stock, and we get to deduct contributions to the plan as compensation expense. Thus, the employees "earn" the shares.[38]

2. An Employee Stock Purchase Plan could be created that would permit all employees to purchase shares periodically through payroll deduction. The shares could be offered at a discount price and the company could match the shares purchased according to some formula. For example, the company could give one share to the employee for every four purchased. There could even be a time delay to the share gift; say one year. That would provide an incentive for the employee to stay with the company, particularly with a rising share price.

3. We could, as you indicate, just give the shares to the employees.

4. The gift of shares or options could be tied to a bonus plan as an incentive for employees to work hard.

In fact, there are many other creative ways to link employee compensation to shareholdings or shareholder value performance. At this stage, I'd suggest we not get too fancy with our compensation system. That can come later. I do think we should establish something along the lines of the second plan I mentioned."

Jerry still seemed unconvinced, "I don't know, Bob. Are there any examples of companies that have succeeded with such stock purchase plans?"

Bob smiled and spoke, "Sure. Many successful companies have established employee stock purchase plans. Probably the most famous are Wal–Mart, Microsoft, and Starbucks. Wal–Mart insists that all of its employees own stock. And virtually all of Microsoft's and Starbuck's permanent workforce owns stock. These companies have made many of their employees millionaires. But they became millionaires only because these companies produced enormous shareholder value. If we can get all of our managers and employees to act like shareholders, we'll be a much better company."

---

[38]We are *not* advocating that an individual should hold *only* the stock of his/her employing firm. Interest diversification in one's investment accounts is a "tried and true" component at any sound saving/retirement strategy.

Jerry was beginning to see Bob's viewpoint now. But he persisted, "Your arguments make sense. But wouldn't we dilute the number of shares outstanding if we move to an employee stock purchase plan?"

Bob pressed on. "Keep in mind, Jerry, I am recommending a stock purchase plan. This means employees buy our stock. This will generate cash that will aid our efforts to finance our explosive growth. I further suggest that we allow the managers and employees to purchase the shares at a 10% share price discount through a payroll deduction plan. After one year of employment, we will match their purchased shares one for four, i.e., they will receive one share at no cost for every four shares they purchased a year earlier. This incentive should help cut down our already low employee turnover. If dilution of your ownership position is a serious problem for you, Jerry, we can repurchase our shares in the open market to obtain the shares needed for the program. Thus, the total number of shares outstanding could remain constant with no dilution."

Jerry still had an emotional wall between himself and Bob's proposal, "I still don't see why it is in my benefit to have the managers and employees own shares."

Bob sensed that what he needed was to put the finishing touches on his argument. "The way you have to see it is that the actions taken by the managers and employees will be taken with a shareholder value focus. That should increase the value of the firm. Even if you suffer some dilution, your wealth is likely to be greater than it would be if the managers and employees did not have the shareholder focus and took actions that evaporated value.

"In my view, it is almost a crime in some public companies that even the top management, including the board of directors, own but a few shares. That creates a danger that key decision makers may grow indifferent to shareholder value and mismanage the Value Sphere. We can't let that attitude of shareholder value indifference and the resulting Value Evaporation creep in here. At least you and Sallie still own a large block of stock. Let's go forward with the stock purchase plan and align the motives of all employees with shareholder value."

Jerry seemed to be convinced now. "Okay, Bob. Go ahead and implement the plan."

Main Lessons

- There are many ways for value to evaporate at companies. Some of these ways become so deeply ingrained in the company's culture that most employees see no alternative to behaving that way. However, all these ways to evaporate value

Elements of Value Sphere	Consequence

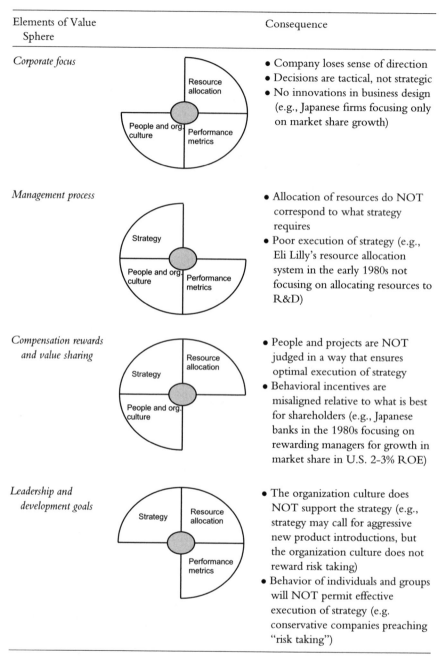

Corporate focus

- Company loses sense of direction
- Decisions are tactical, not strategic
- No innovations in business design (e.g., Japanese firms focusing only on market share growth)

Management process

- Allocation of resources do NOT correspond to what strategy requires
- Poor execution of strategy (e.g., Eli Lilly's resource allocation system in the early 1980s not focusing on allocating resources to R&D)

Compensation rewards and value sharing

- People and projects are NOT judged in a way that ensures optimal execution of strategy
- Behavioral incentives are misaligned relative to what is best for shareholders (e.g., Japanese banks in the 1980s focusing on rewarding managers for growth in market share in U.S. 2-3% ROE)

Leadership and development goals

- The organization culture does NOT support the strategy (e.g., strategy may call for aggressive new product introductions, but the organization culture does not reward risk taking)
- Behavior of individuals and groups will NOT permit effective execution of strategy (e.g. conservative companies preaching "risk taking")

Fig. 5.5.   Consequences of lack of synchronized Value Sphere.

fall into four broad categories: employees do not understand the strategy, they operate in a bad management system, they lack the tools to decide and lead, and they do not feel like owners.

- Even successful companies are not immune to Value Evaporation. Stemming the tide of Value Evaporation often requires careful introspection and a willingness to change. This is particularly difficult if the company is successful.

- A strong internal audit staff is no guarantee that Value Evaporation will not occur because Value Evaporation is not limited to fraud or visible violations of company policies and procedures. In fact, policies and procedures could contribute to Value Evaporation.

- Value evaporation essentially occurs because the Value Sphere is not synchronized, as shown in Fig. 5.5. This diagram depicts the consequences when each element of the Value Sphere is missing (not synchronized) and how this relates to Fig. 5.4.

- The best way to guard against Value Evaporation is to clearly communicate corporate strategy to employees, give them a good management system to work with, provide the necessary tools to help employees decide and lead, and make all employees shareholders so that they make decisions consonant with shareholder value maximization.

End-of-Chapter Exercises

1. Gather a group of 10 employees in your organization who represent two to three levels in the reporting hierarchy. Provide them with the four broad categories of Value Evaporation discussed in this chapter. Ask each employee to list the most prominent examples of Value Evaporation in your company in each category. Collect the list and then, as a group, choose the five that evaporate the most value. Then estimate how much value is evaporated each year by each practice. Now develop an organizational change plan to eliminate these five practices. Calculate the resulting improvement in value retention.

2. Describe the ways in which your organization attempts to align all employees with shareholder value. Are all elements of the compensation system consistent with optimizing the Value Sphere?

3. What are the main lessons for your organization from the various Value Evaporation cases discussed in this chapter?

Practice Problems

1. What are the four high-level reasons why value evaporates at companies? How are these reasons linked to the Value Sphere?
2. Which of these reasons is linked to the agency costs of equity covered in the previous chapter? Explain your answer.
3. Can making employees act like owners completely eliminate Value Evaporation? Why or why not? To what extent can it help?

Strategy

Chapter 6

THE SOURCE OF VALUE:
STRATEGY

1. Stock Price Goes Down

Jerry was happy that Bob implemented the stock purchase plan for managers and employees. Managers and other employees enthusiastically embraced the plan because they had witnessed the profitable expansion of the company firsthand. In fact, 68% of those who were eligible chose to participate. Many employees and managers personally told Jerry how pleased they were to be able to purchase stock. They seemed to exude confidence about the future of the company. However, to Jerry's surprise, the stock price dropped after the stock purchase plan was initiated. Jerry called Bob.

"Bob, why is our share price going down? I thought this stock purchase plan was intended to increase shareholder value."

Bob seemed unconcerned as he replied, "Jerry, the stock purchase plan is intended to have a long-run impact on share prices. But it is *not* a panacea. In the short run, there could be other factors that drive our share price."

"Bob, can you look into what these factors are right now? I'm a bit concerned."

"I'm on it, Jerry," Bob responded.

About one week later, Bob phoned Jerry and scheduled a lunch meeting in the boardroom to discuss the matter.

2. A Business Threat Arises

"Jerry, I discovered we are facing a new business threat and that may explain why our share price has been weak. What I have come up with is based on extensive discussions with Doug.[39] He couldn't make it to this meeting, but he was enormously helpful in helping me prepare for it. Let's eat lunch first and then we can talk."

Later Bob continued, "I've discovered that we are facing some stiff competition from Mickey. He has been setting up competing stores very close to ours. In fact, I am told that he plans to expand into all of the same cities where we have operations."

"Well," Jerry responded, "we have a better product, excellent locations, attractive prices, and loyal customers who would never dream of doing business with Mickey. Customer satisfaction is consistently high for us. The customer surveys we conduct always show us to be highly regarded by our customers. We don't have to fear Mickey. We'll crush him in the marketplace!"

"I agree, Jerry, that our customers like our products. However, I have to tell you that we are losing market share to Mickey's in those cities where we compete head-on."

"How can that be? We've never had a problem with Mickey before. Is he buying our customers?"

"You're on the right track, Jerry. I've taken a close look at the data for two stores where we clearly compete head-to-head with Mickey; one in Cincinnati and the other in Indianapolis. Mickey's strategy in both cities is similar — he is doubling his advertising and promotion expenditures and cutting prices. His price cuts are 10% in Cincinnati and 15% in Indianapolis. The monthly reports for our locations confirm that our customers are defecting. Last month sales were down 15% in Cincinnati and 20% in Indianapolis."

"Have you got any ideas, Bob?"

Bob responded, "As I began to think about this issue, I decided to investigate what the leaders in strategy had to say. What I first learned is that **strategy is all about matching opportunities to capabilities and core competencies**. The term "core competency" was coined by Gary Hamel and C.K. Prahalad (1990) in a famous article,[40] and I will define it in a minute. But let's begin with Fig. 6.1 which sketches a framework for strategy organization, and incentives." Bob put up the diagram on the overhead projector.

---

[39]Bob was referring to Doug Harris, Vice President of Strategic Planning at Jerry's Lemonade, Inc.

[40]C.K. Prahalad and Gary Hamel, "The Core Competency of the Corporation," *Harvard Business Review*, May-June 1990.

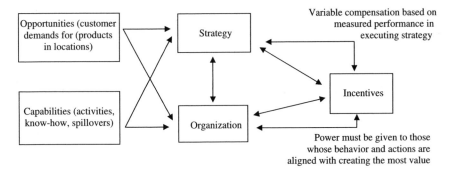

Fig. 6.1.   Framework for strategy, organization, and incentives.

"The basic point of this diagram, Jerry, is that our business opportunities and organizational capabilities should determine both our strategy and how we structure our organization." Bob continued, "And then we should design incentives for our people so that they are consistent with our strategy and organizational structure. Of course, incentives include both those that are provided through the compensation system and through the distribution of power among different employees. Thus, this perspective is an elaboration of the key dimensions of the Value Sphere."

After Jerry had finished looking at the diagram,[41] Bob continued, "To understand how to come up with the best strategy in this framework, we need to first examine all the interacting players who impact the formulation and execution of strategy. For that, let's talk about the game theory approach to strategy.[42] Essentially, this approach views business as a sophisticated game." Given below is a summary of Bob's presentation on this approach, beginning with Fig. 6.2.

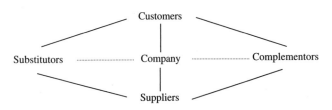

Fig. 6.2.   A company's value net.

---

[41] This diagram appears in David Baron and David Besanko, "Strategy, Organization and Incentives: Global Corporate Banking at Citicorp," *Industrial and Corporate Change*, 10-1, 2001, pp. 1–36.

[42] Adam M. Brandenburger and Barry J. Nalebuff, "The Right Game: Use Game Theory to Shape Strategy," *Harvard Business Review*, July–August 1995, pp. 57–71.

- The *value net* represents all the players in the game and the interdependencies among them. The vertical axis details the company's transactions with *customers* and *suppliers*. The horizontal axis notes the players with whom the company interacts but does not transact: *substitutors* and *complementors*.

- Substitutors and complementors transact with customers and suppliers, but not with the company. Substitutors are essentially competitors, i.e., those whose products can substitute for ours. The term substitutors is used because it is considered less provocative than competitors. Complementors are those products and services that complement our own. Computer software companies are complementors of computer hardware companies. What is important is that these roles are *not* cast in stone. A substitutor can also be a complementor. For example, airline companies are each other's substitutors with respect to customers (passengers), but are each other's complementors with respect to aircraft suppliers (Boeing). The larger the number of airplanes ordered by airline companies, the lower is Boeing's cost of manufacturing each aircraft.

- Once the value net portraying all the interdependencies of the strategic game has been understood, then all of the five game elements must be specified as follows:

  o *Players*: these are the participants in the game. The customers, suppliers, substitutors, and complementors are not fixed, and can be strategically altered to one's advantage.

  o *Added values*: these are the value enhancements that players bring to the game. One can use strategic creativity to change the values different players add to the game.

  o *Rules*: these are the implicit and explicit norms by which the game is played. There are no universal rules to structure a game. Law, custom, practice, and contracts all affect the rules that govern a game. These rules too can be changed to the advantage of one of the players.

  o *Tactics*: these are the specific moves players make based on their perception of the game. Tactics take the scope of the game as given, and then attempt to maximize the payoff to the player employing the tactics.

  o *Scope*: this is what defines the boundaries of the game. For any company, the definition of scope is a choice variable, and it defines who the players in the game will be.

The acronym for these five elements is PARTS.

Within this overall framework, the essence of what leading thinkers in strategy have prescribed can be simply summed up as follows: **Too often, firms focus excessively on tactics and don't think enough about the scope of the game. Good strategy must think more expansively about the right scope. Moreover, a good strategy typically distinguishes the firm sharply from its competitors. But this does not necessarily mean all-out war with your competitors. In fact, the more you can cooperate with the other players in the industry the better.**

3. Business Strategies that Lead to Value

Bob continued, "One of the most influential thinkers on strategy, Michael Porter, has made this point repeatedly. A summary of his writings is given below."[43]

- Too many companies focus on operational effectiveness (tactics) rather than strategy. While operational effectiveness initiatives–such as manufacturing quality, business process reengineering, speed to market and benchmarking–are clearly important, operational effectiveness is not strategy.
- Strategy must establish a preservable distinction between the company and its competition. Gains resulting from improvements in operational effectiveness are typically imitated in a relatively short period of time by competitors and thus are not sustainable.
- A preservable distinction is likely to result from performing activities that are different from those of competitors or from performing similar activities in different ways. This is only possible if the company chooses a strategy that distinguishes it from its competitors and allows it to make choices that deliver unique value to customers, employees, and shareholders.

Bob continued, "Just look at the companies that have created significant shareholder value. Coca-Cola, Microsoft, Starbucks, McDonald's or Wal-Mart. Each had a distinct strategy that separated it from its competitors. None of them played by the rules of the game that were already in place. They all did innovative things that created exceptional value for their customers."

Jerry nodded his agreement. "Bob, I like the idea that customer value is at the heart of value creation. Since the founding of our business, this has been my guiding philosophy. What else?"

---

[43]Michael Porter, "Competition in Global Industries: A Conceptual Framework," in *Competition in Global Industries*, (Michael Porter, editor), Harvard Business School Press, 1986.

In response, Bob proceeded to summarize the work of Kenichi Ohmae, who makes interesting observations about dealing with the competition.[44]

- Beating the competition should *not* be the goal of strategy. Rather, it should be to serve the real needs of your customers. If the focus of strategy is about beating the competition, it is unsustainable in the long run. In other words, a focus on tactics rarely yields a *sustainable* competitive advantage since successful tactics are usually imitated by your competitors.
- As the Chinese philosopher Sun Tzu observed many years ago, the great virtue in war is to *avoid* the competition. The goal is to achieve your objectives without having to fight. It economizes on resources and minimizes risk. This calls for differentiating yourself from your competitors by redefining the scope of the game so that you do not confront your competitors head-on.
- Competitor-focused strategies inevitably lead to disruptive and expensive fights and reactive planning. Such strategies are not customer focused. Of course, in *evaluating* strategic choices, one must consider what competitors are doing and how our strategies will create a lasting advantage relative to our competitors. However, the mindset should be to do this by focusing on the customer rather than the competitor.

Jerry looked out of the window pensively as he asked, "Bob, does this mean we should plan to avoid meeting Mickey head-on as he attacks our business in Cincinnati and Indianapolis?"

Bob replied, "That is one implication, Jerry. However, we need some further discussions before we can formulate a specific strategic response. In particular, some would object to your use of the word "plan." Many observers believe that strategy is not amenable to the usual planning at most companies. In fact, Gary Hamel and C.K. Prahalad, who I mentioned earlier, have made the point that a good strategy is rarely about "linearly extrapolating the present reality." It is about seeing the future. This doesn't mean speculating about what might happen. Rather, it is about understanding the revolutionary potential of what is already happening. Unfortunately, the usual "linear" strategic planning process at most companies tends to come up with evolutionary rather than revolutionary thinking."

Jerry was getting a bit puzzled now. "Bob, this sounds good, but I'm not sure how one becomes a revolutionary without being an anarchist. And I'm not interested in being that in my own company."

---

[44]Kenichi Ohmae, "Getting Back to Strategy," in *Strategy: Seeking and Securing Competitive Advantage* (Cynthia A. Montgomery and Michael E. Porter, editors), Harvard Business School Press, 1991, pp. 61–76.

Bob agreed with Jerry and then proceeded to summarize for him what Professors Hamel and Prahalad recommended for those who wanted to inject revolutionary thinking into their strategy deliberations. One must embrace the following three perspectives:

1. *Systematically deconstruct the orthodoxies and dogmas that rule a business:* When people sit down and think about strategy, too often they take 90–95% of industry orthodoxies as a given and as a constraint. This almost invariably leads to a discussion of tactics within the context of the existing game rather than an introspective look at the best way to redefine the scope of the game. Moreover, it leads to strategies that are very similar across competing firms. This often creates "hyper-competition" and diminished value creation.
2. *Understand the discontinuities in the environment at present and how they can be leveraged to our advantage in remaking the industry:* A discontinuity is a confluence of events that substantially changes the structure of an industry or "the rules of the game." A discontinuity: (i) is an intersection of trends, (ii) affects business or life styles, (iii) creates new rules, (iv) creates opportunity for those who adopt the new rules, and (v) can be a new source of revenue and profit.
3. *Develop a sense of product market domain that is expansive and broad enough to be linked to the company's core competencies, and not limited to the present conception of what is possible today:* A core competence is defined as a bundle of skills and technologies that yield a fundamental customer benefit, as shown in Fig. 6.3.

A core competence is something that gives the company a sustainable competitive advantage. Basic business requirements, values/norms, or assets are important. But they are capabilities or "the price of admission," not core competencies.

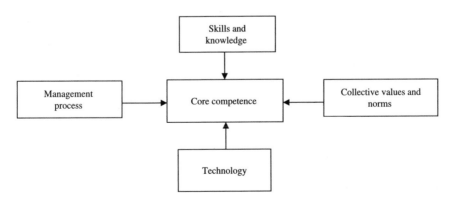

Fig. 6.3. Core competence.

The secret to formulating an effective strategy is then to: (i) identify the discontinuities in the environment that are relevant to you; (ii) determine your core competencies; (iii) determine the discontinuities that your core competencies will permit you to exploit effectively; and (iv) develop a strategy to exploit these discontinuities.

4. What does It All Mean for Jerry?

As Bob finished, he sensed that Jerry seemed enthusiastic about these ideas. Bob began putting his slides away, but stopped as Jerry asked, "So, what does all this mean for us, Bob?"

"I'm not entirely sure, Jerry," said Bob. "Doug is working on that as we speak. My guess is he'll have a strategy proposal for you in a few weeks. His hope is that the proposal will serve as a starting point for deliberations by the Executive Committee on our new strategic blueprint. I believe you and he have had some discussions about this, haven't you?"

Jerry smiled, "Just a couple. But I'm interested in what your thoughts are at this stage."

Bob looked up at the ceiling for a minute as he gathered his thoughts. He then spoke, "There are a few general observations that I have. I don't mean to suggest that they should represent our strategy. But they're just some initial thoughts I have." Bob then proceeded to summarize:

- We have been too focused on operational planning (tactics) and not enough on strategy. For example, our training manual, which is excellent, is all about operations. We need some breakthrough thinking to get back on track. It is likely that we do not have a very good understanding of either the discontinuities facing us or our core competencies. Developing such an understanding will be essential if we are to change the rules and the scope of the game.
- In the past we have done an excellent job of serving our customers and meeting their needs. However, I think it is time to rededicate ourselves to them. We have become too inwardly focused and we need to reorient ourselves to the customers once again. It could be that we need to investigate pricing, since Mickey appears to be hurting us by undercutting us. Perhaps our customers are more price sensitive than we think. We need to examine the added values we bring to the game relative to those that Mickey brings.
- Mickey needs to understand that we intend to keep our customer base. However, we want to avoid an all-out war with Mickey, since we are likely to both wind up losers. We need to think about ways in which we can view Mickey not just as

a substitutor/competitor, but also perhaps as a complementor. Perhaps the whole market for our products will grow.

Jerry nodded in apparent agreement as he spoke, "That's a good start. Let's wait for Doug's report before we continue this discussion at the Executive Committee level."

Main Lessons

- Before you can formulate a strategy, you must understand the business game you are involved in, including the identities of the players in the game and the scope of the game. Thus, understanding your business game must precede the development of your Value Sphere.
- Operational effectiveness is a component of tactics and hence not a complete statement of strategy. Breakthrough strategies do not come from incremental improvements in current operations.
- Coming up with breakthrough strategies requires changing the scope of the game. This often requires a deep understanding of customers, the discontinuities in the company's environment and the company's core competencies.
- Cooperation in a competitive game can be more desirable than a strategy to crush the opponent. However, in most situations, explicit cooperation is not (legally) possible. Tacit cooperation requires a certain level of sophistication on the part of the players involved. And a resolve to not change industry dynamics for short-term gain in a manner that escalates long-term competitive pressures.

End-of-Chapter Exercises

1. What is your strategy? How did you arrive at it?
2. Who is the central focus of your strategy: customers, competitors, suppliers, employees or _____?
3. Can you clearly write down the PARTS for the game you are involved in? What does it teach you about the appropriate tactics? How often have you redefined the scope of your game and how?
4. What are your core competencies? What are the major discontinuities in your environment? Which ones do you wish to exploit and what is the strategy that will enable you to do so? How different is this from your existing strategy and the strategies of your major competition?

Practice Problems

1. Why would a company's stock price be linked to investors' perception of its strategy?
2. What are the key attributes of a good strategy? Explain how each attribute contributes to value creation.
3. What is a "value net" and what is its usefulness in thinking about strategy?
4. What is the difference between a "capability" and a "core competence" and what is the relevance of this distinction in formulating strategy?

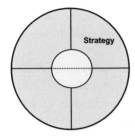

Chapter 7

RISK AND VALUE: WHY SHOULD JERRY CARE?

1. Jerry Has Global Ambitions

"Twins! Can you believe we're having twins?" Jerry asked Sallie rhetorically as they drove out of the hospital parking lot. They were heading toward their favorite restaurant after the ultrasound examination.

While at the restaurant, the conversation naturally revolved around the ultrasound results. But Sallie noticed that Jerry looked somewhat distracted. She finally asked, "How is business, Jerry?"

Jerry nearly burst at the seams, "I'm glad you asked. I have fantastic news. Jerry's Lemonade is going global! I just listened to a proposal yesterday given by the marketing group. You remember Doug Harris, don't you?"

Sallie nodded nervously. "Of course I do." Jerry, Doug, and Bob had been very good friends ever since high school. Jerry had invited Doug to join the firm about the same time he brought on Bob.

"Well, Doug's now our vice president in charge of strategic planning and he's come up with a plan for Jerry's Lemonade to be introduced to Europe, India, and China! Can you believe it?" He looked at Sallie, anxiously awaiting her enthusiasm to match his own.

She asked hesitantly, "When is this going to happen?"

"Can't happen soon enough, as far as I am concerned," he replied. "Our existing businesses have been incredibly profitable over the last couple of years, but there's a limit to the size of our domestic market. And we are bumping up against Mickey. I think we're ready to go at this full steam and see what lies for us beyond our shores."

"Jerry, I don't want to be a kill-joy, but that sounds really risky," she stated firmly. "I'm sure you know your business a lot better than I do. But we have kids on the way. What if this goes sour? Couldn't the main ship sink while you're trying to expand the fleet?"

The more she talked, the more nervous Sallie became. "Besides, the last thing I want to see you do is increase your travel load! Our kids aren't going to benefit from worldwide lemonade sales if they never see their father."

Jerry became a little sheepish. "I don't want to be a part-time father either, Sallie. But if I have done one thing right along the way, it's been to surround myself with good people. I certainly won't change that approach for something this big. If it goes through, I will place people like Doug abroad to run the day-to-day operations and my traveling will be minimized," Jerry said as he slowly regained his confidence. "And, although I do agree there are a lot of risks involved in this expansion, I think I have that covered. Bob has agreed to sit down with me tomorrow and go over the risks of this plan. We certainly don't want to evaporate the value we've built up in the business over the years."

2. Jerry Gets a Lesson in Risk

The next morning, Jerry arrived at the office bright and early. Sallie must have gotten his subconscious working. Now *he* was a little nervous about this global strategy.

He quickly settled into his desk and began poring over the proposal Doug had given him a few days earlier. This has to be the right course to take, he thought to himself. Looking up at the clock, he saw that it was 8:15 a.m. The meeting with Bob was not until 10:00, so he thought he would better clear his desk of some outstanding matters in the meantime.

Bob showed up on schedule. "How did the ultrasound go?"

"We're going to have twins," beamed Jerry. "You know, I'm amazed how technology has advanced such that we can know these things so early."

"Congratulations! That's terrific. I'm thrilled for you and Sallie," said Bob with a smile. "It must be nice to resolve the uncertainty, though."

Jerry got up from his chair and began pacing the room. "Yeah. But speaking of uncertainty, let's talk about the risks in our global expansion."

"Well Jerry, I can't lie to you. This is the biggest risk we have faced thus far. Bigger than quitting your job all those years ago to go sell lemonade. We are going to face a lot of new uncertainties, such as political risks, foreign exchange risk, interest rate risk, ..."

Jerry thought to himself, "this isn't helping."

Bob went on, "But you know Jerry, I think we can handle it. Risk is an essential part of our strategy. What we need is a system for handling all our risks. A risk management system. I have been doing some reading and came across a research paper[45] in which the authors were looking at designing risk management systems."

"Hold on a minute," Jerry interrupted. "Are you proposing that we devise a system in which we might use things like derivatives to hedge risks?"

Bob nodded. "Yes, I'm sure we will need to use some derivatives to manage risks."

Jerry almost exploded. "Bob, the last thing I want to see is a group of individuals using our assets to speculate on whether interest rates will rise or fall in the next year. I don't want us to be the next Procter & Gamble, Barings, or Orange County that lost millions of dollars in derivatives trading. Talk about value evaporation!"

Bob waved his hands in the air to calm Jerry down. "Jerry, we are getting a bit ahead of ourselves here. There are going to be some pitfalls. Deadly ones in fact. However, that is exactly why we need to talk about a risk management system and what it is designed to do. Many firms, such as Lukens and MCI, have successfully managed their risks without the 'business headline' losses that you mentioned."[46]

Bob followed up by beginning to describe what such a system might be like. He described the three basic premises upon which such a system rests:

- The key to creating corporate value is making good investments.
- The key to making good investments is generating enough cash internally to fund those investments. When companies do not generate enough cash, they tend to cut investments more drastically than their competitors do.
- Cash flow — so crucial to the investment process — can often be disrupted by movements in external factors such as exchange rates, commodity prices, and interest rates, potentially compromising a company's ability to invest.

A risk management program, therefore, should have a single overarching goal: to ensure that a company has the cash available to make value-enhancing investments that help execute the strategy.

Bob went on, "Jerry, it all comes back to strategy. For us to manage the risks of Doug's plan, or any of our other strategic plans, we should understand the factors

---

[45]Bob was referring to Kenneth Froot, David Scharfstein, and Jeremy Stein, "A Framework for Risk Management," *Journal of Applied Corporate Finance*, Fall 1994, 22–32.
[46]See "Bank of America Roundtable on Derivatives and Corporate Risk Management," *Journal of Applied Corporate Finance*, 8–3, Fall 1995, 58–74.

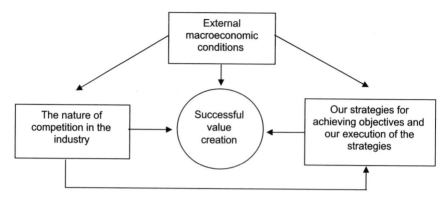

Fig. 7.1.   Factors affecting value creation.

that affect value creation. Only then can we come up with a way to minimize value evaporation. Let's look at Fig. 7.1."

Bob went on to briefly describe the boxes. "The box representing "Our Strategies …" is something we control. You will recall we discussed it earlier (Chapter 6) in connection with our conversation about strategy. The other two boxes represent external factors, or risks if you like, that we cannot control directly."

Bob continued. "Now if we can understand these factors, perhaps through game theory and other analyses, we should be better prepared to manage them."

Bob described these latter two boxes in greater detail, paying particular attention to how these risks affected Jerry's Lemonade now and in the global future. Bob characterized what could be thought of as a roadmap, which would allow him and Jerry to formulate a risk management system. This roadmap is summarized below.

3. What are the External Factors Affecting Value Creation?

3.1. *External macroeconomic conditions*

Anticipated macroeconomic conditions — the growth rate of the economy, interest rates, money supply, unemployment, etc. — affect a company's strategic plans and profit plans because these conditions help determine the total size of its product market as well as the total demand for each product. Moreover, during a strategic planning cycle or a year, macroeconomic conditions can change unpredictably, making it necessary to change the forecasts and specific components of the strategy.

To this end, Bob prepared the following list of key questions that Jerry's Lemonade, Inc. must answer about macroeconomic conditions.

- What are economic growth rates expected to be, domestically and internationally?
- Has there been a recent reversal in economic trends? If so, how long will the reversal last?
- What is the current rate of inflation and what is the forecast for future inflation? How will this affect our cost structure and the demand for various products?
- What is the current interest rate environment? What will be the effects of future interest rate movements on the food and beverage business overall and on our individual products? Is the price of gasoline affecting the ability of our customers to visit our stores?
- Is consumer spending up or down? What is consumer sentiment? Are consumers optimistic or pessimistic about the future?
- Are demographic trends favorable or unfavorable? Is our customer base changing along with the demographics?
- What are anticipated changes in governmental regulations, such as through the Federal Food and Drug Administration (FDA)? How will these affect the prices and ingredients of our products and the demand for them?
- What impact will tax laws and government incentives programs have on our business results?
- What is the potential impact of currency risk on our business?

3.2. The nature of competition in the industry

Bob began, "To understand the nature of competition, let's turn to Professor Michael Porter,[47] who I mentioned during our previous strategy discussions. He has identified five forces that determine the nature of competition in any given industry:

- Intensity of rivalry among existing competitors
- Threat of new entrants
- Threat of substitute products
- Bargaining power of suppliers
- Bargaining power of buyers.

---

[47] See Michael E. Porter, "How Competitive Forces Shape Strategy," *Harvard Business Review* March–April 1979 and Michael E. Porter, *Competitive Strategy: Techniques for Analyzing Industries and Competitors*, Free Press, New York, 1980.

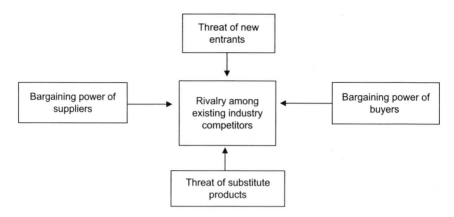

Fig. 7.2.   The five forces affecting industry competition.

Simply put, our value creation opportunities will be small if the industry rivalry is intense, if new entrants can enter the market easily, if there are numerous close substitutes for our products and services, if suppliers have considerable bargaining power over us, or if buyers have considerable bargaining power. These five forces are shown in Fig. 7.2."

Bob went on to describe how these forces related to Jerry's. The discussion again revolved around a series of questions.

3.3. Rivalry among existing industry competitors

What is the commitment of our major competitors to the flavored drinks business? What percentage of their corporate revenues comes from such sales? What is the free-cash-flow position of each competitor? For example, a competitor like Mickey, who is exclusively focused on flavored drinks, represents formidable competition.

- What is the amount of capital invested in the food and beverage business by each of our major competitors? Where has this capital been invested?
- What is the industry capacity utilization? What is the capacity utilization by product area for each of our major competitors? The lower the capacity utilization, the greater are the competitive pressures on pricing and margins. For example, in the home appliance industry, capacity utilization for the industry is between 65% and 70% in North America and the market is growing only at about 2% per year. This makes it difficult for appliance manufacturers like General Electric, Maytag, and Whirlpool to consistently create shareholder value in this

industry, even though these firms have done a remarkable job in consistently improving their cost efficiency and product quality.[48]

- What is the industry concentration identified by the market share of the top five firms? A highly concentrated industry can sometimes help reduce rivalry.

3.4. Bargaining power of buyers/customers

- What alternatives do our customers have to buying from us? The greater the number of alternatives they have, the lower is our bargaining power. That is, the more we look like our competitors, and the more of them there are, the less bargaining power we have over our customers.
- What percentage of our total business does each of our customers represent? The less diversified our customer base the less power we have over them. That is, the larger the percentage of our total business that a particular customer represents, the lower is our bargaining power over that customer.
- What are the trends in the evolution of distribution channels? The more consolidated the distribution channel and the greater its importance to us as a buyer that intermediates between us and the ultimate customer, the less bargaining power we have over the channel as a buyer. For example, manufacturers of specialty home products and home appliances do not have much bargaining power over buyers like Wal-Mart.

3.5. Bargaining power of suppliers

- How vertically integrated are our competitors as technology evolves? For example, might our competitors acquire their own fruit farms and cut costs? How will this affect us?
- How concentrated are the industries from which we source our raw materials? Greater concentration gives suppliers potentially greater power.
- How global is our procurement? The more global we are in our procurement, the less power suppliers have over us. McDonald's has created significant value for its shareholders by globally procuring inputs like sesame seeds. However, we must determine which product inputs should be procured globally. Obviously, there would be problems in shipping 40 tons of lemons from Florida to Beijing. Could they be kept fresh? For example, McDonald's looks for regional, rather than global, sources of beef.

---

[48]In fact, Maytag has recently (Summer of 2005) experienced such financial performance that they are subject to a takeover fight. It appears that Whirlpool has won the battle for Maytag. The domestic appliance market is further consolidating.

3.6. *Threat of new entrants*

• How attractive is this industry in terms of the returns to shareholders of the major competitors? The higher these returns, the greater the threat of new entrants. The success of Starbucks invited a host of new entrants to the specialty coffee business, such as Costa Coffee and Seattle Coffee Co.

• What are the barriers to entry? What are the minimum capital requirements to enter the industry? What are the economies of scale, proprietary product differences, distinct brand identities and customer loyalties by brand? The greater the minimum capital requirements, economies of scale, product differences, brand identities and customer loyalties, the smaller the threat of new entrants.

• What are the exit barriers? If the costs of exiting the industry are high, the threat of new entrants will be smaller. However, our present competitors are likely to hang around longer even if the profit potential is poor.

3.7. *Threat of substitute products*

• What kind of products could as-yet unidentified latent competitors develop that could partially substitute for our products? What if firms like Coca-Cola or PepsiCo bring out their own line of ready-made, high-quality lemonade and smoothies?

• What is the affordability of our products in light of the purchasing power of customers? The lower is the affordability, the greater is the threat of substitute products.

Bob summarized by saying, "You know, when you juxtapose Porter's Five-Forces analysis with what we discussed earlier about strategy, one overarching message emerges. **From the standpoint of our customers, the more we look like our competitors, the stronger will be the competitive forces that depress our profit margins and value creation potential, and increase the risk of not creating sustained shareholder value. Thus, the key to value creation for us will be to come up with strategies that truly distinguish us from our competition on a sustained basis."**

4. Jerry Wants to Get Started Right Away

As Bob finished his summary Jerry said, "This is very useful Bob. You know, we can answer these questions in due course. But that doesn't tell us how to cope with them."

"I agree," Bob remarked, "It turns out there are a lot of theories on how to manage the various risks of a business. However, we have to determine for ourselves the extent to which we want to hedge these risks. We may choose to bear some of these risks."

Jerry was perplexed, "What do you mean we may want to bear some of these risks?"

Bob responded, "Well, our choice depends on the magnitude of the risk and how much it would cost to hedge it. It will cost us more to hedge greater amounts of risk. Some firms are quite aggressive in how much risk they choose to bear. For example, Lukens — which is a producer of carbon, alloy, and stainless steel — sometimes chooses to take on some risks in the hope of turning a profit.[49] What this implies for them is that when their risk management group has an opinion on the future developments in say, the market for nickel, then they will actively trade in line with their view."

"Isn't that just speculation Bob?" Jerry asked.

"Looks that way, doesn't it? Unfortunately, the line between hedging and speculation is sometimes blurred," Bob responded. "However, Lukens appears to go about this very carefully. They have a group of senior executives who must unanimously vote in favor of taking any position. With careful monitoring and reporting to the board, they will probably be just fine. After all, they do possess competencies in this business."

"I will have to think a little bit about that one. Now, tell me what this has to do with us."

Bob replied, "Simply put, we have two issues. First, we will have to decide which risks we want to hedge and which we want to bear. A good rule is that we should bear those risks that are innate to our business and hedge all other risks. For example, we probably shouldn't worry about hedging the risk that the demand for our lemonade may be too low. But we may want to hedge foreign exchange risk or the risk that sugar prices may be too high.

"Second, there are going to be situations in which we can't determine upfront the amount of hedging needed. For instance, at the beginning of the year, MCI Communications used to hedge 100% of its one-year cash flows associated with foreign contracts.[50] This means risks more than a year out remain unhedged. By contrast, The Walt Disney Co. hedged its yen royalties in 1985 for a period of ten years. So, there is no right answer to how far out we should go with our hedging.

---

[49]See "Bank of America Roundtable on Derivatives and Corporate Risk Management," *Journal of Applied Corporate Finance*, 8–3, Fall 1995, 58–74.
[50]Ibid.

We just need to make sure that our risk management is aligned with all the other components of our Value Sphere."

"Okay, let me see if I have this right," Jerry said. "Our policy will be designed to manage risks, not to eliminate them, right?"

"Exactly," Bob replied.

"I think I would like to hear an example. Can you describe a situation of why we would want to, and how we could hedge, say fluctuations in foreign exchange rates, if we opened up our operations in another country?" Jerry asked.

"Absolutely," Bob replied. To highlight the main points on foreign exchange risks, he put the following slides on the projector.

4.1. Foreign currency and valuation

- Our global operations expose us to foreign exchange risk, necessitating an understanding of spot and forward exchange rates, currency exposure, and hedging.

- An exchange rate is simply the price of one currency in terms of another currency. That is, it represents how many units of one currency will be needed to purchase one unit of another currency. For example, the exchange rate between the US dollar and the British Pound may be $1.50/£1. This exchange rate implies that it takes $1.50 to purchase £1 or analogously, if you sell £1, you would receive $1.50.

- Exchange rates that apply to current transactions involving different currencies are called spot rates. These rates are listed daily in any financial newspaper and include most major world currencies.

- Forward rates exist at present for a foreign exchange transaction to be undertaken in the future. For example, one could buy a forward contract today to exchange US dollars for Euros, in six months. Forward exchange rates are affected by the market's expectation of the future spot rate. It is important to note that if one enters into a forward contract to exchange two currencies, both parties are obligated to fulfill the contract.

- Currency exposure represents a real business risk for any global firm. The risk that a firm faces is that the currency in one country may move against the home currency. For example, consider a US-based firm which has some of its sales generated in Japan. These profits are then exchanged from Japanese yen to US dollars. If the yen weakens against the dollar (i.e., it takes more yen to buy $1), then the firm will receive fewer US dollars than it would have if the yen had remained strong. This potential loss is an example of currency exposure.

  Since currency exposure can represent a severe risk to firms, many companies attempt to hedge these risks. There are many financial instruments available to hedge against such losses. Examples of such instruments include forward contracts, money market (or balance sheet) hedges, option contracts and futures contracts. Most hedging instruments attempt to lock in an exchange rate so that losses are not incurred if a currency moves in an adverse manner relative to another currency.

Bob warned, "Now, these are just the 'nuts and bolts' of hedging foreign exchange risk. In reality, we are going to need a risk management group within our treasury department to be responsible for all corporate hedging."

"How many special teams and task forces do we need to run a company anyway?" Jerry asked. "It seems like we have more of these than we have people in total!"

"You may have a point, Jerry," Bob conceded. "But it's going to be pretty difficult to argue against this particular team. There are so many ways to manage these risks now — interest rate swaps, barrier options, swaptions, FRAs (Fixed Rate Arrangements), forward and futures contracts, etc. — we're going to need a couple of high-tech finance types just to keep up with the investment bankers. We should probably benchmark our efforts against firms like Lukens, FMC, W.R. Grace, and The Stanley Works."[51]

Jerry nodded. A risk management group was probably critical to the success of any business, especially a global one. "I'm sure you're right," Jerry replied. "Am I right in assuming that most firms engage in such hedging?"

"Absolutely," Bob responded. "In fact, I just saw the results from a survey[52] the Wharton Business School carried out. They found that 59% of large firms were actively engaged in hedging foreign currency risk through derivative securities like options and futures contracts."

"OK, OK," Jerry muttered, "you've convinced me! I say we get your team to start addressing the questions about 'external risk factors' ASAP. Or do you have that covered already?" Bob nodded affirmatively, with a bit of a smirk. He'd already briefed his team to start formulating answers to these questions before the meeting.

"Just one last thing..." Bob said as he sensed Jerry was about to close the meeting.

5. Micro Risks Which Jerry Can Impact

"We need to say something about internal risks, as well as the risk of Mickey and the like," Bob said. "What I am referring to here are the micro risks."

Bob explained that micro risks are those that arise from uncertainty about product-specific factors that affect the product's profitability. For example, forecasts of sales and costs could be wrong, leading to an underestimation of a product's profit potential. One would then mistakenly abandon the product. Or one could overestimate profit potential, resulting in an investment in a money-losing venture. The

---

[51] See John Morris, "Are You In This Together?" *Treasury and Risk Management*, September 1994.

[52] See G. Bodnar, G. Hayt, and R. Marston, "1995 Wharton Survey of Derivatives Usage by U.S. Non-Financial Firms," *Financial Management*, 25-4, Winter 1996, 113–133.

profit potential of the product may also suffer from implementation risks, including unanticipated delays in product launch that not only postpone the realization of profits, but also yield valuable turf to competitors.

"Is there an easy way to quantify what you are saying?" Jerry asked.

Bob nodded, "Sure. The easiest way to think about this is to construct probability distributions. So whenever you have some variable — or project input, if you like — that can take one of a number of different values, you want to think of it in terms of a probability distribution."

Jerry interrupted, "Can't I think of these probability distributions as ranges of values that could occur?"

"Absolutely," Bob replied. "For now, let's consider three distributions — the uniform, triangular and normal distributions."

Bob then put on the document camera. He began to explain each distribution. "The distribution chosen for any variable depends on the behavior of the variable. For example, the uniform distribution is appropriate when only a range between minimum and maximum values can be specified for the variable, and all values of the variable within that range are equally likely.

"On the other hand, the *triangular distribution* is useful when the analyst is able to specify the variable's minimum, most likely and maximum values. The variable can take any value from the range between the minimum and maximum values, but not with equal probabilities. The most likely value has the highest probability of occurrence, and the probabilities decline as the variable moves away from the most likely value and approaches the minimum and maximum values.

The normal distribution is appropriate when you can specify the mean (or average) and standard deviation of the variable, and the variable can take any value, with values around the mean being more likely."[53]

"I can see how thinking about distributions would be quite useful," Jerry remarked. "I suppose this is what weather forecasters use when they tell us that there is a 95% chance of snow tomorrow. In our case, I guess I could think about our lemon prices per pound as being uniformly distributed from 99 cents to \$1.21."

---

[53] A relatively simple approach to determine the mean and standard deviation for a normal distribution can be derived from the lessons of statistical quality control. A process is under control as long as the measurement variable lies between statistically specified minimum and maximum values. For the normal distribution, a common control limit standard is the 95% level; i.e., establish the limits such that 95% of the occurrences lie between them. The same limits can be utilized in the case of normal distribution inputs for subjective date. The provider of the input must be willing to assert that 95% of occurrences of this normally distributed variable lie between specified upper and lower limits. With this data, the analyst can then calculate the mean as: (upper limit + lower limit)/2 and the standard deviation as (upper limit–lower limit)/4.

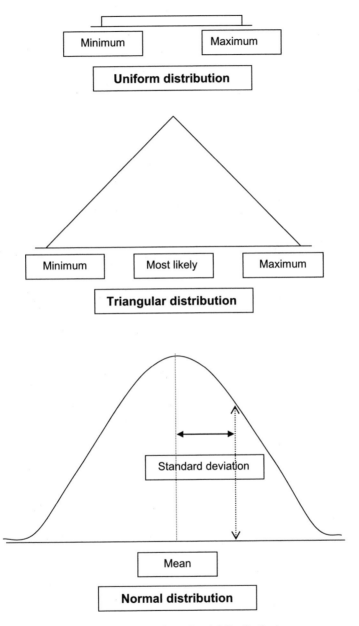

Fig. 7.3.   Three commonly used probability distributions.

"Just about right, Jerry," Bob said. "Although you have to keep in mind that to use a uniform distribution we have to be confident that the price could never be less than 99 cents or more than $1.21."

"Point taken," Jerry conceded. "Now, didn't you say something about competitor risks?"

"Yes, I did. While probability distributions are a useful way of thinking about the risk and uncertainties we face, I think we can go a lot further. Particularly in terms of how we think about project risks and especially, the risk of our pal Mickey," Bob exclaimed as he glanced up at the clock on the wall. "However, I see that we are out of time. Why don't you take a look at this." Bob handed Jerry a report in memo form.[54]

Jerry quickly scanned the cover sheet and replied, "Looks interesting. We can talk about this next week then. But before that I'll see you at the golf course this weekend. Bring your best game. I feel sharp."

When Jerry returned to his office, he quickly checked his diary. Luckily, he still had the next 25 minutes open. He immediately began to read Bob's memo.

INTERNAL MEMO

To: Jerry Wyman, CEO

From: Bob Butterfield, CFO

Subject: Project and Competitor Risk

In thinking about the micro risks of our business, we must first examine our current strategy and assess its performance in terms of maximizing shareholder value. Importantly, our strategy also defines a fundamental trade-off in our capital budgeting practices. This is the trade-off between product cycle time and risk.

We can envision this trade-off as follows. The more time and resources we are willing to commit to collecting information about new product ideas, the more we can learn about the project's cash flows before we invest. This will lower our informational risk exposure, making it less likely that we pour funds into value-evaporating ideas. However, this risk reduction comes at the expense of a longer cycle time, as shown in Fig. 7.4.

In Fig. 7.4, the curve given by points ABCD represents the cycle time-risk efficiency frontier for a new product initiative like a new flavored lemonade. Observe that it is impossible to lie below the frontier, given our existing human capital, organization structure, and technology.

(Continued)

---

[54]See also John A. Boquist, Todd T. Milbourn, and Anjan V. Thakor, "How Do You Win the Capital Allocation Game?" *Sloan Management Review*, Winter 1998, pp. 59–71.

(*Continued*)

Now for any point that is off the frontier, say E, there is another point on the frontier that we would prefer. For example, B represents a shorter cycle time with the same level of risk as E. And C represents a lower level of risk with the same cycle time as E. Depending on the cycle time-risk tradeoff we desire, we would prefer either B or C to E.

As a starting point, we should take the frontier as a given. Where along the frontier we wish to be is a matter of strategic choice. If we choose to be more tolerant of informational risk, we may prefer B. However, if we choose to be less tolerant of informational risk, we may prefer C. Holding the efficiency frontier fixed, then by choosing B, we will be more error-prone in identifying customer tastes, estimating market demand, and so on. But when we're right, we will have a competitive first-mover advantage over, say Mickey's, if they prefer to be at C.

This is an important aspect of time-based competition. A shorter cycle time has a competitive edge, but it also means bearing more risk. The quality of the information on which our capital budgeting is based will not be as good as that of a firm willing to tolerate longer cycle times.

As an example, it is often claimed that Japanese companies — like Toyota — have preferred shorter cycle times (and consequently greater risk) than US companies — like General Motors — when it comes to introducing new products. In fact, Japanese automakers typically take only 18 months to bring a new idea to market. American automakers, on the other hand, often take up to 36 months to do the same. United States automakers are now trying to shorten the time it takes to introduce a new model.

Of course, we need not take the frontier as given. We could try to push the frontier down, say to A1 D1. But this will require a fundamental reengineering of our corporation and attention to a process orientation. However, if this can be achieved, it can give us a powerful competitive advantage. This is the essence of time-based competition.

Firms that perceive different frontiers may also make different decisions about product introductions. To see this, suppose that Mickey's deemed R the acceptable level of risk, just like us. Now if Mickey's believed that they were on the efficiency frontier ABCD, they would view their cycle time as T2. We, on the other hand, may be on the frontier A1 D1, and would view our cycle time as T1. With the shorter cycle time, we would be spending less money prior to product launch and bringing the product to market faster. Naturally, we would assess a higher value from this product than Mickey's. The value could well be positive for us and negative for Mickey's, so that they would reject the product while we introduced it.

The basic conclusion is that, whatever the efficiency frontier, our company's strategy determines the point along that frontier where we want to be. The implications of this strategic choice for cycle time and risk should be clearly communicated to our project teams.

Just as importantly, when we are screening capital requests and allocating capital, we must make sure that our screening criteria are consistent with our company's overall strategic choice. Breakdowns will occur if our strategy is decoupled from our project-ranking criteria, i.e., if risk management is not aligned with the other components of the Value Sphere.

(*Continued*)

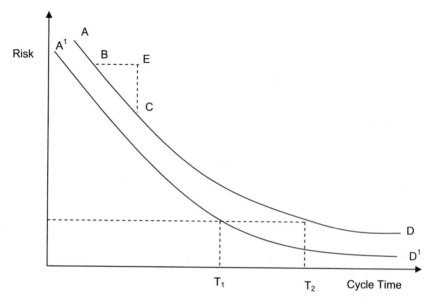

Fig. 7.4.   The cycle time-risk efficiency frontier for a new product.

(Continued)

For example, if we choose to embark on the strategy to grow aggressively through global expansion, our key capital budgeting criterion cannot be to discriminate against projects with payback periods longer than two years. Alternatively, if our strategy is to introduce a new product every year, then the demands on the quality of market research data used to support the sales volume assumptions in investment planning cannot be so great that it is impossible to achieve the cycle time-risk trade-off consistent with the strategy.

6. Concluding with the Biggest Risk

Jerry really liked the thinking behind Bob's report and looked forward to discussing it with him next week. Perhaps they would chat about it a bit during their golf game Saturday. However, it got him thinking about a different, but related, issue. To a certain extent, the risks we are exposed to depend on the capital investments we make and the products and markets we choose. But how do we judge which investments, products and markets are best from a risk-return standpoint? (This is taken up in Chapter 9.) He decided to call Bob.

"Bob," began Jerry, "how do we actually work this risk assessment into our choice of capital investments?"

"Well, Jerry," replied Bob, "that's a whole new discussion. First, we need to determine how to reflect risk into our cost of capital (see Chapter 8). Then, we need to design an appropriate resource allocation system."

Jerry tapped on his desk. "I suppose that's something we'll have to work on. But how do we quantify the risk of obsolescence? You know, someone inventing something to replace lemonade or to provide it more effectively to the customer?"

Bob stood speechless for a moment. How could he have ignored this risk in his discussion?

"Jerry, you're absolutely right," he began. "That is the biggest risk we face. It is the risk of value migrating away from us because someone comes up with a brand-new business paradigm that creates more value. I am not sure that we can quantify it precisely, but what we can do is make that thinking an integral part of our strategy. Perhaps we should have someone working on a project to come up with a new business design that can make our current business design obsolete."

Jerry, looking troubled, asked, "Does anyone do that?"

"Sure," said Bob, now regaining his composure. "Jack Welch, the former CEO of General Electric, had teams engaged in precisely that exercise for the various business units of the company. If you do come up with such a business design, the advantage is that you can prepare for it before someone else comes up with a similar design. Or you may decide to adopt it yourself and throw out your old design. Either way, you win."

Jerry looked a bit more reassured now. "Ok, I'll put someone to work on it right away."

Main Lessons

- All companies face risks, but not all manage them effectively to maximize value retention.
- The overarching goal of any risk management system is to insure that the company has sufficient cash flow to execute its value-creation strategy. What is done in risk management should be aligned with the other components of the company's Value Sphere.
- Firms must identify the external factors that may affect the execution of the strategy, and determine the portion of the risks they create that they would like to hedge, and those they would like to bear.
- Micro risks arising from the misestimation of revenue and cost items can also be very costly. How large this risk is depends on the firm's choice of where to be along the cycle time-risk efficiency frontier of new-product introduction. This is

a matter of strategic choice. The longer the product development cycle time, the smaller will be the risk that we will misestimate revenues, costs and investments and thus invest in projects that evaporate value. But, the higher is the likelihood that we will lose first-mover advantage in introducing the new product.

- All risks should be explicitly modeled using appropriate probability distributions to capture the possible range of future outcomes.
- The biggest risk a firm faces is that a competitor shifts the paradigm in a way that makes the current business design obsolete.

End-of-Chapter Exercises

1. Does your firm have an explicit risk management system? How does your system stack up when evaluated on the three basic premises of a sound risk management system as suggested by Bob in Section 2?
2. From the viewpoint of your company, answer the questions in Section 3 related to (i) external macroeconomic conditions and (ii) competitors' market positions.
3. From the section on Porter's "Five Forces" affecting industry competition, again answer the questions from your company's perspective. Give your company a score from 1 (low) to 5 (high) on each of the five forces. For example, a score of 1 would mean that our suppliers have very low bargaining power over us, whereas a score of 5 means they have enormous power over us. Then compute a total score.
4. Based on your answers to Questions 2 and 3, what did you learn about your company's competitive position? If your total score in Question 3 was above 12, perhaps you should consider strategically repositioning your company. Write down a new strategic plan for a business unit or for the company that gives you a score under 12.
5. Write down the risks associated with your current strategy (score > 12) and the new strategy developed in Question 4 (score < 12). Which strategy has greater risk? Why? How would you manage the risks in the chosen strategy to maximize value retention?
6. If your firm operates globally, how are you affected by "global risks" in your current position? Is there a risk management group within the organization that copes with these risks, or are you expected to do so?
7. Based on Bob's memo about "Project and Competitor Risk," where would you place your company (or division) along the cycle time–risk efficiency frontier? Where do you believe your major competitors lie along this frontier? Could value be created by a shift along (or away from) the existing frontier? What specific steps would be necessary for such a move?

8. Do you know the business design that can make your current way of doing business obsolete?

Practice Problems

1. Which risks should a company hedge and which risks should it not hedge? How should one decide?
2. What is the "cycle-time-risk efficiency frontier"? What is the usefulness of this concept?
3. What is the biggest risk any company faces? Why is this the biggest risk?
4. What are the elements of a sound risk management system?
5. What are Porter's 5 forces? How do they help us evaluate a company's risks and value-creation potential?

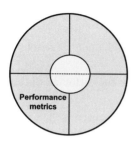

Chapter 8

WHAT DO OUR INVESTMENTS
REALLY COST US?:
THE COST OF CAPITAL

1. How to Proceed?

Jerry now had a risk management system in place. Bob had recruited Nancy Whitmore, an MBA who was working at Citigroup, to head their risk management team. Things seemed to be in place. But the competitive threat from Mickey had not diminished. Jerry thought that he had to keep the company growing to cope with this threat and prevent disruptions to the Value Sphere. Investments in new products or new geographic regions could be the company's future lifeblood. But such investments also carried with them the risk that capital would be committed to value-evaporating projects. Firms suffering from such Value Evaporation often grew but destroyed shareholder value. Jerry wanted to make sure his company did not make similar mistakes. He called Bob into his office to share his concerns.

2. The Capital Markets

Bob began, "The secret to capital allocation in any company is to constantly ask the question: What would the capital market want us to do? The capital market communicates to us by establishing required rates of return for various investments. Our task is to interpret what the capital market is telling us and use it in our decision making. The way we do this is by linking the rate of return established by the capital market — called the cost of capital — to the internal performance metrics that are a

124

part of our Value Sphere. It is the theory of the cost of capital that links the capital market to our business."

"How is that linkage created, Bob?"

Bob replied, "Let's create the linkage by starting with the business and its balance sheet. The typical balance sheet, in summary form, is given below.

Typical balance sheet

Current assets	Current liabilities
Cash	Accounts payable
Marketable securities	Accrued expenses
Accounts receivable	Bank loans
Inventory	Current portion of long-term debt
Fixed assets	Long-term debt
Gross fixed assets	Equity
Less accumulated depreciation	Common stock
	Retained earnings
Total assets	Total liabilities and equity

Since total assets must equal total liabilities plus equity, any decision to add assets must be accompanied by a corresponding increase in liabilities or equity. Any decreases in assets are accompanied by liability or equity decreases. Another way to say this is that total uses of funds (asset increase, liability decrease, or equity decrease) must equal total sources of funds (asset decrease, liability increase, or equity increase) during any period of time.

For example, it may be informative to look at the sources and uses of funds for the business over the past 3 years since the IPO as shown in Fig. 8.1. Basically it tells us that our investments in assets (current assets, equipment, and facilities) were financed with increases in bank debt, current liabilities, and equity."

Jerry nodded and said, "That is very interesting, Bob, but I still don't see where the capital market fits in."

Bob replied, "I'm getting there, Jerry. Consider the transformed balance sheet shown below:

Transformed balance sheet

Current Assets	IBCLS
− NIBCLS	+ Debt
+ Net fixed assets	+ Equity
= Net assets	= Invested capital

Balance sheets

Assets	Year 1 (in $)	Year 4 (in $)	Liabilities and equity	Year 1 (in $)	Year 4 (in $)
Cash	120,000	567,000	Accounts payable	380,000	3,997,000
Accounts receivable	60,000	246,000	Taxes payable	—	987,000
Inventory	450,000	4,600,000	Accrued liabilities	—	373,000
Current assets	630,000	5,413,000	Current liabilities	380,000	5,357,000
Gross fixed assets	1,700,000	24,387,000	Bank debt	800,000	2,555,000
Accumulated depreciation	(150,000)	(3,432,000)	Public debt	—	—
Net fixed assets	1,550,000	20,955,000	Shareholders' equity	1,000,000	18,456,000
Total assets	2,180,000	28,368,000	Total liabilities and equity	2,180,000	26,368,000

Statement of funds flow: Years 1 through 4

Sources of funds	(in $)	Uses of funds	(in $)
Accounts payable	3,617,000	Cash	447,000
Taxes payable	987,000	Accounts receivable	186,000
Accrued liabilities	373,000	Inventory	4,150,000
Current liabilities	4,977,000	Current assets	4,783,000
Bank debt	1,755,000	Gross fixed assets	22,687,000
Public debt	—	Accumulated depreciation	(3,282,000)
Shareholders' equity	17,456,000	Net fixed assets	19,405,000
Total sources	24,188,000	Total uses	24,188,000

Fig. 8.1.　Three years after IPO.

"Wait a minute, Bob. This NIBCLS and IBCLS stuff sounds like a foreign language."

Bob responded, "It's actually not too bad. I did talk about this earlier (Chapter 2). NIBCLS stands for non-interest bearing current liabilities and IBCLS stands for interest-bearing current liabilities. We separate the current liabilities into two parts: those that have a stated interest rate (IBCLS) and those that do not (NIBCLS). For example, accounts payable would be classified as a NIBCLS since they do not carry an explicit interest rate, whereas bank loans would be classified as an IBCLS.

"The reason we transform the balance sheet in this way is so that we can determine the returns the capital market requires for the right-hand side of the balance sheet. Our bank lenders, the bondholders providing us long-term debt, and our shareholders are all capital market providers of funds. Our goal is to determine the cost of the funds provided. This cost represents the minimum return expected by our financiers. It is in essence a capital markets benchmark. This means we should only invest in assets that promise expected returns that exceed this minimum return."

"It all makes sense to me Bob. We can only create value if the returns we earn on the capital we invest exceed the cost of that capital. But one thing is puzzling. Why don't we consider accounts payable, one of the NIBCLS you mentioned, to be part of the funds provided by the capital market? Aren't our suppliers also providing financing by giving us extended payment terms?"

"That is an excellent question, Jerry. Extended payment terms are, in fact, a credit arrangement. However, it is fundamentally different from a bank loan in at least one very important aspect: trade credit does not carry a stated rate of interest."[55]

"On the other hand, you can be sure that our suppliers are smart enough to price their goods and services to include the financing expenses associated with giving us extended payment terms. So, the cost of the funds supplied by trade creditors is already in the price they charge for goods and services and is, therefore, deducted as an expense when we calculate our income. Since this cost is already accounted for in the cost of goods sold, we don't consider it a separate financing charge. A similar logic holds for accrued expenses and other NIBCLS."

"Well, Jerry, we are now in a position to determine the cost of capital. Or more precisely, the weighted average cost of capital (WACC). The theory of WACC builds upon the risk discussion we started earlier. The capital market operates under

---

[55] Of course, if we continually delay payments to suppliers, they may require us to sign formal notes with them that carry a stated interest rate.

one basic truth: higher perceived risks for an investment require higher expected returns. If you reconsider the transformed balance sheet, the job of the capital markets is to assess the risk and hence the required return expected on our sources of funding; both debt and equity."

3. Cost of Debt Financing

Jerry began: "Isn't the cost of debt financing easy to determine, Bob? Just calculate the interest rate we pay on the past borrowings and use that as the cost of debt financing?"

Bob explained patiently, "You are close, Jerry, but it isn't quite that easy. The relevant cost of debt finance is its marginal cost. This is related to the next dollar we raise. Thus, we would not use the interest rate we pay on past borrowings to determine the cost of the next dollar of borrowing. As interest rates change, the rate on past borrowings will differ from the cost of funds today."

"I agree Bob, but on your transformed balance sheet you have listed two different kinds of debt: IBCLS and long-term debt. Are the costs the same for both types of debt?"

Bob replied, "Actually, they are not. But as a practical matter, most companies use the same rate for IBCLS and long-term debt.[56] The reasoning is straightforward. We are generally concerned with the value of long-term projects and strategies. Thus, any short-term debt included in IBCLS will need to be rolled over and refinanced to provide long-term funding.

"In the long run, the cost of rolling over short-term debt approximates the cost of long-term debt. Any advantage or disadvantage in short-term rates relative to long-term rates will be dissipated over the long horizon. So, we set the cost of IBCLS equal to the cost of long-term debt. This is consistent with what some call the expectations theory of the term structure of interest rates."

"That certainly simplifies matters," Jerry responded.

"Yes it does, but we may want to make further adjustments to the cost of debt financing. In particular, debt financing has a tax advantage since interest expense is deductible from income before calculating corporate income tax. Because of this deduction for interest expense, the government effectively shares in the expense. After adjusting for corporate taxes,[57] the effective after-tax cost of debt financing is

---

[56]For example see Chapter 8 in *Valuation: Measuring and Managing the Value of Companies*, 2nd edition, by Tom Copeland, Tim Koller & Jack Murrin, John Wiley & Sons, 1996.
[57]Some theorists also adjust for personal taxes. See Merton H. Miller, "Debt and Taxes," *Journal of Finance*, 32, May 1977, 261–276.

given by the following equation:

Pre-tax cost of debt [1 − tax rate] .

For example, our current interest rate is 10% and our tax rate is 40%. So our after-tax cost of debt is:

$$10\%(1 - 0.4) = 6\%.$$

The tax deduction for interest expense reduces the effective cost of debt financing."

"Wait a second, Bob. I don't quite see the point. Can you give me an example of the effect of the tax deduction for interest expense?"

"Sure, Jerry. It's just like the interest deduction for the mortgage on your home. You have an 8% interest rate. But since your effective personal tax rate is about 35%, your real interest cost is only 5.2% = 8% (1 − .35). Consider a company that has an income statement that looks like this without and with $100 in interest expense.

	Without interest (in $)	With interest (in $)
Revenues	1000	1000
Cost of goods sold	400	400
Gross margin	600	600
SG&A	200	200
Earnings before interest and taxes (EBIT)	400	400
Interest expense	0	100
Earnings before taxes (EBT)	400	300
Tax (0.4)	160	120
Earnings after taxes (EAT)	240	180
+ Interest expense	0	100
Cash flow to capital providers	240	280

"There are two important aspects to this example, Jerry. First, in the case where there is $100 in interest expense, the taxes paid are lower by $40 ($160 vs. $120). Since a total of $100 in interest is paid, but $40 less in taxes, the effective cost of this debt is $60 ($100 − $40), or $100 × (1 − 0.4) = $60.

"Second, the total cash flow to all capital providers, earnings after-tax to shareholders and interest to lenders, are $40 higher ($240 vs. $280). Note that the increase in payments to a capital providers, both equity and debt, of $40 is equal to $100 × (0.4). In symbols, the amount is iDT, where iD is the interest paid, calculated by multiplying the interest rate, i, times the amount borrowed D, and T is the corporate tax rate. This increase in the firm's total cash flow because of the tax deductibility of debt interest is important to the valuation of the firms. Firms that borrow money have higher valuations than those that do not borrow, everything else equal."

4. Equity Financing

Bob began, "Now, let's look at the cost of equity. The most widely used method of determining the cost of equity financing is to use the capital asset pricing model, known as the CAPM.[58] The CAPM specifies that the cost of equity capital is equal to the return expected on the firm's common stock, and can be written as:

Equity cost of capital

= Risk-free rate + [Stock's beta × Market risk premium]

where the 30-year US Treasury bond rate is used to proxy for the risk-free rate.

"In this model, it is the beta coefficient that is unique to each stock. Everything else is common to all stocks traded on US exchanges."

"Hold on, Bob. You need to slow down and explain this beta and risk premium stuff," said Jerry.

Bob responded quickly. "Sure, Jerry. The cost of equity capital has two elements: the first is compensation for the pure time value of money which is represented by the risk-free rate. And the second is compensation for the risk in investing in a particular stock that is given by beta times the market risk premium. Note that the market risk premium is the additional return over and above the risk-free rate that investors demand for investing in the stock market as a whole. An example of an overall stock market risk is that occurring after the internet bubble collapsed. A stock's beta measures how risky the stock is relative to the whole market."

Jerry nodded. "Bob, I want to know a bit more about this beta coefficient. It is a mystery to me."

Bob smiled reassuringly, "The beta coefficient is a risk measure, identifying how responsive a stock's return is relative to movements in the entire stock market. What investors have found is that when the market goes up or down, almost every stock tends to move in procyclical fashion with the market, although different stocks move by different amounts. You know the old saying: 'A rising tide lifts all boats.' So, it is with the stock market. This is why the risk represented by beta is called systematic risk. For relatively few stocks, such as gold mining shares, the relationship with the

---

[58]There are other models to determine the cost of equity capital and WACC. See *The Search for Value* by Michael C. Ehrhardt, Harvard Business School Press, 1994.

market may be negative, meaning that a rise (fall) in the market is accompanied by a fall (rise) in the stock. For the vast majority of stocks, however, the relationship is positive."

"How is beta determined, Bob? Is it an objective number? Or is it subjectively determined?" asked Jerry.

Bob replied, "Beta is objectively calculated for each stock based on statistical estimation. The calculation relies on historical return data for the market and the stock over a long-time period. For example, returns could be calculated over weekly intervals for the past two years, or monthly for the past five years. The return on a stock is the change in stock price plus any dividends paid over that time period all divided by the initial stock price, for example:

$$\text{Return on the stock in a given month} = \frac{\text{Price appreciation during the month} + \text{Dividends}}{\text{Beginning price}}$$

"Similar return information is obtained for the entire market for the same time period. We then stack up the returns on the stock and on the market over months, and statistically analyze this data.[59]

"Perhaps the best way to see what is going on is to plot the data as shown in Fig. 8.2. The return on the market is plotted on the horizontal axis and the corresponding return on the stock on the vertical axis. Statistical analysis called regression is applied to this data, to produce a line that best fits the data as shown in the diagram.

"The slope of this regression line is the beta coefficient we are looking for. It identifies how responsive the stock return is to the return in the overall market. A beta of 1.0 indicates that the stock behaves just like the market. If the market moves up 10%, loosely speaking we'd expect the stock to move up 10% too. On the downside, if the market goes down 10%, we'd expect the stock to go down 10%. A beta coefficient of 0.5 would indicate that the stock's return is only half as responsive to market returns; whereas a beta of 2.0 would be twice as responsive. Seen this way, beta is a measure of a stock's return volatility relative to the market."

Jerry shook his head, "I see how beta is calculated, Bob. But that seems like a lot of hassle to go through each time you want to determine the cost of equity capital. Besides, I don't see how this measure is related to risk."

---

[59] With large computerized databases such as CRSP, produced by the Center for Research in Security price at the University of Chicago, the task is not as daunting as it seems. The website Yahoo Finance also provides such stock return information for all publicly-traded companies.

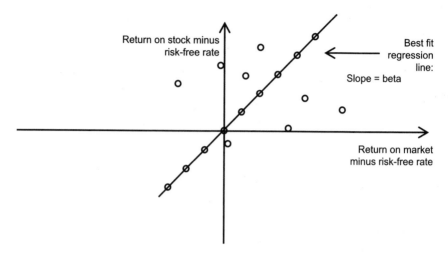

Fig. 8.2.   Regression analysis of return data to calculate beta.

Bob spoke as he paced the room, "Your first question is easy to answer, Jerry. We don't have to actually do the regression calculation each time we want to measure the cost of equity capital. Many investor services, such as Value Line, Standard and Poors, Bloomberg, Yahoo Finance, and Barra, publish their estimates of beta coefficients. So do most brokerage houses. It is also available from the Internet at sites such as Yahoo Finance. The key is to check a few of these sources. And if their estimates are close, use the average number in the analysis. To give you some idea of the beta coefficients for commonl- traded stocks, I have drawn Fig. 8.3 using data from Yahoo Finance.

"As you look at this list, Jerry, note that the higher betas are associated with biotechnology and computer companies, while the lower betas are for utilities and supermarkets. These rankings fit our intuitive notion of risk. Since we are unable to predict the market as a whole, we are left with the risk of how the company's stock reacts to the market movements."

"Why is this so, Bob?" asked Jerry.

Bob responded, "Because we'd expect biotech and computer companies to be more volatile relative to the market than utilities and supermarkets. You always need energy and food."

"In addition, there are individual risks associated with an investment in a single stock, i.e., a fire at a key plant, the unexpected landing of a major contract, etc. These risks are called idiosyncratic or unsystematic, and represent the points (stock returns) that are above or below the line in Fig. 8.4. These risks can be diversified away by

Company	Beta
Eli Lilly	0.44
Abbott Labs	0.16
3 Com Corporation	1.56
Exxon	0.86
Advanced Micro Devices	1.82
BP	1.19
Disney	0.66
Dow Chemical	0.78
Apple Computers	2.91
General Motors	1.48
IBM	0.81
Kroger	0.47
Safeway	1.07
Biogen Idec	0.44
Coca–Cola	0.48
General Electric	0.74
McDonald's	1.01
Microsoft	1.13

Fig. 8.3.   Value line betas for selected companies.
Source: Yahoo Finance, October 17, 2008.

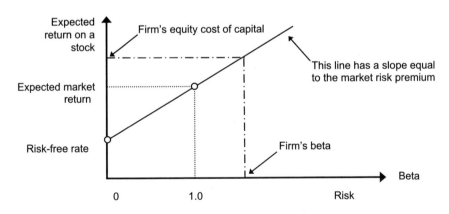

Fig. 8.4.   Expected return and risk.

investors who buy sufficiently diverse portfolios of stocks?[60] Since systematic risk can't be diversified away but unsystematic risk can, it is systematic risk that gets priced in the market."[61]

Jerry wanted to get back to the issue for Jerry's Lemonade. "Speaking of the cost of equity capital, Bob, are we in a position to calculate it now?"

Bob replied, "Just about, Jerry. Remember the equation:

Cost of equity capital

= Risk-free rate + [Beta × Market risk premium]

"We have talked about all terms except the last one, the market risk premium. It represents the amount by which the market returns are expected to exceed the returns on long-term risk-free bonds. Over 1926–2004, the historical arithmetic average of this value is about 7.0% in the US market.[62] Estimates on a forward looking basis are currently 3% to 3.5%, but I prefer to use the historical average.

"Since this is a measure of the historical returns over a long period of time, it is reasonable for investors to expect the stock market to earn this 7.0% spread over government bond returns in the future. Whatever the current risk-free bond return is, investors expect to earn 7.0% more by investing in the entire US stock market. For example, if the current risk-free rate is 5.5%, investors who buy a well-diversified stock mutual fund, such as an index fund, would expect to earn 12.5% (i.e., 5.5% + 7.0%) on their investment.

"We can now take advantage of the facts that the overall market has, by definition, a beta coefficient of 1.0 and the risk-free government bond a beta of 0. Let's plot these two points in Fig. 8.4 that specifies the x axis as risk measured by beta and the y axis as expected return.

"As shown in the diagram, a beta of 0 is expected to generate the risk-free rate of return and a beta of 1.0 is expected to generate the overall market expected return. Given these two points, we can write the equation of the straight line

[60]Research suggests that 20 randomly chosen stocks are typically sufficient for portfolio diversification. See Meir Statman, "How Many Stocks Make a Diversified Portfolio?" *Journal of Financial and Quantitative Analysis*, 22, 353–364 (September 1987). Since mutual funds have at least 20 securities from different companies, they may offer effective diversification, although their securities are not chosen randomly, so it may take more securities to diversify.

[61]Some of the services that publish betas adjust them to reflect the empirical tendency for them to revert to a value of 1.0 in the future. A common way to adjust for this tendency is to weight the calculated beta by 2/3 and the market beta of 1.0 by 1/3, i.e. β adjusted = $(1/3)$ β calculated + $(1/3)(1.0)$. This is considered a better predictor of future betas than historically estimated betas.

[62]See Ibbotson Associates, *SBBI Valuation Edition, 2005 Yearbook*, Chicago, Illinois. Note that Ibbotson also provides estimates of a size premium that can be added to determine the equity cost of capital for a small firm.

connecting them:

Equity cost of capital for a firm

= Expected return on the firm's equity

= Risk-free rate + [Beta × Market risk premium]

This is how the CAPM works."

Jerry understood now. "Bob, I think I understand the CAPM! But is this a practical way to measure our cost of equity capital?"

Bob nodded. "The model is well received by both academic and practitioners. In fact, the developers of the model, William Sharpe and Harry Markowitz, won the Nobel Prize in Economics for their contribution. Portfolio managers and corporations use the model routinely.

"Let's use it to calculate our cost of equity capital. The current government long-term borrowing rate is 4.5%, and our company's beta is 1.15. Thus, according to the CAPM, our cost of equity capital is:

$$4.5\% + 1.15\ (7.0\%)$$
$$= 4.5\% + 8.05\%$$
$$= 12.55\%.$$

"As you can see, Jerry, the model is very easy to use. We can now use it to determine our Weighted Average Cost of Capital (WACC)."

5. The Weighted Average Cost of Capital

What Bob explained to Jerry is summarized below.

The formula for WACC is:

$$\text{WACC} = \left\{ \begin{array}{l} [\text{After-tax cost of debt} \times \text{debt as a fraction of total assets}] \\ + [\text{Cost of equity} \times \text{equity as fraction of total assets}] \end{array} \right\}$$

Let's talk about the fractional weights for debt and equity. These weights are different from those found in the transformed balance sheet. For WACC purposes, the values of debt and equity must be stated at *market values*, not book values. Market values represent the value of investors' debt and equity positions in the firm. The way to think about this is the fact that investors could sell their investments at anytime and collect the market value.

The market value of debt can be obtained if it is traded. If it carries an adjustable rate of interest, the book value of the debt should approximate its market value.

If the debt is not traded, and carries a fixed rate of interest, the market value can be inferred by calculating the present value of the promised debt payments for interest and principal, by using the value of i, the interest rate on the next dollar borrowed, as the relevant discount rate. (See Chapter 2 for a review of present value methods.)

Since IBCLS are short-term debts, their book values will often approximate their market values, although this may not always be true. In addition to the market value of IBCLS and debt, the value of non-capitalized lease payments should be included in the market value of debt. If you know the series of future minimum lease payments, they can be discounted at i, the interest rate, in order to determine the amount to add to the market value of debt. A shortcut used sometimes is to simply multiply the minimum annual lease payment by 8 and add it to the market value of debt. This is the calculation we performed in Chapter 3.

For a traded company, it is easy to determine the market value of equity. You would simply multiply the share price by the number of shares outstanding.

5.1. Calculating WACC

Jerry asked, "What is your estimate of our cost of capital, Bob?"

Bob replied, "Before calculating it, I need to make one more clarification. The weights for debt and equity capital could be determined from the market values of each. Alternatively, we could state a policy on debt usage and use that. As the top managers of the company, we have control over our leverage position. This is what I would call a long-run target capital structure."

"Can you remind me what we agreed would be our target capital structure, Bob?" asked Jerry.

Bob nodded affirmatively. "Recall that we did our IPO because our debt levels, including operating leases, were quite high. In fact, debt usage at that time was too high, given our growth plans. We issued equity to bring the leverage position more in line. Over the long run, I'd say our target capital structure, on a market value basis, is about 40% debt and 60% equity."

"How did you come up with that number?" Jerry asked.

Bob's response was brief. "It is consistent with other small firms in our industry and with our growth aspirations. Recall our earlier discussion of sustainable growth. With 40% debt, we can finance our growth and take advantage of the tax deductibility of interest payments without excessive financial exposure. We could use more sophisticated models,[63] but this is fine for now. So, given a 10% pre-tax

---

[63]See Damodaran, Aswath, *Corporate Finance*, John Wiley & Sons, Inc., 1997.

cost of debt and a 40% effective tax rate, our WACC is roughly 10%." Bob then proceeded to put up the following slide.

$$\text{WACC} = [(0.4) \times 10.0\% \times [1 - 0.40]] + [(0.6) \times 12.55\%]$$
$$= 2.4\% + 7.53\%$$
$$= 9.93\% \text{ or rounded off to } 10\%$$

"I'd suggest we use 10% as the discount rate for capital project analysis," concluded Bob.

5.2. International projects

"Well, Bob, I think I understand this cost of capital idea. I do have a question, however. What happens now that we have gone overseas with our business? Would we have the same required return on our capital investments in other countries?" questioned Jerry.

Bob said enthusiastically, "Great question, Jerry. Your intuition is correct. Most companies make adjustments for international investment projects since they tend to be more risky than domestic projects in the United States. This is particularly true for the emerging markets, like in Latin America and Asia. If we expand into Mexico, Brazil, or Argentina, we would have to recognize the increased risk in these countries and adjust our cost of capital accordingly. Fortunately, it is possible to determine the return we should require on such investments.[64] Given our knowledge of the CAPM, the adjustments are relatively easy."

"Bob, do we need any unusual data to make the calculations?"

"Not really, Jerry. The data are readily available," said Bob and proceeded to summarize the key steps for Jerry.

1. Estimate all of the project cash flows in dollars. The translation of local currency flows into dollars can be accomplished by:

   (1) Using forward exchange rates, or
   (2) Estimating exchange rate scenarios, or

---

[64] This section draws on the article "A Practical Approach to Calculating Costs of Equity for Investments in Emerging Markets," by Stephen Godfrey and Ramon Espinosa, *Journal of Applied Corporate Finance*, Fall 1996, pp. 80–89.

(3) Adjusting the exchange rate for inflation by using the purchasing power parity condition

2. Implement an adjusted CAPM to account for sovereign risks and commercial risks in the country of choice:

Equity cost of capital

$$
= \left\{ \begin{array}{l} \text{(Risk-free rate in US + Credit spread for the country)} \\[1em] + 0.6 \left(\dfrac{\text{Market volatility in foreign country}}{\text{Market volatility in US}} \right) \\[1em] \times \left(\text{US Market premium} \right) \times \text{Beta} \end{array} \right\}
$$

Determine the weighted average cost of capital, WACC, as before and use it to discount dollar-denominated cash flows and determine the NPV of the investment project in the emerging market.

Jerry looked lost and laughed derisively, "Sure. This is a piece of cake! No, seriously, I'm going to need a little help with that formula, Bob."

Bob replied: "No problem, Jerry. The first term adds the extra cost of financing in the chosen country to the government bond rate in the United States. That is, the credit spread is the amount by which the borrowing rate for the government of the country in question is greater than the borrowing rate of the US government. One has to be careful in determining the credit spread to not include the exchange rate risk."

Jerry remarked: "You mean you just can't compare interest rates, Bob?"

Bob swiveled in his chair and turned to face Jerry. "Exactly. If government bond rates are 6% for dollars in the United States and 11% for pesos in Mexico, it is incorrect to suggest that the credit spread for Mexico would be 5%. This is because the peso interest rate includes expectations about the future movement of the peso relative to the dollar as well as any difference in credit quality between the two countries. This credit quality difference is related to the sovereign risk of investing in Mexico.

"In order to determine sovereign risk, we must isolate the credit quality spread. Fortunately, many countries have issued sovereign bonds in traded currencies like the US dollar.[65] In these cases, one can simply compare the yield on that country's

---

[65] For example, Yankee bonds in dollars, Euro-bonds in dollars, Brady bonds in dollars, Samurai bonds in yen, or Euro-bonds in Duetsch Marks.

dollar-denominated government bonds with the yield on US government Treasury bonds; the difference represents the credit spread for the country because the exchange rate effect has been removed in this comparison.[66]

"If the country has not issued traded-currency bonds, then other procedures can be employed.[67] The authors report credit spreads of 3.8%, 4.1%, and 4.0% for Mexico, Brazil, and Argentina, respectively. Thus, these Latin American countries are seen to be very similar in sovereign risk."

Jerry was beginning to see the logic now, "I think I understand the sovereign risk term, Bob. I suppose we could call up our investment banker or a consultant to find out the latest credit quality spread on a specific emerging market. But that second term relating to commercial risk seems tougher. Can you explain it?"

Bob was truly in his element now, "Note that in the second term,

$$0.6 \left(\frac{\text{Market volatility in foreign country}}{\text{Market volatility in US}} \right) \times (\text{US Market Premium}) \times \text{Beta}$$

the market risk premium is the same that we would use in the United States. You recall that was 7.0% based on the average (arithmetic) historical returns of the US stock market over government bonds. The other term, (0.6 (Ratio of market volatility in foreign country to that in United States)), is an "adjusted" beta to reflect the business risk in the chosen country. The commercial risk is captured by how volatile the equity market in that country is relative to the US market, where the volatility of the equity market is estimated by the standard deviation of the annualized returns earned in the market. The business risk measure captures the overall riskiness of investing in the market. The 0.6 multiplier is included so as to not double count risk in both the credit spread and the standard deviation used to assess commercial risk. It turns out that about 40% of the variation in market volatility across different emerging markets is explained by variation in credit quality (0.6 = 1 − 0.4). Finally, the beta in this term is simply the beta of the company in the foreign country with the stock market in that country."

"What does this all mean for our Latin American investments, Bob?"

---

[66] In Brady-style debt reschedulings of sovereign debt, countries are often required to post US Treasury securities as collateral. This lowers the yields on these securities. Thus, to compute the credit quality spread, one should be careful to assess the stripped yield on the bond, i.e., the yield that would exist without the collateral.

[67] See the Godfrey-Espinosa article mentioned earlier for suggestions.

Bob continued, "The numbers in Fig. 8.5 are based on 1991–96 data and assume the US risk-free rate is 5.0% and the equity market risk premium is 7.0%.[68] The resulting costs of equity capital are, I believe, in line with our thinking about the risks of entering these markets. For example, Mexico is less risky than Brazil or Argentina."

6. The Impact of Leverage

Bob also explained to Jerry how the company's financial leverage would affect its WACC. Suppose we start with a situation in which the firm is unlevered. Then, it will have an equity cost of capital that reflects only its business risk. If it now takes on some leverage, its (levered) equity cost of capital is given by:

Levered equity cost of capital

$\quad$ = Unlevered equity cost of capital + Financial risk premium

where financial risk premium

$$= \left\{ \begin{array}{c} [\text{Unlevered equity cost} - \text{cost of debt}] \\ \times \left[\dfrac{\text{Debt}}{\text{Equity ratio}} \right] \times [1 - \text{tax rate}] \end{array} \right\}$$

We can determine the equity cost directly by first adjusting beta for leverage using the following formula (assuming riskless debt):

$$\text{Beta levered} = \beta \text{ unlevered} \left[1 + (1 - \text{tax rate}) \times \frac{\text{Debt}}{\text{Equity ratio}} \right]$$

Of courts, the debt/equity ratio is determined on a market value basis. Then the beta can be inserted into the CAPM formula to calculate the levered equity cost of capital.

The WACC can now be calculated as usual.

One can also go directly from the unlevered equity cost of capital to the WACC as follows:

$$\text{WACC} = \text{Unlevered equity cost}$$
$$\times \{1 - [\text{Tax rate} \times \text{Debt to total assets ratio}]\}$$

---

[68] All of the data in Fig. 8.5 would have to be periodically updated to reflect current market conditions.

Country	Credit spread	Market volatility in foreign country	Ratio of foreign country to US market volatility x0.06	Cost of equity if Beta = 1.0
Argentina	4.0%	54.74%	3.39	$= 5\% + 4\% + 3.39\% \times 7\% = 32.73\%$
Brazil	4.1%	53.75%	3.33	$= 5\% + 4.1\% + 3.33 \times 7\% = 32.41\%$
Mexico	3.8%	36.56%	2.26	$= 5\% + 3.8\% + 2.26 \times 7\% = 24.62\%$
United States	—	9.68%aa	1.00	$= 5\% + 1 \times 7\% = 12\%$

Fig. 8.5.　Estimated costs of equity capital in latin America.

These formulas are useful to determine WACC if a company intends to change its target capital structure.[69] In that case, the debt ratio in the formula above would be the target.

7. Jerry Needs Time to Let it All Sink In

Jerry's discussions with Bob about the cost of capital had provided Jerry with his toughest mental challenge to date. However, while he could not claim to be an expert on all the details, he at least has an intuitive grasp of the key ideas. These were that his company's cost of capital was related in a systematic way with how cyclical the company's returns were relative to the whole stock market and how much debt it had on its balance sheet. That would do nicely for a start.

Main Points

- The cost of capital is a critical input to resource allocation decisions. It specifies the minimum return required by the capital markets on our investments and is an essential component of the internal performance metrics that are a part of a company's Value Sphere. It establishes the capital market bench mark to gauge company's financial performance.
- The cost of debt capital is tax-advantaged because interest expense is tax deductible. The after-tax cost of debt is the one that should be used in computing our overall WACC.
- The cost of equity capital can be determined with the Capital Asset Pricing Model (CAPM). The cost of equity is not tax advantaged and is determined by adding to the risk-free return on government bonds to a risk adjustment that equals our equity "beta" times a risk premium for the whole market.
- Our beta measures how volatile our stock's return is relative to that of the whole US stock market.
- The WACC, is determined by weighting the after-tax cost of debt and the cost of equity by the proportions of each in the firm's capital structure. The proportions are given by market value weights for the existing capital structure or the target structure of the firm.
- If a company changes its capital structure the costs of debt and equity will change with the change in leverage.

---

[69]Note that these formulas are consistent with the Modigliani and Miller valuation framework. See R. Hamada., "The Effects of a Firm's Equital Structure on the Systematic Risk of Common Stocks," *Journal of Finance*, May 1972, 435–452.

• The cost of equity capital for international projects can be determined by a formula that adjusts for the incremental credit risk (relative to US government bonds) associated with the government bonds in the country in which the investment is being considered and the volatility of that country's stock market relative to that of the US stock market.

End-of-Chapter Exercises

1. What is your company's target capital structure? Is it specified in book value or market value terms? How did you arrive at this capital structure?
2. Please complete the following table for your company and three of its major competitors.

Company	Equity Beta	After-tax cost of debt	Capital structure	WACC
Your company				
Competitor 1				
Competitor 2				
Competitor 3				
Average				

Practice Problems

1. What is the WACC for XYZ company that has collected the following data:

Cost of borrowing = 10.2%

Beta = 1.2

US Government 20-year bond rate = 6%

Effective tax rate = 40%

Market risk premium = 7%

Target capital structure = 30% debt, 70% equity

2. What is the cost of equity capital if XYZ changes it capital structure to 50% debt? Why is the cost of equity different?

3. Are international investments always riskier than similar industry investments in the United States? Why or why not?

4. Comment on the following statement made by one of Bob's finance staff members.

"If we borrow the money to finance the investment, it costs us only 6% after tax. Since the investment has a rate of return of 8% we should take it!"

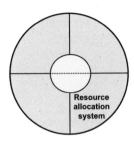

Chapter 9

HOW TO KNOW WHICH PROJECTS
ARE GOOD: PROJECT SELECTION
CRITERIA

1. Sorting Out the Wheat from the Chaff

It was a beautiful Saturday morning. Crisp and cold, the way Jerry liked it. The sky was a deep blue, and it was absolutely clear. Jerry's mind, unfortunately, was not. The week had ended in a flurry of capital allocation requests. It seemed that his people had responded all too zealously to his charge for new product ideas. How will we sort through this pool and pick only those that contribute to the wealth of our shareholders? Jerry wondered to himself.

He decided to give Bob a call.

He waited for a couple of seconds before Bob answered. "Hey, Jerry. What's up?"

Jerry filled him in on what was troubling him. As it turns out, Bob had been having similar concerns about the practical implications of trying to sift through the project idea pool. "Actually, Jerry, I have been working on a report about what other firms do when assessing financial performance to optimize Value Sphere management. Unfortunately, I won't be done for another two weeks or so."[70]

"Well, I guess we'll have to wait then," Jerry said somewhat dejectedly.

Bob has a thought. "Well, if you're feeling really ambitious this weekend, you could go back and read through our capital budgeting manual. We haven't touched that document in a while."[71]

---

[70] We will present the finding of this report in Chapter 11.

[71] As we describe later in Chapter 13, Bob and Jerry eventually discover that the capital budgeting system outlined in this outdated document may be contributing to the evaporation of value. That is, while the

"That's a great idea, Bob. Sallie and the twins are off to her mother's tomorrow, so I will have the afternoon free. It will probably do me good to review them, in light of the report you are preparing." Bob agreed. "Thanks, Bob. Have a nice weekend."

That Sunday Jerry brushed up on his capital budgeting. Below is a summary of the concepts he read about that day.

2. The Existing Capital Budgeting Manual

Choosing which projects to take and which ones to forego is arguably the most fundamental decision that our firm faces. It is a part of our overall resource allocation process. However, there are many criteria by which we can make these decisions. In this manual, we discuss the following methods:

- Net present value (NPV)
- Internal rate of return (IRR)
- Return on net assets
- Economic profit[72]
- Payback
- Discounted payback.

For each method, we provide a definition and outline the decision rule. Where appropriate, we highlight any disadvantages. We conclude with a practical example for a hypothetical project, applying each of the methods to this project.

Collecting the Necessary Information: The first step in evaluating any project, regardless of the selection criterion, is to collect the following information:

- sales revenue forecasts for each year of the project life
- manufacturing costs for each year
- investments in property, plant and equipment each year, along with a depreciation schedule
- anticipated marketing outlays
- the effective tax rate
- yearly investments in net working capital

---

project selection theory contained there was certainly correct (as it is presented in this chapter), the error in not keeping the manual a "living document" was proving to be a problem.

[72]Economic profit is also called economic value added (EVA), which is a registered trademark of Stern Stewart & Company.

- anticipated residual (or salvage) value at the end of the project's useful life
- the appropriate risk-adjusted discount rate (WACC for the project).

2.1. *Project Selection Criteria*

• NPV Criterion

Definition: The NPV of the project can be calculated using the "free cash flow" approach as[73]:

Net present value = the present value of free cash flows for all periods
computed using the WACC as the discount rate *minus*
the initial investment
plus the present value of the after-tax residual value of
the project's net assets at the end of the project
computed using the WACC as the discount rate.

Decision rule: The NPV decision rule is simple: accept all projects for which the NPV is greater than zero. This is quite intuitive in that WACC represents the minimum expected return demanded by our creditors and shareholders. Thus, generating an NPV above zero implies that the project return exceeds shareholders' expectations.

Special notes: Sunk costs have to be treated appropriately. Any cost that has already been incurred, and for which there is no alternative use, is treated as sunk when one considers a decision regarding the project. That is, a sunk cost should not affect the forward-looking decision.

• IRR Criterion

Definition: The IRR is defined as the discount rate that generates an NPV of zero.

Decision rule: Given a project profile, the decision criteria for the IRR method for project selection is straightforward. Accept only those projects that have an IRR greater than the WACC.

Special notes: The NPV and IRR criteria sometimes produce conflicting results. If cash flows change from negative to positive (or positive to negative) more than once during the life of the project, there may be more than one IRR for the project. Unfortunately, there is no scientific way to know which IRR

---

[73]See Chapter 2 for a review of calculating free cash flow.

is the "correct" one to choose. In such cases, one should rely on NPV as the correct measure of project value. Likewise, if projects are mutually exclusive, such that only one of them can be accepted, the ranking based on NPV may be different from that based on IRR. Again, one should rely on the NPV criterion if it happens to conflict with the IRR ranking.

For example, with a weighted average cost of capital of 10%, a project with an IRR of 15% on an investment of $10 million yields a higher NPV than a project with an IRR of 100% on an investment of $10,000. In sum, always rely on NPV as the unambiguous measure of the benefit of the project to the shareholders.

In fact, the NPV calculation represents the increase in shareholder value expected by investing in the project. That is, our firm's total share value will move (up or down) exactly by the amount of the project's NPV provided that:

- investors *agree* with the assessment of the project;
- investors had not already *anticipated* this project's contribution to shareholder value in the current stock price and
- capital markets are efficient. That is, the necessary information is available to investors.

• Return on net assets (RONA) criterion

Definition: The RONA for any period is defined as the NOPAT generated in a period divided by the net assets invested at the beginning of the period, where net assets = net fixed assets + net working capital. That is,

$$\text{RONA in a period} = \frac{\text{NOPAT produced during that period}}{\text{Net assets deployed at the start of the period}}$$

Recall that NOPAT was defined in Chapter 2.

Decision rule: A project is good for shareholders if in period t, RONA is greater than the WACC. That is, when the rate of return on the project exceeds the cost of funds given by the WACC, shareholder value is created.

Special notes: Observe that over a single period, RONA is not very informative. In fact, to assess a project's worth to shareholders, one would have to compare RONA to WACC across all periods of a project's life. Additionally, to measure the dollar value of wealth created (or destroyed) by the project, the spread of (RONA–WACC) must be multiplied by the amount of capital invested. We turn to just such a measure next.

- **Economic profit criterion**

  Definition: The economic profit for any period t is defined as:

  Economic profit for a period

  $= \text{NOPAT}$ for the period

  $- [\text{WACC} \times$ Net assets or capital deployed at the start of the period].

  An equivalent way to express economic profit is:

  Economic profit $= [\text{RONA} - \text{WACC}] \times$ Net assets or capital.

  To assess the incremental value of the project, one should calculate the NPV of the project using the yearly economic profit as:

  $\text{NPV} = $ Present value of future economic profits, where the WACC is used as the discount rate.

  Decision rule: Just as in the NPV method above, accept all projects with $\text{NPV} > 0$.

  Special notes: In terms of selecting projects, calculating the NPV as the present value of the operating free cash flows offers exactly the same answer as calculating the NPV as the present value of the future economic profits.

  If these methods give the same answer, why do both? Practically speaking, since the NPV based on economic profit gives the same answer as the one from free cash flows, there is no new information provided by an economic profit calculation for selecting projects. However, there are other compelling reasons for doing both.

  First, calculating the yearly economic profit provides a picture of how the shareholder value created — captured by the absolute dollar amount of the NPV — unfolds over time. That is, economic profit highlights the yearly additions to shareholder wealth.

  Second, calculating the NPV of a project under both methods provides a useful "check" on the analysis. Since theoretically these two values should match perfectly, a "mismatch" informs the analyst that a mistake has been made somewhere in the analysis.

  Third, economic profit can be used for employee compensation, whereas NPV can not. Thus, we can use the same performance measure to evaluate projects and people. This is useful in aligning employees' interests with those of shareholders. These issues are discussed in greater depth in Chapter 10.

- **Payback criterion**

  Definition: The payback of a project is defined as the number of years of operating free cash flows it takes to recover the value of the initial investment. That is, starting with the first year of the project and moving along year by year, calculate the cumulative value of the free cash flows. The time (that is, the year or point in the year) at which the cumulative free cash flow reaches zero defines its payback period.

Decision rule: Accept all projects with a payback of less than a specified period of time. However, what should this period be . . . three years? Four years? Five years?

Special notes: Alas, we have presented our first project selection criterion with no well-defined decision rule. Although other firms may specify a payback cutoff of say, four years, for their typical projects, this number is arbitrary. This is obviously a drawback of using payback to select projects.

There are further drawbacks. The payback criterion completely ignores the time value of money. That is, it treats cash flows in all years identical. Moreover, the payback criterion ignores any (potentially positive and significantly large) cash flows beyond the payback year.

In payback's defense, the payback period of a project does offer a rough assessment of the risk of a project. Projects with longer payback periods are usually riskier than projects with shorter payback periods. This is reasonable in that the economic environment specific to a project can change over time. Therefore, projects with shorter payback periods have a lower downside risk of not recovering our initial investments.

- **Discounted payback criterion**

    Definition: The discounted payback of a project is defined as the number of years of discounted operating free cash flows it takes to recover the value of the initial investment. That is, first calculate the present value of each year's operating free cash flow. Then, starting with the first year of the project and moving along year by year, calculate the cumulative present value of the operating free cash flows. The point at which the cumulative discounted free cash flow reaches zero defines its discounted payback.

    Decision rule: Again, there is no well-defined decision rule for the discounted payback criterion as the cutoff period is arbitrary.

    Special notes: Discounted payback suffers from the same drawbacks as payback, with the sole exception of the time value of money. The discounted payback method does not treat cash flows in different years identically. Rather, it cumulates the present value of each year's cash flows. Thus, it can be said that discounted payback provides a slightly more theoretically sound assessment of a project's risk.

2.1.1. Example

We now offer an example of how to calculate each of these measures for a simple capital budgeting problem. All the necessary information for project "Lemonade Sticks" is contained below:

- Plan to sell 15,000 units in the first year, growing at a 5% rate for 6 years
- Price per "stick" will be $1.50, growing at 5% per year, each year
- Manufacturing costs will be $1.20 per unit, growing at 5% per year
- Investment of $8,200 in equipment is depreciated on a 5-year MACRS schedule
- There is no residual value
- No net working capital is needed
- Effective tax rate is 40%
- WACC is 10%.

We can capture all of this information, as well as calculate yearly revenues, costs, and net asset levels in the following spreadsheet.

	Year 0	Year 1	Year 2	Year 3	Year 4	Year 5	Year 6
Project Lemonade Sticks							
Sales units		15,000	15,750	16,537	17,364	18,232	19,144
Price		1.50	1.58	1.65	1.74	1.82	1.91
Sales revenue		22,500.00	24,808.25	27,348.89	30,152.15	33,242.75	36,650.13
Cost per unit		1.20	1.28	1.32	1.39	1.45	1.53
Depreciation expense		1,640.00	2,624.00	1,574.40	944.64	944.64	472.32
Total operating expenses		19,640.00	22,469.00	23,453.51	25,066.36	27,538.84	29,792.42
Net operating profit		2,860.00	2,337.25	3,895.38	5,086.70	5,730.91	6,857.71
Taxes at 40%		1,144.00	934.90	1,558.15	2,034.32	2,281.56	2,743.08
NOPAT		1,716.00	1,402.35	2,837.23	3,051.47	3,422.35	4,114.62
Gross fixed assets	8,200.00	8,200.00	8,200.00	8,200.00	8,200.00	8,200.00	8,200.00
Depreciation rates		20.00%	32.00%	19.20%	11.52%	11.52%	5.76%
Accumulated depreciation		1,640.00	4,264.00	5,838.40	8,783.04	7,727.68	8,200.00
Net fixed assets	8,200.00	6,560.00	3,936.00	2,361.60	1,416.96	472.32	—
Total net assets	8,200.00	6,560.00	3,936.00	2,361.60	1,418.96	472.32	—

Now, given the NOPAT and Net asset levels, we can calculate our project selection criterion in order of their appearance above. First, we calculate the NPV of the free cash flows and the project's IRR.

	Year 0	Year 1	Year 2	Year 3	Year 4	Year 5	Year 6
Project Lemonade Sticks							
NOPAT		1,716.00	1,402.35	2,837.23	3,051.47	3,422.35	4,114.62
Total net assets	8,200.00	6,560.00	3,936.00	2,381.60	1,418.96	472.32	—
Change in net assets	8,200.00	(1,640.00)	(2,624.00)	(1,574.40)	(944.64)	(944.64)	(472.32)
Free cash flow	(8,200.00)	3,356.00	4,026.35	3,911.63	3,996.11	4,366.99	4,586.94
NPV (FCF)	9,147.50						
IRR	41%						

As the project is acceptable since the NPV is greater than zero and the IRR is greater than the WACC. Next, we calculate the yearly RONAs and economic profit. Observe that we can also re-derive the project's NPV using the present value of economic profit.

	Year 0	Year 1	Year 2	Year 3	Year 4	Year 5	Year 6
Project Lemonade Sticks							
NOPAT		1,716.00	1,402.35	2,837.23	3,051.47	3,422.35	4,114.62
Total net assets	8,200.00	6,560.00	3,936.00	2,381.60	1,418.96	472.32	—
RONA		20.93%	21.38%	59.38%	129.21%	241.53%	871.15%
Capital charge (IC)		820.00	656.00	393.60	236.15	141.70	47.23
Economic profit		896.00	746.35	1,943.63	2,815.31	3,280.65	4,067.39
NPV (Economic profit)	9,147.50						

The RONA is greater than the WACC in each year of the project's life, indicating that it creates shareholder value. The positive economic profit each year indicates the same thing. Naturally, the NPV based on economic profit is $9,147.50 — as we derived using free cash flows — and highlights the project's contribution to shareholder value. Lastly, we calculate the project's payback and discounted payback as follows:

	Year 0	Year 1	Year 2	Year 3	Year 4	Year 5	Year 6
Project Lemonade Sticks							
Free cash flow	(8,200.00)	3,356.00	4,026.35	3,911.63	3,996.11	4,366.99	4,586.94
Cumulative FCF	(8,200.00)	(4,844.00)	(817.65)	3,093.998	7,090.09	11,457.08	16,044.02
Payback	2.21						
Discounted FCFs	(8,200.00)	3,050.9091	3,327.562	2,938.8632	2,729.3998	2,711.5545	2,589.21
Cumulative discounted FCF	(8,200.00)	(5,149.09)	(1,821.53)	1,117.33	3,846.73	6,558.29	9,147.50
Discounted payback	2.62						

Assessing the project's true worth from either payback measure is impossible. However, both the payback (2.21 years) and discounted payback (2.62 years) periods are quite short, indicating a relatively quick recovery of the initial cash invested.

3. Practical Interpretations of the Analysis

There are two ways to graphically capture the project's characteristics with respect to its NPV. These are the *cumulative discounted free cash flow* and *NPV Profile* graphs. The first re-expresses the NPV formula by investigating the cumulative NPV of a project over time. This graph is given for our example in Fig. 9.1.

This plot first captures for our project the initial cash outflow in year 0, followed by the cash inflows in all years thereafter. The last point on the smooth line gives the NPV of the project. The crossover point on the time line is the discounted payback period, i.e., the length of time it takes to recover the project investments on a present value basis.

Another useful NPV-related graph is the NPV profile. An NPV profile displays the NPV of a project for a range of discount rates. An example of an NPV profile is given by Fig. 9.2.

Such a graph is useful in that it allows for the analyst to judge the sensitivity of the project's NPV to changes in the discount rate. Moreover, the NPV profile gives the internal rate of return (IRR) of the project. That is, the IRR is the discount rate at which the NPV becomes zero. As we calculated above, this occurs at a discount rate of 41%.

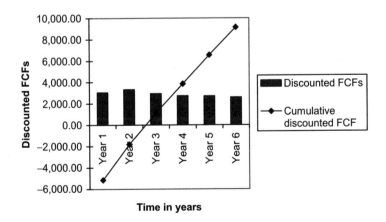

Fig. 9.1.   Cumulative discounted free cash flow over time.

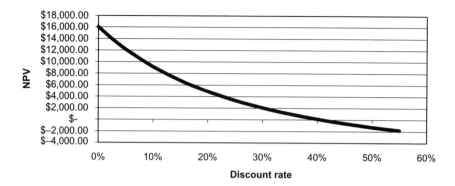

Fig. 9.2.   NPV profile for project.

4. Important Capital Budgeting Issues

Given the basics of project selection criteria and their interpretations above, we now turn to a discussion of some important issues related to *obtaining* the components of cash flow in the first place. These issues are:

- Defining the "Base Case"
- Accounting for cannibalization and competitive entry
- Clearly identifying the mutually exclusive alternatives
- Determining the time horizon of the explicit forecast period
- Estimating the residual value.

Defining the "Base Case": The most fundamental concept of capital budgeting analysis is to identify the *incremental* free cash flows generated by a new project. That is, what are the free cash flows that the project will generate *above and beyond* the existing projections of free cash flow (i.e., the cash flows that would be generated without the project)?

The question we are posing is: *What are the projected free cash flows if we continue our operations as they are?*

Answering this question is called "defining the base case." Great care must be taken to define it properly if we are to correctly assess the value of the proposed investment to our shareholders.

The *base case* is a description of the scenario that would occur in the absence of the new project. That is, it represents what would prevail if we did nothing but continue with our present activities. Identifying the base case can sometimes be difficult. But errors at this stage often cannot be overcome later, no matter how sophisticated the subsequent analysis. To see how critical this step is, consider the following example.

Problem set-up

- Suppose we are thinking of investing $3 million to alter some features of our ice shavers.
- The modification will take 1 year to complete.
- We currently sell 5,000 units of the present version of this shaver annually, with an after-tax margin of $100 per unit.
- We estimate that the $3 million investment will permit us to increase sales volume to 7,500 units per year forever without reducing margin.

Defining the base case — Example one

- If the base case here is defined as 5,000 units per year with an after-tax margin of $100 per unit, the $3 million investment is not worthwhile on an NPV basis with a 10% cost of capital. Why?
- NPV = Present value (Extra units sold × After-tax margin) − Initial investment
- NPV = (2,500 × $100)/10% − $3 million = −$500,000.

Defining the base case — Example two

- It may be the case, however, that in about a year, a major competitor will introduce significant new product features in its own ice shaver.
- If this happens, our sales will probably decline to 2,000 units per year and our after-tax margin to $80 per unit for the existing line.
- But, with the proposed feature modifications, suppose we believe that we can sustain annual sales of 7,000 units at a margin of $100 per unit, even if the competitor introduces its new model.
- Obviously, the base case changes now. It should be defined to reflect the reality of competitive entry.
- If the competitor is sure to enter, then the base case is 2,000 units per year with a margin of $80 per unit. The $3 million investment now appears attractive on an NPV basis. Why? Examine the assessed incremental value now.
- NPV = Present value (7,000 × $100) − Present value (2,000 × $80) − $3 million
- NPV = $7 million − $1.6 million − $3 million = $2.4 million!

Two points are worth noting. First, defining the base case incorrectly can cause a firm to miss potentially profitable opportunities. In the example, this could happen if we assume that the probability of new product introduction by a competitor is very low, thereby making the base case the preferred alternative.

Second, we can also fall into the trap of investing in bad projects by creating an imagined threat that undermines the cash flows of the base case. If we overestimate the probability that a competitor will enter and steal market share on our existing project, then we are implicitly making a case to invest in the new project. A discussion of how to treat this issue is covered next.

One must always guard against the propensity to make the base case appear bad in order to make the new project look good. The point is that in capital budgeting, only incremental cash flows matter, and the size of these flows critically depends on how the base case is defined.

Dealing with cannibalization and competitive entry: Estimating the likelihood of competitive entry should involve game theory and probabilistic scenario determination.[74] This should then lead to a probability distribution of competitive entry, along with its impact on project cash flows. This information can then be integrated into capital budgeting in a precise manner.

Cannibalization is defined as the cash flows that are lost on existing projects due to the introduction of (similar) new products. That is, a new product may *cannibalize* the sales revenue of one of our existing lines.

Estimates of cannibalization do not involve game theory, since we do not need to conjecture our competitors' decisions to determine cannibalization. But these estimates should incorporate probabilistic estimates that impact the cash flow projections. Importantly, the impact of cannibalization on NPV depends on the competitive-entry assumptions. This *interrelationship* is often erroneously ignored. The following example highlights the importance of recognizing the potential interdependence between the competitive entry and cannibalization assumptions.

Problem set-up

Example

- Suppose we are considering introducing a new product that requires an investment of $6 million and is expected to produce a perpetual after-tax cash flow of $1 million per year.
- However, it is also expected that introducing the new product will cannibalize our existing product line to the extent of $500,000 in after-tax cash flows per year perpetually.
- There is also a 0.8 probability that a competitor will enter with its own new product. If this happens, our existing product line will suffer an after-tax cash flow decline of $600,000 per year perpetually. This happens regardless of whether we introduce our new product or not, and our new product will suffer an after-tax cash flow decline of $100,000 per year perpetually.
- The question is: Should we introduce the new product when our WACC is 10%?

(Continued)

---

[74]Recall our discussion in Chapter 6. See also Adam M. Brandenburger and Barry J. Nalebuff, "The Right Game: Use Game Theory to Shape Strategy," *Harvard Business Review*, July–August 1995, 57–74, and F. William Barnett, "Making Game Theory Work in Practice," *The Wall Street Journal*, February 13, 1995.

(*Continued*)

Problem solution

- Suppose first that we take into account the cannibalization impact of the new product introduction, but ignore the possibility of competitive entry. Then, the NPV of introducing the new product is:

$$\left[\frac{\$1}{0.10}\right] - \left[\frac{\$0.5}{0.10}\right] - \$6 = -\$1 \text{ million or negative } \$1 \text{ million,}$$

which means we would forgo the new product.

- But now suppose that we also account for the impact of competitive entry. Then, the NPV of introducing the new product if the competitor enters is:

$$\left[\frac{\$1 - \$0.1}{0.10}\right] - \$6 = \$3 \text{ million}$$

where we have not charged the new product for cannibalizing the existing product line because the competitor's new product already impacts the existing product.

- If the competitor does not enter, then the NPV of the new product is −$1 million (calculated earlier). Thus, the expected NPV of the new product is: $(0.8 \times \$3) - (0.2 \times \$1) = \$2.2$ million.

- This means that considering cannibalization and competitive entry simultaneously *changes* the decision. We would now introduce the new product to fight the competition. In fact, if we enter the market first, it may lower the probability that others will enter later.

Clearly identifying the mutually exclusive alternatives: This step challenges the financial analyst to determine whether there are as-yet-unstated alternatives to the proposed project that could be uncovered. However, even when all the alternatives have been identified, it is sometimes difficult to list them appropriately. But proceeding through this step correctly is crucial if the subsequent NPV calculations are to make sense. Consider another example.

Problem set-up

- Suppose Federal Electric has the opportunity to build a new plant to manufacture a high-technology washing machine.

- However, it faces the strategic constraint that it can do this only if it liquidates an existing plant that makes conventional washing machines. Let the NPV of liquidating the existing plant be $2 million.

- Federal Electric can invest $15 million or $20 million in the new plant. And these two investments have different cash flow implications because their manufacturing capacities would be different. How do we define the mutually exclusive alternatives here?

(*Continued*)

(Continued)

Problem solution

- Observe first that Federal Electric faces an *extreme* cannibalization problem here because the new plant requires liquidation of the old plant.
- The base case is continuing with the old plant. But what are the mutually exclusive alternatives? The four alternatives here are:

  1. Continue with the old plant and do not invest in the new plant (base case).
  2. Liquidate the old plant and do not invest in the new plant.
  3. Liquidate the old plant and invest $15 million in the new plant.
  4. Liquidate the old plant and invest $20 million in the new plant.

- Federal Electric can choose only one of these four alternatives. However, the decision problem is now simplified in that they only need to compute the NPV of each alternative and choose the one with the highest NPV.
- The NPV of (1) is given by the present value of expected future cash flows from the old plant, less any investments (including working capital). Observe that they must also be sure to include (if necessary) the effects of potential competitor entry in determining the cash flows associated with the existing plant.
- The NPV of (2) is given as $2 million (this should be net of liquidation costs and taxes).
- In computing the NPV of (3), Federal Electric first computes the NPV of investing $15 million in the new plant and then adds the NPV from (2).
- The NPV of (4) is similarly computed.

Problem discussion

- Some might balk at the thought of *crediting* the new plant with the proceeds from liquidating the old plant. Remember, though, that the new plant will have to have a positive NPV on its own or else it will not beat out the NPV of (2).
- Thus, defining (2) as a distinct alternative (as is proper here) not only justifies, but also necessitates, defining (3) and (4) in the manner we have done here.
- Note that deleting (2) as an alternative, and not including the old-plant-liquidation NPV in (3) and (4), would be incorrect. The reason for this is that in this example, building a new plant necessarily results in Federal Electric capturing the net proceeds from liquidating the old plant. A mistake like this one would bias the decision in favor of continuing with the old plant.

As the example demonstrates, a good financial analyst must explore the full range of possible alternatives and provide senior management with the maximum possible flexibility in making its eventual decision.

Determining the time horizon of the explicit forecast period: The determination of the time horizon for estimating the cash flows of a proposal has two aspects. The first aspect is to define the explicit forecast period that includes detailed forecasts of revenues, costs, taxes, competitor reactions, and the like.

The second aspect is to formulate a period long enough to permit a reliable estimate of the residual value at the end of the explicit forecast period. In practice, the explicit forecast period should be sufficiently long to ensure that the project reaches an economic steady state in order to calculate the residual value.

A steady state occurs when:

1. The project is completed and all assets dedicated to it are sold or deployed elsewhere in the company. This would be the case for project investments such as labor-saving equipment, computers, vehicles, etc. These investments have fairly well-defined economic lives that should be captured in the forecast period.
2. The project cash flows enter a fairly predictable cycle. For example, the project is an investment in a new product for which sales are expected to decline linearly or stay relatively constant beyond the explicit forecast period. The likely steady-state pattern will normally hinge on the expected competition in the market or the anticipated advance of technology. Most new products follow a typical life-cycle pattern of sales.

If the project forecast is sensitive to general economic conditions, the forecast period should be long enough to capture a complete cycle for the industry. Otherwise, the analysis may only reflect the up or down cycle effects and thereby fail to capture all of the relevant project economics.

Estimating residual value: The residual value of a project at the end of the explicit forecast period can significantly affect the overall valuation of the project. Particularly if the forecast period is short. Thus, the residual value estimate deserves special attention.

The exact determination depends on the specifics of the project. For instance, if the project is to be terminated at the end of the explicit forecast period and the assets scrapped, the estimate of the residual value is straightforward.

- The expected selling price of the asset ("scrap value") is compared to the asset's book value in order to establish a gain or loss on the sale.
- If sold at book value, there is no gain or loss to recognize for tax purposes. A sale at book value is appropriate for the net working capital released at the end of the project's life. There may also be other assets that can be sold at book value. But the asset sale will generate a gain if sold for more than book value and a loss if sold for less. These gains (or losses) are typically taxed at the company's effective tax rate.
- For example, suppose that we had assets with a book value of $1,000 at the end of the project life. If we found a buyer for these assets at $1,500 and we faced a tax rate of 40%, what is the after-tax residual value?

- Since we sold the assets for $1,500 when their book value was $1,000, our after-tax gain on the assets is ($1,500 − $1,000) × (1 − 40%) = $500 × 60% = $300. Therefore, our total after-tax proceeds from the sale of the assets are $1,000 (the book value) + $300 (the after-tax gain on sale) = $1,300.

- One possibility is to consider three residual value estimates: selling the assets at book value, sales at less than book (pessimistic valuation), and sales at more than book (optimistic valuation).

In other circumstances, the project may be expected to provide economic value beyond the forecast horizon. The estimation of residual value is now more complex. The reason is that we are now concerned with how we would value the assets as an ongoing business concern in the future.

For this valuation, the issue is the pattern of cash flows over some time period beyond the forecast period. Since the project is assumed to reach a steady state by the end of the forecast period, the cash flows beyond the forecast period may be expected to be growing, declining or constant over some time period. In fact, if warranted, the cash flows could be forecasted in perpetuity.

A useful formula for assessing the residual value as the continuing value of a project as of the terminal date N is:

Residual value as of year N

$$= \frac{\text{Free cash flow (FCF) in year } N \times [1 + \text{perpetual growth rate in FCF beyond year } N]}{\text{WACC} - \text{perpetual growth rate in FCF beyond year } N}.$$

It is important to remember a few things when applying such a formula. First, recognize that under this method you are assuming that the business generates positive free cash flows every year, forever! Second, the growth rate should be stated in nominal terms. That is, it reflects both the expected real rate of growth and the expected rate of inflation. The expected real rate of growth is often estimated by taking the historical average of the real growth rate in GDP, which is approximately 3%. In periods of relatively low inflation,[75] one can use the following approximate formula:

Nominal growth rate = real growth rate + expected rate of inflation.

Another useful way to assess the ongoing concern value of a project is to use economic profit. Essentially, the analyst should answer the question: Over how

---

[75]Technically, the normal growth rate = real growth rate + inflation + (real growth rate × inflation). Periods of low inflation imply that the third term is quite small, and thus it is often ignored.

many years can I expect this project to generate positive economic profit, and what are these economic profits?

In a competitive marketplace, generating positive economic profit in perpetuity for a project is quite uncommon. However, extended (yet finite) periods of competitive advantage are possible. Thus, we can assess the continuing value of a project as of the terminal date N to be:

Residual value in year N

$\quad =$ Book value of assets in year N

$\quad +$ Present value of economic profits beyond year N.

To use this formula, the analyst first calculates the future economic profits of the project. Typically, one would benchmark these predictions against the expected economic profit in the final year of the explicit forecast period (N). The analyst then discounts these future economic profits, thereby capturing the shareholder value to be created in the following years, and adds this to the value of the net assets.

Intuitively, this formula says that a project — or a business for that matter — has ongoing concern value that consists of two components. One is the book value of the project's net assets, and the other is the economic (shareholder) value created from those assets.

In applying this formula, the analyst need only forecast the future economic profit that is expected to be positive, ignoring the rest. There are two justifications for this.

- First, even if the project lives forever, once the economic profit becomes zero and remains at that level, there are no further additions to shareholder wealth.
- Second, if the project's economic profit would turn negative, we would rationally abandon the project. This means we would not actually suffer these negative economic profits.

5. Jerry Thinks He Has Found a Shortcut

After he finished reading about residual values, Jerry sat back in his chair to catch his breath. This break was cut short, however, by a knock at his door. Who could this be on a Sunday afternoon? Jerry thought to himself. "Come on in."

"Afternoon, Jerry," Ray Burns said. "Doing a little catching up?"

Ray was a recent addition to the "new products" team. In fact, he had been hired away from Mickey's. "Hi Ray. What can I help you with?"

"Actually, I came by to drop off our team's three latest project proposals," Ray responded. "When I saw the light on, I just thought I would say hello. Hope I am not disturbing you."

Jerry thought to himself, Great, more proposals. But instead of expressing that frustration, he engaged in some small talk, including a discussion of how much leasing was done at Mickey's to finance acquisitions of capital equipment.

The two chatted for a while longer before heading their separate ways for home. Jerry was anxious to talk to Bob on Monday.

On Monday morning Jerry called Bob on the phone. "Bob, how much leasing do we do?"

"Actually, we do some. Why do you ask?" responded Bob.

Jerry continued, "I had a conversation with Ray Burns, our new products guy, yesterday. Ray said that Mickey is able to invest a lot more in capital projects by leasing assets. Why don't we do this? I know that you've explained to me (see Chapter 3) that leasing is really the same as borrowing. But that means leasing can't cost more than say seven to eight percent, on a pre-tax basis. And all our project proposals seem to clear that hurdle."

"Seems like we have an obvious omission in our manual," Bob said. "We can't confuse financing decisions with capital budgeting decisions. Investing in an asset is a capital budgeting decision. It is distinct from how the investment will be financed. Whether we lease or buy is really part of our overall financing strategy. I'd like our Treasury folks to make that call, rather than people like Ray. I'd like our product people to think about whether an investment is a good idea, assuming that we would have to buy the asset. If the project is a good idea under those assumptions, we'll then see if we can then do better by leasing."

"Okay, now I see," Jerry replied. "Since leasing is like borrowing, the leasing decision is really one that deals with the mix of debt and equity we will use to finance acquisition of the asset."

Bob was pleased, "That's exactly right, but now you've got me a little worried that some of our project teams are thinking about leasing as the solution to perceived capital constraints. I better quickly write an addendum to the manual to cover this."

"Sounds like a good idea," Jerry replied. "Are we still on for two?"

"Absolutely," Bob said enthusiastically. "I have something I want to run by you about how we look at projects."

"Okay, see you then."

Bob's addition on leasing to the capital budgeting manual is given below.

Leasing: The analysis of a leasing situation is carried out in two steps. The first step answers the question, "*Can we justify the asset?*" This is exactly the question we have addressed in our capital budgeting manual, and which should therefore be examined using the tools described there. All leasing decisions must pass through the same approvals as any other capital budgeting project. If the NPV is positive, then proceeding further makes sense.

Assuming that the asset can be leased, the next step is to evaluate the lease alternative and compare it with the alternative to buy the asset. Lease analysis requires an understanding of a fundamental concept, namely that lease payments are fairly close substitutes for debt service payments.

Viewed in this manner, leasing is a funding alternative to debt financing of the asset that has the following attributes:

- Leasing requires contractual payments for the lease term.
- Leasing has an opportunity cost of lost tax shields on depreciation (and investment tax credits if available). Leasing has an additional opportunity cost of the lost residual, or salvage, value of the asset at the end of the lease term.

These attributes suggest a straightforward way to value the incremental cash flows of leasing:

NPV (Lessee) = Initial investment
  minus the after-tax present value of the lease payments
  minus the present value of the depreciation tax shield
  minus the present value of the asset's after-tax residual value.

In addition, there may be adjustments for other expenses, such as maintenance, that are included in the lease payments. These would have to be separately provided if the asset were owned.

What is the decision rule now?

If the NPV (Lessee) > 0, then lease the asset because the analysis confirms that the after-tax cost of lease financing is less than the after-tax cost of borrowing. In other words, it is less expensive to make lease payments and surrender the tax and residual value of ownership. An NPV (Lessee) < 0 occurs when the after-tax cost of leasing is greater than the after-tax cost of borrowing.

Observe that the after-tax lease payments and the depreciation tax shields are discounted at the after-tax cost of debt. This cost of debt should be taken from an equivalent loan to reflect the company's borrowing alternative to the lease contract. The appropriate equivalent loan for lease analysis is one that has similar terms and maturity as the lease. Note that one can also compute the IRR from leasing relative to buying. An IRR exceeding the after-tax lease discount rate indicates a negative NPV, implying that the leased funds are more costly than the borrowed funds.

One controversial issue in lease analysis relates to the appropriate discount rate to use for the after-tax salvage value of the asset. Two viable alternatives are the after-tax cost of debt and the WACC. It is best to think of the choice of the residual value discount rate as being determined by the amount of risk inherent in the salvage value estimate. The discount rate should be specified as the after-tax cost of debt if:

- the salvage value is subject to little uncertainty;
- the estimate is the minimum salvage value that the asset can take; or
- the lease term is long relative to the economic life of the asset.

In the other cases, the salvage value is subject to sufficient uncertainty and should be discounted at the WACC.

An example of a complete lease analysis is shown in the following addendum to this chapter. However, it's useful to remember the following checklist when examining the merits of lease alternatives.

- First determine the value of the cash flows from the asset according to standard capital budgeting analysis. That is, can you justify the asset?
- Next, perform the NPV (Lessee) calculation to determine whether it is better to finance the asset with a series of lease payments rather than debt payments.
- Recall that lease payments are perfect substitutes for a series of debt service payments on an equivalent loan. Contact the Treasury department if you are unsure of what rate to use.
- Always treat leasing as a decision of how to finance the acquisition of the asset. By contrast, acquiring the asset is a decision that should make sense in its own right.
- Carefully consider the risk inherent in the salvage value estimate at the end of the lease term.
- Finally, consider other features, such as valuable cancellation options when technology is changing rapidly, that may be associated with the leasing alternative.

6. Jerry Reflects on Project Selection Criteria

Jerry met with Bob at two o'clock. They discussed the existing capital budgeting manual. Jerry had a few points of clarification with Bob that they dealt with in about an hour. Jerry spent the rest of the day reflecting on the various discussions he had had with Bob, as well as the old manual he had reviewed. In Jerry's mind there seemed to be some merits in each of the different project selection criteria he had studied. What did other firms do? He wondered to himself, and what do they do once the projects are taken? He had have to wait for Bob's report to get an answer.

Main Lessons

- Capital budgeting is a part of the resource allocation process segment of the Value Sphere.
- Good capital budgeting must focus on incremental cash flows. Estimating incremental cash flows requires properly defining the base case, which is the status quo, considering the effect of competition.
- Of all the project selection criteria, the NPV method is the best because it is always consistent with shareholder value. Using other criteria can cause Value Evaporation.
- Estimates of residual values are critically important in NPV calculations. These estimates must reflect anticipated future growth rates in cash flows or economic profits.
- Never confuse investment and financing decisions in capital budgeting.
- The decision of whether to lease or purchase is a financing choice. This means leasing should be considered as an alternative only if there is a capital budgeting justification for acquiring the asset.

End-of-Chapter Exercises

1. Of the six project selection methods listed in Section 2, which of these does your company use to evaluate new projects? If several measures are required for a capital allocation request, does any one measure (or subset of measures) tend to get more "weight" in the decision to fund a project? Could this lead to Value Evaporation?
2. Assuming that there are some measures listed in Section 2 that you are not required to calculate, try calculating these for a project analysis you have done in the past. Would your recommendation have been any different given these results?
3. For the same project you used in Question 2, create an NPV profile for the project. What does this graph tell you about your assumption on the project's cost of capital? How likely was it for value to evaporate if you misestimated the project's risk-adjusted required rate of return?
4. How do you account for potential competitive entry and cannibalization in your project analysis? Are your methods similar to the ones described in this chapter? If they differ, would your recommendation differ (or have differed) if you followed the proposed methods in this chapter?
5. What is the standard assumption made for estimating a project's residual value? In light of the discussion of residual values in this chapter, can you identify what

assumptions are (implicitly) being made in your company's current models? Is value retention being compromised because of these assumptions?

6. Does your company lease a significant percentage of its assets? Is a lease–versus–buy analysis along the lines of the methods in this chapter required for all leasing decisions? If not, can you identify a lease arrangement that was taken to "avoid the capital budgeting process"? How did value evaporate in that situation?

Practice Problems

1. You are considering an investment which has the following cash flows. If you require a 5-year payback period, should you take the investment?

Year	0	1	2	3	4	5	6
Cash flow	−$30,000	$10,000	$5,000	$5,000	$7,500	$10,000	$20,000

2. What is the discounted payback of the following project cash flows if the required return is 14%?

Year	0	1	2	3	4	5
Cash flow	−$60	$22	$22	$25	$10	$5

3. What is the IRR of an investment that costs $18,500 and pays $5,250 a year for 5 years?

4. Jordan, Inc. is considering a proposal to manufacture high-protein milkshakes. These milkshakes are nutritionally sound for the active individual and contain protein, carbohydrates, creatine, and a variety of other muscle-building and recovery supplements. The project would use an existing warehouse, which is currently rented by another firm. The next year's rental charge on the warehouse is $100,000, and will remain at that level each year. You can assume that the warehouse would be rented out again starting in year 5.

   In addition to using the warehouse, the proposal envisages an investment in plant and equipment of $1.2 million. This could be depreciated for tax purposes straight-line to zero over 10 years. However, Jordan, Inc. expects to terminate the project at the end of four years and to resell the plant and equipment in year 4 for $700,000. Finally, the project requires an initial investment of net working capital of $350,000. Thereafter, net working capital is forecast to be 10% of sales in each of years 1 through 4.

   Sales of the high-protein milkshakes are expected to be $4 million in each of the four years of the project's life. Manufacturing costs are expected to be 85% of sales, and profits are subject to corporate tax of 35%. The appropriate weighted average cost of capital for the life of this project is 12%.

   What is the NPV today of Jordan, Inc.'s proposed idea?

Addendum: Illustrative lease vs. buy analysis (5-year lease of $1,000,000 in equipment, Equivalent loan interest of 5.6%, tax rate of 40%)

	Total ($)	Year 0 ($)	Year 1 ($)	Year 2 ($)	Year 3 ($)	Year 4 ($)	Year 5 ($)
1. Lease option cash flows							
Lease payment	(750,000)	0	(150,000)	(150,000)	(150,000)	(150,000)	(150,000)
Tax shield of lease payments	300,000	0	60,000	60,000	60,000	60,000	60,000
Lease payment net of tax shield	(450,000)	0	(90,000)	(90,000)	(90,000)	(90,000)	(90,000)
2. Buy option							
Cost of purchased equipment	(1,000,000)	(1,000,000)	0	0	0	0	0
Depreciation tax shield (7 year MACRS) (TxDEP$_t$)	310,800	0	57,200	98,000	70,000	50,000	35,600
Other expense (after tax effect)	0	0	0	0	0	0	0
Tax effect from (Gain)/Loss @ Disposal	(110,800)	0	0	0	0	0	(110,800)
Est. market value @ End of period	500,000	0	0	0	0	0	500,000
Marketing/disposition costs	(10,000)	0	0	0	0	0	(10,000)
After-tax cash flow	(310,000)	(1,000,000)	57,200	98,000	70,000	50,000	414,800
Incremental cash flows	(140,000)	1,000,000	(147,200)	(188,000)	(160,000)	(140,000)	(504,800)
Present value of cash flows: 3.4% discount rate	(13,867)	1,000,000	(142,415)	(175,976)	(144,898)	(122,664)	(427,914)

Lease vs. Buy cash flow comparison:

Leasing advantage/(Disadvantage) = NPV$_{lessee}$

= Initial investment if equipment purchased

– Present value of after-tax lease payments

– Present value of foregone depreciation tax shield

– Present value of asset's after-tax residual value integration associates.

IRR = 3.77%. Breakeven residual market value = $472,735.

Chapter 10

MORE ON ECONOMIC PROFIT

1. Getting Introduced to Economic Profit

After his discussions with Bob about the capital budgeting manual, Jerry began to read one of the articles on economic profit that Bob had left for him.

The two equivalent ways of expressing economic profit (see Chapter 9) stared back at him from the page in the manual that he had copied and put in front of him:

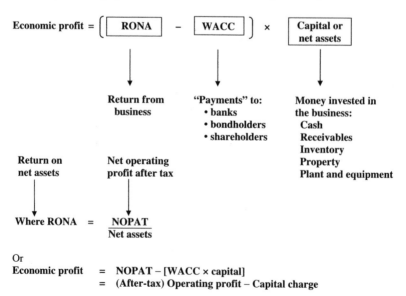

After what seemed like just a few minutes, his secretary Katie's voice on the intercom interrupted his thoughts.

"Bob is here for your meeting, boss."

"Boss"! Jerry still had a hard time getting used to the word. Bob was here already? But the meeting wasn't until — Jerry looked at his watch. It was 11:00 a.m. already! He'd been intermittently reading the article and thinking about how economic profit could be used in his firm for almost an hour now. Wow! He didn't realize he'd been that engrossed."

When Bob sat down, Jerry asked, "So, what's up, Bob?"

"Well," began Bob, "I wanted to get your signature on this memo we're sending out which says that henceforth we'll capitalize all operating leases for capital budgeting purposes."

Jerry looked a bit surprised, "Can't you just send it out with your signature?"

"I could," responded Bob with a smile, "but I wanted to make sure you hadn't changed your mind on this issue. Besides, if you change CFOs, perhaps the new CFO won't be quite so quick to change this policy if it has your signature as well."

Reaching for the article he'd just put down, Jerry said, "No, I haven't changed my mind, so I'll sign it. And you're not wiggling your way out of this job quite that easily. But if we're done, I want to talk about Economic Profit."

"Sure," said Bob. This was one of his favorite topics.

"I know how it's defined and all that. It's laid out quite clearly in our manual," said Jerry. "What I want is a concise summary of why a company like ours should consider using it."

Bob walked over to the white board in Jerry's office to explain. He began with an overview.

"Jerry, I believe there are five important reasons why Economic Profit is a good performance measure to include in our Value Sphere. First, as an internal operating performance measure, it seems conceptually well aligned with the way stock market analysts look at firms for valuation purposes. Second, it is an excellent tool for strategic resource allocation. Third, it can be used effectively in capital budgeting because it never conflicts with net present value (NPV). Fourth, it lends itself nicely to value-driver analysis of components of shareholder value. Finally, it fosters an ownership mindset when tied to compensation and performance assessment. This last advantage is the most important. Economic profit is first and foremost a behavioral tool."

Bob then proceeded to explain each advantage in detail. A summary of his conversation with Jerry is provided in the following sections.

2. Economic Profit and Shareholder Wealth Creation

There are many different ways to measure shareholder wealth creation. One is total shareholder return, which measures the return earned by the shareholders in price appreciation and dividends over any chosen time period.

The other is market value added (MVA), measured as the difference between market value and adjusted book value. This could be a measure we could define over any time period we choose.

Let us consider the first way to measure shareholder wealth creation. To deliver to the shareholders the total return they expect based on the risk they are exposed to, internal decisions must strive to deliver consistently positive and growing economic profit. This link between capital market expectations and managerial decision making within the firm is shown in Fig. 10.1.

But does the stock market performance of firms really improve when they align the incentives of their managers with the goal of consistently increasing economic profit? Research has shown that it does. Figure 10.2 displays how much additional

Standard & Poors 500 performance quartiles
Percent of total

Legend:
- ■ Returns lower than cost of capital
- ■ Returns higher than cost of capital

	1st Quartile	2nd Quartile	3rd Quartile	4th Quartile
10-yr ave returns to shareholders	24%	15%	11%	3%
Revenue growth	15%	7%	7%	7%
EPS growth	16%	8%	4%	(0.3%)
Returns on net assets	16%	11%	9%	7%
Returns on net assets above (Below) Cost of capital	4%	1%	(1%)	(4%)

Fig. 10.1.   Linking the capital market to internal decisions: Economic profit focuses managers on what matters.
Source: Textron strategic planning.

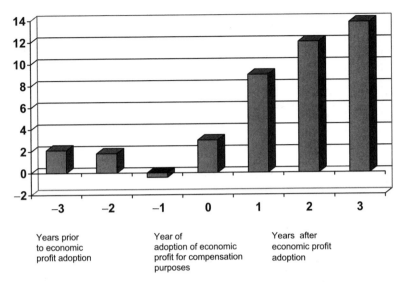

Fig. 10.2. Economic-profit-adopting companies outperform their industry peers: Median abnormal returns of economic-profit adopters relative to media industry peer.

Note: Abnormal return in a particular year is defined as average total shareholder return (dividends plus price appreciation) for economic-profit adopting companies minus average total shareholder return for the industry in that year.

Source: Robert Kleiman, "Some New Evidence on EA companies," *Journal of Applied Corporate Finance*, 12(2), Summer 1999, pp. 80–91.

total shareholder returns are generated for companies that tie managerial compensation to economic profit relative to industry peers that do not. In the time period prior to implementation of economic profit (years −3 through −1), there is little difference between the stock market performances of economic-profit-companies and that of their industry peers. But the story is very different in the three years after the adoption of economic profit. Those who adopt economic profit deliver significantly higher shareholder returns than their industry peers. Moreover, as Fig. 10.3 and Fig. 10.4 show, the correlations between economic profit and stock prices are unmistakable in the cases of some companies.

Portfolio managers, who are on the "buy side" in the stock market, are also increasingly embracing economic profit as a tool for selecting companies to hold in their portfolios. Given below are two quotations that emphasize this.[76]

---

[76]Source: Al Ehrbar, EVA: *The Real Key to Creating Wealth*, John Wiley & Sons, 1998.

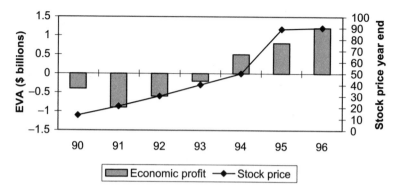

Fig. 10.3.   Economic profit and stock price correlation: HEWLETT PACKARD.

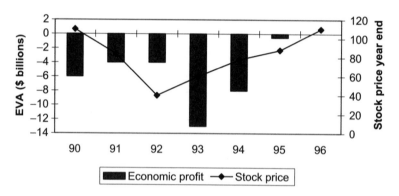

Fig. 10.4.   Economic profit and stock price correlation: IBM.

Anthony Kreisel, manager of Putnam Growth and Income Fund II and co-manager of the Putnam Fund for Growth and Income, has said, "EVA has become my most significant analytical tool. I couldn't care less what next quarter's earnings are going to be."

Economic profit has also been adopted by California Public Employee Retirement System (CalPERS), the largest institutional investor in the United States Bob Boldt, senior investment officer, is quoted as saying, "I wasn't satisfied that we were seeing [poorly performing] companies early enough. I concluded that we should look at a more direct economic measure to see how management was managing from an economic point of view, and I zeroed in on EVA as the best measure of economic performance."

Moreover, investment banks are also taking an economic profit perspective, as the letter in the following box shows.

GOLDMAN SACHS

February 5, 1998
To Our Clients:

Economic value added (EVA®) models have been gaining greater acceptance by corporations and investors in recent years. At its core, EVA® is an analysis of a company's return on capital, its cost of capital, and the spread between the two. The EVA® spread can aid the analyst in assessing the profit performance of a company, its capital efficiency, and the capital allocation process.

Over the past 18 months, we have sponsored client conferences on EVA® and have published several reports applying EVA® to stock markets in the United States, Europe, Japan, and Asia.

We have completed an EVA® analysis for 45 US industries and 625 US companies. This report represents one of these pieces and is being sent to you because you have indicated an interest in this industry. The last page of this report lists all of the EVA® industry publications, and if you would like to receive any of them, please contact your Goldman Sachs sales representative.

Our plans for industry and company EVA® analysis are as follows: First, we intend to publish reports like this one a quarterly basis. Second, our written industry and company analysis will more systematically integrate EVA® analysis. Third, we intend to extend EVA® analysis to our universe of non-US stocks. Fourth, we are in the process of developing company-specific valuation models based on EVA®.

We hope you find our EVA® research useful. As always, we welcome any suggestions or comments you may have.

Steve Einhorn
Director of Global Investment Research

---

3. Economic Profit and Strategic Resource Allocation

Strategic resource allocation is about deciding where to invest our resources and how much to invest. There are many financial tools that can help us with strategic resource allocation, but economic profit seems to be a particularly useful tool for this purpose.

There are four key questions to ask when examining how resources are allocated:

- Are we allocating incremental resources to business units in proportion to the assets these units already have in place?
- Are our investments driven solely by the desire to grow profits/earnings?

- Are our investments driven by rates of return on capital? If so, should we invest more in a business in which our rate of return on invested capital is falling?
- What are the overall implications of performance measure for how we allocate capital?

Let us consider each of these questions in turn.

A. Are we Allocating Incremental Resources in Proportion to those Already in Place?

It is common practice for some companies to allocate incremental capital to business units based on capital that is already in place. This means larger business units typically get more dollar amounts of capital each year. A simple way this happens is if the company reinvests in each unit an amount at least equal to depreciation. Larger asset bases carry more depreciation, everything else equal.

This would be fine if your large business units happen to be the ones that are also creating the most value.

But what if your large business units are destroying value?

A better approach is to use the economic profit generated by each business unit as a guide to determine how much additional capital it should receive.

This is illustrated in Fig. 10.5, which shows an economic profit approach to capital allocation. The prosperity diamond helps us to see the relationships.

In this figure, the x axis plots the capital invested in the asset or the business unit, whereas the y axis plots the difference between the return on net assets (RONA) and the weighted average cost of capital (WACC). We call this difference the "wedge." The amount of invested capital increases as you move from the left to the right, and the wedge increases as you move from the bottom to the top.

The figure is divided into four quadrants, with each quadrant further divided into two segments, giving us a diamond with eight segments. The shrinkage quadrant, containing segments I and II, has assets with negative wedges so these assets are destroying value. And lots of it too since the amount of capital invested in these assets is large. The overall strategy here should be to either divest or shrink the asset base.

The *productivity improvement quadrant*, containing segments III and IV, also has assets that are destroying value because the wedge is negative. But the value destruction is more modest than in the previous quadrant because the invested capital is small. Here, the overall strategic focus should be on improving profit margins.

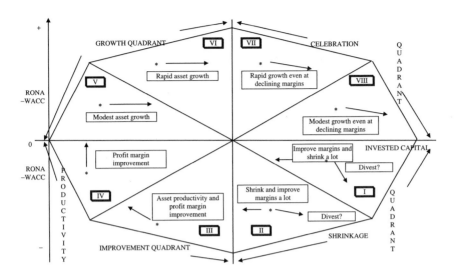

Fig. 10.5.   The prosperity diamond: Using economic profit for resource allocation.
Notes: I: Underperforming gluttons; II: Dropout wannabees; III: Waiting passengers; IV: Dysfunctional and skinny assets; V: Growing puppies; VI: Underfed highefliers; VII: Still-being-fed highfliers; VIII: Champions.

The *growth quadrant*, containing segments V and VI, has assets that are creating value because the wedge is positive. But the value creation is modest because the capital investment is small. The strategic focus here should be on asset growth.

Finally, the *celebration quadrant*, containing segments VII and VIII, "has it right." There is value creation due to a positive wedge. And lots of it since the invested capital is large. These assets should be "role models" for the rest of the organization. The strategic focus should be on continued growth and the protection of profit margins.

Within each quadrant, however, there are subtle distinctions to be made across segments. Segment I has the *under-performing gluttons*. For these assets the wedge is negative but only slightly so. The principal source of value destruction is that lots of capital is invested at this negative wedge. So, one should first ask for a credible plan for profit margin improvement. It may not be all that difficult to come up with such a plan since RONA may have to improve only a little bit to push it over the WACC. If such a plan is not possible, one should divest. If such a plan is available, the main strategic focus should be on rapid reduction invested capital while margin improvement (as the secondary strategic focus) is occurring.

Segment II has the *dropout wannabees*. These assets are actually more likely candidates for divestiture than segment I assets. Here the wedge is negative by a large amount, so it is likely to be more difficult to come up with a credible plan to make it positive. But if such a plan does exist, then the principal strategic focus should be on profit margin improvement while reduction in invested capital (as the secondary strategic focus) is occurring.

Segment III has the waiting passengers. This is a "way station." A sort of midway point in the journey of shrinkage quadrant assets — particularly segment II assets — as they travel to gain respectability as value creators. One would want to check to see how many of the segment II assets have actually made it to segment III as a sort of "progress check." The strategy in segment III is, therefore, an extension of that in segment II. Keep up the intense focus on profit margins. Also continue to reduce invested capital, albeit at a slower pace now than when these assets were in segment II.

Segment IV is the home of the dysfunctional and skinny assets. These assets are value destroyers because of their negative wedge values, but they have relatively small amounts of invested capital. The strategic focus here should be almost exclusively on improving profit margins. Measures such as cost productivity initiatives, price increases, reductions in overheads, etc. should be aggressively pursued. It is the profit and loss statement that receives all the attention in this segment.

Segment V has the growing puppies. These are value-creating assets with positive wedges. That is the good news. The bad news is that there is an inverse relationship between the size of the wedge and the capital invested in that asset. The highest-wedge assets in this segment have the lowest amounts of invested capital, and the assets with the smallest (but positive) wedges have the highest capital among the assets in this segment. The strategy to pursue is transparent. Grow the amount of capital invested in all the assets in the segment, but grow it cautiously. Monitor how the wedge changes as you invest more in the asset. Grow the assets with the highest wedges the fastest.

Segment VI has the underfed high-fliers. Assets here have high positive wedges but too little capital invested in them. Capital should be aggressively invested in these assets to grow fast. Otherwise competitors may recognize the opportunity and expand it aggressively.

Segment VII has the still-being-fed high-fliers. These assets are like the segment VI assets in terms of their wedges, but they have more capital invested in them. However, the amount of capital is still not enough. The assets in this segment should be grown fast by aggressively increasing the capital committed to them.

Finally, segment VIII has the champions. These assets have high positive wedges and relatively large amounts of capital invested in them. The crown jewels. These are the assets worthy of emulation. But they are hardly the assets to be complacent about. Capital invested in these assets should be grown further since the wedge on each is still positive. However, one should be prepared for diminishing margins, so the growth here should be relatively modest. Profit margins and the wedge should be closely monitored as invested capital expands and we witness diminishing marginal returns on the added investments.

B. Are Our Investments Driven Solely by Our Desire to Grow Profits/Earnings?

If the answer to this question for your company is in the affirmative, you are in a death trap. You need to get out of it fast.

It is not difficult to "manufacture" earnings if you do not care about how much capital you invest to do it. But if you are in the shrinkage or productivity improvement quadrant and attempting to grow earnings by investing more capital, you are systematically destroying shareholder value with every additional dollar you invest.

One reason why companies sometimes do this is that they use flawed incentive compensation systems. For example, at one company, executives were compensated based on earnings growth. During a discussion about growth targets, one of their executives remarked, "I don't mind investing a million dollars in capital to generate an additional dollar in earnings." We hope he was being facetious, or trying to point out how ridiculous the compensation system was. But you never know!

As Fig. 10.6 shows, the stock market rewards companies that focus on economic profit growth.

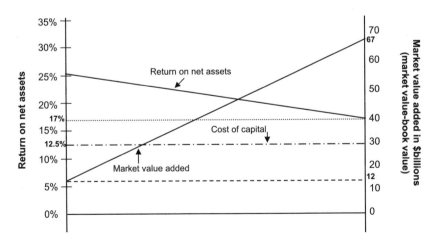

Fig. 10.6. Wal-Mart's performance during 1987–92.

C. Are Our Investments Driven by Rates of Return on Capital?

An improvement over basing strategic resource allocation on earnings or profit growth is to consider rates of return on capital. After all, RONA is a component of economic profit. But is RONA enough to guide us? The answer is NO.

To see this, consider the following question: Should we invest more in a business in which our rate of return on invested capital is falling? If the goal is to maximize RONA, the answer to this question is a resounding NO. But what does economic profit say? Rather than answer this question directly, let us see what Wal-Mart did during the late 1980s and early 1990s.

A couple of points about Fig. 10.6 are worth noting.[77] First, even though Wal-Mart's RONA is falling during 1987–1992, its economic profit is growing. How is this possible? To see this, note that if Wal-Mart had held its invested capital fixed, there is no way its economic profit could grow when its RONA was falling. So, the secret to this puzzle must be that Wal-Mart was rapidly growing its capital base, i.e., doing what a business in quadrant III should do. That is exactly what the company did during this time. It opened a significant number of new stores. The other secret to the puzzle is that for economic profit to grow while RONA is declining, it must also be true that RONA was above WACC all through this period. So, the key to deciding whether the business should grow is not to look at whether RONA will fall if we grow. Rather, it is to look at whether RONA can be maintained above the cost of capital.

The second point worth noting is that through this time period, Wal-Mart experienced negative free cash flows. Now, there are two reasons why a company may experience negative cash flows. One is that it is doing badly and earnings are poor. The other is that it is doing well and needs so much capital to reinvest that it seeks additional debt and equity financing after exhausting all internally generated cash flow. This latter reason describes Wal-Mart.

The stock market definitely recognized the value of Wal-Mart's strategy. Its market value added grew from $12 billion in 1987 to over $67 billion in 1992. In 2004 it reached over $135 billion.

Another example of where a RONA focus would have led to the wrong strategy is Coca-Cola. In the 1980s, it had to decide whether to introduce product line extensions. The RONA on its core products was 25%. The forecasted RONA on product-line extensions was about 20%. RONA indicated that the company should reject these product line extensions. But with a WACC well below 20%, economic profit considerations told the company to go ahead with these extensions. It did.

---

[77] This discussion is based in part on G. Bennett Stewart III, *The Quest for Value, Harper Business*, 1990.

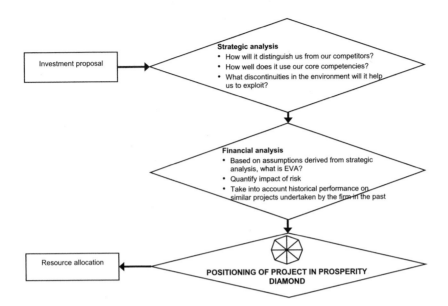

Fig. 10.7.   Using strategy and economic profit for resource allocation.

To summarize, while RONA and cash flow are useful as strategic resource allocation tools, they are not as useful as economic profit.

D. Overall Implications for Strategic Resource Allocation

We can now bring together all of the ideas discussed thus far into a comprehensive picture of how we should think about strategic resource allocation. This is done in Fig. 10.7.

4. Using Economic Profit in Capital Budgeting: Avoiding the "Inverted Pyramid of Ignorance"

One of the virtues of economic profit is that it can be readily integrated into a company's capital budgeting system. This means that one can use it in conjunction with free cash flow. The fact that NPV calculated from economic profit is the same as NPV calculated from free cash flow means that we have a useful reconciliation tool. If these two NPVs do not match, there is an error somewhere in the analysis.

This is important on two counts. First, using a tool for strategic resource allocation or performance assessment or incentive compensation that conflicts with

NPV is terribly problematic. Why? Because it creates tensions between capital budgeting recommendations and what people end up doing. This, in turn, diminishes the usefulness of the capital budgeting analysis. Even worse, it may corrupt the whole process.

Second, the ability to detect analytical errors through the attempt to reconcile the two NPVs is a powerful tool. Our own experience is that a vast majority of corporate capital budgeting spreadsheets contain errors of some kind. Often they go undetected. Why? Because the person making the error has no way of knowing that an error has occurred. And those above in the hierarchy do not rerun the spreadsheets. They typically challenge the assumptions. So, we have an "inverted pyramid of ignorance." As the project moves up the corporate hierarchy, it gains increasing credibility. But the analysis remains just as flawed as it was at the first stage!

We provide below a simple example in the following box to show how the reconciliation works.

Calculating economic profit and NPV for a project: An example.

Item	Year 1	Year 2
Operating costs, excluding depreciation	$95,000	$105,000
Depreciation	$20,000	$10,000
Operating income	$30,000	$35,000
Interest	$5,000	$5,000
Earnings before taxes	$25,000	$30,000
Taxes @ 40%	$10,000	$12,000
Net income	$15,000	$18,000

These are all year-end figures, i.e., net income is stated as of end of year 1 and end of year 2.

Balance sheet at year end

Item	Year 0	Year 1	Year 2
Current assets	$40,000	$70,000	$60,000
Gross fixed assets	$70,000	$100,000	$100,000
Depreciation reserve	$10,000	$30,000	$40,000
Net fixed assets	$60,000	$70,000	$60,000
Total net assets	$100,000	$140,000	$120,000
Interest-bearing debt	$30,000	$45,000	$45,000
(Non-interest bearing) Current liabilities (NIBCLs)	$20,000	$30,000	$30,000
Shareholders' equity	$50,000	$65,000	$45,000
Liabilities and net worth	$100,000	$140,000	$120,000

Again, these are year-end figures. Thus, total assets are \$100 at the end of year 0, \$140 at the end of year 1, and \$120 at the end of year 2.

Assume that book value of capital can be recaptured at the end of year 2.

$$\text{Cost of capital} = \text{Hurdle rate} = 10\%.$$

What is the NPV of this project?

SOLUTION

With this data, we can calculate the NPV of the project.

First calculate capital. . . .

Beginning of year 1	= Net current assets at beginning of year 1 +
	Net fixed assets at beginning of year 1
	= Current assets − NIBCLs
	+ Net fixed assets
	= \$40,000 − \$20,000 + 60,000
	= \$80,000
Beginning of year 2	= \$70,000 − \$30,000 + \$70,000
(or end of year 1)	= \$110,000

Next, we calculate NOPAT for each year:

Year 1 NOPAT	= Year 1 Operating income × [1 − Tax rate]
	= 30,000 × 0.6
	= \$18,000
Year 2 NOPAT	= Year 2 Operating income × [1 − Tax rate]
	= 35,000 × 0.6
	= \$21,000

NPV Using economic profits

Year 1 Economic profit	= Year 1 NOPAT
	−WACC × Beginning year 1 capital
	= \$18,000 − 0.1 × 80,000
	= \$10,000
Year 2 Economic profit	= Year 2 NOPAT
	− WACC × Beginning year 2 capital
	= 21,000 − 0.1 × 110,000
	= \$10,000
NPV	= PV of Economic profits

$$= \frac{\$10,000}{(1.1)} + \frac{\$10,000}{(1.1)^2}$$

$$= \$17,355.$$

It is important to remember that for calculating economic profits we use beginning-of-the-year capital, and the capital at the beginning of year 1, for example, is the same as the capital at the end of year 0.

Free Cash Flow Method

Net working capital

Year 0 net working capital (NWC)

$$= \text{Current assets} - \text{NIBCLs}$$
$$= \$40,000 - \$20,000 = \$20,000$$

Year 1 NWC = $70,000 − $30,000 = $40,000

Year 2 NWC = $60,000 − $30,000 = $30,000

Thus, increase in NWC in Year 1

$$= \text{Year 1 NWC} - \text{Year 0 NWC}$$
$$= \$40,000 - \$20,000 = \$20,000$$

Increase in NWC in Year 2

$$= \text{Year 2 NWC} - \text{Year 1 NWC}$$
$$= \$30,000 - \$40,000 = (\$10,000)$$

Investments in fixed assets

In any given year, investments made in fixed assets

$$= \text{Increase in net fixed assets during the year}$$
$$+ \text{Depreciation during the year}$$

For Year 1, increase in net fixed assets (NFA)

$$= \text{NFA End of year 1} - \text{NVA End of year 0}$$
$$= \$70,000 - \$\ 60,000 = \$10,000$$

For Year 2, increase in NFA

$$= \text{NFA End of year 2} - \text{NFA End of year 1}$$
$$= \$60,000 - \$70,000$$
$$= (\$10,000)$$

Thus, investment in net assets:

Year 1 = $10,000 + $20,000 = $30,000

Year 2 = ($10,000) − ($10,000) = ($20,000)

Initial investment at start of year 1:

$$= \text{NFA at end of year 0} + \text{NWC at end of year 0}$$
$$= \$60,000 + \$20,000 = \$80,000$$

Terminal book value (residual value) of assets at end of year 2:

$$= \text{NFA at end of year 2} + \text{NWC at end of year 2}$$
$$= \$60,000 + \$30,000 = \$90,000$$

Cash flow source	Year 1	Year 2
NOPAT (+)	$18,000	$21,000
Investment in net assets (−)	($30,000)	$20,000
Cash flow	($12,000)	$41,000

Thus,

$$\text{NPV} = \frac{\text{CF1}}{1+\text{K}} + \frac{\text{CF2}}{(1+\text{K})^2} + \frac{\text{Capital end of year2}}{(1+\text{K})^2}$$
$$- \text{Initial investment at start of year 1}$$
$$= \frac{(\$12,000)}{1.1} + \frac{\$41,000}{(1.1)^2} + \frac{\$90,000}{(1.1)^2} - \$80,000$$
$$= \$17,355.$$

5. Economic Profit and Value Driver Analysis

The purpose of adopting a metric such as economic profit is not just to use it for high-level corporate strategy. We would also like to be able to use it to drive our day-to-day decisions. This is where economic profit's role in value-driver analysis comes in.

Figure 10.8 shows how to think about value driver analysis conceptually using economic profit. The question every manager must ask is: What can I do to increase economic profit? It turns out that, at a very high level, the ways to increase economic profit correspond to the four quadrants in the prosperity diamond.

Figure 10.9 shows how one can then drill down into the micro drivers of value to show how smaller pieces of the value-creation chain from the profit and loss statement and the balance sheet all add up to economic profit.

6. Economic Profit is not a Financial Tool: Using Economic Profit to Create an Ownership Mindset

In our opinion, economic profit is first and foremost a behavioral tool. It is all about minimizing the agency costs that are the source of friction and Value Evaporation in corporations (see Chapters 4 and 5).[78]

---

[78]See Jeff Bacidore, John Boquist, Todd Milbourn, and Anjan V. Thakor, "EVA and Total Quality Management," *Journal of Applied Corporate Finance*, 10(2), Summer 1997, pp. 81–89, for more on this.

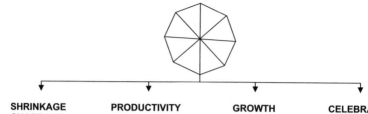

SHRINKAGE QUADRANT: Segments I and II	PRODUCTIVITY IMPROVEMENT QUADRANT: Segments III and IV	GROWTH QUADRANT: Segments V and VI	CELEBRATION QUADRANT: Segments VII and VIII
• *Divest losers* that do not show significant potential for earning positive economic profits in future • *Reduce capital* invested in assets producing negative economic profits historically and at present	• Focus on improving *asset productivity* by using less capital, e.g., lower inventories, less receivables, and longer payment terms • Focus on improving *profit productivity* by improving gross margins and operating margins through cost reductions, price increases, etc. • *Reduce WACC* by increasing debt	• *Rapidly increase invested capital* to grow the business	• *Increase invested capital* modestly by devoting more resources to asset producing economic profit at present and promising to do so in the future. Do this even at declining margins

Fig. 10.8. The prosperity diamond suggests that there are only four high-level ways to increase economic profit.

When an employee maximizes economic profit, he takes into account all the things that owners do. Indeed, he is acting as a de facto owner of the asset he is managing. This means that tying performance assessment and compensation to economic profit should create an ownership mindset. This enhances shareholder value.

In fact, economic profit is a decentralization mechanism. In a large organization, it is usually difficult for individual employees to see how they can have an impact on the corporate bottom line. And without a clear link between their actions and shareholder value, they find it hard to get motivated by speeches of senior executives telling them they should attend to shareholder value.

This is where economic profit can play its most valuable role. By tying an employee's compensation to the economic profit of the assets being managed, and by assigning him the responsibility to maximize economic profit, we can effectively decentralize a large organization into smaller decision-making units. Each unit does what is best for the economic profit of that unit — subject, of course, to some

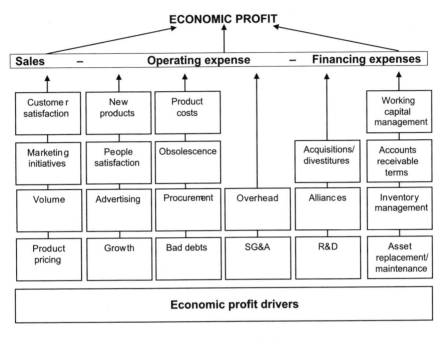

Fig. 10.9.   Economic profit drivers.

coordination constraints to ensure that individual units' decisions do not suboptimize at the level of the whole company.

Most of the other performance measures fall short in this regard. This failure of performance measures other than economic profit to motivate people appropriately is nicely illustrated in the following quote by C.B. Rogers, former CEO of Equifax:[79]

It is very difficult to tell a manager down the line, 'Harry, we're going to measure you on EPS.' Harry doesn't have a clue as to how he can help EPS, particularly if he has a small business unit and he knows that the guys in credit reporting are carrying much of the water.

This is why we believe that economic profit is fundamentally a human resource (HR) tool. It should come into organizations through the HR group rather than finance.

---

[79]Source: Al Ehrbar, *EVA: The Real Key to Creating Wealth*, John Wiley & Sons, Inc., 1998.

7. When does Economic Profit Fail to Deliver?

As useful as economic profit is, there are circumstances in which it fails. Here is a brief list:

1. When it is viewed purely as a financial tool with no link between economic profit and compensation. In this case, it ends up being viewed as nothing more than a number generated by the finance staff. There is no meaningful behavioral change.
2. When the company focuses too much on the accounting adjustments and being accurate to the "second decimal point" in accounting for the capital in each economic profit unit should be held accountable for.
3. When the company keeps talking about it but does not implement it expeditiously.
4. When economic profit is used in an inappropriate way for units that do not have a top line (revenue) responsibility, i.e., staff support functions.
5. When discussions about issues related to shared assets and synergies across business units get bogged down and lead to acrimony, not results.
6. When there is insufficient communication with employees and not enough training to teach employees how they can make value-enhancing changes.
7. When the company is considering highly risky projects with a significant chance of failure but potentially huge payoffs associated with success. Examples are R&D, breakthrough products, entering emerging markets, etc. Such initiatives may make sense even though they have negative economic profits and NPVs. That is, their high option values may offset their negative NPVs (see Chapter 14 for more on this).
8. When economic profit is "oversold" and its adoption is viewed as both a necessary and sufficient condition for value creation. Adopting economic profit may be necessary for some organizations to create value. It is not sufficient. Creating value requires attending to all aspects of the Value Sphere.

8. Jerry is Impressed with Economic Profit

When Bob had finished, Jerry said, "Wow! Looks like economic profit is a pretty impressive measure. How long do you think it would take for us to implement it?"

"Whoa! Hold it there, Jerry. I didn't say we should adopt it right away. There are a lot of excellent companies, like Wal-Mart for instance, that have created enormous shareholder value without using economic profit. After all, economic profit is but a metric. It's not going to create value by itself. Its biggest virtue is that it doesn't stand in the way of value creation. We need to think carefully about what we should do. Unfortunately, I've got too many things on my plate right now. Let me clear some of them and give this some more thought. I promise I'll get back to you."

"Fair enough," said Jerry. The meeting was over.

Main Lessons

- Avoiding a multiplicity of measures to deal with multiple issues is generally a good idea. There is a great deal of virtue in simplicity. The economic profit measure provides that simplicity.
- Economic profit is a unifying metric that is perfectly aligned with NPV and shareholder value creation. It has the highest statistical correlation with average market value added.
- Economic profit is useful for:

    (i) employee compensation
    (ii) value-driver analysis and ongoing decision making
    (iii) strategic resource allocation
    (iv) capital budgeting

- For these reasons, economic profit is a useful component of the Value Sphere.

End-of-Chapter Exercises

1. Make a list of all the performance measures your company uses. Then construct the following table.

Performance measure	Behavior it produces	With which other behaviors does this behavior conflict?
(1)		
(2)		
(3)		
(4)		
(5)		
(6)		

2. How many conflicts were you able to identify? What can you do to minimize the confusion?

3. List the five practices/behaviors in your organization that you believe are diminishing the organization's economic profit. Then write down how economic profit is being destroyed. Would a compensation system designed to reward managers based on improvements in economic profit help to eliminate these practices?

4. Draw a prosperity diamond like that in Fig. 10.9. Then conduct an economic profit analysis of all the major assets (products, business units, brands, geographies, etc.) in your company and determine which of the eight segments each asset belongs to. Is your resource allocation aligned with the optimal strategy identified with each segment in Fig. 10.9?

Practice Problem

(1) Consider a firm that is thinking of investing in a project that requires an initial investment (at date $t = 0$) of \$1,000. The relevant project financials are given below:

Date	$t = 0$ (End of 1st period)	$t = 1$ (End of 1st period and start of 2nd period)	$t = 2$ (End of 2nd period)
Earnings before interest and taxes (EBIT)	—	\$100	\$200
Net working capital	\$400	\$450	\$400
Net fixed assets	\$600	\$650	\$550
Weighted average cost of capital = 10%			
Tax rate = 40%			

Assume that the net working capital and net fixed assets will be liquidated at book value at $t = 2$.

a. What are the free cash flows (FCFs) of this project and its NPV based on FCFs?

b. What are the economic profits (or EVAs) of this project and its NPV on this basis?

c. Can you explain the intuition behind why the two NPVs are identical? What can you conclude if they do not match?

Addendum for Chapter 10

Proof that present value of expected future EVA = NPV based on free cash flow (FCF)

We need some notation. Let:

I_0 = initial investment or net assets
I_t = investment (net assets) at the end of time (say year) t
I_N = investment (net assets) left in the project at the end of its N-year life
x_t = NOPAT at the end of time (say year) t
k_w = weighted average cost of capital.

Now note that at the end of the first period, FCF_1, is:

$$FCF_1 = x_1 - [I_1 - I_0]$$

Since $(I_1 - I_0)$ is the increase in net assets during the first period (year). The general expression for FCF_t, the free cash flow at time t, is:

$$FCF_t = x_t - [I_t - I_{t-1}] = x_t + I_{t-1} - I_t.$$

Then,

$$NPV = \frac{x_1 + [I_0 - I_1]}{1 + k_W} + \frac{x_2 + [I_1 - I_2]}{(1 + k_W)^2} + \cdots + \frac{x_N + I_{N-1} - I_N}{(1 + k_W)^N} - I_0$$
$$+ \frac{I_N}{(1 + k_W)^N} - I_0 + \frac{I_N}{(1 + K_w)^N}$$

Since we subtract the initial investment and add the present value of the terminal value to obtain the NPV with FCF. We can now write.

$$NPV = \frac{x_1 + [I_0 - I_1] - I_0[1 + k_w]}{1 + k_w} + \frac{x_2 + [I_1 - I_2]}{(1 + k_w)^2} + \cdots$$
$$+ \frac{x_N + I_{N-1} - I_N}{(1 + k_w)^N} + \frac{I_N}{(1 + k_w)^N}$$
$$= \frac{x_1 - k_w I_0}{1 + k_w} + \frac{x_2 + [I_1 - I_2] - I_1[1 + k_w]}{(1 + k_w)^2} + \cdots$$
$$+ \frac{x_N + I_{N-1} - I_N}{(1 + k_w)^N} + \frac{I_N}{(1 + k_w)^N}$$

$$= \frac{x_1 - k_w I_0}{1 + k_w} + \frac{x_2 - k_w I_1}{(1 + k_w)^2} - \frac{I_2}{(1 + k_w)^2} + \frac{x_3 - k_w I_2}{(1 + k_w)^3} + \cdots$$
$$+ \frac{x_N + I_{N-1} - I_N + I_N}{(1 + k_w)^N}$$

$$= \frac{x_1 - k_w I_0}{1 + k_w} + \frac{x_2 - k_w I_1}{(1 + k_w)^2} + \frac{x_3 - k_w I_2}{(1 + k_w)^3} + \frac{x_{N-1} - k_w I_{N-2}}{(1 + k_w)^{N-1}}$$
$$- \frac{I_{N-1}}{(1 + k_w)^{N-1}} + \frac{x_N + I_{N-1}}{(1 + k_w)^N}$$

$$= \frac{x_1 - k_w I_0}{1 + k_w} + \frac{x_2 - k_w I_1}{(1 + k_w)^2} + \frac{x_3 - k_w I_2}{(1 + k_w)^3} + \cdots$$
$$+ \frac{x_{N-1} - k_w I_{N-2}}{(1 + k_w)^{N-1}} + \frac{x_N - I_{N-1} - I_{N-1}[1 + k_w]}{(1 + k_w)^N}$$

$$= \frac{x_1 - k_w I_0}{1 + k_w} + \frac{x_2 - k_w I_1}{(1 + k_w)^2} + \frac{x_3 - k_w I_2}{(1 + k_w)^3} + \cdots$$
$$+ \frac{x_{N-1} - k_w I_{N-2}}{(1 + k_w)^{N-1}} + \frac{x_N - k_w I_{N-1}}{(1 + k_w)^N}$$

$=$ PV of expected future EVAs, since the EVA at time t is $x_t - k_w I_{t-1}$.

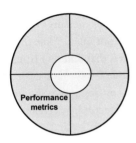

Chapter 11

PERFORMANCE MEASURES: JERRY IS INTRODUCED TO THE "ACRONYM WARS"

1. The Alphabet Soup of Performance Measures

"Come in," Jerry shouted. In walked Bob for their meeting, armed with two thin, bound documents.

"Good afternoon, Jerry." Jerry hardly looked up from a stack of paper at his desk, muttering only a half-hearted hello. Bob asked, "What are you so deeply involved in there?"

Jerry let out an enormous sigh and announced, "EPS, CFROI, NPV, EVA, CVA, TSR, SVA, the acronyms seem to never end. I thought I understood the Value Sphere concept. But now I'm not sure. I really think the consultants have exhausted every possible combination of the letters of the alphabet. No, wait, they have yet to coin SMTM!"

Bob willingly took the bait. "What's that?"

"Come on Bob, it's an easy one. 'Show Me The Money!' SMTM, for short," Jerry quipped. "I think our shareholders would like it."

"I think you are spending a little too much time in the office."

Jerry smirked. "Well, that may be. But I am finding it terribly difficult to keep these straight in my head. I know I'm not a finance guy. But the fact of the matter is that it shouldn't be that hard. Unless I am completely missing the point, aren't all these performance measures simply designed to tell me whether I am creating wealth for my shareholders?"

"Well, yes, but —"

Jerry cut him off. "Then how in the world could so many measures be necessary?"

"I understand your frustration," Bob answered. "The fact is that a few of the performance measures you mentioned are different labels for the same thing. However, people argue that there is actually a need for having a diversity of measures based on two fundamental principles." Jerry looked curious, so Bob continued. "The first relates to how firms create shareholder value. And the second is that different firms suffer from different problems." Bob paused, and then continued.

"At a basic level, firms create wealth for their shareholders by doing two simple things. First, by investing only in projects that create value. And second, by retaining only those projects that continue to create value. Sound familiar?"

Jerry nodded. "Yeah, but I thought you said that the NPV rule was all you ever needed."

Bob was expecting this. "In a perfect world, NPV is all you need. But in reality, you have to be careful. First, other project selection criteria, such as payback period, can often provide information above and beyond what NPV tells you. More importantly, however, the NPV rule is not equipped to judge ongoing financial performance, at least in the manner in which companies like ours need it." Jerry looked puzzled. "You know, for things like performance-based compensation and running diagnostics on the business."

"Can you elaborate?" Jerry asked.

Bob was quick to respond, "Of course. Consider the following. Suppose one of our business units came to us with a great idea for a new product with an NPV of $4 million. If we believed the assumptions, we'd invest in the project in a heartbeat." Jerry nodded his agreement.

Bob continued, "But the problem is that we can't reward this business unit for adding $4 million to our shareholders' wealth because this $4 million is little more than a promise of things to come. Nothing has happened yet. We can assess business unit performance and reward our people only on the basis of actual performance. Not promises. But NPV is not a measure of ongoing performance. What we need for that are flow measures of performance — like cash flow or earnings or economic profit — rather than a stock measure like NPV."

Jerry looked pensively out the window as he spoke, "So you're saying we need this alphabet soup of financial measures for purposes of performance measurement, rather than deciding which projects we should invest in."

"Absolutely!" Bob replied. "NPV is often enough for project selection. But flow measures of performance are needed to see how we're doing on an ongoing basis, to determine compensation, and to incent people to focus on the drivers of shareholder value. Let me give you an example of how Dell Computer uses several measures as a means to achieving one primary goal — measuring and facilitating cash flow generation.[80] One component of generating cash is obviously given by the return on net assets. Now recall how we define our net assets."

Jerry interrupted him. "Net assets are given by the sum of net fixed assets and net working capital."

"Yes! And given how net working capital is defined, Dell's asset manager, Danny Caswell, summarized their cash flow goals with the following statement.[81]

> Basically, we focused on ways to convert what we sell directly to the marketplace as quickly as possible into cash.

How they did this was to develop a set of internal benchmarks. One example is something called the Cash Conversion Cycle."

"Oh, I think I see where you're going," Jerry said slowly. "They must have broken down all the ways in which net working capital was converted into cash, and then tracked these individually."

Bob nodded. "Since net working capital is given by current assets less non–interest bearing current liabilities, they calculate their cash conversion cycle as the sum of days sales outstanding and days sales in inventory, less days payables outstanding."

"So how have they done?" Jerry wondered out loud.

"Very well. In fact, Dell was awarded the CFO Magazine and MasterCard Corporate Products 1997 REACH Award for the best reengineered Treasury Operations. As an example of their progress, Dell has reduced its Cash Conversion Cycle from 40 days in late 1996 to a minus five days by the end of 1997! Pretty amazing, huh?"

"I'd say," Jerry said, almost in awe. "How did they achieve this?"

Bob replied enthusiastically, "They managed to bring their average accounts receivables down by improving their order processing and collection activities. This reduced their days sales outstanding from 42 to 37 days. They also went on to reduce average inventory levels dramatically by asking their vendors to hold more of the inventory instead of holding it themselves. This change brought their days sales in inventory down from nearly 31 days to 13!"

"Well, if my math is correct, that only reduces their cash conversion cycle by 23 days,"[82] responded Jerry. "How did they manage to squeeze an extra 22 days or so out of their suppliers?"

---

[80] See Russ Banham, "Upgrading Cash Flow at Dell," *CFO Magazine*, December 1997.

[81] Ibid.

[82] These 23 (saved) days are given by the reduction of five days in days sales outstanding and 18 days in days sales in inventory.

Bob gazed at the expressionist painting on the wall as he spoke. "As it turns out, they were often paying their bills too early. Danny Caswell admits that they simply weren't paying attention to the credit terms they were given. This allowed them to increase average accounts payable by increasing their days payables outstanding from 33 days to nearly 55 days. This generated the extra 22 days saving."

"That's pretty interesting." Jerry then recalled Dell's performance. "Hey, wasn't 1997 a banner year for Dell's stock?"

"Certainly was," Bob replied. "Their stock was up 200% at one point in the year. The company has been the darling of Wall Street and international money managers. Their CFO, Tom Meredith,[83] is convinced that these stock price increases were highly correlated with the improvements in their Cash Conversion Cycle!"

"So which measure, or should I say measures, do we want to use?" Jerry asked anxiously.

Bob rapped his knuckles on the two documents he had brought in with him and said, "Hopefully, these will make it a little easier for us to decide."

Bob had put together a report of the project selection criteria used most often by firms in practice. Further, he had compiled a list of popular financial performance measures. Each of these latter measures was defined, along with a discussion of their merits and weaknesses.

2. What are These Measures Then?

Bob handed one copy of the study to Jerry. It was essentially a series of presentation slides.

Bob broke the silence, "Let's quickly run through the project selection criteria, as there isn't a lot of variation among firms here. A majority of firms focus on four project selection criteria for new capital investments.[84] Not too surprisingly, these are NPV, IRR, payback period and average rate of return. Take a look at Fig. 11.1 where I have summarized some of their findings relevant to us."

Jerry gave Fig. 11.1 a quick glance and said "Seems like, on average, firms are getting a little more sophisticated in their capital budgeting techniques over time. It's kind of interesting when you look at our industry. As a group, we are more likely to use NPV than the average, but it seems that we have been reluctant to let go of measures like payback and accounting rates of return."

---

[83]See footnote 3.

[84]See E. Gilbert and A. Reichert, "The Practice of Financial Management among Large United States Corporations," *Finance Practice and Education*, 5(1), Spring/Summer 1995, pp. 16–23.

Industry/year	NPV (%)	IRR (%)	Payback (%)	Average rate of return (%)
1991 Average	84.7	81.8	63.3	45.8
1985 Average	82.8	79.6	75.9	59.3
1980 Average	68.1	66.4	79.9	59.1
Food, beverage, and tobacco industry	86	70	71	62

Fig. 11.1.　Project selection criteria. (Percentage of 151 fortune 500 companies to use each measure.)

"You're right," Bob replied. "But it's a pretty small data set and I think there are really only two things we want to take away from this. First, it appears that firms use at least a couple methods for evaluating new projects. That is, they rely on a 'basket' of selection criteria. Second, there has been a pretty significant increase in the percentage of firms using the NPV method."

"Fair enough," Jerry said. "Have you got similar data on how firms judge performance after the projects have been accepted?"

"Yes," Bob replied. "I was just getting to that. The most popular of these measures seems to be Stern Stewart's Economic Value Added (EVA), or economic profit, as we have called it.[85] You remember our earlier discussion (Chapter 10) and the Fortune article 'EVA — The Real Key To Creating Wealth'?[86] In that article, firms like Briggs and Stratton, Quaker Oats, and Coca-Cola, were cited as using EVA as a financial performance measure."

"Oh yes! I do remember. The Coca-Cola story is impressive" Jerry said. "During 1985–95, didn't they earn over 20% a year in total shareholder return?"

"Yeah. Coca-Cola was ranked as having created the most shareholder wealth in 1996, measured as the difference between its total market and book values. This difference was over $125 billion for Coca-Cola. Larger than for any other publicly-traded company," Bob replied. "But firms like AT&T have also tried economic profit, and it certainly didn't solve all their problems. In fact, AT&T ultimately abandoned economic profit.

"I think it is also important to keep in mind that there are numerous successful companies, like Walt Disney after the Saul Steinberg raid, that appear to have excelled with their product market strategies and sound financial management but haven't explicitly used any of the celebrated measures like economic profit. These firms have kept a keen eye on the generation of cash and the returns generated by

---

[85]EVA is a registered trademark of Stern Stewart and Company.
[86]See Shawn Tully, "EVA — The Real Key to Creating Wealth," *Fortune*, September 20, 1993.

their assets. I've looked through many annual reports for Disney, and I've never seen any fancy performance metric mentioned even once. In fact, all you'll ever see are terms like growth in earnings per share, rates of return on investments, and, ultimately, shareholder returns earned through dividend yields and share price appreciation."

"I should have known it couldn't be as easy as copying Coca-Cola," Jerry said.

"All right then," Bob replied. "To make the most efficient use of our time, let's just focus on a few key measures and how they work. You'll recognize a lot of these from our earlier discussions."[87] Bob settled on the following performance measures for their discussion:

1. Earnings per share (EPS)
2. Return on (Book) equity (ROE)
3. Return on net assets (RONA) or Return on invested capital (ROIC)
4. Economic profit or economic value added (EVA) or Shareholder value added (SVA) or Cash value added (CVA)
5. Return on gross investment (ROGI) or Return on gross assets (ROGA)
6. Cash flow return on investment (CFROI)

In evaluating these, Bob thought it was best to judge these on the basis of whether each measure:

- was based on accounting or economic values (economic values are better);
- included an estimate of how much capital was invested in the business;
- used WACC as the opportunity cost of these funds and
- was simple to calculate.

A summary evaluation of performance measures along these dimensions is presented in Fig. 11.2.[88]

Bob continued. "I think Fig. 11.2 will make more sense after some definitions. If you could turn the page, the next figure (see Fig. 11.3) that runs across several pages should be enlightening." He and Jerry then began discussing the following material.

3. Which One Should We Use?

Jerry took another look through the figure. "There certainly seems to be an ordering in terms of complexity here, but what about compatibility and efficiency?" Jerry wondered.

---

[87] See Chapters 2 and 9.

[88] This is based in part on R. Myers, "Measure for Measure," *CFO*, November 1997, pp. 43–56.

Measure (proprietor)	Accounting vs. Economic values	Includes capital base	WACC used in derivation	Simplicity to calculate and understand
EPS	Accounting	No	No	Simple
ROE	Accounting	Yes, but only a part of it	No	Simple
RONA/ROIC	Both	Yes	No	Simple
Economic profit or EVA (similar to CVA and SVA) [*Stern Stewart*]	Both	Yes	Yes	Simple
ROGI [*Boston Consulting Group — BCG*]	Both	Yes	No	A little complex
CFROI [*Holt*]	Both	Yes	Yes	More complex

Fig. 11.2.   Evaluating the evaluation measures.

"If I interpret your question regarding 'compatibility and efficiency' to mean what problems do these measures address," said Bob, "and how well do they do it, then the answer is yes. Turn the page for a tabulated summary of the answers (see Fig. 11.4)."

"Well, Bob, that was very helpful," Jerry said encouragingly. "Looks like we have our work cut out for us on this one."

Bob nodded his head in agreement.

4. What Makes A Good Financial Management System?

"Anything else we need to keep in mind?" Jerry asked.

"Yes, I think there is something critical that I want us to take away from this meeting. If we create shareholder value by doing only two things, choosing the right projects and then retaining only those that are performing well, then our financial criteria for doing both of these have to be explicitly linked. This fundamental observation would move me towards either an economic profit-based measure or CFROI."

"Why is that?" Jerry asked.

"Because they are both consistent with the way we select projects in the first place — the NPV rule. However, I think my group better take a little more time on this one. Just like Dell, we may come up with our own set of benchmarks to use."

"Do companies really keep these two financial systems relating to project selection and project retention separate?" Jerry asked.

Measure	Formal definition/intuitive definition/benchmark for comparison
EPS	$=$ Net Income/# of Shares outstanding
	• EPS roughly gives the per-share funds available to invest in the business (via new/replacement assets) *and* to pay shareholders.
	• EPS realizations can be compared to either zero or earlier EPS forecasts as a means of judging the implications for performance.
ROE	$=$ Net income/Book value of equity
	• ROE gives a marginally informative view of the rate of return on the *book value* of equity, i.e., what percentage of the equity is being turned over into net income.
	• Loosely speaking, ROE could be compared to the required rate of return on equity (R_E) offered by the CAPM (see Chapter 9), but remember that R_E is a market-derived number, and *not* an accounting number.
RONA	$=$ NOPAT/Net assets
	• RONA (or ROIC) is the rate of return on a firm's asset base; that is, it reveals the rate at which assets are turned over into after-tax profits. These profits can then be used to invest in more assets, as well as compensate the bondholders and shareholders.
	• Assuming the net asset base is adjusted to reflect the *economic* value of the assets, RONA should be compared to the firm's WACC to assess performance.
Economic profit	$=$ NOPAT $-$ Capital charge where capital charge $=$ Net assets $\times$ WACC
	Economic profit can also be expressed as:
	$=$ (RONA $-$ WACC) $\times$ net assets
	• Economic profit answers the question: Did the firm (division, project, etc.) generate enough after-tax operating profits (NOPAT) to cover the *absolute* opportunity cost of the asset base (capital charge)?
	• In a narrow sense, if economic profit is positive, then value has been created. If not, it's been destroyed.
	• In a broader sense, a negative economic profit is positive, then value has been created. If not, it is been destroyed.
	• In a broader sense, a negative economic profit for a single year (especially a year early in a new project's life) is not bad, as long as the present value of future economic profits is positive.

Fig. 11.3.   Performance measure definitions.

Measure	Formal definition/intuitive definition/benchmark for comparison

ROGI = Gross cash flow/Gross cash invested

= Net income + interest + depreciation/Net assets + accumulated depreciation

- BCG presents ROGI as a simplified CFROI, and it can be interpreted as the *cash* return on the *cash* value of assets.
- The meaningful comparison would be to WACC, but BCG warns that ROGI may be overstated. However, it is unclear why ROGI may be overstated.

CFROI = ROGI adjusted for inflation, asset life and salvage value

- In other words, CFROI is the IRR generated by the cash investment of the business, over the economic life of the business.
- CFROI can be compared to WACC to assess whether the opportunity cost of capital is being covered with the current deployment of assets.
- Theoretically, CFROI is a very sound measure of the value of the firm's strategy. However, it appears to be more a valuation tool than an *ex post* performance measure.

Fig. 11.3. (*Continued*)

"Sometimes they do. Quaker Oats has been cited as doing just that when it evaluated its infamous Snapple acquisition. And I quote[89]:

Quaker didn't use Economic Profit to calculate its $14 per-share offering price for Snapple. According to company spokesman Mark Dollins, Quaker uses a discounted cash flow model to evaluate acquisitions and divestitures, and merely uses Economic Profit as an incentive compensation tool.

"Now Jerry, does this make any sense in light of what we have talked about?"

"No," Jerry said emphatically. "Aren't valuations based on discounted future cash flows identical to valuations based on discounted future Economic profits?"

"Absolutely!" said Bob, "If the valuations don't match, you've got an error somewhere in one of them. The issue is that if we price our acquisitions based on a financial metric that differs from the metric by which we judge and reward our people, then we dilute accountability. Perhaps that's what happened at Quaker Oats. We will have to be careful not to make the same mistakes."

Jerry remembered something. "You know, this reminds me of my conversation with Ray Burns a couple weeks ago. Remember my leasing question?"

---

[89]Ibid.

Problem/ Situation	Order of the problem (i.e., does the problem typically arrive first, second, ...)	Recommend performance measure [Caveats]
Need to ensure generation of positive profits.	• Can be first-order problem if the business cannot even find projects that generate revenues in excess of their operating costs.	• EPS—Will focus attention on raising net income (earnings). [Caveat: Earnings may (and probable will) come at the expense of asset efficiency and shareholder value.
Need to promote balance sheet (capital) awareness — because of a problem with *overinvestment* in capital.	• Normally a first-order problem. Positive profits are insufficient to cover capital costs.	• RONA and ROGI, CFROI raises awareness of the balance sheet. Normally, improvements in the efficiency of net working capital management are realized first. • Note: The main difference between RONA and ROGI is in the estimate of the asset base. ROGI implicitly assumes that if the asset is still in use, it has not depreciated in an economic sense. [Caveat: Hurdle rate may be raised *too* high, i.e., positive NPV projects with more modest IRRs may go unfunded.]
Need to promote capital efficiency *and* the assets of the business are *not* well captured by adjustments to the balance sheet.	• As with economic profit, it is a response to a first- or second-order problem. But the need for CFROI also depends critically on the nature of the assets used in the business.	• As with RONA and ROGI, CFRPI raises awareness of the balance sheet. Moreover, if the spread between CFROI and WACC is multiplied by the "investment," then it provides an absolute measure like economic profit. • The apparent advantage of CRFOI is that it attempts to give credit today for the NPV of one's decisions. This completeness can be quite valuable in different situations. [Caveat: Using CFROI as a performance measure may be more difficult given its complexities. However, it appears to be theoretically sound on its own.]

Fig. 11.4.   Matching measures to problems.

Bob nodded, hoping that since he would sent out his addendum to the resource allocation manual, the correct methodology was being applied to leasing decisions now.[90]

"Well, Ray shared some more of his experiences with Mickey's new products division that fit exactly with what you are talking about. He was trying to understand how he would be judged after his projects were accepted. I could tell he didn't feel comfortable asking me directly about compensation, so he simply described how it worked at Mickey's."

Bob jumped in. "From what I've heard, don't they give bonuses mainly on the basis of market share and total sales revenue?"

"Yes, they do. But even I thought this seemed a little odd in light of the fact that they mainly used the project's NPV to decide whether they invested in the project. When I pushed Ray on the behavioral consequences of selecting projects on NPV and compensating employees on sales revenue, he admitted that there may have been some massaging of the capital budgeting numbers."

"That is an excellent example of how value evaporates," Bob chimed. "Massage the numbers to make your projects look good on an NPV basis, knowing full well that you will be judged in the future on sales, not NPV."

Jerry smiled. "Seems like their teams then had carte-blanche on capital expenditures after their projects were accepted. Ray claimed that they never had much trouble meeting their bonus targets! However, in Ray's defense, he admitted that he wasn't always sure that the system benefited shareholders."

This reminded Bob of another example that he decided to share with Jerry. In 1995, Texaco Incorporated embarked on a mission to completely restructure its planning process.[91] Part of the impetus for change came from the observation that there were frequent, and often enormous, disconnects between the strategic plans and the tactical plans. The strategy led them to invest in many projects that were not expected to generate positive cash flows for eight to ten years. Forecasts would be generated for the full life of these projects. But by the time they got to the second year, the forecasts had often already lost touch with reality.

What would this imply for year three and onwards?[92] Without tying compensation to the actual performance of a given project, there is no way to insure that the right projects are taken in the first place.

---

[90] In Chapter 9, Jerry discovered why using leasing as a means of circumventing the capital budgeting process could allow for value evaporation.

[91] See Cathy Lazere, "All Together Now," *CFO Magazine*, February 1998.

[92] As we discuss in Chapter 12, part of Texaco's reengineering efforts were to explicitly link the budgeting and forecasting decisions to planning decisions, as well as to ultimate performance.

One firm that has attempted to rectify this type of problem is Eastman Chemical.[93] They now use only one measure for their bonus-based pay, return on capital. Prior to 1994, Eastman used a basket of different performance measures to assess and ultimately reward their employees.

What is interesting, though, is the fact that Eastman still uses a host of other measures. These include customer satisfaction, labor costs, inventory levels, and sales revenue. However, these measures are tracked because they fundamentally drive the firm's return on its capital. By rewarding managers on one of the end results — return on capital — these managers seek out the drivers that they can actually control. Importantly, what drives a project's anticipated NPV before it is accepted is then monitored after its adoption.

5. Jerry and Bob Close with an Eye on the Future

"Well Bob, that is a lot of information to digest," Jerry said. "I think your team better get to work." Stay tuned for Bob's proposal.[94]

Main Lessons

- Many firms suffer from a disconnect between the set of performance measures they use to assess project proposals and the set of measures used to assess projects and performance on an ongoing basis. Such a disconnect disrupts the Value Sphere by diminishing value retention.
- Depending on the type and severity of investment distortions that firms suffer from, there are numerous economically sound measures available to address specific problems (see Fig. 11.4).
- Of the available measures, those such as economic profit and CFROI are consistent with discounted cash flow techniques such as NPV.

End-of-Chapter Exercises

1. How does your firm measure financial performance? Are the same measures used to evaluate your particular area (or division) as those used to evaluate the company as a whole? If different measures are used, can you think of situations in

---

[93]See Bill Birchard, "Closing the Strategy Gap," *CFO Magazine*, October 1996.
[94]We present Bob's recommendation in Chapter 12.

which conflicts arose because of the disparity in measures? Does value evaporate as a consequence?

2. Are the financial performance measures used to judge the business on an *ongoing* basis similar to those that are used to judge new project requests? If not, does value often evaporate? Can you determine why?

3. Using Fig. 11.4, does your company (or division) suffer from any of the three problems identified in the first column? Has the senior management team identified your answer as a problem? If so, what steps have been taken as a means of solving it?

4. Is managerial pay tied to performance? Are the measures used for compensation the same as those used to judge the financial performance of the business itself? If not, can you identify sources of Value Evaporation that occur in your company due to the inconsistency of the measures for pay and company performance?

5. How many financial performance measures do you use? Why do not you pick just one?

Practice Problems

1. Evaluate the different performance measures described in this chapter in terms of their consistency with creating shareholder value.

2. Despite the fact that some of these measures may not be consistent with the NPV rule, why do firms use them?

3. Against each measure, list at least one way in which Value Evaporation could result due to a use of the measure.

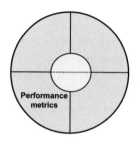

Performance
metrics

Chapter 12

A NEW FINANCIAL MANAGEMENT SYSTEM USING SHAREHOLDER VALUE

1. Do We Expand the Boundaries of the Business?

"Bob is here to see you," announced Katie, Jerry's secretary. This interrupted Jerry's morning musings.

"What's happening in the world of finance, Bob?" asked Jerry.

"With all the turmoil in the Russian, Asian, and Latin American financial markets, there's a bit too much for me to keep up with, Jerry. But I want to talk about a couple of proposals that my strategic planning folks have come to me with. Do you have a little time?" responded Bob.

When Jerry nodded, Bob began to explain the proposals. The first was in response to Bob's memo — sent in the fall — that everybody had to think of ideas to cut costs. Since the major component in the cost of lemonade was the cost of lemons, one proposal was for the company to have its own lemon grove. There was a nice 25-acre lemon grove just outside town that Bob's people could go and check out. It had 2,500 lemon trees that grew approximately 3,750,000 lemons each year.

"You know, Jerry, this won't satisfy all of our lemon needs, but it could be a nice way to experiment with a fraction of what we need," said Bob. "If this works, then we could consider buying more lemon groves."

Jerry chewed on his cigar for a while, then said, "Bob, isn't it true there is a lot of scientific evidence that diversification and vertical integration are not good ideas? Doesn't diversification decrease value retention by increasing the complexity of the Value Sphere?"

"That's true," responded Bob, "and I do believe we have to stay focused. I also know that farming is risky. But this is different. We have a lot of people who have experience in managing lemon groves, and our deep relationships with our suppliers have really given us a great understanding of this business. I've already had my people run the numbers, and they look pretty good."

Jerry felt a twinge of excitement. It was always fun entering into businesses he had not run before. But this could be risky, his instincts warned him.

"Isn't there a safer way to do this? Could we not consider a partnership with our lemon growers, some sort of an alliance?" was the way Jerry verbalized his ambivalence.

Bob responded. "Sure we could, and we ran the numbers on that too. The bottom line is, it doesn't do the trick for us. We give up some of our operating control and provide capital, without being able to fully implement our management philosophy. Besides, we also have to worry about whether our partner shares our vision for the business. There have been many joint ventures and alliances by American companies in China, for example, that have been disasters because the Chinese partners did not share the strategic vision that their American partners had.[95]

You know there has actually been research done on when it's good to have alliances and when it's good to just acquire the firm. The punch line of this research is that when you need a lot of coordination across two units, it's better to have them as part of the same firm rather than have an alliance.[96] With the amount of coordination that we will need across the lemon grove and the rest of our business to ensure that we truly lower the cost of lemons grown in this grove, I think we should buy this grove if we are going to do anything with it."

"You're thorough, as usual," marveled Jerry, "so I promise to think about this."

As Bob prepared to leave, Jerry had a flash of insight. "Bob, what if we bought this lemon grove and converted it into a farm restaurant? You know, instead of using the whole lemon grove to grow lemons, we could use perhaps an acre or two to create a variant of one of our lemonade locations. We could give it a real country feel, and make customers feel as if they are in a little country store in the middle of a farm."

Bob's eyes lit up as he said, "Yeah, and perhaps we could expand the concept to a nutritional restaurant. One where you can buy bananas, carrots, cottage cheese, and

---

[95]See Wilfried Vanhonacker, "Entering china: An Unconventional Approach," *Harvard Business Review*, March–April 1997, pp. 130–141, which cites numerous examples of failed joint ventures in Chains.

[96]See Henry W. Chesbrough and David J. Teece, "When is Virtual Virtuous?" Organizing for Innovation," *Harvard Business Review*, January–February 1996, pp. 65–74.

egg-beater omelets, besides lemonade. I think the market is ready for a nutritional restaurant."

Bob was excited about this too, and left with a promise to have it investigated more fully.

2. The Lemon Grove Sparks a Discussion of Performance Measures

A few days after Jerry's conversation with Bob about the lemon grove, Bob called again and suggested lunch. He was few minutes late and obviously had a lot on his mind. First he described what he had discovered since they met last, then continued, "Basically, this is a good idea, and I think we can make it work. But I found out that in the lemon-growing business, people's performance and rewards are based on the volume of lemon output and the per-unit cost of the lemons. It essentially translates into a profit measure of sorts because generally the more lemons you grow, the lower your per-unit cost and the larger your output. The problem is, we're using a different set of measures, with our focus on quality, product innovation and customer satisfaction."

Bob was worried about the company getting bogged down in too many performance measures. He recalled the previous discussion about how having too many performance measures could lead to Value Evaporation. When Jerry asked him what was really bothering him, Bob said, "You know, as we have grown as a company, so have the performance measures that we use. We just keep adding new performance measures as we add new activities. It seems to make sense in isolation. But when we put it all together, I see emerging problems." Bob listed what he had in mind:

- "Our set of performance measures is now so complicated we are spending more and more time in training our people to just understand these measures. Our manual of performance measures has over 50 pages of definitions, illustrations, and explanations.
- Even our finance people sometimes get confused. The other day I was in a meeting of our group accountants and financial analysts. As our meeting progressed, discussion seemed to get muddled. I finally called "time out" and asked people how they defined gross margin, which is about as basic as you can get. You know what? There were eight people in the room, and I heard six different definitions of a term that is defined on the second page of our manual! We have to simplify.
- We also have so many new project ideas — like the lemon grove acquisition — that it seems like everybody is using their own pet measures to justify their

pet projects. There is just too much flexibility in the system with so many measures.

- Our performance assessment and reward system is not closely tied to the financial performance measures we are using to evaluate our capital investments. We're using IRR and NPV for our capital investments. And for rewarding our people we use a whole basket of measures, including new product ideas and customer satisfaction.

- I also get the feeling that our people think capital is free. We're generating so much cash flow that we are able to fund a lot of projects from our free cash flow. I don't think our performance measures focus the attention of our people on how expensive capital really is."

This was a lot for Jerry to absorb. But he knew Bob was right. He was also a bit confused, however. What Bob was talking about went way beyond what he covered in his finance course at the university. Or what they had discussed earlier. It was also beyond what Jerry had learned through experience running his business.

"I think I understand the first two issues you talked about, Bob. In fact, you have so thoroughly convinced me about the virtues of Economic Profit that perhaps we could just use that instead of all our other measures. But what about the performance assessment and reward issue? I remember reading an article by Alfie Kohn in which he claims that rewarding people in the workplace for superior performance is counterproductive.[97] If he's right, then why worry about our performance assessment and reward systems?" asked Jerry.

Bob paused for a minute, trying to recall his impressions of Kohn's arguments. Once he had done that, he proceeded to lay out for Jerry his reasons for believing in the power of incentives and reward systems in positively affecting employee behavior. His main points were as follows:

- Kohn's argument against individual rewards and incentive compensation is based on the notion that they encourage competition rather than teamwork. They are intrinsically demotivating because any reward to an individual is an implicit punishment for others, Kohn argues. He views incentive compensation as an instrument of control, and states, "Offering good things to people on the

---

[97] Alfie Kohn, "Why Incentive Plans Cannot Work," *Harvard Business Review*, September–October 1993 and Alfie Kohn, *Punished by Rewards*, Houghton Mifflin Company, Boston and New York, 1993.

condition that they do what you tell them is, almost by definition, a way of trying to exert control."[98]

Kohn suggests that employees would work much better if they were driven by their intrinsic motivation. This is the challenge and enjoyment of working creatively, not extrinsic rewards.

Bob observed that a central assumption in Kohn's thesis is that employees know exactly what they should do to maximize the firm's value creation, and that they will do this because of intrinsic motivation. Nothing beats self-direction in this case.

But Bob did not believe this. That is why he insisted on the employee stock purchase plan as the company was getting started. His research and experience showed that employees need and want direction. The assumption that every employee knows what should be done is simply wrong. The sorts of signals provided by an incentive compensation plan tied to the drivers of shareholder value speak much louder than preaching by senior executives.

Consider Quaker Oats before it adopted economic value added (EVA) for performance measurement and incentive compensation. Its performance measurement and reward systems were like those of countless other companies. Each unit was measured based on its stand-alone contribution to the bottom line.

Manufacturing was judged on (per unit) conversion cost. How do you minimize it? By manufacturing the largest volume possible. Economies of scale!

Of course, to manufacture a lot you need lots of inputs that the procurement function needs to buy for you. What is this function judged on? Per-unit purchase cost. And how do you minimize this? By purchasing very large quantities and taking advantage of volume discounts. So, procurement is happy to purchase as much as manufacturing wants.

Now let us think of the sales and distribution function. They have to sell all the goods manufacturing churns out. Sales and distribution is typically judged on some measure of on-time product availability/delivery. Having large quantities of goods to sell obviously helps here. So sales and distribution is delighted that manufacturing is producing so much.

Every individual function is responding to the way its performance is judged. And not just because of the narrow self-interest of the managers of these functions who want to maximize their compensation. Rather, if a function is judged to be doing well based on a particular performance measure, and its managers are rewarded, then it is an unambiguous signal that senior executives — who presumably

---

[98]See, "Rethinking Rewards", Perspective, *Harvard Business Review*, November–December 1993, pp. 37–49.

better see the big picture of what is good for the firm as a whole — view the function as doing the right thing. It is the innate desire to do well that motivates each function.

Unfortunately, in this case the performance measurement system is sending the wrong signals. Although each individual function is optimizing, there is global sub-optimization. Quaker Oats churned out huge quantities of Gatorade, Rice-a-Roni and other products. Much more than they could profitably sell. The consequences were the need for huge warehouses to store the gigantic quantities being produced, and large amounts of inventory. Very capital intensive!

Finally, when the inventory had to be sold, the company had to resort to "trade loading." This is a euphemism for dumping large quantities of product on the market — loading up the trade channels — with special discounts and promotional incentives provided to get people to buy.

The overall outcome was Value Evaporation, as described in Chapter 5. The prodigious amounts of capital consumed by Quaker Oats made it virtually impossible for the company to earn enough to cover its cost of capital.

The moral of the story for Jerry is this: Rewards and performance measurement systems matter. They matter because they provide tangible direction for employees by generating signals about the right thing to do.

Bob recalls for Jerry a quote from an article he read by Donita Wolters, Manager of Human Resources at JMM Operational Services Inc., in Denver, Colorado[99]: "Incentives are neither all good or bad. Although not the right answer in all cases, they can be highly effective motivational tools."

- A second aspect of Kohn's hypothesis is the assumption that what gives employees the greatest innate satisfaction will also necessarily be in the best interests of the firm. Bob knows this is not always so. He reminds Jerry about their earlier discussion regarding the agency costs that arise in organizations (see Chapter 4).

For example, are employees acting in the company's best interest when they pay vendors before they are required to in order to make sure that their budget for the year is completely spent before the year is over?[100]

Are employees acting in the company's best interest when they massage the numbers to get their projects approved?

---

[99]See, "Rethinking Rewards," Perspective, *Harvard Business Review*, November–December 1993, pp. 37–49.
[100]The idea is that if you do not spend what you are allocated, it is likely that less will be allocated next year.

Are employees acting in the company's best interest when they do not disclose bad news in a timely manner that would enable the company to minimize its losses?[101]

Were US federal regulators acting in the best interests of taxpayers when they refused to close down "zombie" savings and loan associations with negative net worth, eventually costing American taxpayers over $100 billion?[102]

No. Employees and other agents do sometimes pursue self-interest in ways that conflict with what is best for shareholders.

It is not that employees are evil or that they do not want to do what is best for shareholders. It is just that a company's performance assessment, resource allocation, and reward systems end up generating incentives that spawn unproductive conflicts between what employees want to do and what they should do.

The message for Jerry is simple. Whether he has an explicit performance assessment and reward system or not, the way resources are allocated in his company and the way talent is evaluated for promotions — or even the assignment of tasks and responsibilities — will create an implicit measurement system to which his employees will respond. If the implicit system is ignored and happens to mis-align the incentives of employees relative to those of shareholders, there will be Value Evaporation. Thus, the Value Sphere dictates that Jerry explicitly design a performance assessment and reward system that produces the desired incentive alignment.

Jerry is pretty convinced by now. He sees that performance measurement systems and incentive compensation will not by themselves create any value in the business. Value creation is his task and that of his operating managers. They cannot use the company's reward systems as a crutch. But how performance is measured and rewarded (both implicitly and explicitly) can have a profound impact on how much of the value created in the business is evaporated. That is, performance measurement and incentive compensation systems are an integral part of Value Sphere, and are a complement to stock ownership plans.

The question now is: What is the best way to design the company's performance measurement and incentive compensation, particularly in light of the possible acquisition of one or more lemon groves? Jerry asks Bob to carefully consider this and meet again the following week. Bob agrees. Stay tuned.

---

[101] The reason for not disclosing bad news in a timely manner is that there is always a chance that the employee could "resolve" the problem eventually and thus nobody would know that there was ever a problem. See Arnoud W. A. Boot, Todd T. Milbourn and Anjan V. Thakor, "Sunflower Management and Capital Budgeting," *Journal of Business*, March 2005, pp. 501–528.

[102] See Arnoud W. A. Boot and Anjan V. Thakor, "Self-Interested Bank Regulation," *American Economic Review*, May 1993, pp. 206–212.

3. A New System is Recommended

A week later, Bob had prepared his recommendations for Jerry in the form of a report. This report is given below.

MEMORANDUM

TO: Jerry Wyman — CEO

FROM: Bob Butterfield — CFO

RE: Performance measures and incentive compensation

Overall analysis

The situation we are faced with is how to develop an appropriate "scorecard" for our business, given its rapid growth. We run the risk of increased complexity in the set of financial and non-financial performance measures we use, and consequently Value Evaporation.

The questions are as follows

- Should we use a common set of measures for capital allocation and incentive compensation? That is, should we use the same scorecard to determine where we invest our money and how we reward our people?
- What should guide our choice of these measures?
- What measures should we use?
- What should be the next step after we decide on an appropriate set of measures?

My recommendations are as follows

- We should use essentially the same set of measures for capital allocation and incentive compensation. We need an integrated system in which we use a simple scorecard with a very small set of measures that everybody can understand. Internalizing how one can positively impact each measure should be the key for each employee.
- Our choice of measures should be guided by three considerations:
  - How well does the measure correspond to shareholder value as judge by the market?
  - How does the measure promise to affect our employees' behavior?
  - How simple is the measure?
- My recommendation is to use economic profit.

If you approve this proposal, then I believe the key next steps are as follows

- I should ask my staff to come up with a new design for you capital allocation system that is built around economic profit.

Details

I believe that our internal "scorecard" must take an external perspective. The external perspective relies on capital market data, and my favorite external measure is total shareholder return (TSR).

(*Continued*)

(Continued)

Our internal measures should focus on the drivers of shareholder value that we can manage to improve shareholders' returns. For example, the "balanced scorecard" approach emphasizes the importance of employees, customers, and business processes as drivers of shareholder value. While many of the internal measures are nonfinancial, they are viewed as being positively correlated with "bottom-line" financial performance as reflected in TSR. Most companies, particularly those listed on US stock exchanges, state their corporate goal as the creation of significant shareholder value. Thus, even though a variety of financial and nonfinancial measures are used internally to assess the performance of managers and to compensate them, it is TSR, an external measure, that is the key metric for judging financial performance.

It is easy to use TSR as a metric for judging a firm's financial performance. But it is problematic to use it for assessing the performance of our managers and for compensating them. The reason is that TSR depends in part on comparing stock prices at two points in time, and since prices are forward-looking, TSR is strongly influenced by how the market's expectations about the firm's future performance have changed.

Clearly, past performance affects perceptions of future performance. But the latter is also driven by exogenous factors such as changes in the outlook for the overall economy, interest rates, exchange rates, inflation expectation, and so on. This means that if we used TSR as a measure by which to judge managerial performance in every period and compensated our managers accordingly, we would be rewarding and punishing managers for things well beyond their control. So if we want to judge managerial financial performance in corporations, TSR should be used only as a long-run measure of financial performance. Not as a period-by-period measure for performance assessment and compensation.

What we need are measures that rely on realized performance and yet correlate positively with TSR. Perhaps the most publicized measure is economic profit. I have examined some data on how well economic profit do in terms of their correlation with TSR.

A research study shows that economic profit is positively correlated with abnormal returns to shareholders — defined as TSR minus the expected rate of return — accruing to shareholders over a given period.

Further, in investigating the list of Stern-Stewart 1,000 firms over the five-year period 1991–1995, Bacidore and Thakor (1997) find that only 362 of the 1,000 companies generated an average economic profit that was positive.[103] The list of companies with positive economic profits includes Coca-Cola, Intel, Microsoft, and Wal-Mart. The average economic profit for Coca-Cola, for example, was $1.35 billion per year. The average annual total shareholder return was 26.15%, which far exceeds Coca-Cola's cost of equity capital. Qualitatively, this is typical of the stocks with positive average economic profits.

The average annual TSR for the "positive economic profit" group was 24.52%, well above the average equity costs of capital for these firms. On the other hand, 636 companies in the top 1,000 had a negative average economic profits, which suggests that the majority

(Continued)

---

[103] See Jeffrey Bacidore and Anjan V. Thakor, "Poor Financial Performance," in *The Pressing Problems of Modern Organization: Transforming the Agenda for Research and Practice* (Robert Quinn, Regina and Lynda St. Clair, eds.), 1999.

(*Continued*)

of companies destroyed shareholder value over this period, according to economic profit. Consistent with the predictive ability of economic profit, the average TSR for this group was lower, 13.94%.

We should then work with the operating unit heads to determine the key value drivers in their businesses that most impact their economic profit. The compensation of the people who report to them should then be tied to those value drivers. At the end of the day, everybody's compensation should be explicitly linked to something that impacts economic profit. But the key is that the operating unit heads will take care to ensure that the people reporting to them do not globally suboptimize as they manage the value drivers. The reason is that the operating unit heads are, and people below them are compensated based on economic profit, not just the value drivers of these variables.

This means that for our new products people, compensation should be tied to the incremental contribution of their new product ideas to the company's economic profit; not on how many new product ideas per se they generate, but how much value these ideas create.

For our manufacturing people, it would be the incremental contribution of changes in total manufacturing costs (including capital costs) to economic profit. Thus, if they buy new equipment to lower per-unit manufacturing cost, then they would be judged on whether the total conversion cost — manufacturing cost plus the cost of capital including that of the new equipment — is lower than before.

For purposes of capital budgeting, I recommend we use only four measures: Economic profit, NPV, IRR, and discounted payback. Those analyzing individual projects will use only NPV to determine the acceptability of the project, but will report economic profit and discounted payback for senior management use.

Main Lessons

- The fewer the performance measures a company uses, the more the employees will be able to focus on creating value and the less they will be distracted by the measures themselves. That is, reducing the number of performance measures helps to manage the Value Sphere better by reducing the complexity of the performance metrics segment of the Value Sphere.
- Whatever internal performance measures are used, they should be highly correlated with total shareholder returns, and the same measures that are used to evaluate the allocation of capital should be used to judge and compensate employees.
- The best performance measures appear to be economic profit and TOPS.

End-of-Chapter Exercises

1. What measures do you use to judge business unit and individual performance? Are these the same measures by which you judge capital investments? If not, why not?

2. How well do your employees understand the performance measures you use? How do you determine how well they understand these measures and whether they aid or impede their management of the company's Value Sphere? Have you educated your employees — especially those outside the finance function — in how their decisions affect their measured performance?

3. How do your competitors measure performance? Do their performance measures give them a competitive advantage over you?

Practice Problems

1. How can performance measures cause Value Evaporation?

2. Why is it that, beyond a certain point, having more performance measures is counter productive?

3. What are the key elements of a good financial performance measurement system? Why do you believe these elements are important?

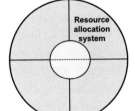

Chapter 13

DESIGNING A WORLD-CLASS
RESOURCE ALLOCATION
PROCESS

1. Is all this Growth Really Good?

Bob was sitting in his office reflecting on the tremendous growth of the business. All of this growth has strained the company's resources, with competing demands for personnel, office space, expense budgets, capital budgets, promotional expenditures, travel, and the like. Bob knew of the dangers of fast organizational growth — managerial hubris, poor resource allocation, and, worst of all, Value Evaporation. He knew he needed to discuss with Jerry how they should allocate resources so that value retention was maximized going forward. He called Jerry's secretary to schedule a meeting.

2. Early Signs of Impending Danger: Bob and Jerry Discuss Preventive Measures

Bob began his meeting with Jerry by talking about his recent conversation with a group of CFOs. He handed Jerry a piece of paper on which he had written down something one of the CFOs had told him that had made a big impression on him. It read:

> In our company we have a strict 20% hurdle rate for our capital investments. No project is approved unless its IRR exceeds 20%. The average IRR for the projects we invest is probably around 30%. And yet our RONA has consistently hovered around

215

8–9% and our WACC has been around 10–10.5%. How are we creating negative economic profits and destroying shareholder value, year in and year out, when every project we invest in has positive NPV?

When Jerry had finished reading it, he asked Bob, "So, what did you tell him?"

Bob smiled, "I told him it was probably all the corporate overheads, including his salary, that were draining value. He wasn't amused.

"But seriously," continued Bob, "I believe the problem is that, like many companies, they probably have a poorly designed resource-allocation system that creates perverse incentives for employees. And the many actions they take collectively destroy value even though projects look good on paper."

Jerry looked at his watch. He wondered why Bob was going into all this.

"So, Bob, what does this have to do with us?"

"Everything," replied Bob, "I believe we're beginning to have some of those problems as well. For example, you'll recall that on the "Jumbo Cookie" factory that has been proposed to be built in Birmingham, the projected present value of cash flows was $22 million, with an investment of $10 million, giving an NPV of $12 million at the time of investment."

"Sure," nodded Jerry.

"Unfortunately," continued Bob, "we've had a lot of unanticipated expenses during the last year. Our original plan was for $5 million in market research, product development, pre-investment tooling and engineering, etc. so that the NPV net of these expenses would be $12 − $5 = $7 million. But three months into the test marketing, after our new product development people had the $5 million, they came back for an additional $2 million. We approved that because it made sense in light of the fact that the $5 million was already sunk."

Jerry had a frown on his face now, "I hope that was the end of it."

"Not quite," replied Bob, "I now have a request pending for another $5.5 million that we'll need to complete the testing and for a major ad campaign. The ad campaign will need to start a month or so before product launch and will continue through the first year of the product launch."

"So, what does it all mean?" quizzed Jerry.

Bob looked out the window as he spoke, "What it means is that the project has a "fully-loaded" NPV of minus $500,000. That is, if we'd correctly anticipated all of these costs, we'd have known that the total outlay would be $22.5 million and the total present value of cash flows was only $22 million. Unfortunately, because many of these expenses were not anticipated and were sequentially incurred, it always made sense to approve each expense because the previous expense was correctly viewed as being sunk. For example, in the case of the pending $5.5 million request, what we have to ask ourselves is whether we want to spend that plus the $10 million in property, plant and equipment — a total of $15.5 million — to gain a $22 million present value of cash flows. The answer is yes."

"But that doesn't change the fact that the overall NPV is negative, does it?" asked Jerry.

"No, it doesn't," nodded Bob. "You see, that is how we can take a project with a positive NPV of $12 million at the time of project approval and still destroy shareholder value. What worries me is that people may be playing games, either postponing certain expenses or not disclosing all the money they would need at the outset."

Bob then went on to tell Jerry about the research he had done on the subject as well as his proposal for a new resource allocation system for the company. He began by reviewing some of the background material.

An important distinguishing factor between the winners and the losers in shareholder value creation is the quality of investment decisions. This critically depends on the soundness of the firm's resource allocation system. Unfortunately, the history of corporate America is littered with examples of poor investment decisions. Examples of distorted corporate investment policies range from investing too little in positive NPV projects, and too much in negative NPV projects[104] to investment myopia.[105]

Investment distortions such as these distract companies from doing what they do best, possibly causing them to sink millions of dollars in the wrong products and ideas. Even Coca-Cola, an example that Bob often used as one for "best practices", has had some missteps along the way in managing their Value Sphere. In the early 1980s, Coca-Cola invested in pastas and wines. As it turned out, these products produced rates of return that were not only well below those of its core soft-drinks business, but also below its cost of capital. What Coca-Cola found out was that these were businesses in which the company had little comparative advantage. Hence, it divested them.

Jerry cut in. "Couldn't you argue that Coca-Cola simply wasn't sure at that time of everything they might be good at? That is, they were trying to learn, and ultimately did?[106] We have to give our people the freedom to fail sometimes."

---

[104]See William Fruhan, "Pyrrhic Victories in Fights for Market Share," *Harvard Business Review*, September–October 1972, pp. 100–107.

[105]See Anjan V. Thakor, "Investment 'Myopia' and the Internal Organization of Capital Allocation Decisions," *Journal of Law, Economics and Organization*, 6, Spring 1990, pp. 129–154.

[106]See Arnoud W.A. Boot, Todd T. Milbourn, and Anjan V. Thakor, "Megamergers and Expanded Scope: Theories of Bank Size and Activity Diversity,"*Journal of Banking and Finance*, 23, 1999, pp. 195–214.

Bob nodded, "Jerry, this is exactly the reason why we need a world-class resource allocation system. Only then will our Value Sphere be synchronized. We need to develop a system that gives our managers the freedom to explore new ideas and take risks. But as we have learned from our 'jumbo-cookie' experience, we need a system that is consistent with shareholder value over time. Learning is great, but we have to learn faster."

Bob continued. "And I cannot overemphasize the importance of having an effective resource allocation system. I agree completely with the following quote by Ronald Lieber. 'Of all the things a manager can do, figuring out the best way to allocate capital is probably the most important.'"[107]

"So why do companies continue to fail? One strong possibility is that they have flawed resource allocation systems and are evidently blind to the flaws. Other firms may know that their resource allocation analyses are weak. However, they may view them as individual problems rather than as fundamental deficiencies in the system. In these cases, the attempts to mitigate the problems are often misdirected, ultimately producing greater frustration. As a result, corporate strategy and resource allocation become misaligned and remain so, despite disappointing financial performance. The blame is then often placed on senior management for failing to provide the appropriate leadership and strategic guidance."

"What one ends up with then is often what Jack Welch, CEO of General Electric, once described as a firm '...with its face toward the CEO and its ass toward the customer.'"

3. A Process Orientation Must Precede Adopting a Resource Allocation System

After a brief coffee break, Bob and Jerry continued their discussion. Jerry turned to Bob, "So what kind of a proposal for a resource allocation system do you have for us, Bob?"

"Before we get to that Jerry, I want to emphasize that we need a process orientation first. Without it we won't have the organizational culture to effectively implement what I'm proposing."

"I'm not sure what you're getting at, Bob," said Jerry with a puzzled look.

"Well," began Bob, "a process orientation is simply a belief that horizontal, cross-functional processes are essential to sustained shareholder value creation in today's turbulent business environment.

---

[107]See Ronald B. Lieber, "Secrets of the Superstars," *Fortune*, September 29, 1997, pp. 43–44.

"Unfortunately, people have different views of what a process orientation means to them. Senior management often sees a process orientation as a way to get uniformity. To the front-line (middle) managers, a process often seems bureaucratic, with layers of management that soak up time and energy. In such an environment, the middle managers end up discarding or abusing the process. Consequently, information reaching top management is filtered by product champions who are in competition. Resources inevitably end up being allocated to charismatic leaders who are skilled at organizational politics. And the resulting poor investment decisions lead to Value Evaporation."

Bob's concern is clearly illustrated in the following statement by Craig Weatherup, then CEO of Pepsi-Cola, North America.[108]

> We struggled at first with a process orientation. Pepsi has always been an action-oriented organization with a "take-the-hill, get-it-done, can-do" mentality. Results were what mattered, whether you got them in an ad hoc or an orderly fashion. At the start, people were afraid that processes would slow them down. It took time to overcome these concerns.

The kind of process orientation that it took to change people's mindset at Pepsi-Cola is described in Fig. 13.1.

The key observations from this process orientation are:

- Improvement is not limited to large-scale processes. Capital and expense allocations can all be improved.
- Processes are not a constraint to slow down the organization. Good processes save time in the long run.
- A process orientation provides discipline and the elimination of ambiguity. Everybody clearly understands the rules by which things get done when there is a good process.
- A process orientation requires constant communication and continual reinforcement by senior management. It will not occur spontaneously. For example, Paul Allaire, one-time CEO, Xerox, says,[109]

> Unless each function has a different customer — and in our business they don't — you have to link together activities that

---

[108]See David A. Gavin, "Leveraging Processes for Strategic Advantage," *Harvard Business Review*, September–October 1995, pp. 77–90.
[109]Ibid.

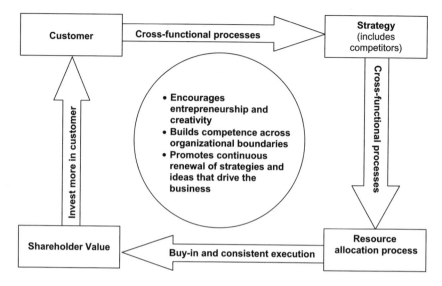

Fig. 13.1.   A process orientation.

were always run separately. They're not going to integrate themselves; they haven't for a hundred years.

Bob continued, "In other words, Jerry, it is our job as senior managers to make the process orientation happens. We not only need to design an effective resource allocation system, but also need to constantly reinforce the need for process orientation," said Bob.

"Won't the resource allocation process conflict with our other processes?" Jerry wondered.

"On the contrary, Jerry. If correctly done, the resource allocation process integrates the other key processes in the business as shown in Fig. 13.2. This is at the heart of having a well-synchronized Value Sphere."

4. Going from a Process Orientation to an Effective Resource Allocation System

"Unfortunately," Bob continued, "most resource allocation systems have some problems, generally because they are missing key features. The problems associated with missing features are shown in Fig. 13.3."[110]

---

[110]Source: John A. Boquist, Todd T. Milbourn, and Anjan V. Thakor, "How Do You Win the Capital Allocation Game?" *Sloan Management Review*, 39(2), Winter 1998, pp. 59–71.

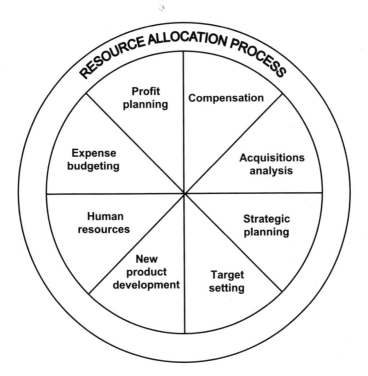

Fig. 13.2.   Resource allocation integrates other processes.

The common drawbacks of resource allocation systems that are indicated by the Fig. 13.2 are:

- Misalignment between strategy and resource allocation
- Lack of dynamic structure for resource allocation and lack of attention to options
- Finance not viewed as a strategic partner in a cross-functional team
- No connection between compensation and financial measures
- Lack of training of financial analysts who then exhibit deficiencies in analytical techniques
- Poor base case identification
- Competition and cannibalization issues
- Inadequate treatment of risk
- Non-uniform assumptions
- Inadequate post-audits to support organizational learning.

After listing these drawbacks, Bob proceeded to elaborate on each.

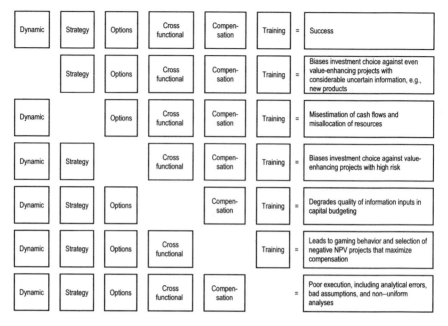

Fig. 13.3.   What is the impact of features missing from the resource allocation system?

4.1. *Misalignment Between Strategy and Resource Allocation*

As noted in Chapter 1, most companies have a well-articulated vision statement or corporate goal, followed by a description of the strategy for attaining that goal. However, the design of the resource allocation system is often disconnected from the strategy. This is one of the most important causes of disruption in the Value Sphere.

For instance, the corporate strategy may be to grow aggressively through new product introductions. Yet, what happens if its capital budgeting practice encourages the analysis to focus on potential revenue losses arising from new products cannibalizing old ones?[111] Clearly there is a disconnect between the intent of the strategy and its execution. The importance of linking the resource allocation process to strategy was emphasized by Paul Allaire, then CEO of Xerox.[112]

"You can't redesign processes unless you know what you're trying to do strategically. What you're after is congruence among strategic direction, organizational design, staff capabilities, and the resource allocation processes you use to allocate

---

[111]Put another way, to understand a company's *true* strategy, do not read what the CEO says it is — look at where the company allocates its capital.

[112]Same as Footnote 5.

your resources and ensure that your people are working together to meet the company's goals."

4.2. Lack of Dynamic Structure for Resource Allocation and Lack of Attention to Options

A good resource allocation system must involve an analysis of capital allocation requests both at the stage at which the project is executed as well as the stage at which there is a need to generate preliminary information.[113]

This is important for two reasons. The first relates to the proposed "Jumbo-Cookie" project and its cost overruns. These overruns could be avoided if a detailed project analysis is required at the early dates of a project's examination.

Second, the preliminary analysis should take into account the options inherent in most capital budgeting opportunities. For example, the project could be abandoned or expanded in the future. Options analysis can lead to different decisions from those arrived at with the NPV rule. Having a dynamic capital resource allocation system is necessary to account for these options.

Unfortunately, many companies lack dynamic resource allocation systems that view market research and product development outlays as investments in options. Moreover, these companies often fail to integrate the determination of how much to spend on these activities within their overall resource allocation systems.

For Jerry and Bob, this point was driven home as they thought about their lemon grove investment.[114] In that case, the original investment in purchasing the lemon grove could have been viewed as an option on buying more lemon groves. Or as an option on opening a farm restaurant, as well as an option on opening more nutritional restaurants.[115]

4.3. Finance Not Viewed as a Partner in a Cross-Functional Team

Sometimes the financial analysts involved in capital budgeting are viewed more as "traffic cops" than business partners. Consequently, financial analysts end up (at best) playing only an auditing role. In these cases, they are brought in near the end of the project analysis simply to rubber-stamp a conclusion reached earlier by a marketing or manufacturing line executive.

---

[113]Bob had recently seen a quote from Jeff Staley, a principal at Mercer Management Consulting, stating that "the truly superior companies have a portfolio-planning process that operates continuously, not a rigid, once-a-year budget cycle." See Ronald B. Lieber, "Secrets of the Superstars," *Fortune*, September 29, 1997, pp. 43–44.

[114]See Chapter 12.

[115]See Chapter 14 for a fuller discussion of real options.

In other companies, financial analysts may be involved from the outset. However, if the numbers they come up with are not "high enough," they are sent back to their spreadsheets with the command, "only projects with a 25% rate of return get approved in this company!" This invites massaging of the numbers.

The process of capital budgeting is then relegated to an exercise in identifying project components that produce the desired answer. Obviously, the quality of the information is seriously compromised.[116] Compounding this is the problem that non-financial people often do not understand how the information they are providing will be used. Hence, their inputs are often biased one way or the other and less useful than they should be.

4.4. No Connection Between Compensation and Financial Measures

As pointed out in Chapter 12, unless an employee's compensation is tied to the financial measures by which the performance of projects is judged, the risk of Value Evaporation is likely to be high.

In many companies, projects may be judged on the basis of a measure like economic profit, but employees are judged on the basis of earnings or profits. This tempts them to grow earnings or profits without worrying about the capital needed to do that. Whether employees actually do this or not, such a system invites them to promise whatever economic profit it takes to get projects approved, and then focus all their attention on maximizing earnings or profits. This gaming behavior leads to Value Evaporation.

4.5. Lack of Training of Financial Analysts

When financial analysts are poorly trained, many problems occur, which are discussed below.

- Poor base case identification: Capital budgeting focuses on incremental cash flows. These are always defined relative to a base case, i.e., the status quo. If the base case is not correctly identified, the incremental project NPV will also be misestimated. We discussed this quite extensively in Chapter 9, so we will just review it briefly here.

For example, suppose we are considering whether to invest $1 million in an advertising campaign. It is estimated that product sales without this ad campaign will

---

[116]This issue was raised by Patrick Barwise, Paul R. Marsh, and Robin Wensley, "Must Finance and Strategy Clash?" *Harvard Business Review*, September–October 1989, pp. 85–90.

generate cash flows with a present value of $3 million, and that sales with the ad campaign will generate cash flows with a present value of $5 million. Thus, the incremental present value of cash flows is $5 − $3 = $2 million. This exceeds the $1 million in advertising needed to generate the incremental cash flows. Thus, the NPV of the ad campaign is $2 − $1 = $1 million.

But what if the base case is wrong? What if cash flows without the ad campaign really have a present value of $4.5 million?

Clearly, the incremental present value of cash flows due to the ad campaign is now only $0.5 million and the ad campaign has negative NPV.

The problem here is that if we misidentify the base case and invest in the ad campaign, we will never know we made a mistake. The reason is that as soon as the investment is made, the base case disappears! We will only see cash flows with a present value of $5 million, exactly what we expected with the ad campaign.

Knowing this, a clever analyst may be tempted to knowingly misrepresent the base case to make his incremental project look more attractive.

- **Competition and Cannibalization:** In computing the NPV of a new product, many companies subtract from the projected sales of the proposed new product the amount by which the sales of an existing product will decline if the new product is introduced. This is known as cannibalization. Again, we will be brief because this issue is also covered in Chapter 9.

While this is theoretically sound, one must be careful to account for the potential impact of competitive entry. For example, if a competitor would enter with a new product anyway, then why worry about cannibalization? The existing product may be doomed regardless of whether we introduce the new product.

A nice illustration of this is the experience of US automakers. They resisted developing small, fuel-efficient cars in the 1960s for fear of cannibalizing the sales of their product line of high profit margin gas guzzlers. And then along came the Japanese car manufacturers in the 1970s with their compact cars to take significant chunks of market share away from US automakers.

- **Inadequate treatment of risk:** There are two main types of risk in capital budgeting:
- The business and financial risk in cash flows that is reflected in the discount rate (see Chapter 8)
- The risk in estimating expected cash flows.

The first risk can be thought of as arising from the distribution of cash flows around a known statistical mean. The second risk arises from the analyst's lack of knowledge of the statistical mean of the cash flow distribution; this is an informational uncertainty. Recall the discussion in Chapter 7. Understanding this type of risk often requires sophisticated simulation analysis.

- Non-uniform assumptions and lack of consistency: Many multidivisional firms find themselves with an unwanted variety in both the assumptions their financial analysts use and the presentation of the financial analysis findings. The non-uniformity typically involves assumptions about residual values, market shares, inflation rates, cycle times, the amounts of capital required, and so on.[117] With different assumptions in different capital allocation requests, all presented in different manners, senior management is forced to allocate capital across projects while comparing "apples and oranges."

While Jerry and Bob probably should have thought about all these inconsistencies when they developed their original framework, the most important point that they overlooked was the value of managerial training. We visit this issue in Chapter 15. As Bob and Jerry discussed these issues, the importance of having a world-class resource allocation system was brought home forcefully to Jerry.

- **Poor post-auditing procedures:** Post-auditing in a capital budgeting context refers to three things:

  - Examining the outcomes of previous investments
  - Comparing these to projections contained in the capital request
  - Documenting the causes of the observed deviations.

When credibly utilized, post-auditing provides an invaluable learning device, facilitating continuous improvement in both operating performance and financial analysis. It also prompts a review of the base case assumptions, thereby stimulating a reassessment of competitive dynamics. This is particularly true if some rejected proposals are also reviewed. Knowing what we know now, should we have accepted the proposal? If instead the process ends up being viewed as only a policing device, suspicion and mistrust will undermine the whole system.

---

[117]Bob recalled that some of his analysts in one region consistently assumed that the assets invested in new products had no residual value after their useful lives. On the other hand, he had analysts from other regions who would assign a *growing perpetuity value* to the residual value of the project. He wondered how much value had been evaporated based on this inconsistency.

5. The Discussion Continues: Key Observations are Summarized

Jerry agreed with Bob that an effective resource allocation has to be designed from the ground up. Companies that are recognized as leaders in this field include:

- GlaxoSmithKline
- Motorola
- General Electric
- Merck.

A number of key observations emerge from studying these successful companies and others:

1. If fewer projects are undertaken, cycle time is reduced on each project.
2. Uniformity of assumptions and approaches coupled with the elimination of process variation is both disciplining and liberating:
   - Time is released to focus on the creative parts of the task
   - Firms that adhere to uniform processes reduce average new product development times by 30%–50%.
3. The resource allocation process depends on the transparency of the valuation process. Everyone should know:
   - The assumptions
   - The information quality — how it was generated, and by whom
   - The complexity and risk of the proposal.
4. The process must be credible to all of the company's management team.

6. The Proposed Resource Allocation System

The resource allocation system consists of the procedures by which projects and capital allocation requests are prepared, evaluated, and approved. A world-class resource allocation system is a multitollgate, dynamic evaluation system that provides well-defined checkpoints to examine whether projects are consistent with the company's strategy. Figures 13.4–13.7 sketch such a system.

This system has four phases and three tollgates. Approval requires a project to pass through all three tollgates, with a review at each tollgate.

Phase 1: The first phase, New Ideas, is when new ideas are generated. This is a multifunctional process, and we should set up "advanced product concepts" groups that are formally charged with this task. Ideas should be screened at the strategic

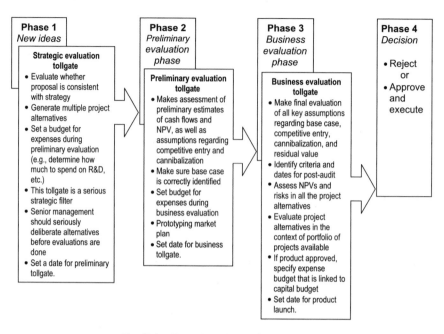

Fig. 13.4.   Dynamic project evaluation system.

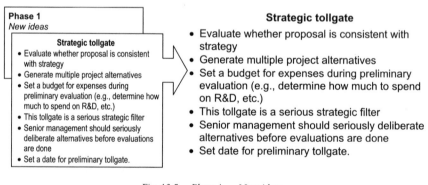

Fig. 13.5.   Phase 1 — New ideas.

evaluation tollgate (SET) for consistency with our strategy. These ideas should be presented only as proposals that explain how each proposed idea is consistent with the strategy and how it will create shareholder value.

Phase 2: The second phase is the preliminary evaluation phase. During this phase, the idea should be shaped into a practical reality. Also, multiple ways to do the

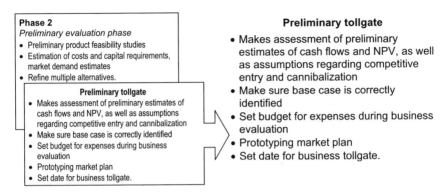

Fig. 13.6. Preliminary evaluation.

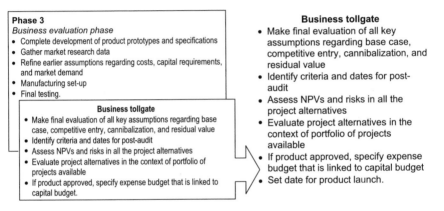

Fig. 13.7. Business evaluation phase.

project should be explored. The latter requires developing a set of project alternatives.[118] These alternatives should include four ways to do the project: (i) abandon it, (ii) leave the current plan as is, (iii) adopt a scaled-down version of the plan, and (iv) adopt a scaled-up version of the plan. Of course, there may be more than one alternative in each version of the plan.

A budget must also be determined for expenses to be incurred during the preliminary evaluation phase. We should also set a date for the next tollgate, the preliminary evaluation tollgate (PET). This will ensure consistency of the cycle time (see Chapter 7) between the SET and the PET with the strategy.

---

[118]See Paul Sharpe and Tom Keelin, "How Smithkline Beecham Makes Better Resource-Allocation Decisions," *Harvard Business Review*, March–April 1998, pp. 45–57.

Next, the team should attempt to provide a preliminary valuation of each plan. This includes the following:

- Obtain preliminary estimates of costs and capital requirements.
- Formulate explicit assumptions regarding market demand for the product under each scenario.
- Clearly identify the base case and highlight the assumptions regarding competitive entry and cannibalization.

This should lead to preliminary estimates of cash flows and NPV for each alternative. At this stage we will begin to pare down the set of alternatives to the most desirable one. Conditional on this decision, we then begin to look forward.

To this end, the analysis should identify whether additional information must be acquired. This determines the necessary expense budget and the length of the following phase, the business evaluation phase. Observe that the expense budget for the business evaluation phase includes the amounts allocated for information acquisition and product development.

The amount allocated for information acquisition should be viewed as the price of purchasing an option. This option gives the firm the right, but not the obligation, to fully invest in the project at the business evaluation tollgate. Naturally, the greater the informational risk in the project, the more we should be willing to invest in information acquisition.

The decision made at the PET may be that committing further resources to this project is not worthwhile. In this case, we will terminate the project. However, if the decision is to go through the business evaluation phase, then we must make sure that the expense budget committed to this phase, in addition to the prescribed length of the phase, is consistent with the cycle time–risk tradeoff implied by the firm's strategy.[119] The information to be provided at the PET is indicated in Fig. 13.8.

Phase 3: The majority of our information gathering efforts are conducted during the third phase, the business evaluation phase. Product specifications should be completed, prototypes developed and tested, market research conducted, and all of the earlier assumptions regarding costs and capital requirements refined. Ultimately, the purpose of this phase is to fully implement the approved information acquisition strategy developed during the previous phase.

Information gathering during this final phase is again a multifunctional task. Our finance group, teamed up with counterparts from manufacturing, technology,

---

[119]See Chapter 7 for the development of the cycle time–risk tradeoff.

1. A brief description of proposed product.
2. Well-defined set of alternatives directly related to the proposed product (multiple ways to do the project).
3. Base case definition.

Then, for each alternative:

4. A summary of key inputs — data on volume, price, costs, assets, etc.
5. A justification of assumptions underlying key inputs and a description of who generated the information and the way it was generated.
6. Lease vs. Buy analysis, where applicable.
7. Total anticipated capital outlay in the business evaluation phase.
8. Product development outlay.
9. Risk reduction outlay.
10. NPV and IRR if project continued with only product development outlay.
11. NPV and IRR if project continued with both product development and risk reduction outlays.

And finally:

12. Recommendation at preliminary evaluation tollgate.

Fig. 13.8.   Contents of financial analysis at PET.

and marketing, should elicit information in a manner that permits both an accurate estimation of future cash flows and an assessment of risk.

However, if the information provided to the financial analyst from the other members is in the form of point estimates, the financial analyst cannot obtain ranges and probabilities of possible future outcomes. Thus, the method by which information is elicited is critically important. An important change to our current system will be the adoption of some computer software that will allow our analysts to more easily increase the sophistication of their project assessments.[120]

Additional tasks to be done during this phase include:

- Revisit the original base-case assumptions for their current relevance
- Use probabilistic estimates to consider the impact of competitive entry on project cash flows
- Evaluate the joint impact of cannibalization and competition
- Determine the date of the first post-audit, as well as the key components of the project's cash flow to be tracked

---

[120] An example of such software is Risk-Strategist[TM] from *Value Integration Associates*, 216 W. Allen Street, Suite 140, Bloomington, IN 47403. The website is www.risk-strategist.com.

1. A brief description of proposed product.
2. Base case definition.
3. Incremental case rationale — include discussion of cannibalization and competitive responses.
4. A summary of key inputs — data on volume, price, costs, assets, etc.
5. A justification of assumptions underlying key inputs and a description of who generated the information and the way it was generated.
6. Product development investment in the business evaluation phase.
7. Risk reduction outlay in the business evaluation phase.
8. NPV for new project.
9. Eva for each year (based on expected cash flows) for new project.
10. Probabilistic distribution of NPVs (based on randomness in cash flows for new project.
11. Analysis showing sensitivity of NPV to changes in the discount rate and the residual value for new project.
12. A graph that shows in a single display how sensitive the new project NPV is to key inputs (see Tornado Chart in Fig. 13.10).
13. Lease vs. Buy analysis, where applicable.
14. Necessary expense budgets in each year of project's life.
15. NPV of new project inclusive of preliminary and business phase expenses.
16. Overall recommendation.

Fig. 13.9.   Financial information to be provided at BET.

- Stipulate the expense levels in each year of the project's life that will be needed to support the cash flow assumptions.

The end of this phase is marked by the BET. A summary of the key items to be presented at the BET are included in Fig. 13.9.

We will also require a brief synopsis — called the top sheet — of the key value drivers and financial performance measures for the project. The performance measures could include the project's NPV and the economic profit for each year of the project's life. Moreover, the risk analysis could include probability distributions and sensitivity analysis of the NPV. A sample top sheet is included as Fig. 13.10.

The final decision about the project is made at the BET. The criteria and dates for post-audits are established and links between capital and expense budgets are forged. The result is a complete business plan for the idea:

1. Background Information
   - A complete description of the preferred alternative
   - The base-case definition
   - The project rationale
   - The recommendation.

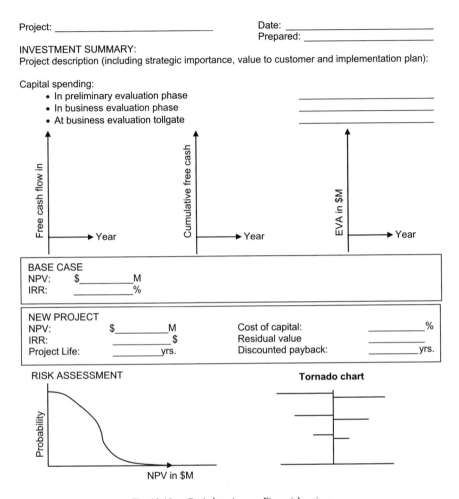

Project: _____   Date: _____
                                    Prepared: _____

INVESTMENT SUMMARY:
Project description (including strategic importance, value to customer and implementation plan):

Capital spending:
  • In preliminary evaluation phase   _____
  • In business evaluation phase   _____
  • At business evaluation tollgate   _____

BASE CASE
NPV: $_____M
IRR: _____%

NEW PROJECT
NPV: $_____M   Cost of capital: _____%
IRR: _____$ Residual value   _____
Project Life: _____yrs.   Discounted payback: _____yrs.

RISK ASSESSMENT   **Tornado chart**

Fig. 13.10. Capital project — Financial review.

2. Data input summary

  • Volume, price, cost, asset investments and other key operational data
  • Justifications for assumptions and description of how information was generated
  • Development expenditures and outlays for risk reduction.

3. Financial analysis

  • NPV, IRR and economic profit for base case and the recommended alternative

- Summary graphs
- Risk analysis based on probability distribution of NPV or IRR.

7. Reflecting on the Potential Benefits of the New System

As Jerry absorbed the details of the new system, Bob summarized what he viewed as its potential benefits:

- The process requirement of consistency of analysis across all units means that creativity at the business unit level is focused on the best way to execute the project rather than on how to analyze it. This optimizes the Value Sphere.
- Tracking expenses throughout the process ensures discipline in the project sponsor's spending on the idea.
- The extensive documentation, peer review, and challenge of assumptions replaces snap judgments by senior executives and gives more weight to carefully researched ideas.
- All capital spending, including mergers and acquisitions, as well as expense spending are consistently screened to ensure shareholder value creation and to minimize Value Evaporation.
- The system provides opportunities for learning. Effective post-auditing generates information from past projects that can improve the quality of the assumptions used in future projects.

8. Jerry's Lesson: The Value Sphere, The Process, and The People

Jerry had learned two very valuable lessons over the past three months. First, successful firms need sound resource allocation processes that are perfectly aligned with the strategy, so the Value Sphere is well-synchronized. Second, successful firms need well-trained people. And this can only be achieved by committing resources to managerial training.

To solidify these insights in his mind, Jerry kept a copy of the following quote[121] on his desk:

> Highfliers find creative, low-cost ways to perform research and development, invest disproportionately in training and technology, and are not afraid to bet the farm.

---

[121] See Ronald B. Lieber, "Secrets of the Superstars," *Fortune*, September 29, 1997, pp. 43–44.

Main Lessons

- A sound resource allocation system must be both dynamic and sophisticated.
- Assumptions underlying cash flow forecasts must always be challenged and tested for credibility.
- A good financial analysis also delineates the benefits of the product to the consumer and focuses on the strategic fit of the product.
- Management involved in resource allocation must view themselves as accountable for their analysis and recommendations.
- Standardization in assumptions, presentation and financial software are critical to the successful execution of the strategy.
- Managerial training is one of the most important investments a firm can make.
- A process orientation to resource allocation is better than a functional approach. It saves time in the long run and insures all ideas and associated alternatives are systematically analyzed on a uniform basis. Many times resource allocation is misaligned with corporate strategy, resulting in shareholder Value Evaporation. The problem is magnified if the allocation is done on a political basis.
- A multiphase evaluation process is frequently used to evaluate major projects. The multitollgate system ensures that essential project information is acquired within budget at each evaluation point. The process also structures a post-audit to enable organizational learning from the project.
- A well-designed resource allocation process increases the prospects for a successful implementation of strategy. The resulting business plan can be thought of as the road map for the execution of the strategy. These are essential elements of a well-balanced Value Sphere.

End-of-Chapter Exercises

1. Write down a description of your company's current resource allocation system. Does your system have features similar to the one ultimately implemented at Jerry's? What elements are similar? What elements are different? What are the value creation and retention implications of the differences?
2. Can you readily identify any of the seven deficiencies in your system (Fig. 13.3) that Bob and Jerry observed in theirs? How could these deficiencies lead to the evaporation of value in the capital allocation process? Have they?
3. When submitting a capital allocation request, are you required to include a financial review topsheet (Fig. 13.10) such as the one required by Bob and Jerry? What are the possible benefits of such a top sheet?

4. Critically appraise the assumptions that are typically made by those in your firm who.

Practice Problems

1. Why does a sound resource allocation system need to be dynamic?
2. Why is it important to standardize the assumptions, presentation and financial software used for the financial analysis undertaken to execute the strategy?
3. What is the importance of management training?
4. What is a process orientation to resource allocation? Why is it better than a functional approach?
5. What are the benefits of a multiphase project evaluation system?

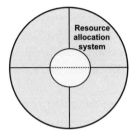

Chapter 14

WHAT TO DO WHEN NPV FAILS: A REAL OPTIONS APPROACH TO PROJECT SELECTION

1. Is It Ever Good to Make a Negative NPV Investment?

Bob and Jerry settled into the conference room to discuss some new issues that surfaced in the implementation of the new dynamic resource allocation system now in place at the company. Doug Harris, the V.P. of Strategic Planning, was invited to the meeting. He was concerned that the new planning system did not adequately capture the strategic benefits of developing new business opportunities.

Doug walked in the conference room and began, "I am glad we are having this meeting. All week long I have been studying the market potential for coffee-flavored yogurt smoothies, an exciting product that has come out of our development labs. I just don't see how to fit this new product idea into our planning system. What we are talking about here is the prospect to develop a huge new market for our company. The Value Sphere implications of this product are enormous. I don't want its potential to be snuffed out by a couple of bean counters in finance and accounting."

Bob responded. "Wait a second, Doug. I would argue that our dynamic resource allocation process is designed specifically to handle the investment opportunity you just mentioned. The key is to break the project up into its logical stages of investments that match our tollgate system. Let's see how your coffee-flavored yogurt project would fit within the system."

"As I understand the project," Bob continued, "it has passed our Strategic Evaluation Tollgate (SET). The project is clearly consistent with our strategy. And it appears to be a feasible addition to our current product offerings. Unfortunately,

Doug, this is a pretty risky project. We have assessed the likelihood of success to be 25%, and the likelihood of failure to be 75%. If we invest and the product is successful, we estimate the NPV to be $300,000. But if the project is a flop, the NPV will be –$300,000."

"That does sound risky, Doug. Why are you promoting this idea?" Jerry asked.

"Because we have a strategy of growing organically," said Doug with a hint of irritation in his voice. "And we're not going to do that if we don't introduce new products. In my experience, there aren't too many new product ideas that are as safe as investing in US government bonds."

"Wait a minute, "Bob interjected. "Let's first come to a decision based on our normal line of thinking. Let's first calculate the expected NPV of investing in the idea, given the uncertainty we have specified."

Bob showed Doug and Jerry the following NPV calculation:

$$\text{NPV} = \text{Probability (success)} \times \text{NPV (success)}$$
$$+ \text{Probability (failure)} \times \text{NPV (Failure)}$$
$$\text{NPV} = 25\% \times \$300,000 + 75\% \times (-\$300,000)$$
$$\text{NPV} = \$75,000 - \$225,000 = -\$150,000.$$

Doug had seen these numbers before. He could not hide his annoyance as Jerry turned to Bob and asked, "We should obviously dump this idea if these numbers are correct, right?"

"Absolutely, if we stopped there," Bob agreed. "However, the project is now at the Preliminary evaluation tollgate (PET), and we need to make a further assessment of the idea. Suppose we could spend $10,000 on a market test and identify whether these smoothies would succeed in the market. That is, the test marketing would give us a lot more information about whether the smoothies would succeed before we had to commit to a full-scale investment."

"Well, that's reasonable," Jerry said. "But why throw any more money after a project that the NPV rule says to drop in the first place?"

Doug, who was convinced now that Bob was just setting the whole thing up to make sure the project was killed for good, tried to look nonchalantly outside the window to keep his temper under control.

"Take a look at the following picture." Bob showed Jerry and Doug Fig. 14.1.

Bob started to explain. "This diagram highlights the fact that if we run the test market, we can avoid investing in the project when it is likely to fail. That is the whole idea behind the PET."

"Oh, I see, Bob. We basically get to avoid all negative NPVs. Right?" quizzed Jerry rhetorically.

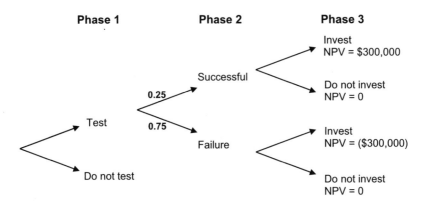

Fig. 14.1.   Coffee-flavored smoothie project.

"Yes! If the test marketing indicates a failure, we will not invest. We have the option to abandon the idea. Now, we can evaluate the NPV of whether to invest the $10,000 in a market test, knowing how we will react to its findings." Bob showed Doug and Jerry the following calculations.

Project NPV with test marketing

= Probability (success) × NPV (investing in successful project)

+ Probability (failure) × NPV (not investing in failing project)

− Cost of Test Market

Project NPV with test marketing = 25% × $300,000 + 75% × $0 − $10,000

Project NPV with test marketing = $65,000.

Doug looked in surprise at the number. What the heck was Bob trying to do anyway? But he could not help smiling as he said triumphantly, "So now we should go ahead with this project."

"Not so fast. All this calculation says is that we should go with the test marketing. Only if the test is successful would we go further with the idea and evaluate it at the Business Evaluation Tollgate (BET). After all, the test results may change our thinking about the project. It could be worse or better than we initially thought."

"Of course," Jerry responded. "This is a pretty interesting way to look at this project. What you've shown us is that we would never do this project without test marketing because of the negative $150,000 NPV. But we would be willing to do the test marketing to see if we want to invest in the project."

"Bob, you're a clever devil. I'm beginning to see how this new dynamic, multi-tollgate resource allocation system will help us," Doug said enthusiastically.

2. What are Real Options?

"Well, you've just been introduced to real options.[122] In fact, assessing this project's merits under this approach told us to continue with the project when basic NPV analysis told us not to. The beauty of the options approach is that risk can actually be a good thing."

"How so?" Doug asked.

"Let me allow you to answer that for yourself. Tell me, what is the "risk" in this project anyway?" Bob asked.

"Whether the project succeeds or fails. That is the risk!" Doug said confidently. "That is always the problem with new products. The biggest risk is that the product might flop. And you don't find out until you introduce the product."

"Absolutely. Now, would you say that this project would be even riskier if the NPV in the successful state was doubled to $600,000 and the NPV in the failure state was also doubled to minus $600,000?" asked Bob.

Doug conceded, "Of course. We stand to lose even more if the project bombs."

"What's really interesting," continued Bob, "is to see how our thinking changes now. Look at these calculations." Bob exposed a new page of numbers on the flip chart.

$$\text{Project NPV without test marketing} = 0.25(\$600,000) + 0.75(-\$600,000)$$
$$= -\$300,000$$
$$\text{Project NPV with test marketing} = 0.25(\$600,000) + 0.75(0) - \$10,000$$
$$= \$140,000$$
$$\text{Increased value due to test marketing} = \text{Project NPV with test marketing}$$
$$- \text{Project NPV without test marketing.}$$
$$= \$140,000 - (-\$300,000)$$
$$= \$440,000.$$

When Doug and Jerry had finished going over the calculations, Bob cleared his throat to speak. "So you see how things change, gentlemen. There are two important lessons from this for us. First, as the project becomes riskier,[123] the value added by test marketing improves. You saw how this "value added" went up from

---

[122]For an extended discussion of real options, see Avinash K. Dixit and Robert S. Pindyck, "The Options Approach to Capital Investment," *Harvard Business Review*, May–June 1995, pp. 105–115.

[123]The statistical notion of risk is standard deviation. In this example, the risk of the project NPV increases as its standard deviation increases.

$215,000 to $440,000 as we made the project riskier. Second, the project NPV with test marketing also increased from $65,000 to $140,000."

"What's the story behind these numbers?" asked Jerry.

Bob turned to face Jerry, "Well, there are two ways to look at what's going on. One way is to think of our investment in test marketing as buying an option to invest in the project. We know that options on riskier securities are more valuable. So the value added by test marketing increases from $215,000 to $440,000, due to the greater risk in the project.

The other way to look at this is that investing in test marketing gives us the ability to avoid making the mistake of investing in the project when its NPV is negative. So, as we increase the risk of the project and thus the amount of money we could lose by making a mistake, the value of avoiding the mistake also goes up."

"Bob, are there any examples of companies that do this?" Jerry asked.

"There are lots of companies doing this," Bob said, sitting back in his chair. "Firms in the pharmaceutical and natural resource industries are good examples. Merck and FedEx are just two examples of companies that use option pricing in their capital budgeting decisions.[124] Jonathan Lowell of New England Electric captures the whole idea behind real options in a quote. He said, '[N]ever do anything today if you can wait until tomorrow to decide'."[125]

"Just like our coffee-flavored smoothies," Jerry responded. "There we put off the final decision of whether to fully invest until after the test marketing."

"That's right," Bob said with a smile. "Of course, we may have to worry about what the competition will do while we are testing, but I believe the options approach to evaluating projects would be a great complement to the other tools we have to manage our Value Sphere. It will allow us to bring greater rigor to our assessment of the risks we should take to implement our strategy. I see that we are out of time. But I will leave both of you with more material on approaching this kind of analysis. I will also provide another example, in written form."

Bob gave Doug and Jerry a write-up on real options. The next section contains that writeup.

3. Real Option Concepts

There are two categories of options, "financial" options and "real" options. Financial options are those offering the opportunity to buy or sell financial assets such as stocks, bonds or currencies. In contrast, real options offer the opportunity to buy

---

[124]See Linda Corman, "To Wait or Not to Wait," *CFO Magazine*, May 1997.
[125]Ibid.

or sell real assets such as real estate or capital investment projects. An option to buy a real or financial asset is a "call option," which allows the option holder to buy the underlying asset or security at a specified price for a stated period of time. Alternatively, an option to sell a real or financial asset is a "put option," which allows the option holder to sell the underlying asset or security at a specified price for a stated period of time. In either case, the option holder has the right, but not the obligation, to complete the transaction. The ability for an option holder to let a worthless option expire unexercised is what makes it an option.

Success in utilizing real options analysis in business decision-making requires the early identification of when options exist. Businesses are frequently confronted with multiple options. For example, Fig. 14.2 lists typical real options faced by firms.

4. How do we Value Real Options?

The key to option valuation is the recognition that risk adds to the value of the option. Consider a call option with an exercise price of $100. As shown in Fig. 14.3, the call option is more valuable if the probability distribution of possible future values is A rather than B, because there is a greater probability of the future value exceeding the exercise price of $100.

It is also true that the prospect of achieving a low value is also higher in the case of distribution A. But this does not matter here because if the future value outcome is on the low end, the option holder will let the option expire worthless. The ability to let the option expire unexercised is what allows the option holder to take advantage of the upside potential of a risky bet without worrying about the downside possibilities. The value of the option thus increases with the riskiness of the underlying security.

This understanding leads to a relatively simple valuation model to price options. Consider the hypothetical case where everybody is risk neutral. Risk neutrality means that asset pricing is independent of investor risk preferences. Assets can then be valued easily, since the value of any asset is the expected value of its cash flow discounted at the risk-free rate.

Consider an example where the risk-free rate of interest is 8%. An investment in Zott+Co, currently valued at $100, offers one of two outcomes at the end of one year: increase 50% to $150 or decrease 20% to $80. Given this information, the probability of a price increase in our risk-neutral world can be calculated as

Category	Description	Important in:
1. Option to *defer*	Firm can invest in the project now or later	• Natural resource extraction • Real estate development • Framing • Paper products • Entry into foreign markets
2. *Time to Build* option (staged investment)	Staging investment as a series of outlays creates the option to abandon the project in midstream if the new information is unfavorable	• All R&D-intensive industries (e.g., pharmaceuticals) • Venture capital investments • Long-term development capital intensive projects
3. Option to *alter operating scale* (i.e., to expand or contract; to shut down and restart	Depending on market conditions, the firm can adjust its operating scale	• Natural resource industries like mining operations • Facilities planning and construction in cyclical industries (fashion apparel, consumer goods, commercial real estate, etc.)
4. Option to *abandon*	If market conditions decline severely, management can abandon current operations permanently and realize resale/liquidation/divestiture value	• Capital intensive industries (e.g., airlines, railroads) • Financial services • New product introduction for any company
5. Option to *switch* (e.g., outputs or input)	If prices or demand change, management can change the output mix of the facility (product flexibility) or produce the same outputs using different inputs (process flexibility)	• Output shifts: any goods produced in small batches or subject to volatile demand (e.g., consumer electronics, toys, specialty paper) • Input shifts: any industry with input/process flexibility (e.g., feedstock-dependent facilities like oil, electric power, chemicals, etc.) • Flexible manufacturing sites
6. Growth options	Any early investment that opens up future growth opportunities	• R&D • Entry into a new/foreign market (e.g., China or India) • New product development
7. Multiple interacting options	Real-life projects often involve options of many different types that interact so that the total value of these options exceeds the sum of the individual option values	• Many real-life projects, especially new product ideas with multiple testing, marketing and production alternatives

Fig. 14.2. Option categories and uses.
Source: Adapted from Table 1.1 in Lenos Trigeorgis, *Real Options in Capital Investment*, Lenos Trigeorgis, Praeger, 1995.

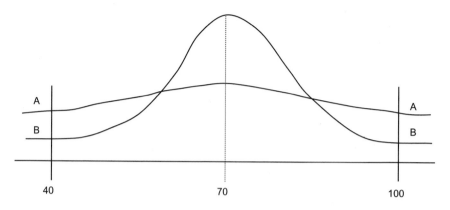

Fig. 14.3.   Probability distributions of future values.

follows:

$$\text{Expected Return} = (\text{probability of increase})(\% \text{ increase})$$
$$+ (1 - \text{probability of increase})(\% \text{ decrease})$$
$$8\% = p(50\%) + (1 - p)(-20\%)$$
$$0.08 = 0.5p - 0.2 + 0.2p$$
$$0.28 = 0.7p$$
$$p = 0.4 = 40\% = \text{probability of a price increase.}$$

Of course, people are not really risk neutral. Since most people are risk averse, we just need to make a simple adjustment. In that case, the 40% calculated above should not be interpreted as the actual likelihood of a price increase. Rather, it is called a "risk-neutral probability." That is, it is a number that helps us use the "no-arbitrage" relationship between the current price and possible future prices. This is the relationship that ensures that the current price is not out of line with possible future prices, permitting someone a risk-free arbitrage opportunity. With risk aversion, the actual probability of a price increase would be something else, say 50%. The risk neutral probability depends on the actual probability and how risk-averse investors are.

Now consider a call option that enables the buyer to purchase Zott + Co in one year for a price of $110. Thus, if the value of Zott + Co declines to $80, the call option will be worthless. If the value increases to $150, the option will be worth $40, i.e., ($150–$110). The expected value of the option in one year is, therefore:

Expected Option Value = (risk-neutral probability of increase) ($payoff)

+ (1 − risk-neutral probability of increase) ($0)

= 0.40($40) + (0.60)($0)

= $16.

Since this is the value of the option in one year, we must discount it at the risk-free rate to determine its present value:

Option value today = Option value in 1 year/[1 + risk-free rate]

$$= \frac{\$16}{1.08} = \$14.81.$$

This simple arbitrage-free valuation approach to options is a powerful construct. It leads to a generalized formula to value options when there is a continuous distribution of investment values. Our example was very simple because there were only two possible outcomes for the future value of the investment. In general, when there is a continuum of values, we end up with a more complex valuation model. Such a model was developed by Fisher Black and Myron Scholes.[126] The formula they derived is:

$$\text{Call option value} = PN(d_1) - Xe^{-R_{ft}}N(d_1)$$

where:

$$d_1 = \frac{\log(P/X) + R_{ft} + [\sigma^2 t/2]}{\sigma\sqrt{t}}$$

$$d_2 = \frac{\log(P/X) + R_{ft} - [\sigma^2 t/2]}{\sigma\sqrt{t}}$$

N(d) = cumulative normal probability distribution

X = exercise price of the option

t = time to exercise the option

P = price of stock at present

σ = standard deviation of the return on the stock per unit of time

(continuously compounded)

---

[126]Fisher Black and Myron Scholes, "The Pricing of Options and Corporate Liabilities," *Journal of Political Economy*, Vol. 81, May–June 1973, pp. 637–654.

R_f = (instantaneous) riskfree rate of interest per unit of time

(continuously compounded)

$\sigma\sqrt{t}$ = volatility = standard deviation of stock return × square root of time.

The good news is that it is rather easy to use this complex formula. The Black–Scholes option valuation model can be simplified to two dimensions: standard deviation of returns multiplied by the square root of time, and current value of the investment divided by exercise price (P/x).[127] The numbers in Table 14.1 give the value of the option as a percent of the current value of the investment. We will use the Black–Scholes approach in a case study to follow.

5. Black–Scholes Option Pricing: A Resource Allocation Case Study

To illustrate the use of the Black–Scholes model, consider the following research and development project.

Case Study

ABC Company is a large, mid-western manufacturing firm that is in the business of producing automotive parts for the "big three" US automobile manufacturers. They compete for this supply business with other large concerns in each of their product areas: drive trains and braking systems. All competitors essentially fight for the same business and the auto companies are famous for playing one supplier against the others. Generally, only one supplier wins each particular contract put out for bids.

Ralph, the manager of the braking systems group, wants to invest in R&D now to develop the ABC Brake, which is a technical advance over the ABC braking system now used in most vehicles. The R&D will be completed this year and next and will produce the cash flows shown in Fig. 14.4 (found at end of the chapter.)

Unfortunately, the NPV of the proposal is −$0.985 million at the company's 10% hurdle rate. Therefore, it does not pass the criteria established for project selection at ABC. However, management has a strong interest in developing the ABC Brake now because it would enable the company to develop the ABC Brake II, which promises an even more advanced braking system that would be a desirable addition to almost all vehicles if it turns out as planned. If the ABC R&D project is not started now, the company will not be able to enter the Brake II market because

---

[127] The two-dimensional table for Black–Scholes option valuation can be found in Richard Brealey and Stewart Myers, *Principles of Corporate Finance*, Fifth Edition, McGraw-Hill, 1996.

Table 14.1. Call option values, percent of share price.

Share price divided by PV (Exercise price)

Standard deviation times square root of time	.40	.45	.50	.55	.60	.65	.70	.75	.80	.82	.84	.86	.88	.90	.92	.94	.96	.98	1.00
.05	.0	.0	.0	.0	.0	.0	.0	.0	.0	.0	.0	.0	.0	.0	.1	.3	.6	1.2	2.0
.10	.0	.0	.0	.0	.0	.0	.0	.0	.0	.2	.3	.5	.5	.8	1.2	1.7	2.3	3.1	4.0
.15	.0	.0	.0	.0	.0	.0	.1	.2	.5	1.0	1.3	1.3	1.7	2.2	2.8	3.5	4.2	5.1	6.0
.20	.0	.0	.0	.0	.0	.1	.4	.8	1.5	2.3	2.8	2.8	3.4	4.0	4.7	5.4	6.2	7.1	8.0
.25	.0	.0	.0	.1	.2	.5	1.0	1.8	2.8	3.9	4.5	4.5	5.2	5.9	6.6	7.4	8.2	9.1	9.9
.30	.0	.1	.1	.3	.7	1.2	2.0	3.1	4.4	5.7	6.3	6.3	7.0	7.8	8.6	9.4	10.2	11.1	11.9
.35	.1	.2	.4	.8	1.4	2.3	3.3	4.6	6.2	7.5	8.2	8.2	9.0	9.8	10.6	11.4	12.2	13.0	13.9
.40	.2	.5	.9	1.6	2.4	3.5	4.8	6.3	8.0	9.4	10.2	10.2	11.0	11.7	12.5	13.4	14.2	15.0	15.9
.45	.5	1.0	1.7	2.6	3.7	5.0	6.5	8.1	9.9	11.4	12.2	12.2	12.9	13.7	14.5	15.3	16.2	17.0	17.8
.50	1.0	1.7	2.6	3.7	5.1	6.6	8.2	10.0	11.8	13.4	14.2	14.2	14.9	15.7	16.5	17.3	18.1	18.9	19.7
.55	1.7	2.6	3.8	5.1	6.6	8.3	10.0	11.9	13.8	15.4	16.1	16.1	16.9	17.7	18.5	19.3	20.1	20.9	21.7
.60	2.5	3.7	5.1	6.6	8.3	10.1	11.9	13.8	15.8	17.4	18.1	18.1	18.9	19.7	20.5	21.3	22.0	22.8	23.6
.65	3.6	4.9	6.5	8.2	10.0	11.9	13.8	15.8	17.8	19.3	20.1	20.1	20.9	21.7	22.5	23.2	24.0	24.7	25.5
.70	4.7	6.3	8.1	9.9	11.9	13.8	15.8	17.8	19.8	21.3	22.1	22.1	22.9	23.6	24.4	25.2	25.9	26.6	27.4
.75	6.1	7.9	9.8	11.7	13.7	15.8	17.8	19.8	21.8	23.3	24.1	24.1	24.8	25.6	26.3	27.1	27.8	28.5	29.2
.80	7.5	9.5	11.5	13.6	15.7	17.7	19.8	21.8	23.7	25.3	26.0	26.0	26.8	27.5	28.3	29.0	29.7	30.4	31.1
.85	9.1	11.2	13.3	15.5	17.6	19.7	21.8	23.8	25.7	27.2	28.0	28.0	28.7	29.4	30.2	30.9	31.6	32.2	32.9
.90	10.7	13.0	15.2	17.4	19.6	21.7	23.8	25.8	27.7	29.2	29.9	29.9	30.6	31.3	32.0	32.7	33.4	34.1	34.7
.95	12.5	14.8	17.1	19.4	21.6	23.7	25.7	27.7	29.6	31.1	31.8	31.8	32.5	33.2	33.9	34.6	35.2	35.9	36.5
1.00	14.3	16.7	19.1	21.4	23.6	25.7	27.7	29.7	31.6	33.0	33.7	33.7	34.4	35.1	35.7	36.4	37.0	37.0	38.3

(Continued)

Table 14.1. (Continued)

	.40	.45	.50	.55	.60	.65	.70	.75	.80	.82	.84	.86	.88	.90	.92	.94	.96	.98	1.00
1.05	16.1	18.6	21.0	23.3	25.6	27.7	29.7	31.6	33.5	34.9	35.6	35.6	36.2	36.9	37.6	38.2	38.8	39.4	40.0
1.10	18.0	20.6	23.3	25.3	27.5	29.6	31.6	33.5	35.4	36.7	37.4	37.4	38.1	38.7	39.3	40.0	40.6	41.2	41.8
1.15	20.0	22.5	25.0	27.3	29.5	31.6	33.6	35.4	37.2	38.6	39.2	39.2	39.9	40.5	41.1	41.7	42.3	42.9	43.5
1.20	21.9	24.5	27.0	29.3	31.5	33.6	35.5	37.3	39.1	40.4	41.0	41.0	41.7	42.3	42.9	43.5	44.0	44.6	45.1
1.25	23.9	26.5	29.0	31.3	33.5	35.5	37.4	39.2	40.9	42.2	42.8	42.8	43.4	44.0	44.6	45.2	45.7	46.3	46.8
1.30	25.9	28.5	31.0	33.3	35.4	37.4	39.3	41.0	42.7	43.9	44.5	44.5	45.1	45.7	46.3	46.8	47.4	47.9	48.4
1.35	27.9	30.5	33.0	35.2	37.3	39.3	41.1	42.8	44.4	45.7	46.3	46.3	46.8	47.4	47.9	48.5	49.0	49.5	50.0
1.40	29.9	32.5	34.9	37.1	39.2	41.1	42.9	44.6	46.2	47.4	47.9	47.9	48.5	49.0	49.6	50.1	50.6	51.1	51.6
1.45	31.9	34.5	36.9	39.1	41.1	43.0	44.7	46.4	47.9	49.0	49.6	49.6	50.1	50.7	51.2	51.7	52.2	52.7	53.2
1.50	33.8	36.4	38.8	40.9	42.9	44.8	46.5	48.1	49.6	50.7	51.2	51.2	51.8	52.3	52.8	53.3	53.7	54.2	54.7
1.55	35.8	38.4	40.7	42.8	44.8	46.6	48.2	49.8	51.2	52.3	52.8	52.8	53.3	53.8	54.3	54.8	55.3	55.7	56.2
1.60	37.8	40.3	42.6	44.6	46.5	48.3	49.9	51.4	52.8	53.9	42.4	54.4	54.9	55.4	55.9	56.3	56.8	57.2	57.6
1.65	39.7	42.2	44.4	46.4	48.3	50.0	51.6	53.1	54.4	55.4	55.9	55.9	56.4	56.9	57.3	57.8	58.2	58.6	59.1
1.70	41.6	44.0	46.2	48.2	50.0	51.7	53.2	54.7	56.0	57.0	57.5	57.5	57.9	58.4	58.8	59.2	59.7	60.1	60.5
1.75	43.5	45.9	48.0	50.0	51.7	53.4	54.8	56.2	57.5	58.5	58.9	58.9	59.4	59.8	60.2	60.7	61.1	61.5	61.8
2.00	52.5	54.6	56.5	58.2	59.7	61.1	62.4	63.6	64.6	65.4	65.8	65.8	66.2	66.6	66.9	67.3	67.6	67.9	68.3
2.25	60.7	62.5	64.1	65.6	66.8	68.0	69.1	70.0	70.9	71.6	71.9	71.9	72.2	72.5	72.8	73.1	73.4	73.7	73.9
2.50	67.9	69.4	70.8	72.0	73.1	74.0	74.9	75.7	76.4	77.0	77.2	77.2	77.5	77.7	78.0	78.2	78.4	78.4	78.9
2.75	74.2	75.4	76.6	77.5	78.4	79.2	79.9	80.5	81.1	81.6	81.8	81.8	82.0	82.2	82.4	82.6	82.7	82.7	83.1
3.00	79.5	80.5	81.4	82.2	82.9	83.5	84.1	84.6	85.1	85.4	85.6	85.6	85.8	85.9	86.1	86.2	86.4	86.4	86.6
3.50	87.6	88.3	88.8	89.3	89.7	90.1	90.5	90.8	91.1	91.3	91.4	91.4	91.5	91.6	91.6	91.7	91.8	91.9	92.0
4.00	92.9	93.3	93.6	93.9	94.2	94.4	94.6	94.8	94.9	95.0	95.1	95.1	95.2	95.2	95.3	95.3	95.4	95.4	95.4
4.50	96.2	96.4	96.6	96.7	96.9	97.0	97.1	97.2	97.3	97.3	97.4	97.4	97.4	97.4	97.5	97.5	97.5	97.5	97.6
5.00	98.1	98.2	98.3	98.3	98.4	98.5	98.5	98.6	98.6	98.6	98.7	98.7	98.7	98.7	98.7	98.7	98.7	98.7	98.8

(Continued)

Standard deviation times square root of time

Table 14.1. (Continued)

1.02	1.04	1.06	1.08	1.10	1.12	1.14	1.16	1.18	1.20	1.25	1.30	1.35	1.40	1.45	1.50	1.75	2.00	2.50	
3.1	4.5	6.0	7.5	9.1	10.7	12.3	13.8	15.3	16.7	20.0	23.1	25.9	28.6	31.0	33.3	42.9	50.0	60.0	.05
5.0	6.1	7.3	8.6	10.0	11.3	12.7	14.1	15.4	16.8	20.0	23.1	25.9	28.6	31.0	33.3	42.9	50.0	60.0	.10
7.0	8.0	9.1	10.2	11.4	12.6	13.8	15.0	16.2	17.4	20.4	23.3	26.0	28.6	31.1	33.3	42.9	50.0	60.0	.15
8.9	9.9	10.9	11.9	13.0	14.1	15.2	16.3	17.4	18.5	21.2	23.9	26.4	28.9	31.2	33.5	42.9	50.0	60.0	.20
10.9	11.8	12.8	13.7	14.7	15.7	16.7	17.7	18.7	19.8	22.3	24.7	27.1	29.4	31.7	33.8	42.9	50.0	60.0	.25
12.8	13.7	14.6	15.6	16.5	17.4	18.4	19.3	20.3	21.2	23.5	25.8	28.1	30.2	32.3	34.3	43.1	50.1	60.0	.30
14.8	15.6	16.5	17.4	18.3	19.2	20.1	21.0	21.9	22.7	24.9	27.1	29.2	31.2	33.2	35.1	43.5	50.2	60.0	.35
16.7	17.5	18.4	19.2	20.1	20.9	21.8	22.6	23.5	24.3	26.4	28.4	30.4	32.3	34.2	36.0	44.0	50.5	60.1	.40
18.6	19.4	20.3	21.1	21.9	22.7	23.5	24.3	25.1	25.9	27.9	29.8	31.7	33.5	35.3	37.0	44.6	50.8	60.2	.45
20.5	21.3	22.1	22.9	23.7	24.5	25.3	26.1	26.8	27.6	29.5	31.3	33.1	34.8	36.4	38.1	45.3	51.3	60.4	.50
22.4	23.2	24.0	24.8	25.5	26.3	27.0	27.8	28.5	29.2	31.0	32.8	34.5	36.1	37.7	39.2	46.1	51.9	60.7	.55
24.3	25.1	25.8	26.6	27.3	28.1	28.8	29.5	30.2	30.9	32.6	34.3	35.9	37.5	39.0	40.4	47.0	52.5	61.0	.60
26.2	27.0	27.7	28.4	29.1	29.8	30.5	31.2	31.9	32.6	34.2	35.8	37.4	38.9	40.3	41.7	48.0	53.3	61.4	.65
28.1	28.8	29.5	30.2	30.9	31.6	32.3	32.9	33.6	34.2	35.8	37.3	38.8	40.3	41.6	43.0	49.0	54.0	61.9	.70
29.9	30.6	31.3	32.0	32.7	33.3	34.0	34.6	35.3	35.9	37.4	38.9	40.3	41.7	43.0	44.3	50.0	54.9	62.4	.75
31.8	32.4	33.1	33.8	34.4	35.1	35.7	36.3	36.9	37.5	39.0	40.4	41.8	43.1	44.4	45.6	51.1	55.8	63.0	.80
33.6	34.2	34.9	35.5	36.2	36.8	37.4	38.0	38.6	39.2	40.6	41.9	43.3	44.5	45.8	46.9	52.2	56.7	63.6	.85
35.4	36.0	36.6	37.3	37.9	38.5	39.1	39.6	40.2	40.8	42.1	43.5	44.7	46.0	47.1	48.3	53.3	57.6	64.3	.90
37.2	37.8	38.4	39.0	39.6	40.1	40.7	41.3	41.8	42.4	43.7	45.0	46.2	47.4	48.5	49.6	54.5	586	65.0	.95
38.9	39.5	40.1	40.7	41.2	41.8	42.4	42.9	43.4	44.0	45.2	46.5	47.6	48.8	49.9	50.9	55.6	59.5	65.7	1.00

(Continued)

Table 14.1. (*Continued*)

1.02	1.04	1.06	1.08	1.10	1.12	1.14	1.16	1.18	1.20	1.25	1.30	1.35	1.40	1.45	1.50	1.75	2.00	2.50	
40.6	41.2	41.8	42.4	42.9	43.5	44.0	44.5	45.0	45.5	46.8	48.0	49.1	50.2	51.2	52.2	56.7	60.5	66.5	1.05
42.3	42.9	43.5	44.0	44.5	45.1	45.6	46.1	46.6	47.1	48.3	49.4	50.5	51.6	52.6	53.5	57.9	61.5	67.2	1.10
44.0	44.6	45.1	45.6	46.2	46.7	47.2	47.7	48.2	48.6	49.8	50.9	51.9	52.9	53.9	54.9	59.0	62.5	68.0	1.15
45.7	46.2	46.7	47.3	47.8	48.3	48.7	49.2	49.7	50.1	51.3	52.3	53.3	54.3	55.2	56.1	60.2	63.5	68.8	1.20
47.3	47.8	48.4	48.8	49.3	49.8	50.3	50.7	51.2	51.6	52.7	53.7	54.7	55.7	56.6	57.4	61.3	64.5	69.6	1.25
48.9	49.4	49.9	50.4	50.9	51.3	51.8	52.2	52.7	53.1	54.1	55.1	56.1	57.0	57.9	58.7	62.4	65.5	70.4	1.30
50.5	51.0	51.5	52.0	52.4	52.9	53.3	53.7	54.1	56.4	55.6	56.5	57.4	58.3	59.1	59.9	63.5	66.5	71.1	1.35
52.1	52.6	53.0	53.5	53.9	54.3	54.8	55.2	55.6	56.0	56.9	57.9	58.7	59.6	60.4	61.2	64.6	67.5	71.9	1.40
53.6	54.1	54.5	55.0	55.4	55.8	56.2	56.6	57.0	57.4	58.3	59.2	60.0	60.9	61.6	62.4	65.7	68.4	72.7	1.45
55.1	55.6	56.0	56.4	56.8	57.2	57.6	58.0	58.4	58.8	59.7	60.5	61.3	62.1	62.9	63.6	66.8	69.4	73.5	1.50
56.6	57.0	57.4	57.8	58.2	58.6	59.0	59.4	59.7	60.1	61.0	61.8	62.6	63.3	64.1	64.7	67.8	70.3	74.3	1.55
58.0	58.5	58.9	59.2	59.6	60.0	60.4	60.7	61.1	61.4	62.3	43.1	63.8	64.5	65.2	65.9	68.8	71.3	75.1	1.60
59.5	59.9	60.2	60.6	61.0	61.4	61.7	62.1	62.4	62.7	63.5	64.3	65.0	65.7	66.4	67.0	69.9	72.2	75.9	1.65
60.9	61.2	61.6	62.0	62.3	62.7	63.0	63.4	63.7	64.0	64.8	65.5	66.2	66.9	67.5	68.2	70.9	73.1	76.6	1.70
62.2	62.6	62.9	63.3	63.6	64.0	64.3	64.6	64.9	65.3	66.0	66.7	67.4	68.0	68.7	69.2	71.9	74.0	77.4	1.75
68.6	68.9	69.2	69.5	69.8	70.0	70.3	70.6	70.8	71.1	71.7	72.3	72.9	73.4	73.9	74.4	76.5	78.3	81.0	2.00
74.2	74.4	74.7	74.9	75.2	75.4	75.6	75.8	46.0	76.3	76.8	77.2	77.7	78.1	78.5	78.9	80.6	82.1	84.3	2.25
79.1	79.3	79.5	79.7	79.9	80.0	80.2	80.4	80.6	80.7	81.1	81.5	81.9	82.2	82.6	82.9	84.3	85.4	87.2	2.5
83.3	83.4	83.6	83.7	83.9	84.0	84.2	84.3	84.4	84.6	84.9	85.2	85.5	85.8	86.0	86.3	87.4	88.3	89.7	2.75
86.8	86.9	87.0	87.1	87.3	87.4	87.5	87.6	87.7	87.8	88.1	88.3	88.5	88.8	89.0	89.2	90.0	90.7	91.8	3.00
92.1	92.2	92.2	92.3	92.4	92.4	92.5	92.6	92.6	92.7	92.8	93.0	93.1	93.3	93.4	93.5	94.0	94.4	95.1	3.50
95.5	95.5	95.6	95.6	95.7	95.7	95.7	95.8	95.8	95.8	95.9	96.0	96.1	96.2	96.2	96.3	96.6	96.8	97.2	4.00
97.6	97.6	97.6	97.6	97.7	97.7	97.7	97.7	97.8	97.8	97.8	97.9	97.9	97.9	98.0	98.0	98.2	98.3	98.5	4.50
98.8	98.8	98.8	98.8	98.8	98.8	98.8	98.8	98.9	98.9	98.9	98.9	98.9	99.0	99.0	99.0	99.1	99.1	99.2	5.00

(*Continued*)

	2002	2003	2004	2005	2006	2007	2008
				Year			
Net sales:							
Units			1,000,000	1,000,000	1,000,000	1,000,000	1,000,000
Price per unit			$25.00	$25.00	$25.00	$25.00	$25.00
Total sales			$25,000	$25,000	$25,000	$25,000	$25,000
Production costs							
Cost per unit			$19.00	$19.00	$19.00	$19.00	$19.00
Total prod. costs			$19,000	$19,000	$19,000	$19,000	$19,000
Gross profit			$6,000	$6,000	$6,000	$6,000	$6,000
Marketing and distribution expense:							
Expense per unit			$3.00	$3.00	$3.00	$3.00	$3.00
Total marketing costs			$3,000	$3,000	$3,000	$3,000	$3,000
General and administrative expense			$2,000	$2,000	$2,000	$2,000	$2,000
R&D Expense	$3,000		$—	$—	$—	$—	$—
Depreciation on facilities			$1,300	$1,300	$1,300	$1,300	$1,300
Profit before taxes	$(3,000)		$1,700	$1,700	$1,700	$1,700	$1,700
Taxes 40%	$(1,200)		$680	$680	$680	$680	$680
Net profit	$(1,800)		$1,020	$1,020	$1,020	$1,020	$1,020
Depreciation			$1,300	$1,300	$1,300	$1,300	$1,300
Cash flow from operations	$(1,800)	$—	$2,320	$2,320	$2,320	$2,320	$2,320

Fig. 14.4. ABC brake analysis.

	2002	2003	2004	2005	2006	2007	2008
							Contract renewal?
Facilities		$(13,000)					
Working capital		$(3,750)					
Total yearly cash flows	$(1,800)	$(16,750)	$2,320	$2,320	$2,320	$2,320	$2,320
Terminal value							$14,255
Total cash flows	$(1,800)	$(16,750)	$2,320	$2,320	$2,320	$2,320	$16,575
PV Factor @ 10%	1	0.909	0.826	0.751	0.683	0.621	0.564
Present value	$(1,800)	$(15,277)	$1,917	$1,743	$1,585	$1,441	$9,356
NPV if ABC gets contract	$(985)						

Fig. 14.4. (*Continued*)

the competition will be firmly established in the marketplace with alternative technologies. If the project is approved now, the company has the opportunity to make the follow-on investments in the Brake II concept that could be highly profitable. Thus, the proposed ABC Brake project gives the company its own cash flow as well as a call option to continue with the subsequent development of the Brake II system. It is that call option which can be a source of strategic value.

Of course, the Brake II project itself could be good or bad, since it is highly uncertain. The preliminary analysis in Fig. 14.5 (found at the end of the chapter) confirms this, because the NPV of the Brake II project as of today is –$1.494 million. It seems strange that one would want to invest in a negative NPV project (Brake I) to have the option to invest in another negative NPV project (Brake II).

However, it is the uncertainty that gives the call option potential value. If the development of the brake technology is successful, ABC stands to make a lot of money. On the other hand, if the development is unsuccessful, ABC has the opportunity to abandon the project. In order to determine the value of the option, Ralph offered the following assumptions in support of his idea to start the ABC Brake R&D now.

1. The decision to invest in the Brake II must be made at the end of two years.
2. The ABC Brake II is double the scale of the ABC Brake market. In other words, the units sold are twice as much as the ABC Brake project.
3. The investment required for the Brake II project is $37.1 million after taxes: $3.6 million for R&D, $26 million for facilities, and $7.5 million for working capital. This total represents the exercise price of the call option.
4. The future value of the Brake II project is highly uncertain. The value is expected to evolve with a standard deviation of 35% per year. This is consistent with the variation of returns for high technology stocks and with the past history of ABC's R&D projects.
5. The annual risk-free rate of interest is 5%.

Solution to Case Study

Using these assumptions, Ralph was able to value the call option of the ABC Brake II project as follows:

$$\text{Asset value} = \text{PV of cash inflows:}$$
$$\text{PV of cash inflows} = \text{NPV} + \text{PV of outflows}$$
$$= -\$1.494 + \$30.661$$
$$= \$29.167 \text{ million from Fig. 14.5.}$$

					Year			
	2002	2003	2004	2005	2006	2007	2008	2009
Net sales:								
Units				2,000,000	2,000,000	2,000,000	2,000,000	2,000,000
Price per unit				$25.00	$25.00	$25.00	$25.00	$25.00
Total sales				$50,000	$50,000	$50,000	$50,000	$50,000
Production costs								
Cost per unit				$19.00	$19.00	$19.00	$19.00	$19.00
Total prod. costs				$38,000	$38,000	$38,000	$38,000	$38,000
Gross profit				$12,000	$12,000	$12,000	$12,000	$12,000
Marketing and distribution expense:								
Expense per unit				$3.00	$3.00	$3.00	$3.00	$3.00
Total marketing costs				$6,000	$6,000	$6,000	$6,000	$6,000
General and administrative expense				$4,000	$4,000	$4,000	$4,000	$4,000
R&D expense			$6,000	$—	$—	$—	$—	$—
Depreciation on facilities				$2,600	$2,600	$2,600	$2,600	$2,600
Profit before taxes			$(6,000)	$3,400	$3,400	$3,400	$3,400	$3,400
Taxes 40%			$(2,400)	$1,360	$1,360	$1,360	$1,360	$1,360
Net profit			$(3,600)	$2,040	$2,040	$2,040	$2,040	$2,040
Depreciation				$2,600	$2,600	$2,600	$2,600	$2,600

Fig. 14.5. ABC brake II analysis.

				Year				
	2002	2003	2004	2005	2006	2007	2008	2009
Cash flow from operations			$(3,600)	$4,640	$4,640	$4,640	$4,640	$4,640
								Contract renewal?
Facilities			$(26,000)					
Working capital			$(7,500)					
Total yearly cash flows			$(37,100)	$4,640	$4,640	$4,640	$4,640	$4,640
Terminal value								$28,511
Total cash flows			$(37,100)	$4,640	$4,640	$4,640	$4,640	$33,151
PV factor @ 10%	1	0.909	0.826	0.751	0.683	0.621	0.564	0.513
Present value of inflows	$—	$—		$3,486	$3,169	$2,881	$2,619	$17,012
Total	$29,167							
Present value of outflows	$(30,661)							
NPV if ABC gets contract	$(1,494)							

Fig. 14.5. *(Continued)*

PV of exercise price using the risk-free rate as the discount rate

$= $ PV of $37.1 in 2 years

$= \$37.1/(1.05)2 = 37.1/1.1025 = \$33.65$

Ratio of asset value to PV of exercise price $= \dfrac{\$29.17}{\$33.65} = 0.87.$

Call value $= 14\%$ of asset value (from Table 14.1 for a cumulative volatility of 0.495 and a ratio of 0.87).

Asset value $= 0.14 \times \$29.167 = \$4.08$ million.

Seen in light of the option possibilities, the total value of the ABC Brake R&D project is approximately $3.1 million (($0.985) + $4.08). Clearly, the project should be undertaken, even though its NPV is negative and the stand-alone NPV of the possible follow-on investment in Brake II is negative as well.[128]

Notes to Real Options Case Study

This case study illustrates how options thinking can improve our analysis of strategic investment alternatives. The high risk of the R&D proposal, captured by the volatility variable in the Black-Scholes model, adds to its value. Since the R&D project is an option to reserve the right to invest in a future business, it can be allowed to expire if the R&D results are not promising. The ability to abandon is what makes high-risk R&D projects valuable. Incremental R&D projects, those with low values of volatility, are less valuable than high-risk R&D projects with the promise of very high payoffs. Thus, the options approach tells us to accept and manage the risk inherent in truly breakthrough projects with high option value that will position the company in a new strategic dimension, even when the NPVs of such projects are negative. The key to value creation is to control the risk during the R&D process.

There are two other issues concerning this project. First, we are assuming that we know the exact details of the follow on investment, i.e., the cost in 2 years, its value, etc. In practice these estimates are likely to change during the two year period. Second, and most important, we are assuming that the projects face no competition. However, if competitors also have similar investment options, then the analysis presented here is too simplified. Our options and the competitor's options would affect each other's value, greatly complicating the analysis. In fact, we would have to consider game theory to accurately map the competitor's response to our initiative.

---

[128]Using Table 1 can be rather limiting because one has to do quite a bit of interpolation to get values that do not show up in the table. There is, however, a software package available that allows one to compute real options values by just pointing and clicking. It is *Risk-Strategist*[TM], available from *Value Integration Associates*, 216 W. Allen Street, Ste. 122, Bloomington, IN 47403. Also visit www.risk-strategist.com.

6. Options Thinking Gives Jerry a Fresh Strategic Perspective

As Jerry finished reading Bob's write-up on options, he realized there was a lot of work to be done. They now had a world-class resource allocation system. They also had an options valuation approach to look at things like new products and R&D. Some of these ideas had earlier been rejected based on NPV analyses, but the options approach would provide a fresh strategic perspective. He agreed with Bob that options would be a good part of their tool kit to manage the Value Sphere. The problem was that there was a big gap between the level of sophistication in these approaches and the skills of the financial analysts in the company. How could the gap be closed?

Jerry asked Katie to set up a meeting with Barb Sidwell, his VP of HR, and Bob. At the meeting, Jerry asked Barb and Bob to develop a training seminar for the financial analysts. Bob turned to Barb and asked, "How many people will we have in the target audience, Barb?"

"Well, including regional controllers, I'd say about 30," said Barb, "although I wonder if we should include some of our key sales and marketing people."

"Why would we want to do that?" asked Jerry.

Barb looked at Bob, paused, and replied, "Because I think it's important to have a cross-functional audience if we're going to have all these different functions involved in our new resource allocation process. Furthermore, our sales and marketing groups need to utilize option thinking when negotiating with large customers and supplies."

"Barb is right," said Bob, "We can't just limit this to our finance and accounting folks."

Jerry gave his OK and the meeting adjourned.

Main Lessons

- Options thinking forces the organization to consider multiple ways to do investment projects. This should lead to greater creativity and a sharper focus on value creation.
- Options thinking promotes contingency planning that leads to better and more efficient project execution. It is thus a useful component of a synchronized Value Sphere.
- Option valuation approaches explicitly recognizes the value impacts of:
  - Time • Flexibility • Staged investment
- Option approaches facilitate investing in high-risk and negative NPV projects but call for careful thinking about ways to control risk.

- The dynamic capital budgeting system is designed to incorporate an options approach to project evaluation because of its requirements of multiple alternatives as projects pass through multiple tollgates.

End-of-Chapter Exercises

1. Identify actual examples of real options embedded in the investment projects at your company. For each example, classify the option element of the project into the categories listed in Fig. 14.2. How was the option value determined?
2. Does your project evaluation system require that multiple project *alternatives* be specified at each stage of the decision-making process?
3. How would you implement options thinking and options valuation techniques in your company? What organizational issues must be dealt with for successful implementation?
4. How would you train your financial analysts to use an options valuation approach in your company?

Practice Problems

1. Determine the value for the following call option to buy stock for $60/share in three years.

   Risk free rate = 6%
   Current stock price = $50/share
   $\sigma = 30\%$

   Comment on the key drivers of value for this option.
2. You calculate the NPV of an investment in a new product to be a negative $2 million. However, the marketing director suggests that you undertake a test market of the product for $1 million after taxes. Currently the product has a 40% chance of success which has an NPV of +$10 million and a 60% chance of failure having a negative $10 million NPV. The test market will unequivocally determine whether the product will turn out to be a success or failure. Is it financially advisable to undertake the test market? What strategic concerns do you have?
3. Your R&D lab has an interesting proposition for you. If you invest $2 million today you will have the opportunity to invest in a project to produce no-carb pizza in three years. At that time the pizza product calls for an investment of $10 million to implement. Unfortunately, the investment currently has a negative

NPV of $3 million, assuming a present value of $7 million for the cash inflows. Nonetheless, it could be highly profitable given the popularity of pizza and low carb diets. The R&D group suggests that a real options analysis may prove that the investment in the pizza R&D is a worthy project. They estimate based on their analysis, including Monte Carlo simulations of the project that $\sigma = 40\%$ and risk free rate $= 6\%$. Should you invest in this R&D? What are your concerns about the pizza projects?

4. Why is risk valuable in a real options analysis? Does this mean companies should undertake a portfolio of risky projects in order to create value for their shareholders?

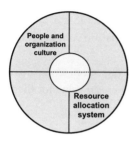

Chapter 15

COMPREHENSIVE RESOURCE
ALLOCATION: A TRAINING
SEMINAR

1. Training the Troops

This chapter contains the case and solution given out during the resource allocation training seminar that Barb and Bob organized and delivered. It illustrates
Jerry's new resource allocation process. The case begins with a summary of the relevant information for a new product idea that was gathered during the preliminary
evaluation phase.[128] Participants in the training seminar were asked to carry out
the financial analysis at both the preliminary evaluation tollgate and the business
evaluation tollgate. Bob's solution — given as his example of best practice —
follows.

2. Preliminary Evaluation Tollgate — December 31, 2003

Jerry's Nutritional Food Division has proposed the introduction of new nutritional
sports drinks. With the ever-increasing demands in today's society to both work
hard and play hard, sport and fitness are becoming important parts of everyday
life. The Project Team (PT) believes that it has developed a new range of drinks
designed to help increase physical performance.

The drinks come in two forms. First, there is the carbonated variety, Nitro
Fitness, with its complex carbohydrates that provide slow-releasing and long-lasting

---

[128]This summary constitutes roughly half the items required by Jerry's team for project proposals being
reviewed at the preliminary evaluation tollgate. See Chapter 13 for a full list of these items.

energy, along with added iron to aid the body in converting the carbohydrates into energy. These drinks will come in a variety of flavors including lemonade, blueberry, raspberry, and strawberry. Because they all contain real fruit, they are all rich in natural vitamin C. The proposed recipe also calls for added vitamin B for stress release. Without relying on the dehydrating and potentially nerve-damaging use of caffeine, Nitro Fitness' special ingredients are intended to help rehydrate the body and replace essential nutrients, thereby increasing energy levels.

Second, the PT plan to introduce a milk-based product as well, Nitro Shakes, offering all the benefits of natural calcium, and vitamin A. Using skim milk as a base, the product remains low in fat but high in protein. This recipe calls for added iron, vitamin C, and zinc to boost the immune system, glucose to replace lost energy, and vitamin B to aid the nervous system. These will also come in a variety of flavors such as chocolate, strawberry and vanilla, as well as the more unusual combinations of peanut butter-banana, blueberry-cranberry, and raspberry-lemonade.

The PT proposes to carry out a broad marketing campaign. Naturally, both drinks will be pitched to the sporting types. However, the PT plans to extensively push the slogan: "You don't have to be a top athlete to make the most out of Nitro drinks." Business executives, rushing between meetings, use up a lot of energy. For these people, Nitro Fitness can help replenish that lost energy. Moreover, Nitro Shakes could be marketed as excellent meal replacements for those too busy to stop for breakfast or lunch.

What is Nitro bringing to the marketplace that is not offered by other sports drinks? The PT proposes to make the centerpiece of its advertising campaign the fact that the recipes call for only organic ingredients, thereby insuring the absence of artificial chemicals and pesticides. Also, many sports drinks contain caffeine, which Nitro does not.

The PT strongly believes that Nitro drinks will prove to be an exciting addition to today's demanding beverage market. For Jerry's, this product provides the gateway to an as-yet-untapped market, moving the firm's beverage operations from its current "refreshments" position to one that includes the "nutritional" beverage market.

3. PET Financials

The PT has conducted a preliminary financial analysis for this project. It is estimated that it will take one year from the approval date for the product to be launched because it will take that long to get the plant set up for full-scale production. Additionally, the PT predicts that all Nitro drinks can be sold at reasonable margins for five years before competitive responses begin to substantially reduce the profitability of the product. Thus, the PT has defined a five-year explicit project life, beginning in the year of the product's launch.

In the analysis, the PT has taken Jerry's weighted average cost of capital to be 10% and the effective marginal tax rate as 40%.

Jerry's existing plants are all currently tied up in the production of other products. Hence, the PT suggests that a new plant be built in Springfield. All drinks will be produced here and shipped nationwide. A possible plant site has already been located. The owner currently uses the land for his trailer home business. However, he plans to retire at the end of 2004 and has agreed to sign a forward contract calling for the land to be sold to Jerry's for $3 million on December 31, 2004. This would allow for the plant construction to begin immediately in January of 2005.[129] The PT believes that the property will retain its value throughout the life of the project.

Since the land is currently used for commercial purposes it complies with all codes regarding sewage, highway access, and water drainage. Therefore, pre-construction times and costs should be minimal. The PT predicts that the plant could be built for $4 million, with another $6 million needed for mixing and bottling equipment. These investments are to be made on December 31, 2004. More details on the equipment purchase are contained in Fig. 15.1.

What will all the capital be worth at the end of the project's anticipated five-year life? The residual value of the project at the end of the explicit forecast period must be estimated to address this question. For a new product such as Nitro, two possibilities exist: the ongoing concern value or the scrap value. The PT suggests that the ongoing concern value be calculated as follows.

Assume the following: If Nitro is creating value in the last year of its explicit life (2010), then Nitro will retain a competitive advantage for four additional years. The economic profits to be earned over this additional period are projected to decay evenly, such that the economic profits in years 2011, 2012, 2013, and 2014 will be 75%, 50%, 25%, and 0% of the realized economic profit in 2010.

Note that this series of economic profits depends entirely on the economic profit in 2010, which is a random variable. The ongoing concern value at year-end 2010 is then the discounted value of these future economic profits, plus the book

Purchase price of equipment	= $6 million
Date of purchase	= Year-end 2004
Depreciation schedule (for tax purposes)	= 7-year MACRS starting in 2005

Fig. 15.1.   Information regarding $6 million of equipment for new plant.

---

[129]The plant will be depreciated straight-line to zero over 39.5 years.

value of the assets as of year-end 2010. The scrap value is simply the book value of the assets as of year-end 2010. Therefore, if economic profit in 2010 is positive, the residual value is the ongoing concern value. If it is negative, the residual value is the scrap value.

If this project passes the preliminary evaluation tollgate, the business evaluation phase of the process must begin by January 1, 2004, in order to stay on track for full product launch in January of 2006. This will allow one year for product development and some test marketing.[130]

The PT estimates that a $0.75 million investment in product development on December 31, 2003, might be necessary to complete the product specifications. Moreover, a $0.55 million investment in test marketing might prove useful in refining the estimates of sales demand. Both of these investments can be expensed for tax purposes.

The PT has also gathered information regarding net working capital estimates over the life of the project. These data are contained in Fig. 15.2. Current assets include inventory and accounts receivable, while noninterest bearing current liabilities include accounts payable and some miscellaneous payable.

The PT believes that the key drivers behind the success or failure of Nitro can be found in the sales and cost estimates. Figure 15.3 contains the expected values of the selling prices, cost variables, and expected unit sales for the explicit forecast period under the median scenario.

The PT has assumed that the two randomly distributed variables in Fig. 15.3 are unit sales and material expense. In the median forecast, unit sales in 2006 are assumed to be drawn from a normal distribution with a mean of 400,000 and standard deviation of 50,000. Moreover, unit sales are assumed to be correlated through time. Specifically, sales in 2007 are a function of actual sales in 2006 plus

Current assets	
Days sales outstanding	24 days
Inventory turnover	2.1
Other current assets	$120,000
(yearly growth rate of 7%)	
Non-interest bearing current liabilities	
Accounts payable as a percentage of sales revenue	10%
Other payables	$90,000
(yearly growth rate of 7%)	

Fig. 15.2.   Net working capital estimates.

---

[130]There will be more discussion on this part of the process later.

	Initial value 2006	Yearly growth rates (2007–2010)			
		2007	2008	2009	2010
Unit sales	400,000	25%	30%	20%	−10%
Case price	$17.00	7%	7%	5%	5%
Labor cost per unit	$2.00	4%	4%	4%	4%
Material cost per unit	$6.50	3%	3%	3%	3%
Selling and administrative cost per unit	$1.80	4%	4%	4%	4%
Fixed production costs	$435,000	3%	3%	3%	3%
Fixed SG&A costs	$279,000	4%	4%	4%	4%
★All entries are expected values					

Fig. 15.3.   Median forecast of sales and costs★ (Units: 24-Can Case).

a random error term, and so forth. The relationships for unit sales through time are defined as follows:

$$S07 = (1.25 \times S06) + e$$
$$S08 = (1.3 \times S07) + e$$
$$S09 = (1.2 \times S08) + e$$
$$S10 = (0.9 \times S09) + e$$

In these relationships e is drawn from a normal distribution with a mean of zero and standard deviation of 50,000. This means, for example, that sales in year 3 are 125% of the sales in year 2 plus a noise term that is expected to have a value of zero and a standard deviation of 50,000.

The material expense per unit is assumed to be uniformly distributed, with a minimum value of $6 and a maximum value of $7 in 2006, with both the minimum and maximum growing at 3% per year (see Chapter 7 for a review of normal and uniform probability distributions).

The PT has also developed two alternative sales and cost structure scenarios. Since the PT has defined unit sales and material expense as two of the key drivers of value, pessimistic, and optimistic distributional assumptions have also been provided for these two variables. This information is contained in Fig. 15.4.

All other numbers and estimates given in Fig. 15.2 and Fig. 15.4 remain the same across all three forecasted scenarios. Moreover, the PT believes that all three of the scenarios (pessimistic, median, and optimistic) are equally likely to actually occur. That is, the probability of occurrence is 1/3 for each scenario.

The uncertainty surrounding the scenarios increases the risk for Jerry's Lemonade. Moreover, it is possible for one variable to be drawn from the optimistic scenario, while the other variable is drawn from the pessimistic scenario. For

Pessimistic scenario:

- Unit sales in 2006 are normally distributed with a mean of 250,000 and standard deviation of 50,000 (2007–2010 unit sales still expected to grow as specified).
- Material expense per unit is uniformly distributed with a minimum value of $7 and a maximum value of $8, both growing at 3%.

Optimistic scenario

- Unit sales in 2006 are normally distributed with a mean of 550,000 and standard deviation of 50,000 (2003–2006 unit sales still expected to grow as specified).
- Material expense per unit is uniformly distributed with a minimum value of $5 and a maximum value of $6, both growing at 3%.

Fig. 15.4. Alternative sales and cost scenarios.

example, unit sales may be very high (i.e., the optimistic scenario is realized), while material expenses per unit are higher than expected (i.e., the pessimistic scenario is realized).

Consequently, different distributional combinations for these two variables imply that there are nine possible scenarios that could be realized in 2006. Given this uncertainty, an investment in risk reduction analysis may be worthwhile. An overall budget of $1.3 million has been allocated for risk reduction analysis. Investments can be made in marketing research and development research to achieve this risk reduction. This amount of $1.3 million is an upper limit on how much money can be spent on risk reduction; the entire amount need not be spent.

If funds are directed towards marketing research, Nitro samples could be placed with consumers and forecasting models can be employed to refine the estimates of future unit sales. On the other hand, an investment in development research would allow Jerry's Lemonade to make the nutritional ingredient mix more appealing to consumers. This, in turn, could improve estimates of variable material expenses. An investment in generating information in one area will yield information such that the true scenario for that respective variable will be known by the end of the business evaluation phase. The $1.3 million may be allocated in any way deemed appropriate.

Class Assignment

Your task at this stage is to determine whether Jerry's should continue with Project Nitro into the business evaluation phase. If the answer to this question is yes, determine the optimal strategy with respect to the test market and development research expenditures.

Financial Analysis Leading up to Preliminary Evaluation Tollgate[131]

The PT has determined that cannibalization can be ignored for Project Nitro. Moreover, because Nitro is a truly new product, the base case is easily defined and valued. The base case is simply not to continue with Project Nitro in any form, and thus has an NPV of zero.

There are, however, several possibilities for progressing with Nitro drinks. These mutually exclusive investment opportunities are:

• Proceed to the business evaluation phase without carrying out any risk reduction analysis.[132]

• Proceed to the business evaluation phase and only invest in the marketing research at a pre-tax cost of $550,000 (this is equivalent to investing in information to refine unit sales estimates).

• Proceed to the business evaluation phase and only invest in the development research at a pre-tax cost of $750,000 (this is equivalent to investing in information to refine material expense estimates).

• Proceed to the business evaluation phase and invest in both the marketing and development research at a total cost of $1.3 million (this is equivalent to investing in information to refine both unit sales and material expense estimates).

In order to determine the optimal strategy going forward, one must calculate the NPV of each of these four alternatives. To assess these, one should first characterize all the potential scenarios that could materialize.

As was mentioned in the previous section, the PT believes that two of the variables that impact the profitability of Nitro, unit sales, and material expense, could have significantly different values that depending on the state of the world. Moreover, these variables are assumed to be independent of one another. For instance, one variable could turn out to be in the optimistic state, while the other is in the pessimistic state. All of the possible states and the likelihood of their occurrence are captured in Fig. 15.5.

The next step is to calculate the NPV of each of these nine possible scenarios that could occur as of year-end 2010.[133] As an example, Fig. 15.6 contains a copy of the financial spreadsheet developed for the "median unit sales/median material

---

[131]This section represents Bob's solution to the first case assignment.

[132]For simplicity, Bob had the groups assume that since the proposed property was not available until the end of 2004, there was no way to start producing Nitro any earlier. Obviously, if it was possible, the PT should assess the value of this alternative moreover, in practice, few firms would let a project requiring $13 million in capital proceed without some investigative analysis.

[133]Eventually, we will discount these year-end 2004 NPV estimates back to year-end 2003.

Probability of unit sales scenario	Unit sales scenario	Probability of material expense scenario	Material expense scenario	Probability of combination	Combination (Unit sales/Material expenses)
1/3	Optimistic	1/3	Optimistic	1/9	Opt/Opt
				1/9	Opt/Med
				1/9	Opt/Pess
1/3	Median	1/3	Median	1/9	Med/Opt
				1/9	Med/Med
				1/9	Med/Pess
1/3	Pessimistic	1/3	Pessimistic	1/9	Pess/Opt
				1/9	Pess/Med
				1/9	Pess/Pess

Fig. 15.5. Unit sales — Material expense scenarios.

expense" scenario. This analysis was performed on a computer using the firm's recently-adopted financial software,[134] Risk-Strategist™, and the assumptions are outlined in Section 2.

Given the financial assumptions used in the analysis, a Monte Carlo simulation was run for 1,000 iterations. The results of this simulation offered an average (or expected) NPV as of the end of the year 2004 (business evaluation tollgate) of $1.544 million.[135]

This process was repeated for the remaining eight scenarios, running the risk strategist software for each set of assumptions. The end result of this exercise was to generate the expected NPV as of 2004 for all nine scenarios. This is given in Fig. 15.7. With the results of Fig. 15.7, one can now calculate the NPV of each of the four mutually exclusive investment opportunities described above.

NPV of Project with No Information

If the PT decides not to invest in either the market research or in development research, in one year it will know no more than it does today. That is, each of the

---

[134] @RISK™ and Crystal Ball™ offer two alternatives for building simulation models from within Excel.
[135] Observe that there is a slight difference between the expected NPV with the simulation and the expected NPV given in Fig. 15.6, which is based on the expected values of the input variables rather than a simulation. This is a natural consequence of generating random numbers. Moreover, the simulated value of the project may also differ due to the abandonment option in 2010. Re-call that the PT assumed that if Nitro was not creating value at the end of its explicit life, the project would be scrapped and the capital recovered. This option to abandon can often times add significantly to the project's value.

	Bus. Eval.	Execution	Launch				
Year	2004	2005	2006	2007	2008	2009	2010
Project year	0	1	2	3	4	5	6
Sales units			40,000	500,000	650,000	780,000	702,000
Price			17	18	19	20	21
Revenue			6,800,000	9,095,000	12,651,146	15,940,444	15,063,718
Labor costs			2	2	2	2	2
Material costs			7	7	7	7	7
Selling and administrative expenses			2	2	2	2	2
Other costs			—	—	—	—	—
Total cost per unit			10	11	11	11	12
Total variable costs			4,120,000	5,323,500	7,153,854	8,874,222	8,256,410
Fixed production costs			435,000	448,050	461,491	475,336	489,596
Fixed SG&A			279,000	290,160	301,766	313,837	326,390
Start-up cost		—					
Depreciation of equipment		857,400	1,469,400	1,049,400	749,400	535,800	535,200
Depreciation of tooling		—	—	—	—	—	—
Depreciation of building		101,266	101,266	101,266	101,266	101,266	101,266
Net operating profit		(958,666)	395,334	1,882,625	3,883,368	5,639,982	5,354,856
Taxes		(383,466)	158,134	753,050	1,553,347	2,255,993	2,141,942
PATOI		(575,199)	237,201	1,129,575	2,330,021	3,383,989	3,212,913

Fig. 15.6.   Financial analysis for project Nitro (Median unit sales/Median material expense).

Year	Bus. Eval. 2004	Execution 2005	Launch 2006	2007	2008	2009	2010
Current assets		2,393,314	3,029,070	3,992,994	4,895,263	4,608,631	4,608,631
NIBCLs		770,000	1,005,800	1,368,156	1,704,298	1,624,343	1,624,343
NWC		1,623,314	2,023,270	2,624,838	3,190,964	2,984,288	2,984,288
Net plant/building	4,000,000	3,898,734	3,797,468	3,696,203	3,594,937	3,493,671	3,392,405
Net equipment	6,000,000	5,142,600	3,673,200	2,623,800	1,874,400	1,338,600	803,400
Tooling	—	—	—	—	—	—	—
Tooling recoveries from customer	—						
Net land	3,000,000	3,000,000	3,000,000	3,000,000	3,000,000	3,000,000	3,000,000
Operating investment	13,000,000	13,664,648	12,493,938	11,944,840	11,660,301	10,816,559	10,180,093
Capital charge		1,300,000	1,366,465	1,249,394	1,194,484	1,166,030	1,081,656
Change in total capital	13,000,000	664,648	(1,170,709)	(549,098)	(284,539)	(843,743)	(636,466)
Economic value without residual value							2,131,257
Residual value of P&E (RV – BV) × (1 – T)							12,914,219
							1,640,476
Economic value	—	(1,875,199)	(1,129,264)	(119,819)	1,135,537	2,217,959	3,771,733
NPV (Economic values)	1,553,786						
FCF = PATOI — Chg. In T. Cap.	(13,000,000)	(1,239,847)	1,407,910	1,678,673	2,614,560	4,227,732	15,669,948
Yearly Discounted FCF	(13,000,000)	(1,127,134)	1,163,562	1,261,212	1,785,780	2,625,089	8,845,277
NPV (FCFs)	1,553,786						
IRR	12.33%						
WACC	10.0%						

Fig. 15.6. (Continued)

Probability of combination	Unit sales	Material expense	Scenario number	NPV as of year-end 2004 (BET)	NPV as of year-end 2003 (PET)
1/9	Opt	Opt	1	$7,952,611	$7,229,646
1/9	Opt	Med	2	$5,718,525	$5,198,659
1/9	Opt	Pess	3	$3,484,050	$3,167,318
1/9	Med	Opt	4	$3,172,101	$2,883,728
1/9	Med	Med	5	$1,544,074	$1,403,704
1/9	Med	Pess	6	($77,939)	($70,854)
1/9	Pess	Opt	7	(1,588,517)	($1,444,106)
1/9	Pess	Med	8	($2,591,749)	($2,356,135)
1/9	Pess	Pess	9	($3,590,635)	($3,264,214)

Fig. 15.7.   Summary of NPVs by scenario[136]

nine possible scenarios could occur. This implies that any one of the NPV figures could occur.

To assess the NPV of this alternative, one must simply calculate the expected value of the project across all possible scenarios. The expected NPV of this alternative is then the sum, across all possible scenarios, of the probability of each scenario occurring times the expected NPV of the project in that scenario. For Project Nitro, each scenario is equally likely, and thus the NPV is given by:

NPV (no information)

$$= 1/9 \times [\text{NPV (Scenario 1)}] + 1/9 \times [\text{NPV (Scenario 2)}]$$

$$+ 1/9 \times [\text{NPV (Scenario 3)}] + 1/9 \times [\text{NPV (Scenario 4)}]$$

$$+ 1/9 \times [\text{NPV (Scenario 5)}] + 1/9 \times [\text{NPV (Scenario 6)}]$$

$$+ 1/9 \times [\text{NPV (Scenario 7)}] + 1/9 \times [\text{NPV (Scenario 8)}]$$

$$+ 1/9 \times [\text{NPV (Scenario 9)}].$$

NPV (no information)

$$= 1/9 \times [\$7,229,646 + \$5,198,659 + \$3,167,318 + \$2,883,728$$

$$+ \$1,403,704 + (-\$70,854) + (-\$1,444,106) + (-\$2,356,135)$$

$$+ (-\$3,264,214)].$$

NPV (no information) = $1,416,416.

---

[136]The 2003 NPVs were calculated by discounting the year-2004 NPVs one year by Jerry's WACC.

Observe that the expected NPV of Project Nitro is positive, even without investing anything in research. However, additional information may add to project value. We turn to this analysis next.

NPV of Project with Unit Sales Information

If the PT invests the (pre-tax) $550,000, it will know precisely at year-end 2004 whether unit sales are described by either the optimistic, median, or pessimistic scenario. However, the PT will still face uncertainty regarding the scenario for material expense.

What will this investment in information allow the PT to do? It will allow them to abandon the project if the expected NPV of the project is negative for any of the unit sales scenarios. Thus, to calculate the NPV of the investment in unit sales information, the PT must first calculate the expected NPV of the project for each unit sales scenario, acknowledging the fact that material expense is still uncertain.[137] This is done by taking the weighted average of the NPVs in each unit sales scenario.

For Nitro, the expected NPV for each scenario is given by:

NPV (optimistic unit sales)

$$= 1/3 \times [\text{NPV (scenario 1)} + \text{NPV (scenario 2)} + \text{NPV (scenario 3)}]$$
$$= 1/3 \times [\$7,229,646 + \$5,198,659 + \$3,167,318]$$
$$= \$5,198,541.$$

NPV (median unit sales)

$$= 1/3 \times [\text{NPV (scenario 4)} + \text{NPV (scenario 5)} + \text{NPV (scenario 6)}]$$
$$= \$1,405,526.$$

NPV (pessimistic unit sales)

$$= 1/3 \times [\text{NPV (scenario 7)} + \text{NPV (scenario 8)} + \text{NPV (scenario 9)}]$$
$$= -\$2,354,818.$$

Next, given the expected NPV for each scenario, the PT must decide in which scenarios it will invest in Nitro and in which it will abandon. If it chooses to abandon the project at any stage, its NPV going forward is then zero. Given the expected NPVs for each scenario, the PT will obviously invest in the project only if the optimistic or median unit sales scenario is realized. That is, the PT will abandon the

---

[137] That is, material expense could still be given by any one of the three scenarios.

project if the market research reveals that unit sales are to be given by the pessimistic scenario, since it has a negative expected NPV in this scenario.

The overall NPV of the investment in information is, then, the sum, across all three scenarios, of the probability of each of the three unit sales scenarios occurring, times the expected NPV of the project in that scenario, less the after-tax cost of the market research. This is given by:

NPV (unit sales information)

= Probability (optimistic unit sales) × Expected NPV (optimistic unit sales)

+ Probability (median unit sales) × Expected NPV (median unit sales)

+ Probability (pessimistic unit sales)

× Expected NPV (pessimistic unit sales)

− After-tax cost of market research.

NPV (unit sales information)

= (1/3 × $5,198,659) + (1/3 × $1,405,526) + (1/3 × $0)

− ($550,000 × (1 − 0.40))

= $1,871,356.

Comparing the NPV of the project with the unit sales information to the NPV of the project with no information, one observes that the unit sales information is valuable. However, the other two information investment alternatives must be examined before any final decision is made.

NPV of Project with Material Expense Information

If the PT invests the (pre-tax) $750,000, it will know precisely at year-end 2004 whether material expense is described by the optimistic, median, or pessimistic scenario. However, the PT will now face uncertainty regarding the scenario for unit sales.

What will this investment in information allow the PT to do? Again it will permit abandonment of the project if the expected NPV of the project is negative for any of the material expense scenarios. Thus, to calculate the NPV of the investment in unit sales information, the PT must first calculate the expected NPV of the project for each material expense scenario, acknowledging the fact that unit sales are still uncertain.[138] This is done by taking the weighted average of the NPVs in each unit sales scenario.

---

[138]That is, unit sales could still be given by any one of the three scenarios.

For Nitro, the expected NPV for each scenario is given by:

NPV (optimistic material expense)

$= 1/3 \times$ [NPV (scenario 1) + NPV (scenario 4) + NPV (scenario 7)]

$= 1/3 \times$ [$7,229,646 + $2,888,728 − $1,444,106]

$= $2,889,756.

NPV (median material expense)

$= 1/3 \times$ [NPV (scenario 2) + NPV (scenario 5) + NPV (scenario 8)]

$= $1,415,409.

NPV (pessimistic material expense)

$= 1/3 \times$ [NPV (scenario 3) + NPV (scenario 6) + NPV (scenario 9)]

$= −$55,916.

Next, given the expected NPV for each scenario, the PT must decide in which scenarios it will invest in Nitro and in which it will abandon. If it chooses to abandon, its NPV going forward is zero. Given the expected NPVs for each scenario, the PT will invest in the project only if the optimistic or median material expense scenarios are realized. The PT will abandon the project if the development research reveals that material expense is given by the pessimistic scenario, since it has a negative expected NPV.

The overall NPV of the investment in development information is, then, the sum, across all three scenarios, of the probability of each of the three unit sales scenarios occurring, times the expected NPV of the project in that scenario, less the after-tax cost of the market research. This is given by:

NPV (material expense info)

$=$ Prob (optimistic material expense) $\times$ Exp NPV (optimistic material expense)

$+$ Prob (median material expense) $\times$ Exp NPV (median material expense)

$+$ Prob (pessimistic material expense)

$\times$ Exp NPV (pessimistic material expense)

$−$ After-tax cost of development research.

NPV (material expense info)

$= [1/3 \times $2,889,756] + [1/3 \times $1,415,409] + [1/3 \times 0]$

$− [$750,000 \times (1 − 0.4)]$

$= $985,055.

Comparing the NPV of the project with the material expense information to both the NPV of the project with no information and with unit sales information, one observes the following. Although the NPV of the project with material expense information is positive, it is smaller than even investing in the project with no information. In other words, the information learned by investing in material expense is simply not worth its cost.

However, it is still possible that the value of having both unit sales and material expense information is greater than the unit sales information on its own. This analysis is carried out next.

NPV of Project with both Unit Sales and Material Expense Information

If the PT invests in both pieces of information, it will know perfectly which of the nine scenarios it turns out to be in. Thus, the PT will be able to abandon the project at any point for which the NPV is negative, not just when the average NPV of a particular combination of points is negative. However, this increased decision making power comes at a cost. The pre-tax cost of this is $1.3 million.

The NPV of investing in both pieces of information is then calculated by first identifying the points at which it will invest, and the point at which it will abandon. Using Fig. 15.7, one observes that the PT will recommend accepting the project for scenarios 1, 2, 3, 4, and 5, and abandon the project for scenarios 6, 7, 8, and 9. Thus, since the probability of each scenario is given by 1/9, we have:

NPV (all information)

$$= 1/9 \times [\text{NPV (scenario 1)}] + 1/9 \times [\text{NPV (scenario 2)}]$$
$$+ 1/9 \times [\text{NPV (scenario 3)}] + 1/9 \times [\text{NPV (scenario 4)}]$$
$$+ 1/9 \times [\text{NPV (scenario 5)}] + 1/9 \times [\text{NPV (scenario 6)}]$$
$$+ 1/9 \times [\text{NPV (scenario 7)}] + 1/9 \times [\text{NPV (scenario 8)}]$$
$$+ 1/9 \times [\text{NPV (scenario 9)}] - \text{After-tax cost of market research}$$
$$- \text{After-tax cost of development research.}$$

NPV (all information)

$$= 1/9 \times [\$7,229,646 + \$5,198,659 + \$3,167,318 + \$2,888,728$$
$$+ \$1,403,704 + (\$0) + (\$0) + (\$0) + (\$0)] - [\$550,000 \times (1 - 0.40)]$$
$$- [\$750,000 \times (1 - 0.40)]$$
$$= \$1,429,288.$$

Again, this NPV is positive. But it is less than the NPV of investing in just the unit sales information. Why is not the knowledge of the material expense scenario, in addition to the unit sales scenario, valuable?

Quite simply, knowing the material expense scenario after the unit sales scenario is already known allows the PT to avoid only one additional negative NPV scenario — scenario 6. The other negative scenarios given by 7, 8, and 9 have already been avoided solely by knowing the unit sales scenario. Moreover, the NPV of scenario 6 is only −$70,854. Although this value is negative, spending an additional $450,000 after-tax on development research to avoid a scenario with a value of −$70,854 — which only occurs with a probability of one-ninth — obviously is not a worthwhile investment.

Final Recommendation at Preliminary Evaluation Tollgate

The optimal recommendation for project Nitro as of the preliminary evaluation tollgate is to go forward into the business evaluation phase. Additionally, the PT should request $550,000 to carry out the market research over the next year, as this alternative has the highest NPV, estimated to be $1,871,356.

4. Results of the Market Research and the Business Evaluation Tollgate

By the end of the second day of the three-day training course, all the participant groups had come to the conclusion described by Bob above. To complete the simulated capital budgeting exercise, on the morning of the third day all teams were given the "results" of their market research that took place during the business evaluation phase. With this information, the participants were given the task of preparing all of the financial analysis required for the capital appropriation request at the business evaluation tollgate. The market research results and final instructions are contained in Fig. 15.8. Bob's solution then follows.

Bob's Solution
Once the new assumptions are entered, Risk-Strategist™ will then produce the following financial review topsheet that highlights the key financial data of Project Nitro. Figure 15.9 contains this top sheet. A copy of the final spreadsheet is then found in Fig. 15.10.

Project Nitro has a significantly positive NPV of $5.68 million. Therefore, the project should be accepted at the business evaluation tollgate, and the $13 million capital appropriation request granted.

- The market research determined that unit sales would be drawn from the optimistic scenario.
- Since development research was not carried out, material expense is still unknown. To input material expense into *Risk Strategist*, enter a uniform distribution with a minimum value of $5 and a maximum value of $8.
- Re-run the simulation for the project using the new information.
- Prepare a financial review topsheet as per the guidelines of our new capital budgeting manual.[139]
- Prepare a copy of the spreadsheet from *Risk Strategist*.
- In addition to copies of the graphs contained in the topsheet, include an NPV profile in appendix form.

Fig. 15.8.   Market research and final guidelines and tasks.

All groups came to the same conclusion. However, Bob pressed them during their presentations to dig deeper into the sources of value for the project. He did this in the context of the discussion of the key financial graphs that were generated by the software. Bob then stressed that a first-rate financial section of a project proposal would not only be prepared and presented in the same way as Nitro was in class, but it would also contain the same level of sophistication and understanding as his interpretation of the financial addendum did. This is presented next in Figs. 15.11–15.16.

Financial Addendum

Starting with the graphs on the financial review top sheet, the first graph displays the free cash flows to be earned in each year of the project life.

As can be seen above, the early year's cash flows beyond the year of investment are relatively small. In fact, the last year of the project's initially forecasted life has the largest free cash flow by far. What does this imply about the speed at which Jerry's Lemonade will recover its initial investment in Nitro? It implies that the project is a relatively long-term investment, as is clearly indicated by the graph of discounted cumulative free cash flow through time.

As this graph shows, the discounted payback on this project is 5.05 years. So where is the value being created in Nitro, a project with an NPV of $5 million? Let us turn to the third graph for more of the story.

This graph shows that essentially all of the value is created in the last three year's of Project Nitro. Importantly, the economic profit for the year 2010 contains the expected value of Nitro as an ongoing concern. That is, if the project is creating value during the year 2010, then the PT's assumptions were that this project

---

[139]See Chapter 12.

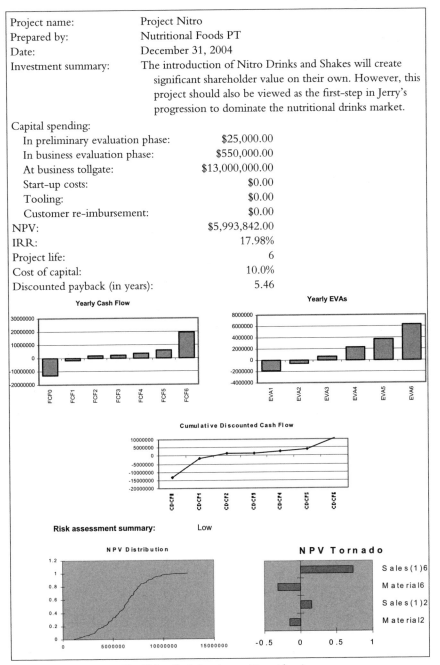

Project name:	Project Nitro
Prepared by:	Nutritional Foods PT
Date:	December 31, 2004
Investment summary:	The introduction of Nitro Drinks and Shakes will create significant shareholder value on their own. However, this project should also be viewed as the first-step in Jerry's progression to dominate the nutritional drinks market.

Capital spending:

In preliminary evaluation phase:	$25,000.00
In business evaluation phase:	$550,000.00
At business tollgate:	$13,000,000.00
Start-up costs:	$0.00
Tooling:	$0.00
Customer re-imbursement:	$0.00
NPV:	$5,993,842.00
IRR:	17.98%
Project life:	6
Cost of capital:	10.0%
Discounted payback (in years):	5.46

Risk assessment summary: Low

Fig. 15.9.   Capital project — Financial review.

Year	Bus. val. 2004	Execution 2005	Launch 2006	2007	2008	2009	2010
Project year	0	1	2	3	4	5	6
Sales units			550,000	687,500	893,750	1,072,500	965,250
Price			17	18	19	20	21
Revenue			9,350,000	12,505,626	17,395,325	21,198,110	20,712,613
Labor costs			2	2	2	2	2
Material costs			7	7	7	7	7
Selling and administrative expenses			2	2	2	2	2
Other costs							
Total cost per unit		—	10	11	11	11	12
Total variable costs			5,665,000	7,319,812	9,836,549	12,202,055	11,352,564
Fixed production costs			435,000	448,050	461,491	475,336	489,596
Fixed SG&A			279,000	290,160	301,766	313,837	326,390
Start-up cost	—						
Depreciation of equipment		857,400	1,469,400	1,049,400	749,400	535,800	535,200
Depreciation of tooling		—	—	—	—	—	—
Depreciation of building		101,266	101,266	101,266	101,266	101,266	101,266
Net operating profit	—	(958,666)	1,400,334	3,296,938	5,944,852	8,289,815	7,907,596
Taxes	—	(383,466)	560,134	1,318,775	2,377,941	3,315,926	3,163,038
PATOI	—	(575,199)	840,201	1,978,163	3,566,911	4,973,889	4,744,558

Fig. 15.10.   Financial analysis for project NITRO (business evaluation tollgate).

Year	Bus. val. 2004	Execution 2005	Launch 2006	2007	2008	2009	2010
Current assets		3,168,128	4,036,813	5,356,436	6,590,978	6,190,454	6,190,454
NIBCLs		1,025,000	1,346,863	1,842,573	2,302,065	2,189,233	2,189,233
NWC		2,143,128	2,689,950	3,513,863	4,288,913	4,001,221	4,001,221
Net plant/building	4,000,000	3,797,468	3,797,468	3,696,203	3,594,937	3,493,671	3,392,405
Net equipment	6,000,000	5,142,600	3,673,200	2,623,800	1,874,400	1,338,600	803,400
Tooling	—	—	—	—	—	—	—
Tooling recoveries from customer	—	—	—	—	—	—	—
Net land	3,000,000	3,000,000	3,000,000	3,000,000	3,000,000	3,000,000	3,000,000
Operating investment	13,000,000	14,184,462	13,160,618	12,758,250	11,833,492	11,197,026	10,180,093
Capital charge		1,300,000	1,418,446	1,316,062	1,283,387	1,275,825	1,183,349
Change in total capital	13,000,000	1,184,462	(1,023,844)	(326,753)	(75,616)	(924,758)	(636,466)
Economic value without residual value							3,561,208
Residual value of P&E							15,765,594
(RV − BV) × (1 − T)							2,741,141
Economic value		(1,875,199)	(578,246)	662,101	2,283,525	3,698,064	6,302,349
NPV (Economic values)	5,728,227						
FCF = PATOI − Chg. In T. Cap.	(13,000,000)	(1,759,662)	1,864,044	2,304,916	3,642,527	5,898,647	19,319,190
Yearly discounted FCF	(13,000,000)	(1,599,692)	1,540,532	1,731,717	2,487,895	3,662,596	10,905,179
NPV (FCFs)	5,728,227						
IRR	17.77%						
WACC	10.0%						

Fig. 15.10.   (*Continued*)

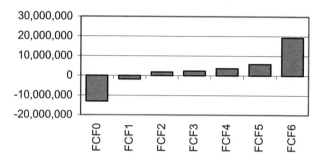

Fig. 15.11.   Yearly free cash flow.

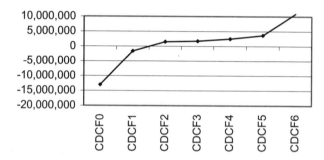

Fig. 15.12.   Cumulative discounted cash flow.

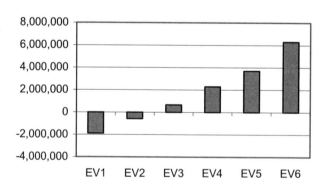

Fig. 15.13.   Yearly economic profits.

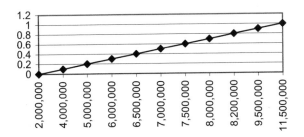

Fig. 15.14.   NPV distribution.

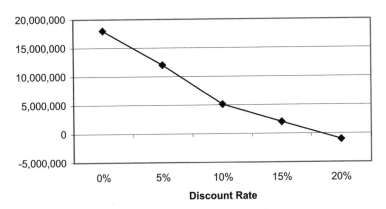

Fig. 15.15.   NPV profile.

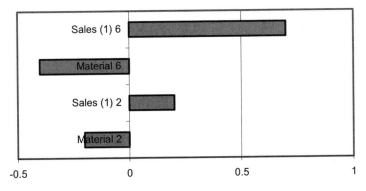

Fig. 15.16.   NPV tornado.

could create value going forward for a further three years before anticipated competitive responses brought the economic profit back to zero. Hence, the project has enormous potential to create significant shareholder value. But it will take a while for this value to be realized.

Should the long-term nature of the payoffs change our perspective on risk? Two graphs are useful in answering this. First, from the financial review top sheet, we have the cumulative distribution of NPVs generated by the simulation. According to our assumptions on Project Nitro, including the results of the $550,000 test market, the probability that the NPV of the project will be positive is nearly 100%, i.e., there is only a very small chance of a negative NPV. On the basis of this, the PT should assign a risk classification of "Low."

Some may object to assigning a "Low Risk" label to a project that is truly a long-term venture. However, if there is still genuine nervousness about this issue, one has to question the reliability of the test market and other information generated by the PT, not the quality of the financial results based on that information. In other words, perhaps the input assumptions need to acknowledge a greater degree of uncertainty in the estimates.

Next, the PT should provide an NPV profile to demonstrate the sensitivity of the project's expected NPV to changes in the discount rate. If interest rates go up in the future, so will the risk-adjusted discount rate. This is given by the following.

This graph shows that for any discount rate less than 17.72% (the project's IRR), the project's NPV is positive. Moreover, the graph also tells us how fast the NPV declines as the cost of capital rises above 10%.

So, what are the risks in this project? To answer this question, the PT should also identify the key value drivers behind the success of the project. Carrying out a sensitivity analysis, as was done when generating the top sheet, best captures this.

According to this tornado graph, the NPV of the project is most sensitive to the sales units in 2010. This is the last year of the product's life. The reason for this is the PT's assumption that the project will be an ongoing concern beyond the year 2010.

5. Jerry Wants to Light up that Stogie

The first resource allocation training seminar was an unqualified success. Having a cross-functional target audience turned out to be essential to the success of the seminar. Barb and Bob had already planned the next one.

Jerry and Bob decided to celebrate with cognac and cigars. Bob relayed to Jerry that he felt all the participants left feeling they had taken away a firmer understanding of the basic principles of project analysis and a greater appreciation for what senior management was looking for in every capital appropriation request. They also knew that senior management was fully committed to the new system. They both looked forward to the next offering of the seminar. More significantly, they both looked forward to reading the first capital request that reflected the lessons learned in the seminar. They were convinced that such seminars touched many components of the Value Sphere — particularly the resource allocation and people and organization culture segments — and were thus important for properly managing the Value Sphere as the group moves forward.

Main Lessons

- Managerial training courses should be as "hands-on" as possible. That is, their design should reflect the processes actually in place at the company. The object of the training should be to enhance on-the-job performance.
- Resource allocation/capital budgeting seminars should not be limited to finance and accounting staff. Capital investments analysis requires cross-functional inputs from a variety of functional areas like manufacturing and marketing. All these employees should be trained as well.
- Managers involved in resource allocation should be fully equipped to conduct risk analysis and utilize advanced simulation techniques to assess probability distributions of possible future outcomes.
- Firms should adopt processes and user-friendly financial software that allow managers to focus their time on the assumptions underlying the analysis and the interpretation of the results, rather than in learning how to use the software.

End-of-Chapter Review Exercises

1. Does your firm provide a resource allocation training course like the one Bob ran? If so, what were the similarities and differences?
2. Are you required to perform a risk simulation analysis for the projects that you propose? Have you ever used simulations in your financial analysis of projects? What could be the benefits of such simulations to you?
3. Have you ever been involved in the analysis of a multistage project such as Project Nitro? Did you ever attempt to value (early) investments in things like test marketing and product development as real options? If so, compare your methods to those developed in this chapter.
4. Take a multistage project for which you provided (or were involved in) the financial analysis. Would your recommendation have been any different if you

applied the techniques employed by Bob? If so, can you identify where (and why) your recommendations would differ? Would you say that value evaporated because of these difference?

5. Take the approach to resource allocation and project analysis developed in this and previous chapters and develop an appropriate process for your company. How would you go about having the process adopted on a company-wide basis? What impediments would you expect? How would you overcome them?

Practice Problems

1. What is an NPV distribution? How would you use it?
2. What is an NPV profile and what use would you put it to?
3. What is an NPV tornado chart? What kind of information would you extract from it for capital budgeting purposes?
4. What can we learn from a graph of cumulative discounted cash flow and how would a CFO use this tool?
5. What are the advantages of a simulation over a point estimate of NPV for capital budgeting?

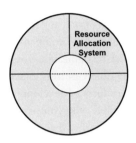

Chapter 16

JERRY HAS A NEW PROBLEM: HOW TO USE A PORTFOLIO APPROACH TO PROJECT SELECTION

1. A New Problem: Prosperity of Ideas

It was 9:00 a.m. Winter had set in once more, and Jerry could see snow from his office window. He was pleased. And with good reason. The business was doing well; annual sales topped $450 million last year and Jerry's Lemonade, Inc. was now a global enterprise.

There was a knock on the door. Jim Lymon, his corporate treasurer, came in.

Jerry asked him by way of conversation, "Jim, how's Nancy Whitmore working out?" Nancy, whom Bob had hired from Citigroup to take care of corporate risk management, reported to Jim.

"She's great," said Jim, "I'm really pleased at the way she's refined our risk management system. Jerry, there's something else I want to talk to you about. I've talked to Bob about this, and he suggested I also discuss it with you. My Mergers and Acquisitions person has identified two potential acquisition targets. One is a bottling firm in St. Louis that we could buy if we wanted to expand into the business of bottling some of our products for retail distribution through grocery stores. The other is Singletary's Health Pub. Do you have a few minutes to chat about this?"

Jerry puffed on his cigar and motioned for Jim to be seated, but he remained silent and pensive. He had nothing marked on his calendar for today and was hoping to spend the day reflecting on the business and its Value Sphere, rather than making decisions. "The tyranny of the routine," as a friend of his once put it, was something he wanted to guard against. You get so caught up in day-to-day stuff and deadlines that it crowds out all the time you have to think. Not good for a CEO.

Jerry's mind wandered to the Russo and Schoemaker book[141] which ends with the premise, "But to advance further down the road to excellence and competitive success, we need to better understand the most important processes of all: the processes of thinking."

Jerry wondered whether that was what Robert Gouizeta, Chairman and CEO of Coca-Cola until his death in 1997, had in mind when he crafted the company's strategy of global dominance. It is said that the second-most recognizable word anywhere in the world is "Coke."[142] Jerry thought about the time Gouizeta asked his people to estimate the potential demand for Coca-Cola products in developing countries. They came back with estimates of the number of people who consumed (or were likely to consume) soft drinks, and Coca-Cola's likely market share.

Gouizeta understood the way they were thinking and he knew it was too limited. He admonished them with the assertion that the potential market for Coca-Cola in these countries included everybody who was human and needed to ingest fluids!

This cognitive breakthrough was central to a reshaped strategy. All of a sudden, the product-line boundaries Coke executives had imposed on their own thinking disappeared with a whoosh. We cannot be sure that this is what led to Coca-Cola getting into the bottled water business. But it is likely that the expanded thinking did not stand in the way of that decision.

Jerry's musings were interrupted by the sound of Jim clearing his throat. Jerry turned to him, "I'm sorry, Jim. I'm just a bit preoccupied this morning. Yes, we can talk about these possible acquisitions. But before we do that, I want to tell you I'm getting very concerned."

"Are we being too aggressive...?" asked Jim, but before he could finish, Jerry cut him off.

"It's not quite that. It's just that our company is a bit like a sparkler right now; we have as many new ideas as a sparkler has sparks. With so many ideas for investing our money, I'm not sure we have the right process in place to handle everything."

Jim looked a bit puzzled. After a brief pause, he asked, "Jerry, are you saying you're not satisfied with the new dynamic resource allocation system that we recently adopted and offered training on for all our key people?"

Jerry could see the growing pain on Jim's face. Jim had personally invested a lot of time in developing the resource allocation manual, and in helping with the training of analysts in how to use the sophisticated new risk analysis tools that were discussed in the manual. Besides, he was also obviously excited about the two potential acquisitions that Jerry seemed to be lukewarm about thus far.

---

[141] Russo, Edward J. and Paul J. H. Schoemaker (1989) *Decision Traps*, Simon and Schuster, New York.
[142] The first is "hello."

Smiling re-assuringly, Jerry said, "Not at all, Jim. But isn't it true that our new resource allocation system looks at each project individually in analyzing its merits? Sort of like a tub on its own bottom? I know we look at all the major projects as a group when they come to the Executive Committee. But even at that stage, we were essentially ranking all these individual projects based on their NPVs. We then bring in our subjective judgment and knowledge of the needs of the overall strategy to decide how many of these projects to fund, given the size of our capital budget.

"I'm concerned that this may not be the best way to do things. For example, when your people run the numbers on these acquisitions they will think of each acquisition as a stand-alone project. Everybody does that. And then when things get to the Executive Committee, we are somehow expected to wave a magic wand and take all the possible portfolio effects into account in making our decisions! But we have no science on which to base it. And we can't fund them all. So after all the hard analysis that goes into examining individual projects, we end up deciding on the portfolio of our investments based, in large part, on gut feel. Don't you think this could cause Value Evaporation and sub-optimize our management of the Value Sphere?"

Jim was beginning to sense that Jerry had touched upon something important, although he did not understand how these "portfolio effects" would impact individual project NPVs. And since their resource allocation system was focused now on Economic Profit and NPV, it was hard to see how anything would change even if "science" could somehow be brought to bear on the portfolio decisions that Jerry and the executive committee had to make.

But, keeping these thoughts to himself, he said, "You may be right, Jerry. Let me talk to Bob and we'll see if we can modify our process to deal with this issue before deciding on these acquisitions."

2. The Search for a Solution

Jim met with Bob and they decided to have a couple of their bright young analysts work on the project. Bob gave them two guidelines:

- Benchmark at least three companies (he suggested Procter and Gamble, Merck, and Starbucks, but stressed that these were just suggestions).
- Contact Professor Steve Showles at the university for advice. Bob gave them permission to hire Steve as a consultant on this. Professor Showles had considerable experience in helping companies design resource allocation systems.

The project team returned a month later with a report prepared with Professor Showles' advice. Bob and Jim read it, met with the team for clarifications, modified the report a bit, and submitted it to Jerry for his approval.

3. The Essence of the Report

Jerry was pleased at how quickly Jim and Bob had been able to come up with a report. He leaned back in his chair and began to read. Halfway through the first page, he had a thought. He flipped on the intercom switch and barked, "No visitors or phone calls until 11 this morning. Not even Bob."

The Report

Objective

The purpose of this report is to describe a resource allocation system that will permit the Executive Committee to take a portfolio approach to resource allocation.

The Problem: The main problem with not taking a portfolio approach is that each project has been analyzed at lower levels as if it were a stand-alone asset to which all the required organizational resources could be dedicated. This way of analyzing each project is obviously correct for our analysts. But we need a scientific way to examine the entire portfolio of projects submitted for approval. The reason is that if we were to invest in all the projects that are estimated to have positive NPVs, we would not have adequate organization resources to support them all. Consequently, project cash flows would suffer and the NPVs estimated for individual projects would not be realized.

By resources, we mean not just financial. We are more concerned about our human resource capabilities to pull it all off. Thus, it is essential that after all the projects have been analyzed individually by our analysts, the Executive Committee adopt a portfolio approach to examining all the requests for capital.

The Overall Approach

We recommend a four-step interactive approach as represented in Fig. 16.1. (Details are given in the following Addendum.)

The Addendum

Step 1: How Fast Do We Want to Grow?   This is clearly a matter of strategic choice. However, whatever growth targets we set should be permanently value-consistent.

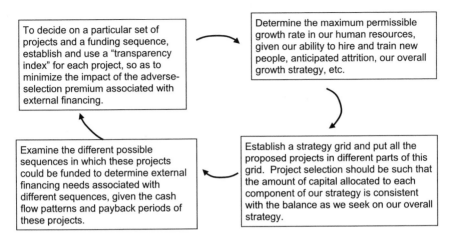

Fig. 16.1. The interactive approach to portfolio selection.

This means that we should not grow now in such a way that we can anticipate having to scale back in the future. Scaling back is very disruptive to the Value Sphere. Moreover, the growth targets should also depend on our existing stock of human resources and how fast we can add to this stock. Absorbing new employees requires training and takes time, too. Finally, our growth targets should take into account industry dynamics and the rate at which we can expect to replace our maturing products with new ones. All of this suggests that we need a closer strategic partnership between our finance and HR functions.

To summarize, four main factors should determine our growth targets:

1. Our overall business strategy
2. Our permanent value-consistent growth rate, i.e., the rate at which we can grow while still ensuring that all our investments yield rates of return exceeding the cost of capital[143]
3. Our existing human resources and the rate at which we can expand these resources
4. Industry and competition dynamics and our anticipated rate of new product development.

---

[143]This differs from the sustainable growth rate covered in Chapter 3. That growth rate was one that could be sustained without external equity financing. There is no such restriction on external financing here.

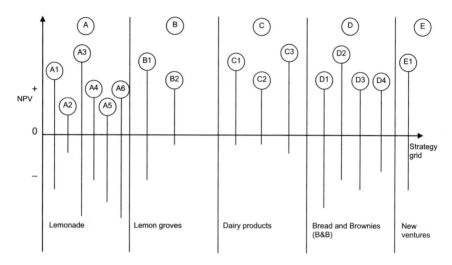

Fig. 16.2.   Strategy grid diagram.

Step 2: A Strategy Grid for Projects[144]   Our resource allocation is the tangible manifestation of our strategy. This means that the way we allocate resources should be consistent with our strategy. One way to develop a systematic framework to achieve this is to develop a grid for our five major product groups (strategy components) as shown in Fig. 16.2.

This strategy grid diagram contains a plot of the possible range of NPVs for each project that is submitted for Executive Committee approval. This range would be generated by using the risk analysis and simulation software (Risk Strategist™) that we have used to train our analysts (see Chapter 15). The project NPV plots are segregated on the basis of the Product Group (strategy component) that originated the request. The plots displayed in the figure are merely illustrative. This analysis then leads to a strategy-resource alignment check, such as that shown in Fig. 16.3.

Again, Fig. 16.3 is only for illustrative purposes; the numbers are hypothetical and meant to represent the capital allocation requests depicted in the previous diagram. Note that Step 1 (How Fast Do We Want to Grow?) would determine the total anticipated resource allocation.

This kind of analysis would readily permit the Executive Committee to see if the portfolio of resource allocation requests is consistent with our strategy. For example, in this illustration, there is far too much capital requested by Lemonade and B&B, and far too little capital requested by Dairy Products and New Ventures.

---

[144]This discussion is adapted from John A. Boquist, Todd T. Milbourn, and Anjan V. Thakor (1998) "How do You Win the Capital Allocation Game?" *Sloan Management Review*, Winter, pp. 59–71.

	Strategy component				
	Lemonade (%)	Lemon groves (%)	Dairy products(%)	B&B (%)	New ventures (%)
Anticipated percentage of total resource allocation according to strategy (given a total capital allocation)	50	5	20	10	15
Actual Percentage of total resource allocation implied by capital requests	60	7	8	20	5

Fig. 16.3.   Strategy-resource alignment check.

This should trigger further examination. If we now look at the Strategy Grid diagram, we can reach two tentative conclusions:

1. The Lemonade Group seems to be more creative and more focused on product expansion and new product development relative to other groups, particularly New Ventures.
2. The Lemonade Group seems to be more risk tolerant than Dairy Products. The Lemonade Group's project proposals have NPV ranges that admit more negative NPV possibilities than those of Dairy Products. Perhaps the Dairy Products Group is killing too many projects relative to the demands of the strategy because they view these projects as having too much uncertainty/unpredictability or perhaps they are too conservative.

In this case, the Executive Committee has two possible courses of action:

A. Discuss these resource allocation requests with the Product Group Vice Presidents (VPs) to see if the requests can be revised to make the overall portfolio more consistent with the predetermined corporate strategy. This may result in groups like Dairy Products submitting additional resource allocation requests and those like Lemonade withdrawing some. In some instances, it may be that the total resources requested by all the groups exceed what we anticipate investing. In this case, resources may have to be rationed, unless we can go back to Step 1 and revise our growth targets.
B. Revise the strategy to move it closer to the resource allocation requests. This is in the spirit of the interactive aspect of Fig. 16.1.

We suspect that in practice, we will do both — have discussions with the Group VPs and also fine-tune the strategy. The basic idea is for us to be constantly aware of the link between strategy and resource allocation and keep them in alignment. Otherwise, the Value Sphere will suffer.

Step 3: Determine External Financing Needs   Based on the projects we currently have, as well as those we have approved in this round of examining resource allocation requests, we can estimate the internally-generated free cash flow pattern for the corporation as a whole over the next few years. This free cash flow would be the difference between the cash flow our operations produce and the cash flow we need to reinvest in the business. That is,

$$\text{Internally generated free cash flow (IGFCF)}$$
$$= \text{NOPAT} - \text{Capital investment} \qquad (1)$$

We can then estimate the cash flow we need to service our debt and pay dividends. Call it cash flow for interest and dividends (CFID).[145] Then, the net free cash flow is:

$$\text{FCF} = \text{IGFCF} - \text{CFID} \qquad (2)$$

In those periods in which FCF < 0, we will need to cover the deficit with external financing.

Clearly, the pattern of our external financing needs through time will depend on the sequence in which we plan to fund our projects. Thus, our recommendation is to prepare a whole range of funding sequences and thereby generate various patterns of expected external financing needs. For example, we might produce something like Fig. 16.4.

Project funding sequences	External financing needs in $ million as identified by negative FCF for period t			
	$t = 1$	$t = 2$	$t = 3$	$t = 4$
(1) Period 1: A1, A2, A4, B1, C2, C3, D1, E1 Period 2: A3, A5, B2, C1, D2, D3 Period 3: A6, D4	$45	$30	—	—
(2) Period 1: A1, A2, B1, C1, D1, D2 Period 2: A3, A4, B2, C2, D3, E1 Period 3: A5, A6, C3, D4	$30	$35	$10	—

Fig. 16.4.   Possible sequences of external financing needs.

---

[145]Of course, any principal payments make would be part of the debt service payment we have in mind here.

Step 4: Establish a Transparency Index for Each Project and Select the Right Sequence of Investments There is an asymmetry of information between us (the managers of the firm) and outside investors. We know more about our projects than our investors do. Moreover, this informational asymmetry varies from project to project.

For example, if the project involves opening a few new stores in a city where we already have stores, without adding to the product line, then investors are likely to know a lot about the project. The informational asymmetry between us and investors will be rather small.

But if the project is a new product, particularly one that no one is offering at present, then we are likely to know considerably more about the project than our investors would. In part, this would be because we have access to all the particulars of the product, market research data, taste-test results, etc. We may choose not to reveal this information to the market because, if we did that we could not keep the information out of our competitors' hands. In this case, the informational asymmetry between us and our investors is likely to be quite significant.

The Transparency Index is merely an attempt to capture this informational asymmetry. The higher this index, the more transparent things are to investors, and the lower the asymmetry. We propose a three-value Transparency Index for our company, as shown in Fig. 16.5.

For every sequence of projects examined in the previous step we should compute two indices: a total transparency index score and an overall expected transparency index for the whole firm for each of the time periods in which we need to raise external financing. That is, at the time that we need to raise external financing, we should know the extent of the informational asymmetry between us and the market.

In short, for each project funding sequence in Fig. 16.4, we will have:

- an external financing need at each future point in time
- a transparency index value that goes with each external financing need at each point in time

Transparency index	Examples of types of projects
High informational asymmetry or low transparency: 1	New product introductions (particularly non-core), projects in the new ventures group, international projects
Medium: 2	Product line extensions based on existing products (e.g., lemonade softies)
Low information asymmetry or high transparency: 3	Maintenance reinvestments in PP&E, replacement of old equipment with new technology upgrades, etc.

Fig. 16.5.   Transparency index values.

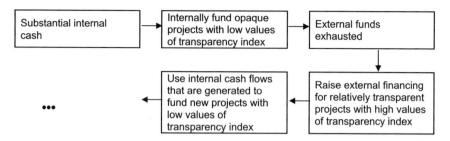

Fig. 16.6.   The optimal project funding sequence.

Research has shown that the degree of informational asymmetry between the firm and the market has an important effect on the cost of external financing.[146] Indeed, every firm pays a premium for this informational asymmetry, called the "adverse selection premium." It is a premium that investors demand, to be compensated for their lack of information relative to the firm's managers.

This has two important implications for us:

1. We should use our financial reporting system to decrease the informational asymmetry between us and the market.[147] This means disclosing as much as we can and as directly as we can without revealing strategic information to our competitors.
2. We should time our external financing to minimize the adverse selection premium. This calls for using the transparency index for each possible project funding sequence in Fig. 16.6 as a factor in deciding which funding sequence to adopt.

4. Overall Recommendations for Our Financial Policy

1. We should not undertake global expansion and significant new product development simultaneously. The reason is that both have low values on the transparency index and will call for external financing that will have attached to it a relatively high adverse selection premium.

[146]See Stewart Myers and Nicholas Majluf (1984) "Corporate Financing and Investment Decisions When Firms Have Information That Investors Do Not Have," *Journal of Financial Economics*, 13, pp. 187–221.
[147]See, for example, Paul B. W. Miller, "Financial Reporting, Meet TQM," *CFO*, 13(11), November 1997, p. 10.

2. We should probably emphasize stable growth projects (with high values of the transparency index) before more opaque projects so that they will throw off cash flows in the future that could be used to fund more opaque projects.

3. Our greatest external financing should be done when we are funding projects that are easy for the market to understand (high values of the transparency index). This suggests that we should perhaps consider our major acquisitions and some global expansion now when we have lots of internal cash. In the next phase of our expansion, we will have used up our internal cash, so that the projects we should consider funding would be those which are more transparent to investors (high values of the transparency index), since these will require external financing, as indicated in Fig. 16.6.

5. The Theory Behind the Report

There are two key theoretical issues raised in the report prepared by Bob Butterfield and Jim Lymon. These are addressed in this section.

A. Is Capital Rationing Rational?

The standard textbook prescription in corporate finance is that capital should not be rationed as long as the firm has positive NPV projects available to fund. For example, while recognizing that many firms do set upper limits on the amount of capital they will allocate, Van Horne's (1992) text states[148]:

Capital rationing usually results in an investment policy that is less than optimal .... If it [the firm] rations capital and does not invest in all projects yielding more than the required rate, is it not foregoing opportunities that would enhance the market price of its stock? ... In the final analysis, the firm should accept all proposals yielding more than their required rate of return.

Thus, capital rationing is viewed as irrational.

At a certain level, this assertion is little more than a tautology. If the firm has a truly positive NPV project available and it denies funds to it, then it is simply leaving money on the table. That just cannot be rational for the shareholders.

Some new theories of capital rationing have emerged that explain it as rational behavior by managers. In a nutshell, the premise of these theories is not to challenge the NPV rule. Rather, they propose that measuring project NPVs on a stand-alone basis — as done in the standard NPV analysis — is incorrect. There are three types of arguments used in these theories.

---

[148]James C. Van Horne (1992) *Financial Management and Policy*, Prentice-Hall, Inc., Englewood Cliffs, New Jersey 07632.

(i) The First Theory: According to this theory, managers will sometimes ask for capital when they should not. This is called the "overinvestment problem."[149] It arises as follows: Because managers are risk-averse, the optimal wage contracts are downward rigid. That means their wages can go up through time but not down. Now suppose the manager's ability to manage projects is unknown and is being gradually inferred from the observed cash flows of the project. Then, if cash flows are higher than expected, the manager's ability will be perceived to be higher than at the outset, and his wages will increase. If cash flows are lower than expected, the manager will be perceived to be less able. But he does not care because his wage can not go down.

What does this mean for the manager's project selection and desire to ask for capital? To answer this question, we must understand what happens when the manger does not ask for capital (and thus does not invest), and what happens when he invests. If the manager does not ask for capital, perceptions of his ability remain unchanged. So his wage remains the same.

Clearly, if the manger has a bad (negative NPV) project, we would like him to refrain from asking for capital. But in this case, since the manager's wage remains unchanged, he is really indifferent between requesting capital and not requesting it.

What happens if he asks for capital? It is possible that the project will produce poor cash flows. People will revise downward their perception of the manager's ability. But nothing happens to his wage. So the manager does not care about the likelihood of poor project performance. On the other hand, there is at least some chance that the project will fortuitously throw off good cash flows. In this case, people will revise upward their perception of the manager's ability, and his wage will rise.

So the manager's wage contract is essentially an option on his human capital. When he gets capital and invests in a project, it's like tossing a coin. If it's tails (bad outcome), nothing happens. If it's heads (good outcome), he comes out smelling like roses and his wage goes up.

What is a rational (self-interested) manager to do? Always ask for capital, of course.

This is a lot like options in financial markets. The value of the financial option increases as the volatility (risk) in the underlying security rises.[150] Similarly, the value of the manager's human capital option is elevated by the gambles the manager takes with the firm's capital. So he overinvests.

---

[149]See Bengt Holmstrom, and Joan Ricart I. Costa (1986) "Managerial Incentives and Capital Management," *Quarterly Journal of Economics*, 101, pp. 835–860.

[150]See Fisher Black and Myron Scholes (1973) "The Pricing of Options and Corporate Liabilities," *Journal of Political Economy*, 81, May–June, pp. 637–654. Also re-call Chapter 14.

How should senior management react if all the managers play this game? By rationing capital.

Thus, from this viewpoint, rationing capital is rational because it allows senior management to scale back overall capital spending to where it should be. Bad projects are pruned in the process.

(ii) The Second Theory: According to this theory, capital may be denied to some projects now in order to conserve it for some projects in the future.[151] The basic idea is as follows: Suppose I have a project that requires a $100 investment. Call it project "Good Fun." The present value of its cash flows is $101. Thus, its NPV is $1. This project will yield its first cash flow two years from now.

Next year, the firm anticipates having another project available. Call it project "Good Times." It will require $120 in investment. If internally financed, its NPV will be $3. However, if external financing is needed, the adverse selection premium will be $3.10. So the NPV of the project will be negative (−$0.10). The firm will generate $20 in free cash flow from its other operations. This could be used for project "Good Times." But this will still call for $100 in external financing, with the accompanying adverse selection premium of $3.10.

The choice is clear. If I can fund "Good Times" with internal funds, it is a good project. But if I am forced to use external financing, it's not.

What is interesting is that whether I can fund "Good Times" internally or not depends on whether I fund "Good Fun" now or ration capital to it. If I fund "Good Fun," I will end up being forced to use external capital for "Good Times," and will therefore reject "Good Times." This costs me the $3 in NPV that "Good Times" brings with it. If I do not fund "Good Fun," then I will have $100 available that I can use for "Good Times." When added to the $20 free cash flow from other operations, this will be just enough to entirely fund "Good Times" internally. Doing this means I forgo the $1 in NPV associated with "Good Fun." But this is less than the $3 in NPV that I gain from "Good Times." So I should ration capital to "Good Fun."

(iii) The Third Theory: Finally, the third theory is along the lines of what was outlined in the Butterfield–Lymon report. Firms experience rigidities in their deployment of human resources. If a firm can not profitably harvest the positive NPVs of all its proposed projects with its existing stock of human capital, then it has only two choices. It can either hire more qualified people, or it can reject some positive NPV projects.[152]

---

[151]See Anjan V. Thakor (1991) "Investment Myopia and the Internal Organization of Capital Allocation Decision," *Journal of Law, Economics and Organization,* 7(2), pp. 278–283.

[152]The projects have positive NPVs only if the necessary human resources can be dedicated to them.

Hiring more people may be problematic if they will not all be needed in the future when there are fewer projects to manage. Then the firm must either pay wages to idle employees or fire some of them. Both actions can be costly. Paying wages to those who do not work seems like an obvious waste of shareholders' money. Firing people can damage the firm's reputation for continuity and stability in the labor market, plus all the training associated with the fired workers is lost.

It may thus be better for the firm to avoid increasing its labor force now, if it can not be sure it can sustain its larger size in the future. Given this, it has no choice but to choke off capital to some projects that look good (positive NPVs) on paper.

B. What is the Adverse Selection Premium?

Mostly, the adverse selection premium arises from the fact that the capital market has insufficient information about the firm and is therefore forced to make guesses. These guesses are in response to informational uncertainty perceived by investors.

This information uncertainty drives up capital costs for at least five reasons[153]:

1. The market perceives additional uncertainty because it is suspicious of managers (what are they hiding?).[154] Uncertainty elevates the minimum return investors require.
2. This suspicion leads the market to make protective (conservative) estimates of the unreported or misreported numbers. This may depress cash flow estimates.
3. These estimates are error-prone because they do not come from primary sources and are unaudited.
4. Investors generate these estimates through costly information acquisition processes. Since they must be compensated for their information acquisition costs, it drives up the minimum required return.
5. All of the above reduce the number of investors potentially interested in holding the security. This diminishes liquidity.

The net effect of these five factors is to drive up the firm's cost of capital. The extent by which the firm's cost of capital is driven up is called the "adverse selection premium." If this premium is high enough, we may be forced to pass up projects

---

[153]See Paul B.W. Miller (1997) "Financial Reporting, Meet TQM," *CFO*, 13(11), November, p. 10.

[154]There is a theorem in economics that if somebody chooses *not* to disclose something, it must be bad news. See Paul Milgrom (1981), "Good News and Bad News: Representation Theorems," *Bell Journal of Economics*, 13, pp. 380–391.

that would have had positive NPVs had they been internally funded. The report provided a specific example of how this could happen.

6. Jerry has Some Questions

Jerry had spent a few hours in his office poring over the report. But he had not absorbed everything fully, so he took it home with him. After dinner he felt compelled to take out Bob's report from his briefcase. There were many things he felt uncomfortable about. He furiously began to jot down all the questions he had.

The next morning, on his way into his office, Jerry told Katie to have Bob see him. Fifteen minutes later, Bob was there.

"I think this is a marvelous report, Bob. You guys have done a great job. But I have a question," started Jerry.

"Sure," said Bob, "shoot."

Jerry began, "I know that we're using discounted payback as one of our project selection criteria. But I've been thinking. Isn't it true that payback has far too many weaknesses to be taken seriously?"

"That's right, Jerry. And I continue to believe that our analysts should absolutely not use payback in deciding whether a project is good or not. They should rely only on NPV. But at the Executive Committee level we should use the payback periods of individual projects to determine our overall cycle of external financing needs. This is because of the adverse-selection premium.

"The point is that if we anticipate investing in a lot of opaque projects with low Transparency Index values in the near future, then we should probably consider investing in faster payback projects now. That way, the projects we take now will throw off enough cash flow in the near future to allow us to invest in those opaque projects without relying on external financing.

"We just want to make sure, Jerry, that we use payback as a piece of information to strategically align our external financing needs to those time periods when there is the smallest informational asymmetry between us and the market."

Jerry began to understand. But he pushed back some more. "You mean all those finance text books are wrong about payback?"

"Well, not entirely," qualified Bob. "It's still true that you never want to invest in a negative NPV project just because it has a short payback period. In that sense, NPV is still king. But payback is useful when you are considering portfolios of projects and the possibility of adverse selection premia."

"I see now," said Jerry. "I like your recommendations. Let's do it."

As Bob prepared to leave, Jerry said, "Thanks for acting so quickly on this, Bob."

Main Lessons

- At the senior management level, relying on conventional capital budgeting analysis to determine which projects to fund can undermine management of the Value Sphere. This is because conventional analysis views each project as a stand-alone project, whereas it is essential for senior management to take a portfolio approach.
- The portfolio approach takes account of the informational transparency of each project to financiers because of its effect on the cost of external funding.
- A project's discounted payback will be relevant in a portfolio analysis of projects.
- A portfolio approach to project analysis leads to an optimal project funding cycle that could result in some positive NPV projects being delayed in order to take other positive-NPV projects with larger near-term cash flows.

End-of-Chapter-Exercises

1. How is project portfolio analysis conducted in your company? Assess the strengths and weaknesses of your process relative to that described in this chapter. Can you identify the Value Evaporation that occurs in your company as a result of an inadequate portfolio analysis?
2. Conduct a post-audit of resource allocation in your company for each of the past 5 years and determine the average dollar amounts and percentages of resources (capital and human) allocated to the different product lines/business units. Now fill out the table given below.

Product line/ Business unit	% of total resources allocated on average for past 5 years	Average $ amount of capital allocated and $ equivalent of human resources	% Rate of growth in $ resources	Average economic profit for past 5 years	Average % economic profit growth rate past 5 years

Study this table and determine whether: (i) the largest percentage of your resources are being allocated to the line/business unit that has the highest average economic profit or the highest growth rate in economic profit; (ii) the growth in resources allocated to a particular product line/business unit corresponds to percentage growth in economic profit.

Summarize what you learned from this analysis and the changes you will make in your company as a result of the analysis.

3. Calculate the transparency index for your firm. How has it changed over time? Have your external financing decisions been correlated with these changes?

Practice Problems

1. Why is it important to consider portfolio effects in evaluating projects?
2. What is the relevance of discounted payback when accounting for portfolio effects?
3. How can portfolio analysts sometimes lead to the firm not investing in a positive-NPV project right away?
4. How does an aggressive competitor affect portfolio analysis at a firm?

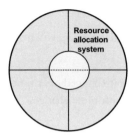

Chapter 17

DIVIDENDS: JERRY CONTEMPLATES A PAYOUT

1. Should Jerry's Lemonade Pay a Dividend?

"Bob, the discussion we had the other day about free cash flows and internally generated funds got me thinking." Jerry said as he sipped on one of his newly formulated lemonade drinks. Jerry always seemed to be searching for new lemonade recipes for the company and Bob had to admit that Jerry had great instincts as to what tasted good with lemonade.

"I have learned to get nervous when you start thinking about something." Bob said with a sigh.

"The hint of lime I put in this recipe tastes very good!" Jerry said as he interrupted Bob.

"Please end the suspense, Jerry, and tell me what is on your mind!" Bob had planned a busy afternoon and he wanted to hear what was on Jerry's mind right now.

"Bob, I think we should consider paying a dividend on our stock. We have been quite successful lately and it appears that our internally generated funds will be healthy in the future. Therefore, this might be a good time to share some of that success with the shareholders. Furthermore, I understand that the tax rate our shareholders have to pay on dividends received is now only 15%, the same rate as on capital gains, instead of the ordinary income tax rates they used to have to pay. For all these reasons, I think we should start paying dividends." From the tone in his voice Bob knew Jerry was enthusiastic about the idea of paying dividends.

Bob decided to address Jerry's enthusiasm head on. "Well you might be right, Jerry, but there are many considerations that go into formulating a dividend policy for Jerry's Lemonade. Since we would be initiating a dividend for the very first time, we must be very careful. We'll have to live with the decision for a very long time because the market will severely punish our stock price if we cut or reduce dividend payments in the future. Once we start paying dividends we must commit to continue paying. Also, we have to consider our future investment needs because dividends are cash payments that must be deducted from the funds we generate. It would be a shame if, in the future, we need to postpone or cancel worthwhile investment projects just to continue an ill-conceived dividend payment. That is, our dividend policy affects the resource allocation quadrant of our Value Sphere. Let's not rush into anything."

"From your comments it sounds as if you think paying dividends is a foolish idea." Jerry said with a noticeable frown on his face.

"I just want us to be careful." Bob interjected. "Let me write up a brief report on dividends, summarizing what the experts are saying now. This will help us in our deliberations. I'll get it to you first thing Monday morning. I'll use the weekend to study the latest research on dividends."

"Okay, Bob. However, be sure to include reasons for paying dividends as well as those against. I want a balanced view." Jerry remarked as he added a bit more lime to his glass of lemonade.

2. Considerations in Paying Dividends

The first thing Monday morning Bob handed the dividend report to Jerry. "I think you'll like this." Bob said with a grin on his face.

As Jerry thumbed through the report he was impressed. Bob had conveniently summarized his thoughts on dividend policy for Jerry's Lemonade. Jerry was delighted to see both the pros and cons presented. As he sipped a glass of vanilla-flavored lemonade he read the report intensely.

3. Bob's Dividend Report

Mature vs. Growing Firms

There are many reasons why firms pay dividends. In general, high growth firms pay no dividends, and mature firms with lower growth rates pay substantial dividends because their internally generated funds greatly exceed their investment needs. High growth firms need to reinvest all of their available funds to fuel their growth. You may recall the sustainable growth calculation we discussed earlier in Chapter 3, when Jerry's Lemonade was considering its IPO. The formula boils down to return on equity times 1 minus the dividend payout ratio ($g^* = ROE(1 - \text{dividend payout ratio})$). At that time, we concluded that the company's strategy called for growth greater than the sustainable rate. Even though all funds were retained, and we did not pay a dividend to our shareholders, we completed the IPO, got the needed funds, and grew very fast. Now that Jerry's Lemonade is an established company, and growth has slowed, it makes sense to consider paying a dividend. However, we need to recognize that money could be paid out to the shareholders either through a cash dividend or a share repurchase.

Cash Dividends and Share Repurchase

Cash payments to shareholders can be made one of two ways;

1. Pay a cash dividend, or
2. Repurchase the company's shares.

Which is preferred? It depends on the financial environment we assume. In a "frictionless" environment where there are no taxes and no costs to issue or repurchase shares, Modigliani and Miller (M&M) proved that dividend policy has no effect on the wealth of current shareholders.[155] In the M&M world, investors can costlessly reproduce any dividend a company pays by selling shares of stock or reinvesting the dividends on their own. If a firm has a positive NPV investment to make, it does not matter if the firm funds it by issuing new shares or cutting dividends.

In the M&M world it does not matter whether a firm pays a dividend or not. Neither does it matter whether it repurchases shares or pays a cash dividend.

Of course, in the real world there are a number of frictions that exist that may cause dividend policy to affect shareholder wealth. Taxes clearly may affect the decision since cash dividends are immediately taxable to the investor as ordinary income. Even if the ordinary tax rate on dividends is the same as that on capital gains, as is the case in the United States now, taxable investors would prefer share repurchase since any capital gain can be deferred, thereby lowering the *effective* tax rate. Another friction to consider is the cost of issuing shares. Investment bankers have to be paid, which is an expense to the current shareholders. In addition, investors may be skeptical about why management is selling shares and therefore

---

[155]Franco Modigliani and Merton Miller, "Dividend Policy Growth and the Valuation of Shares," *Journal of Business,* October 1961, pp. 411–433.

require a price discount before they purchase any new shares.[156] If this is the case, internal equity financed by retentions would create more shareholder wealth than external equity raised by selling new shares to the public.

An important dividend policy consideration is whether or not dividend payments have information content for the market. The initiation of a dividend or an increase in dividend payments may indicate a positive sign to the market about the firm's future earnings, since it would take a sufficiently high level of earnings to sustain the higher dividends.[157] In this case the stock price would rise. By the same token, a dividend cut would carry a negative connotation and lead to a share price decline. Cash dividend payments do have information content and the stock market reacts to management's dividend actions. By making cash dividend payments, a company is committed to distribute cash in the future. This long-term commitment to pay cash via dividends can be seen as a powerful signal of management's confidence in the firm's continued future profitability.

However, share repurchases also carry positive signals for stock prices. For example, Comment and Jarrell report a 2% average abnormal stock price increase when firms announce open market share repurchase programs.[158] When companies offer to buy their stock at a premium through Dutch auction or fixed price self tender offers, the positive signal is even greater, averaging an 11% abnormal price increase. Management's action to repurchase shares at a premium is taken by the market as a very strong signal that the shares are undervalued. This is particularly true if management does not sell any of its share holdings at the higher price.[159] Furthermore, cash that is paid out is less likely to be subject to Value Evaporation, i.e., it solves the "free cash flow problem" of managers unwisely investing excess cash in negative NPV projects for "empire building." Michael Jensen articulated this as a problem in corporations that dividends can help address.

---

[156]Many studies indicate a 3% average price discount for a firm issuing shares. A theoretical justification is provided by Stewart Myers and Nicholas Majluf, "Corporate Financing and Investment Decisions When Firms Have Information That Investors Do Not Have," *Journal of Financial Economics* 13, 1984, pp. 187–222.

[157]For companies initiating a dividend, Healy and Palepu report a 43% increase in earnings in that year. See P. Healy and K. Palepu, "Earnings Information Conveyed by Dividend Initiations and Omissions," *Journal of Financial Economics*, 21, 1988, pp. 149–175.

[158]P. Comment and G. Jarrell, "The Relative Signaling Power Dutch–Auction and Fixed Price Self-Tender Offers and Open-Market Share Repurchases," *Journal of Finance*, September 1991, pp. 1243–1271.

[159]For a theoretical justification, see Ahron Ofer and Anjan Thakor, " A Theory of Stock Price Responses to Alternative Cash Disbursement Mechanisms: Stock Repurchases and Dividends," *Journal of Finance* 42, June 1987, pp. 365–394.

The empirical evidence on dividends is mixed. They seem to signal *future* earnings (supporting the signaling theory) and are also related to *past* earnings (consistent with the "free-cash-flow hypothesis").[160]

How is Dividend Policy Determined?

Unfortunately, there are no hard and fast rules on how companies should set their dividend policies. We do know that in practice dividend policy tends to be conservative. This tendency was first reported in the 1950s by John Lintner, who surveyed corporate managers.[161] He described how dividends were determined by documenting the following:

- Dividend changes are more important than the level of dividends.
- Firms have target dividend payout ratios.
- Companies tend to smooth dividends relative to long-run earnings, i.e., dividend changes are smaller than earnings changes.
- Dividend increases are reversed only as a last resort.

According to Lintner, firms "smooth" dividends relative to earnings, i.e., they increase them less than they expect earnings to go up and they rarely decrease them. Transitory earnings do not affect dividend deliberations. Dividends are reduced in only the most severe circumstances.

For Jerry's Lemonade the research suggests that we must carefully think through the reasons to initiate a cash dividend or to re-purchase shares periodically. If we start paying a cash dividend, we must be committed to continue it.

4. Jerry Meets With Bob

Jerry took a couple of days to read and react to Bob's dividend report. On Friday he called Bob into his office.

"Bob, it sounds like your academic buddies can not come to a conclusion about paying dividends." Jerry loved to needle Bob about his academic background. "Should we pay a cash dividend or not? Should we repurchase shares or not? I see that Microsoft paid a big dividend and repurchased shares. Shouldn't we follow a market leader?"

---

[160] Allen, F. and R. Michaely (2003). Payout policy. *North-Holland Handbooks of Economics.* G. Constantinides, M. Harris and R. Stulz.

[161] J. Lintner (1956) "Distribution of Incomes of Corporations among Dividends, Retained Earnings, and Taxes," *American Economic Review*, May, pp. 97–113.

"You are right," Bob replied, "but you can not generalize from Microsoft's situation. We are still growing quite fast and Microsoft's growth was slowing as the company matured. Furthermore, Microsoft was sitting on a cash hoard of $43 billion at the time they initiated the $0.08 per share annual dividend in March 2003. Microsoft's market dominance in software was throwing off $1 billion a month in free cash flow. We should be so lucky at Jerry's Lemonade!"

"I thought Microsoft paid a much larger dividend than that. Do you have your facts right, Bob?," Jerry inquired.

"You are right, Jerry. After the dividend initiation in 2003, the cash at Microsoft kept piling up until it reached $60 billion in July 2004. In light of this fact the company decided to pay a special one-time dividend of $32 billion and increase its annual dividend to $0.32 per share. They also announced a share repurchase of $30 billion over the next four years. In essence they decided to give the money back to the shareholders with the special dividend and the share repurchase."

"Bob, is this good news or bad news for Microsoft?," Jerry wondered.

"I believe it means the rapid growth is over at Microsoft. In that sense it is bad news. However, they had the courage to return the money to the shareholders, rather than waste it with some value evaporating initiative. As Richard Steinberg, head of Steinberg Global Asset Management, said at the time: "Microsoft could have used the money for some potentially disastrous deals. This eliminates the notion of them doing something stupid with that money."[162] In this sense the payout is good news for the company," Bob opined.

"Okay, Bob, I agree that the Microsoft situation does not apply to us at Jerry's Lemonade. We'll never have a gusher of cash flow like that. Do you think it makes sense to pay a stock dividend rather than a cash dividend? Some of the stocks in my portfolio pay stock dividends and I rather like them."

"Unless something else about the company changes with the stock dividend, the wealth effect will be neutral. The share price will drop in proportion to the stock dividend, i.e. a 10% stock dividend will result in a 10% share price reduction. It works the same way with a stock split. Unfortunately we can not create wealth with a stock dividend or a stock split. We have to create value the old fashioned way, Jerry. By earning it!"

"I have one last question about your dividend report, Bob. You cited an old study by Lintner from the 1950s. Isn't there some more recent information about dividend practice?"

---

[162] Quoted in *Business Week Online*, July 22, 2004, The Microsoft dividend information is taken from this article and another on January 17, 2003.

"Yes there is," Jerry, Bob replied. "The Lintner study is a classic and the results have been durable over time. However, the rise of share repurchases since the time of the Lintner study suggests some additional thoughts are in order. In the 1950s over 80% of the publicly-traded firms in the U.S. paid regular cash dividends. By the late 1990s the percentage had declined to 20%. For NASDAQ companies, which tend to be smaller, faster growing firms, the current percentage of dividend payers is below 10%.[163] Furthermore, firms that do pay dividends tend to pay out a lower percentage of earnings than they did in the past. A recent survey of 384 financial executives by Brav, Graham, Harvey, and Michaely documents this trend.[164] Many of the firms in their sample that do pay dividends wish they did not. Share repurchases are now a very important alternative to cash dividends because repurchases offer flexibility, in the sense that the amount of cash being paid out to shareholders via a repurchase can be altered in response to good investment prospects, without invoking the negative stock price reaction that a dividend cut would. Re-purchases can offset the dilution from stock option exercise. In addition, repurchases offer a simple way to time the return of capital to investors. Executives believe that institutional investors view repurchases as attractive as cash dividends. They conclude that "with respect to payout policy, the rules of the game include the following: there is a severe penalty for cutting dividends, do not deviate far from competitors, maintain a good credit rating, it is good to have a broad and diverse investor base, maintain flexibility, and given that an important portion of investors price stocks using earnings multiples, do not take actions that reduce EPS.[165] These rules summarize their survey findings."

"Sounds reasonable to me. So, tell me: are we ready to establish a dividend policy?" Jerry asked with optimism in his voice.

"Yes!" Bob stated emphatically.

5. Dividend Policy for Jerry's Lemonade

Jerry's Lemonade has come a long way from the early days of rapid growth. The company now has 20 million shares outstanding selling on the NASDAQ for $25/share. The market value of its equity is up to $500 million and it is a dominant force in the lemonade and related beverage market worldwide. Although the

---

[163]The data for the percentages of dividend paying firms is taken from Eugene Farma and Kenneth R. French, "Disappearing Dividends: Changing Characteristics or Lower Propensity to Pay?", *Journal of Applied Corporate Finance*, Spring 2001, pp. 67–79.

[164]Working paper by Alon Brav, John R. Graham, Campbell R. Harvey, and Roni Michaely (2004) "Payout Policy in the 21st Century," June 14.

[165]Page 23, Brav, *et al.*, op.cit.

company still has organic growth opportunities, Jerry and Bob agree that growth has slowed to a modest 7%, this is above the US GDP growth rate, but not the double-digit growth the company had experienced in the past. Any major spike in corporate growth is likely to come from an acquisition. The good news is that Jerry's Lemonade is still highly profitable with an ROE of 18%.

"Jerry," Bob began. "I think we should initiate a yearly cash dividend of 10 cents per share. To minimize mailing and administrative costs I'd suggest we pay the dividend annually instead of quarterly. There is a precedent for this payment pattern: Disney switched to annual dividend payments in 1999."

"Bob, can you give me a quick summary why you are proposing we initiate a cash dividend now."

"Sure Jerry. I just happen to have the major points detailed on a group of slides I prepared for this meeting." Bob proceeded to show Jerry the following bullet points.

- Our growth has slowed and we do not have enough investment projects or trained people to use all of the funds generated internally.
- Standard and Poors indicates that the largest publicly traded firms in our industry (food and non-alcoholic beverages) pay out over 50% of earnings as dividends.
- Major competitors in our area have been paying out 20% to 30% of earnings as cash dividends.
- Some security analysts are asking why we do not pay out dividends like our competitors do. They are concerned that we may waste our cash flow on Value Evaporation activities.
- The initial annual dividend of 10 cents is small compared to our forecast of $1.90 in EPS for next year. The payout ratio is just above 5%, which is a modest beginning.
- Initiating a dividend should be a positive signal of future earnings and should favorably impact our share price.
- In the future, we can also initiate share repurchases for periodic cash distributions to shareholders. These are one-off distributions that will increase our flexibility without disrupting our core dividend policy.
- The initial dividend is so small there is very little chance it will ever have to be cut. Since the share price penalty for a dividend cut is so severe, it makes sense for us to begin at this modest level. The level of 10 cents is in line with Microsoft's initial dividend of 8 cents. We do not have their cash or cash flow, but our earnings are equally stable.

"That pretty well sums it up, Jerry. I'll suggest we pay the dividend to all shareholders on the date of record of December 18. Of course the ex dividend date will be approximately 5 days earlier in order to record the shareholders properly. Investors who buy shares after this date are not entitled to the dividend. The payment date will be February 2 next year. We'll have to run this by the Board of Directors and get their approval. I'll release this information in an announcement to the market assuming the board approves it at their meeting next week."

"Let's do it!" Jerry stated enthusiastically as he rose from his chair.

Main Lessons

- There are two main ways to distribute cash to shareholders: Cash dividends and share repurchases.
- Cash dividends and share repurchases do not affect the value of a company in a frictionless world of no taxes and no transaction costs.
- Taxes on investor income suggest that share repurchases are slightly more tax efficient relative to cash dividends.
- Cash dividends and share repurchases can credibly signal the future performance of the firms. Cash commitments suggest that management will not embark on value evaporating initiatives.
- In practice firms pay dividends conservatively — slowing raising them and reducing than only under severe financial conditions.
- Dividends are typically smoothed relative to earnings.

End-of-Chapter Exercises

1. What is your firm's dividend policy? How was it determined?
2. How does your firm's dividend policy compare with those of your competitors? Do you believe your dividend policy places you at a competitive advantage or disadvantage?
3. Calculate the total dollar amount in dividends your company pays out every year. Are there any deserving projects that could benefit from this capital?

Practice Problems

1. Assuming everybody pays a 15% tax on income and capital gains, would you prefer a cash dividend or a share re-purchase? Why?
2. If dividend policy is simply "residual" — that is, a firm simply pays out the cash that is left over after it has exhausted its investment opportunities — why do stock prices tend to rise when firms announce an increase in dividends?

3. If a company makes a fixed price tender offer to re-purchase half of its stock at a 10% premium, what would be the effect on the firms' share price?

4. Some companies repurchase shares to increase earnings per share. Assume the following information:

Earnings	$1 million
Number of shares	1 million
EPS	$1.00
P/E Ratio	25
Share price	$25

The company repurchases 500,000 shares at $25/share. The number of shares declines to 500,000 and the EPS goes to $2.00/share. Assuming the P/E ratio stays at 25, the share price doubles to $50/share. Do you agree with this conclusion? Why or why not?

Chapter 18

CAPITAL STRUCTURE: JERRY WONDERS HOW MUCH DEBT TO USE

1. Introduction

Jerry picked up the *Wall Street Journal* and began to read it. He had about 15 minutes before his meeting with the Board of Directors. A section on the airline industry caught his eye. It discussed the impending bankruptcy of a major US airline unless creditors were willing to restructure its debt contracts. He read about financial risks arising from a combination of volatile cash flows and excessive financial leverage. He made a mental note to himself to discuss the issue with Bob.

At the end of the Board of Directors meeting, Jerry asked Bob to come to his office. "You know," began Jerry, "I have been thinking about how much debt we have on our balance sheet. With all these firms in financial distress, I wonder if we may be in similar peril if there is a downturn in our business."

Bob look a bit surprised, "Well, we did decide that we would have a capital structure that has 40% debt and 60% equity (re-call Chapter 8). You and the Board approved it, and we've mostly stayed pretty close to it."

"I know," said Jerry, "but didn't we just tap our credit line with the bank and borrow another $40 million? Doesn't that drive up our debt-equity ratio?"

Bob cleared his throat. He had a feeling this was not going to be a quick conversation, "Not quite. Out stock price has been going up recently, so the debt-to-total assets ratio in market value terms is actually still below 40%. I would say we still have some unused debt capacity."

"What does our stock price have to do with our debt-equity ratio, Bob?" asked a seemingly puzzled Jerry.

Bob smiled a bit sardonically, "Because we have defined our optimal capital structure in market value terms. That is, the market value of our debt is to be approximately 40% of our enterprise value, which is the sum of the market values of our debt and equity. So when our stock price goes up and the market value of our debt is unchanged, our debt-to-total assets ratio falls. To re-store it to the long-term target of 40%, we borrow some more."

"I guess that makes sense, and I do remember vaguely now that we'd talked about this a while back," responded Jerry, "But don't most firms raise equity rather than debt when their stock prices are high?"[166]

Bob nodded in agreement, "That's right, Jerry. That does seem to contradict the idea that we issue debt when our stock price is high. However, the way I look at it is this. We should always try to raise capital with the security that will be best received in the market. If we have a bank credit line that we can tap at below-market rates, then that's where we go. If our stock price is high, indicating shareholder agreement with the way we are running the firm, or perhaps overpriced stock, then we should opt for equity.[167] I view these as *opportunistic* security issuance decisions. But these decisions are always taken with an eye on our *long-term* target debt-equity ratio. If our opportunistic security issuance decisions take us too far away from our target capital structure, then we have two choices. One is that we should revise our view of our optimal capital structure, something that may make sense because the very conditions that led to these opportunistic security issuance decisions may dictate that we change our view of what our optimal capital structure is. The other choice is that we keep our optimal capital structure unchanged, but we have to make sure our subsequent security issuances move us back toward our target capital structure."

"Hmm," mused Jerry, "It's a bit much to absorb all at once. I suppose there's a lot of research backing up your views on this."

"That's correct," responded Bob.

Jerry smiled as he spoke, "Well then, it would really help if you could summarize all that in a brief report and we could meet again to review if we have the right capital structure given our present circumstances."

---

[166] This has been empirically documented in numerous research publications. See, for example, Malcolm Baker and Jeffrey Wurgler, "Market Timing and Capital Structure", *Journal of Finance* 57, 2002, pp. 1–32.

[167] This view is developed in Arnoud Boot and Anjan Thakor, "Managerial Autonomy: Allocation of Control Rights, and Optimal Capital Structure", working paper, Washington University in St. Louis, October 2008.

"I had a feeling you might want that. I'll get right on it," said Bob with a wry smile as the meeting concluded.

2. Bob's Capital Structure Report

The basic idea of determining an optimal capital structure is to figure out the way to compose the *liability* side of the balance sheet. In other words, holding the size of the asset side of the balance sheet *fixed*, what is the optimal mix of debt and equity that should be used to finance the asset side of the balance sheet? This question has been at the center stage of research in corporate finance ever since Professors Modigliani and Miller raised the issue in their famous 1958 paper.[168] Many theories have been proposed to address this question and these are briefly discussed below.

The Modigliani–Miller Capital Structure Irrelevance Theorems

Professors Modigliani and Miller specified a set of conditions under which they derived the following two results:

a. In the absence of taxes, a firm's capital structure has no impact on its value and is therefore irrelevant.

b. When corporate debt interest payments are tax deductible but dividend payments are not, the capital structure that maximizes the value of the firm is almost all debt and one share of stock.

The two central assumptions in the derivations of these theorems are that everybody is equally informed and everybody seeks to maximize the value of the firm.

Capital Structure Irrelevance with No Taxes

To see (a), suppose V_U is the value of the firm when it has no leverage and V_L is its value when it has leverage. Suppose the firm's pre-tax cash flow is CF per year and, for simplicity, suppose this is perpetually constant and is paid to investors as dividends each year. Then, it follows that

$$V_U = \frac{CF}{K_W}$$

---

[168] Franco Modigliani and Merton Miller, "The Cost of Capital, Corporation Finance and the Theory of Investment", *American Economic Review* 48–3, 1958, pp. 261–297.

Where K_W is the weighted average cost of capital and $\frac{CF}{K_W}$ is the present value of a perpetuity (re-call Chapter 2). Now, we know that (re-call Chapter 8):

K_W = weighted average cost of capital

$= K_U[1 - TL]$

= unlevered equity cost of capital [1 − {tax rate × leverage ratio}],

where the leverage ratio

$$L = \frac{\text{market value of debt}}{\text{market value of debt} + \text{market value of equity}}.$$

If the tax rate is $T = 0$, then $K_W = K_U$ and we can write:

$$V_U = \frac{CF}{K_U},$$

which remains unchanged regardless of the firm's capital structure.

While this may seem at first like a bit of algebraic black magic, the idea is actually very simple. In a world without taxes and perfect capital markets, there is really nothing to distinguish debt from equity, other than the fact that debt has a priority claim on cash flows over equity. This priority means that the cash flows to debtholders are less risky than those to shareholders. But that means these cash flows are also discounted at a lower rate.

That is,

weighted average cost of capital

$= K_W = L * \text{cost of debt} + [1 - L] * \text{cost of equity},$

and the cost of debt is less than the cost of equity due to the priority of debt. Now, as we increase L by replacing some equity with additional debt, two things happen. First, equity becomes riskier because there is a bigger fixed claim that has priority over equity. Hence the cost of equity goes up. Second, the firm substitutes to a lower-cost financing source in replacing equity with debt, i.e., there is a greater weight attached to debt, and debt is cheaper than equity. When there are no taxes, these two effects exactly cancel each other out and K_W remains unaffected as leverage changes. And leverage changes also have no effect on the firm's total cash flow, CF, since they only determine how the cash flow is divided among shareholders and bondholders, rather than its size. Thus, firm value is unaffected by changes in L.

Professor Miller, who along with Professor Modigliani won the Nobel Prize in Economics for this contribution, explained capital structure irrelevance with the following analogy. Suppose you have a pizza. Then you have just as much pizza if you cut it in four slices as you would if you cut it in eight slices! In other words, in a taxless world, changes in capital structure only affect how a total cash flow is sliced up among shareholders and bondholders, and these changes affect neither the size of the total cash flow nor the weighted average cost of capital used to discount them. Hence, leverage cannot impact firm value.

An All-Debt Capital Structure with Taxes

Now consider (b). With taxes, debt has associated with it a "tax shield." If our tax rate is 40%, then every dollar we pay in debt interest carries with it a 40 cent refund from the tax authorities. Since dividends paid to shareholders do not have a similar tax treatment, the tax code opens up an asymmetry between debt and equity. Debt is more valuable due to the "debt tax shield."

This can be readily seen by looking at the formula:

$$K_W = K_U[1 - TL].$$

It is clear that as L increases, K_W declines. Since changes in L do not affect the firm's cash flow CF, the value of the levered firm, V_L, keeps rising as L increases. The best thing the firm can do is to issue one share of stock to raise the smallest possible amount from shareholders and finance the rest of the firm with debt.

In fact, we can calculate exactly how much value is added by having debt rather than equity in the firm's capital structure. This is given by the formula:

$$V_L = V_U + DT$$

That is,[169]

$$\text{Value of Levered Firm} = \left\{ \begin{array}{l} \text{Value of Unlevered Firm}(V_U) \\ + \text{Present Value of Debt Tax Shield } (DT) \end{array} \right\}$$

This is illustrated in Fig. 18.1.

We can also see what is at work by considering a simple example, such as the one given below.

Example: Consider a firm that is all-equity financed and has $100 in assets. Its pre-tax cash flows are $20/year perpetually. It has an opportunity cost of capital of 10%

---

[169]To show this, observe that $V_L = V_U + \frac{rDT}{r}$.

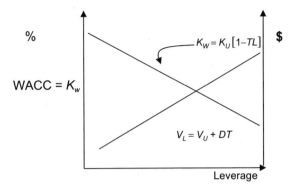

Fig. 18.1. WACC, Firm value, and Modigliani–Miller theorem with taxes. Value of Levered Firm $= V_L$.

and a tax rate of 50%. Now, the shareholders' rate of return

$$= \frac{\$20[1 - 0.5]}{\$100}$$

$$= 10\% \text{ per year.}$$

Now, suppose the firm issues $20 in debt at a 10% yield ($2 in interest per year perpetually). It uses the proceeds to distribute a special dividend to its shareholders. After this capital structure change, shareholders receive

$$\$(20 - 2) \times 10[1 - 0.5] = \$9 \text{ per year.}$$

But their rate of return $= \frac{\$9}{\$80} = 11\%$, which exceeds the 10% earned before.

Alternatively, shareholders can re-invest their $20 at their opportunity cost of 10%. Then their average return $= [0.8 \times 11] + [0.2 \times 10] = 10.8\%$, which also exceeds 10%.

Note that the value of the firm is also higher. In fact, it rises from $100 to $110 with $20 debt and a 50% tax rate. In other words, the value of the firm increases by $DT = \$20 \times 0.5 = \$10$.

Another Example to Illustrate What Happens when a Firm Increases Leverage in a Modigliani–Miller World with Taxes

Consider a firm that has $100 in book equity and is all equity financed. Its unlevered equity cost of capital is 10%. Its earnings before interest and taxes (EBIT) is $20 per year and is expected to be perpetually constant. The tax rate is 50%. What is the value of equity? What is the NPV to shareholders? What is the WACC? Assume that net fixed assets (NFA) and net working capital (NWC) remain perpetually constant.

Solution : $K_W = 0.10$, $EBIT = \$20$

$$(\text{Market}) \text{ Value of equity} = \frac{FCF}{K} = V_S$$

where

$K = $ levered equity cost of capital
$K = K_U = $ unlevered equity cost of capital (since the firm is unlevered)
$\quad = 10\% = 0.10$

Free cash flow $= FCF$

$$FCF = NOPAT - \text{Increase in NFA} - \text{Increase in NWC}$$

$$= EBIT(1 - T) - 0 - 0$$

$$= \$20(1 - 0.5)$$

$$= \$10 \text{ per year perpetually}$$

Thus, (market) value of equity

$$= \frac{\$10}{0.10} = \$100$$

Return on equity (ROE) $=$ net income/Book equity

$$= \frac{\$10}{\$100} = 0.10 = 10\%$$

$$NPV \text{ to shareholders} = \text{Market value of equity}$$

$$- \text{Book value of equity}$$

$$= 0$$

$$WACC = K_W = K_U(1 - TL)$$

$$= K_U \text{ since } L = 0 \text{ (no leverage)}$$

$$= 10\%$$

Additional Data

The firm now issues $20 in debt (say it takes a $20 loan) and uses the proceeds to repurchase $20 of its equity. This reduces book equity to $80 and puts $20 of debt on the balance sheet.

Assume pre-tax cost of debt = 5%

i. What is the new levered equity cost of capital?
ii. What is the new return on equity?
iii. What is the new WACC?
iv. What is the value of the firm?
v. What is the new NPV to shareholders?
vi. Why is the NPV to shareholders going up even though the equity cost of capital is higher?

Solution: Re-call first that the value of the levered firm, V_L, can be written as:

$$V_L = V_U + DT$$

where V_U = value of firm if unlevered

$$= \frac{FCF}{K_U} \tag{1}$$

DT = present value of debt tax shield, where D = debt and T = effective tax rate.

Now let K_d represent the pre-tax cost of debt. Then, in any year, the debt tax shield is $K_d D \times T$ since $K_d D$ is the $ interest paid on $D of debt and $K_d DT$ is the $ amount saved on taxes. The present value of a perpetual stream of $K_d DT$ tax savings is:

$$\frac{K_d DT}{K_d} = \$DT$$

Using Eq. (1) and recognizing that for an *unlevered* firm,

Total firm value = V_U = $100, we have the value of the levered firm:

$$V_L = V_U + DT$$

$$= \$100 + \$20 \times 0.5$$

$$= \$110$$

Since the value of debt $= D = \$20$, the value of the levered firm's equity

$$= V_L - D$$
$$= \$110 - \$20$$
$$= \$90$$

Since book equity (E) $= \$80$ now, NPV to shareholders

$$= \text{Market value} - \text{Book equity} = V_S - E$$
$$= \$90 - \$80$$
$$= \$10$$

The new levered equity cost of capital (re-call the formula provided in Chapter 8)

$$= K = K_U + [K_U - K_d][1 - T]\frac{D}{V_S}$$

That is,

Levered equity cost of capital (K) = unlevered equity cost of capital (K_U)

$$+ \{[\text{unlevered equity cost}(K_U)$$
$$- \text{debt cost } (K_d)][1 - \text{Tax Rate}]$$
$$\times [\text{Debt} - /\text{Equity Ratio}]\}$$

Note that $\frac{D}{V_S} = \frac{20}{90}$ since we must measure capital structure in market value terms for cost of capital.

Thus, levered equity cost of capital

$$K = 10 + [10 - 5][1 - 0.5] \times \frac{2}{9} = 10.56\%$$

Thus, K increases from 10% to 10.56% due to an increase in L from 0 to 20%.

The new $WACC = K_W = K_U[1 - TL]$.

Where the new

$$L = \frac{D}{D + V_S}$$
$$L = \frac{D}{V_L} = \frac{\$20}{100}$$

Thus, $K_W = 10\left[1 - \frac{2}{11} \times 0.5\right] = \frac{100}{11} = 9.1\%$.

This means the *WACC* declines from 10% to 9.1% due to L going up from 0 to 0.2. Return on equity $=$ ROE

$$= \frac{\text{Net income}}{\text{Book equity}}$$

$$= \frac{[\text{EBIT} - \text{Interest}][1 - T]}{\text{Book equity}}$$

$$= \frac{[\$20 - \$1][1 - 0.5]}{\$80}$$

(Where \$1 is the interest on \$20 of debt at 5%)

$$= \frac{\$19 \times 0.5}{\$80} = 11.875\%$$

Thus, ROE increases from 10% to 11.875%.

This example illustrates several general concepts, as discussed next.

Figure 18.2 illustrates that an increase in leverage increases both ROE (re-call the DuPont formula discussion in Chapter 2) and the leveraged equity cost of capital. It leaves the unlevered equity cost of capital unaffected and it reduces the weighted average cost of capital.

Figure 18.3 shows that an increase in leverage decreases both the book and market values of equity as debt replaces equity. However, the *difference* between the market and book values of equity increases, as does the total value of the levered firm.

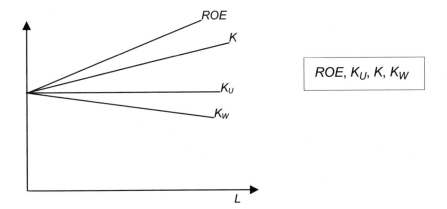

Fig. 18.2.   Impact of leverage on return on equity and various costs of capital.

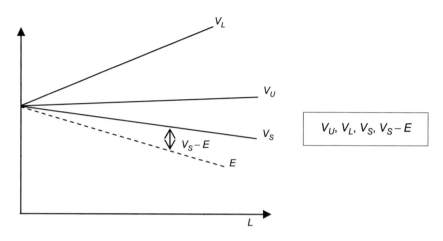

Fig. 18.3.   Impact of leverage on value of firm and value of equity.

We can summarize as follows. As leverage (L) increases, keeping the total book value of assets fixed, the following things happen:

(1) The weighted average cost of capital K_W decreases due to the debt tax shield $(K_W$ would remain constant with increases in L, if $T = 0)$.

(2) The value of the levered firm V_L increases by DT, the present value of the debt tax shield.

(3) The levered equity cost of capital K increases due to an increasing financial risk premium by shareholders associated with higher leverage.

(4) ROE increases even faster than K, making shareholders better off (see the DuPont formula in Chapter 2 for a discussion of how leverage affects ROE).

(5) As L increases, D increases, thereby causing a decline in book equity, E. This is because every \$1 increase in D is replacing \$1 of book equity. Consequently, V_S also declines. However, the NPV to the shareholders = market value of equity $- BV$ of equity $= V_S - E$, is increasing in L.

Thus, the shareholders are better off because their NPV is going up, even though the size of their invested capital and the total dollar value of equity (in both book and market value terms) is going down. In our example, book equity goes down from \$100 to \$80, the market value of equity goes down from \$100 to \$90, and yet shareholders are better off because ROE increases from 10% to 11.875% (an increase exceeding the increase in K from 10% to 10.56%) and their NPV increases from 0 to \$10.

(6) So, from a purely cost of capital standpoint, the firm is better off as L increases. The reason why, it may not pay to increase L indefinitely is something that will be considered next.

Going Beyond Modigliani and Miller: The Impact of Asymmetric Information

A key assumption in the classic Modigliani and Miller analysis is that everybody has the same information. Investors know as much as managers do. Clearly, this is a heroic assumption. Managers often know more about their firms than investors do. They may therefore, have incentives to use this informational advantage strategically.

A situation in which the manager has more information about the firm's future cash flows is called a situation of *asymmetric information* (re-call the extensive discussion in Chapter 16). To see how this can affect the firm's security issuance decision, consider an example.

Suppose a firm's cash flows to shareholders (think of all earnings paid on dividends, for simplicity) are expected to be $9 million per year perpetually. The manager knows this. But investors, lacking the manager's information, believe that the cash flows will be $12 million per year perpetually. Assume that the equity cost of capital for the firm is 10%. Then the *market value* of the firm's equity will be $\frac{\$12 \text{ million}}{0.10} = \$120$ million, whereas the manager knows that it should be $\frac{\$9 \text{ million}}{0.10} = \$90$ million. The firm has 10 million shares outstanding.

Now, suppose the manager wants to raise $10 million in external financing. Everybody expects this $10 million to be invested to yield a return equal to the firm's cost of capital, i.e., it will produce an annual cash flow of $0.10 \times \$10$ million $= \$1$ million perpetually, with a present value $= \frac{\$1 \text{ million}}{0.10} = \$10$ million. A zero NPV investment!

Assume that the firm would incur a small transaction cost to raise the money, say $1,000. What should the manager do?

First, suppose the stock was correctly priced at an aggregate value of $90 million, or $9 per share. Let n be the number of additional shares the manager would need to issue to raise $10 million, then n satisfies:

$$\left[\frac{n}{n + 10 \text{ million}} \right] * \left[\frac{\$9 \text{ million} + \$1 \text{ million}}{0.10} \right] = \$10 \text{ million}$$

That is, those who purchase the n shares will now have a claim to a fraction

$$\left[\frac{n}{n + 10 \text{ million}} \right]$$

of the firm's post-equity-issue cash flow, where $n + \$10$ million is the number of shares outstanding after the equity issue. The post-equity-issuance cash flow per year will be $9 million + \$1 million, where $1 million is the incremental cash flow from investing the $10 million proceeds at 10%. The present value of the new shareholders' share of the total cash flow is then:

$$\left[\frac{n}{n + 10 \text{ million}}\right] * \left[\frac{\$9 \text{ million} + \$1 \text{ million}}{0.10}\right],$$

and this must equal the amount they pay for these shares, $10 million.

Solving this equation yields $n = [1/0.9]$ million $= 1.1111$ million shares. That is how many new shares the firm will need to issue to raise $10 million.

What is the NPV of this to the firm's existing (old) shareholders? Note that the present value of their share of the post-equity-issuance cash flows is:

$$\left[\frac{10 \text{ million}}{n + 10 \text{ million}}\right] * \left[\frac{\$10 \text{ million}}{0.10}\right] - \text{transaction cost of issuing new equity}$$

$$= \$9 \text{ million} - \$1,000$$

That is, they are exactly where they were *before* the equity issue, ignoring the $1,000 transaction cost. The presence of the transaction cost makes them worse off. So if their equity is correctly priced and all they can do is invest the proceeds from a new equity issue in a zero-NPV project, they would rather not issue equity.

But now, suppose the market values the equity at $120 million. What will the manager do now?

The answer depends on how he believes the market will react, i.e., whether investors are rational or irrational. Suppose first that investors are rational. Then they will recognize, using logic similar to that presented above, that the manager will only issue equity when his firm is overvalued. To see this more concretely, suppose investors believe that there is a 50% chance that the firm's annual cash flows will be $9 million perpetually and a 50% chance that they will be $15 million perpetually. The weighted average or expected value across these two possibilities is $0.5 \times \$9$ million $+ 0.5 \times \$15$ million $= \$12$ million, which is the value they use in determining the stock price. That is, investors know that half the firms are overvalued and half are undervalued, but they don't know which is which. So they price at the average.

Investors may be informationally handicapped. But they are rational nonetheless, and recognize their informational disadvantage. Thus, they know that the manager of a firm whose cash flow is $15 million per year will never issue equity. Such a firm would not issue equity even if it was correctly priced, so why would it issue equity when undervalued? But it may be a different story for the overvalued firm.

Suppose, it issues $\hat{n}$ shares to raise $10 million. The value of $\hat{n}$ will depend on which of two possibilities apply.

Possibility 1: Investors are rational and recognize that only the overvalued firm will issue equity.

In this case, as soon as the firm issues equity, investors will view it as a signal of overvaluation and revise their assessment of future cash flow down to $9 million per year. Consequently, $\hat{n} = n = 1.111$ million, and the old shareholders will see their share of the firm drop to $90 million in market value minus $1,000 in transaction cost. The *true present value* of their future cash flows now drops to $90 million $- \$1,000$, which is $1,000 less than before. Since the market value of their equity is $120 million *before* the equity issue, they recognize that they too are better off abstaining from a new equity issue, whether their wealth is measured as the true present value of future cash flows or as market value. Thus, they will instruct the manager to *not* issue equity. In other words, nobody issues equity! The prediction is that equity issues should be quite rare, and when they occur — say during financial duress when debt financing is difficult to obtain — there should be a negative announcement effect, i.e., a drop in the firm's stock price.[170] There is thus a "pecking order" in security issuance. Firm's will finance first from retained earnings, then from debt, and only under exceptional circumstances from equity.

Possibility 2: Investors are Irrational and Do Not Anticipate that only Overvalued Firms Will Issue Equity

What if investors are not as smart as we have assumed? What if they ignore the strategic behavioral incentives of managers? That is, suppose that the issuance of equity does not precipitate an adverse price reaction. A firm that issues equity is still viewed as being capable of generating $12 million per year in pre-issuance equity cash flows. In this case, $\hat{n}$ is obtained as a solution to:

$$\left[\frac{\hat{n}}{\hat{n} + 10 \text{ million}} \right] * \left[\frac{\$12 \text{ million} + \$1 \text{ million}}{0.10} \right] = \$10 \text{ million}$$

This yields $\hat{n} = \frac{10}{12}$ or 0.8333 million shares. Because the firm is overvalued, it needs to issue fewer shares than before to raise $10 million.

---

[170]This "pecking order" theory was developed by Stewart Myers and Nicholas Majluf, "Corporate Financing and Investment Decisions When Firms Have Information that Investors Do Not Have," *Journal of Financial Economics* 13, 1984, pp. 197–221.

What happens to the wealth of the old shareholders?
The true present value of their future cash flows is now:

$$\left[\frac{10.00}{10.8333}\right] * \left[\frac{\$9 \text{ million} + \$1 \text{ million}}{0.10}\right] - \$1,000$$

$$= 0.9231 \times 100 - \$1,000$$

$$= \$92.31 \text{ million} - \$1,000$$

which clearly exceeds the $90 million they enjoyed previously.
In terms of market value, this is:

$$\left[\frac{10.00}{10.8333}\right] * \left[\frac{\$13 \text{ million}}{0.10}\right] - \$1,000$$

$$= \$120 \text{ million} - \$1,000$$

So, while the old shareholders incur a transaction cost of $1,000, their share of the firm's market value is unchanged except for the $1,000 impact. However, their share of the true present value of future cash flows *rises* by almost $2.31 million, from $90 million to $92.31 million–$1,000.

There is a hypothesis, called the "market timing hypothesis," which asserts that the manager will wish to issue equity in this case.[171] What the equity issuance essentially achieves is a $2.31 million wealth transfer from the new shareholders to the old shareholders. This wealth transfer comes about because the firm issues 0.8333 million shares rather than the 1.1111 million it would have to issue if it were not overvalued. Equity issues are thus predicted to be quite prevalent, especially during periods of high stock prices.

It is readily apparent that the "pecking order" and "timing" hypotheses generate diametrically opposite predictions *under essentially the same informational assumptions.* What distinguishes them is that the pecking order hypothesis is based on the assumption that investors know less than managers but are rational, whereas the timing hypothesis assumes that investors are both less informed and irrational.

Going Beyond Modigliani and Miller: Agency Costs and Managerial Autonomy

We saw in our preceding discussion that relaxing the Modigliani–Miller assumption of symmetric information has important consequences. Another direction that the

---

[171] See Malcolm Baker and Jeffrey Wurgler, "Market Timing and Capital Structure", *Journal of Finance,* **57**, 2002, pp. 1–32.

capital structure research has taken is to relax the assumption that all agents — managers, shareholders and creditors — are interested in maximizing firm value. As we saw in Chapter 4, the interests of shareholders, creditors and managers may diverge. Shareholders seek to maximize the value of equity. Creditors seek to protect the safety of their fixed claims. Managers may like perquisites, running larger firms, higher compensation and higher stock prices. The actions of each group will be driven by personal interest. This gives rise to *agency costs* (see Chapter 4).[172]

Consider first the *agency costs of debt*, which arise due to a divergence of interest between the shareholders and the creditors. A simple example will illustrate how this cost can arise.

Suppose a firm can choose between a safe (S) project and a risky (R) project. The safe project will pay off $100 for sure next period, whereas the risky project will pay off $150 with probability 0.5 and nothing with probability 0.5. The firm has debt outstanding that will require a re-payment of $75 next period. The riskless rate is 10% and everybody is risk neutral.

First, note that the value-maximizing project is S. It has a present value of $\frac{\$100}{1.1} = \$90.91$, compared to a present value of $\frac{0.5 \times \$150}{1.1} = \$68.18$ for R. Thus, if value maximization was everybody's goal, S should be chosen.

But now, suppose the shareholders can unilaterally make their project choice and creditors can do nothing to affect it. The present values of *equity* for the two choices are:

$$S : \frac{\$100 - \$75}{1.1} = \$22.72$$

$$R : \frac{0.5[\$150 - \$75]}{1.1} = \$34.09$$

Hence, shareholders prefer R!

Why does this happen? It is because by choosing R, shareholders are able to expropriate wealth from the bondholders. Consequently, rational creditors will *anticipate* this incentive on the part of the shareholders and price their debt accordingly. That is, if there was no agency problem and bondholders could be assured that the value-maximizing choice S would be made, they would be willing to lend $\frac{\$75}{1.1} = \$68.18$ to the firm at the outset in exchange for a promised repayment of $75. But, given the agency problem, they are only willing to lend $\frac{0.5 \times \$75}{1.1} = \$34.09$.

Agency problems associated with debt therefore create two kinds of costs. One is the cost associated with *inefficient investments*. As shown above, the presence of

---

[172]Jensen, Michael C., and William H. Meckling. 1976. Theory of the Firm: Managerial Behavior, Agency Costs, and Ownership Structure. *Journal of Financial Economics*, **3**, no. 4 (October): 305–360.

debt may cause shareholders to invest in projects that do not maximize firm value, such as R. The other is that the availability of debt may be reduced as bondholders will simply refuse to lend beyond a certain point, no matter what the price. Firms may therefore be unable to fully exploit their debt tax shields.

There are also *agency costs of equity* that arise from managers acting in their own self interest to the detriment of shareholders. Addressing these agency costs requires aligning the interests of managers more closely with those of shareholders through equity ownership and compensation design (see Chapters 4 and 5; further discussion will also appear in Chapter 23).

The basic agency cost argument is that the firm's capital structure will attempt to trade off the agency costs of debt on the one hand against the agency costs of equity and the tax advantage of debt on the other hand.

A more recent theory, called "managerial autonomy," argues that managers care about how much autonomy/flexibility they have in making investment decisions. Because bondholders care primarily about protecting the safety of their investments, they will impose restrictive covenants that limit the manager's choices much more than shareholders would. Although equity gives the manager more freedom, to say that the freedom is unlimited is an illusion. If shareholders disagree with the manager's choice, they will react to the decision by lowering the firm's stock price. To the extent that the manager cares about this (perhaps because compensation and job security are tied to the stock price), he will view his investment autonomy as being limited.

A higher stock price means that shareholders are less concerned about the manager making decisions they disagree with, i.e., they have a higher propensity to agree with the manager. Thus, the manager will perceive his investment autonomy with equity as being higher when the firm's stock price is higher. If this autonomy is valued sufficiently high, it will exceed the tax-shield benefit of debt and the firm will issue equity. If the firm's stock price is lower and the autonomy associated with equity is valued less highly, the tax-shield advantage of debt will dominate and the firm will issue debt.

Combining the agency costs and managerial autonomy arguments, we see that the firm's optimal capital structure is determined by a tradeoff of costs and benefits, as shown in Fig. 18.4.

The Empirical Evidence

How do the different post-Modigliani–Miller theories perform empirically?

The pecking order theory finds some empirical support in the fact that on average equity issues are greeted with negative (abnormal) price reactions. However,

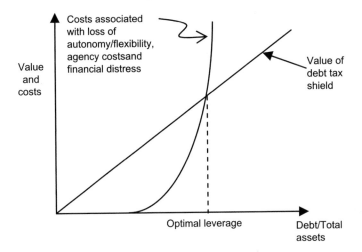

Fig. 18.4.   The tradeoff in optimal capital structure.

recent research has provided strong evidence against this theory. The evidence is that equity issues are not as rare as the pecking order theory predicts, and that a majority of firms appear to issue securities in apparent violation of the pecking order.[173] Moreover, it has also been documented that firms do not seem to issue securities to move toward target capital structures when changes in their stock prices cause them to experience changes in their debt–equity ratios in market value terms.[174]

There is some evidence in support of market timing.[175] It appears that firms tend to issue equity when their stock prices are high, and these issuances seem to have long-term effects on the capital structures of firms.

There is also evidence that managerial autonomy considerations affect security issuance decisions. That is, in addition to market timing, it appears that managers choose which security to issue based on how much investment autonomy it gives them.[176]

---

[173]See Eugene Fama and Kenneth French, "Financing Decisions: Who Issues Stock?", *Journal of Financial Economics*, forthcoming.

[174]See Ivo Welch, (2004) "Capital Structure and Stock Returns", *Journal of Political Economy*, **112**, pp. 106–131.

[175]The strongest evidence in support of timing is provided by Malcolm Baker and Jeffrey Wurgler, (2002) "Market Timing and Capital Structure", *Journal of Finance*, **57**, pp. 1–32.

[176]See Amy Dittmar and Anjan Thakor, (2007) "Why Do Firm's Issue Equity?", *Journal of Finance*, 62-1, February 2007, pp. 1–54.

3. Jerry Reflects on the Report

Jerry sat in the rocking chair on his deck, sipping his favorite lemonade and poring over Bob's report. Fall was here and while it was cooling down, Saturday afternoons were still warm enough to sit on the deck.

This was a thorough report. Perhaps more theoretical and steeped in research findings than Jerry would have liked. But quite extensive and useful nonetheless. There were still holes in Jerry's understanding. And as usual, Bob had said nothing about what Jerry's Lemonade should do. Should they reduce their financial leverage? Were they in financial peril? If most firms issued equity when their stock prices were high, why did we just issue debt? What about the empirical evidence on Modigliani and Miller's theorems? But these were topics for his next meeting with Bob.

4. The Meeting with Bob

"Come on in, Bob," said Jerry cheerfully. "I have a lot of questions about this report."

"I'm sure you do," responded Bob. "Did you find it helpful?"

Jerry smiled, "Oh yeah! It's a wonderful report. Obviously there's a lot of research that has been done and you've covered it well. But my first question is this. You've discussed empirical evidence related to the various theories, but have said nothing about the Modigliani–Miller theorems. Does it mean they have no empirical support?"

Bob nodded, "You're quite right, Jerry. I didn't discuss Modigliani–Miller in that context. One of their strong predictions was that firms should be using a lot of debt due to the tax shield. Some people initially viewed this as *prima facie* evidence against the theory because we don't observe firms using all that much financial leverage. But that is because a lot of managers were sub-optimizing and not borrowing as much as was good for their shareholders. However, at business schools we kept drilling this into our MBA students, and eventually some of them went to Wall Street and invented the Leveraged Buyout (LBO). With an LBO, firms were able to substantially increase their leverage. I view the rise of LBOs in the 1980's as a practical vindication of an important prediction of the Modigliani–Miller theory with corporate taxes."

"Ah! I see," said Jerry, "so agency costs of equity caused managers to have underlevered firms, and LBOs were a way to overcome this and realize value for shareholders through the debt tax shield."

"Precisely," countered Bob.

Jerry smiled as he spoke, "Okay, fine. But now tell me what all this means for our capital structure."

"Well," began Bob, "first I should say that there is *no* formula for optimal capital structure. So I can't give you a number that should be our goal. The theories provide qualitative assessment tools to guide our decision. We are now in a fairly mature phase and our growth and cash flows are quite predictable, unless we change our growth strategy and embark on more rapid growth via, say, acquisitions. Barring that, this stability implies relatively low agency costs of debt and low financial distress costs. Hence, leverage is desirable."

"So you think we should borrow more?" asked Jerry.

Bob shook his head, "No, not really. We just tapped our credit line at the bank and now our debt is about 33% of our total assets in market value terms. We did this in part because the line was accessible at a below-market rate and partly because we're below our target leverage ratio. But the line is now nearly exhausted. Moreover, our stock price is even higher now than before I wrote my report. The managerial autonomy argument suggests we use equity if we need more money."

"But wouldn't that take us further away from our target ratio?" asked Jerry, a little perplexed.

"Yes, it would," replied Bob, "But all that it means is we'll have greater flexibility to make investment decisions as well as modify our growth strategy if necessary. Most firms reserve some flexibility for the future. We will have a fair amount of unused debt capacity. That may be very useful if we decide to make a big play like an acquisition. That is, we may want to revisit the issue of what our optimal capital structure should be once we have redefined our growth strategy, which I suspect we may do before too long."

"Gotcha," said Jerry, "I guess that makes sense. Let's leave things where they are. We don't need investment funds right now, but if we do then we can tap the equity market. It's not so bad to be below our target leverage ratio. I'll sleep easier at night knowing that we face less financial risk."

Main Lessons

- Debt financing provides firms a debt tax shield because interest payments on debt are tax deductible, whereas dividends paid to shareholders are not. This means that the firm's weighted average cost of capital decreases as its leverage ratio increases.
- The value of a levered firm exceeds the value of an otherwise identical unlevered firm of equal size by an amount DT, where D is the amount of debt and T is the

corporate tax rate. The term DT represents the present value of the firm's debt tax shield. A leveraged buyout is designed in part to take advantage of this debt tax shield.

- If investors are rational, asymmetric information creates a disadvantage for equity issues and generates a "pecking order" of securities. Firms are predicted to first rely on retained earnings, then debt, and only in exceptional circumstances, on equity.
- If investors are irrational, asymmetric information leads to firms' preferring to issue equity when their stock prices are high, i.e., when they are overvalued. This is called "market timing."
- A divergence of interests between shareholders and bondholders generates agency costs of debt, which offset the tax shield advantage of debt and may lead to an optimal capital structure.
- Managers desire autonomy/flexibility in making investment decisions. This autonomy is typically greater with equity than with debt. The perceived autonomy of equity increases with the firm's stock price. Thus, the firm's security issuance trades off the relative autonomy benefit of equity against the tax shield advantage of debt.

End-of-Chapter Exercises

1. What is your firm's optimal capital structure? How was it determined?
2. Compare your capital structure with those of other firms in the industry. What does the comparison reveal?
3. In your industry, is having higher leverage than the industry average an advantage or a disadvantage? Why?

Practice Problems

1. Consider a firm with an expected perpetual annual pretax cash flow of $1 million. The tax rate is 40%. The firm's unlevered equity cost of capital is 10%.

   a. What is the firm's value if it is unlevered?
   b. What is the firm's value if it borrows $2 million in perpetual debt (a consol) at a rate of 7%?
   c. What is the present value of the firm's debt tax shield?

2. Describe the Modigliani and Miller capital structure theorems and the empirical predictions they generate.

3. What are the other theories of capital structure? List their empirical predictions and compare them.

4. What do the different capital structure theories imply about the capital structures of firms in the following industries and why?

- Regulated utility
- Computer technology
- Beverages

Chapter 19

ACQUIRING A FIRM

1. To Acquire or Not: That is the Question

Jerry had just started a meeting with his senior executives to go over the company's near-future expansion plans. Present at the meeting were his CFO, Bob Butterfield, his VP of HR, Barb Sidwell, his Treasurer, Jim Lymon, and his Vice President for Strategic Planning, Doug Harris. Bob began the meeting by giving Jerry his overview of what some of them had discussed earlier.

"Jerry, if we are to meet the expansion goals of our strategy that we discussed at our last meeting, it is unlikely that we can achieve that from organic growth alone. To remind everybody in this room, our target is to grow our Market Value Added (MVA) by 10% per year and to gain an increasing share of the total MVA in our industry. Unlike many of the companies in our peer group, we do not state our growth targets in terms of market share or sales revenue. As I've mentioned to some of you earlier, there are numerous examples of companies that have evaporated value by growing sales revenue and market share without concern for shareholder value."

Jerry asked, "Why can't we meet our MVA target through organic growth? Is it because we have financial constraints on growth?"

Bob looked at Barb as he spoke. "It's not so much financial, but rather constraints imposed by the markets we are in, as well as our human resources. As we discussed the other day, our domestic market is rapidly approaching a mature stage and it is going to be difficult for this market to grow much more rapidly than the rate at which the overall U.S. economy is growing. We have estimated only single-digit annual organic growth for our company going forward. This is one reason why we initiated a dividend. In the long run, of course, the market constraints will be relaxed as we execute our strategy and introduce new products in *new* markets. But the human resource constraints are a different matter."

Barb interjected. "That's right. We just can't recruit and develop people as fast as our expansion goals demand. And that's assuming no more than our normal attrition rate. But in recent months, it has been more and more difficult to retain people who get aggressive offers from other companies."

Jerry looked at the group, paused briefly and asked, "So we need to think of acquisitions, right? What's on the list of possible targets?"

Bob distributed a list and said, "I know I probably don't need to say this to this group, but I'll do it anyway. This list is absolutely, strictly confidential. One word of this leaks out, and we're going to have a serious problem. Don't breathe a word of this to anyone in your organization. Or even to your significant other."

Everyone nodded and then spent a few minutes looking over the list. Barb was the first one to speak.

"This may be a silly question, but why isn't Mickey's on this list, Bob?"

Bob smiled and said, "We didn't give it serious thought, Barb, because there is no chance Mickey would be interested. We've had a conversation or two about this in the past. But we all know Mickey hates our guts and wouldn't dream of merging or selling out to us."

Jerry, scratching his cheek, looked pensive as he spoke. "Bob, I'm not sure we should dismiss this possibility so readily. I know Mickey has not been receptive in the past. But his company does offer us the best strategic fit and growth prospects. Adding to our mix the billion dollars in sales Mickey's would bring wouldn't be half bad. And we would find out how they manage to bring new products to market so fast. Especially those products that are similar to some of ours that beat us to the market by weeks."

Bob, a bit surprised, turned to Jerry. "I agree Mickey's would be a terrific addition to our company. And I am also impressed with their new product creation process. But I don't see much chance here, so we could waste a lot of time and also alert Mickey about our strategic initiatives. That will give him yet another opportunity to hurt us."

Jerry was not convinced. "Bob, why don't you run some numbers on Mickey's and let's meet in a few days. If that is our best bet, perhaps we can make Mickey an offer he can't refuse."

"Jerry," said Bob, "I will do that, but please let's remember that the large-sample scientific evidence is that the majority of acquirers do not create value for their shareholders via their acquisitions. Although the shareholders of target firms do well — on average they receive a 20% premium over the pre-acquisition market price in mergers and 30% in tender offers — the shareholders of acquiring firms break even at best, although there are some acquisitions in which acquirers do quite well."

Jerry turned to face Bob, "And why is that?"

"Well," started Bob, "in part it's because many acquisitions have been under-taken for diversification purposes, to reduce earnings cyclicality. Such deals have resulted in value losses on average. They're ill-advised to begin with since share-holders can diversify their investment portfolio cheaper on their own. Not surprising then that refocusing divestitures have led to significant improvements in operating performance and shareholder value. In non-diversifying acquisitions, the problem is often an overestimation of synergies from the acquisition as well as an underes-timation of the importance of cultural compatibility between the acquirer and the target. This is why acquirers often end up overpaying and then fail to fully capture the synergies they had counted on because they are unable to blend the disparate corporate cultures represented by the acquirer and the target."

"Can you give me an example, Bob?" asked Jerry.

Bob tapped on the desk, "Hmm… there are so many. HP-Compaq is one. The clash of cultures and different business models proved to be an enormous challenge and eventually cost CEO Carly Fiorina her job. Daimler-Chrysler is an even more spectacular example. Cultural incompatibility and the consequent loss of key Chrysler employees resulted in value destruction within two years of the merger that exceeded the entire pre-merger value of Chrysler! I think Chrysler was worth around $27 billion before the merger. Eventually, it may have been the reason CEO Jurgen Shrempp stepped down!"

Jerry looked pensive for a moment and then spoke, "This is pretty sobering, Bob. We'll have to move carefully. I trust we'll have more discussions on this."

"Sure," said Bob, "In the meantime, I am going to make sure everyone in my group has carefully gone over this (Bob shook a booklet in front of him, a copy of which is provided in the Addendum) — I call it 'The Blocking and Tackling of M&A'."

After a few other items related to organic growth strategies were discussed, the meeting was over.

2. An Analytical Framework for Acquisitions

Bob had adopted a nine-step process[177] for evaluating potential targets that he read about. The nine steps were:

1. **Discreet initial scan:** A quiet initial scan of the possible motives the target could have to sell out, as well as the strategic fit of the target, should be done.

---

[177] This discussion draws partly upon Tom Copeland, Tim Koller, and Jack Murrin, (1990) *Valuation: Measuring and Managing the Value of Companies*, John Wiley & Sons.

At this stage, it is important to be discreet and ensure that the target does not know it is being studied.

2. **Compare current market value (or value estimated by analysts for privately-held firms) to peer group:** The purpose of this comparison is to determine whether the current managers and owners of the business are likely to view the firm as under- or over-valued. One way to determine this is to compare the firm's cost of capital to the returns it has been delivering.

3. **Estimate liquidation value of the firm:** One should estimate how much the firm would be worth if it were broken up and sold off in pieces. This will permit an assessment of the portfolio synergies in holding these assets in a single portfolio.

4. **Estimate firm value based on historical projections and status quo decision-making:** The idea here is to do a discounted cash flow (DCF) or Economic Profit valuation using forecasts of future cash flows/Economic Profits that are based on the firm being run the way it is now. This value can then be compared with the current market value or analysts' estimates to determine the gap between how the firm is perceived and what it is truly worth. This value should also be compared to the liquidation value from step 3 above. These comparisons can illuminate the assumptions analysts are making about the firm's future.

5. **Estimate firm value with innovative operating improvements:** The goal here is to determine how much the firm's value can be increased by making innovative internal improvements in operations that lead to lower costs, higher margins, higher asset productivity, etc. Improvements may stem from combining the target's operations with those of the acquirer.

6. **Estimate firm value based on selling out the firm and restructuring it:** As a potential acquirer, we would like to know how much additional value, if any, we could create by optimally restructuring the firm. The re-structuring could involve spinning off one or more divisions, or doing a leveraged buyout (LBO), or liquidating the firm.

7. **Estimate maximal firm value under optimal combination:** In practice, a value-conscious acquirer will want to use the optimal combination of (3), (4) and (5), so one should examine the maximum firm value that could be realized through such a combination. This will then serve as the upper limit on how much the acquirer should be willing to pay for the target.

8. **Have bidding firm's CEO approach target firm's CEO:** At this stage, it is important to determine the price range in which negotiations will proceed. There is a large body of scientific evidence that says that, on average, acquirers do not create any wealth for their shareholders in acquisitions. One implication of this is that acquirers overpay on average. Having an opening bid and a walkaway

price firmly determined prior to entering negotiations is important to avoid the common pitfall of paying too high an acquisition premium.

9. **Determine post-acquisition integration plan, including identification of who will lead the target after the acquisition, before making the deal:** It is often too late to think about how to integrate the target into the acquirer's organization once the deal is done. Moreover, having a clear idea of who will lead the target after it is integrated helps to provide a sense of direction, and can also diminish some of the uncertainty perceived by the target's employees about the future. Research has shown that the most successful acquirers often retained a large number of the target firm's senior executives.[178] In the post-acquisition integration plan it is also important to emphasize autonomy for those who will be decisionmakers in the acquired unit, and to tie their compensation to the key drivers of shareholder value. These too are hallmarks of successful acquirers, according to the evidence.

If the acquisition involves a privately-held firm, with family control of operations, then one should be careful to find out whether those presently in control wish to remain involved in managing the firm. The success of the negotiations may depend very much on the acquirer's willingness to accommodate the wishes of an influential family member.

This is not always easy. Firms often become targets because their leaders lack vision or employ poor strategies or just plain mismanage. Many acquirers cannot wait to remove these managers after they take over the firm. But taking a hammer to the task is not always the best solution. A savvy acquirer can create a "figurehead" position or two in the new organization for senior target managers whose preference for staying in control would otherwise torpedo the deal.

Figure 19.1 offers a picture of these nine steps.

3. Bob Applies the First Three Steps of His Process to Mickey's

Rather than just "running the numbers" on Mickey's as Jerry had asked him to, Bob decided to take a little time and apply as much of his eight-step process as he had time for before Jerry would insist on moving ahead.

1. **Discreet initial scan:** Bob asked some of the people he knew who were familiar with Mickey and his privately-held company. He discovered the following:

   • In book value terms, Mickey's debt to total assets ratio was about 50%.

---

[178]Patricia L. Anslinger and Thomas E. Copeland, (1996) "Growth Through Acquisitions: A Fresh Look," Harvard Business Review, January–February, pp. 126–135.

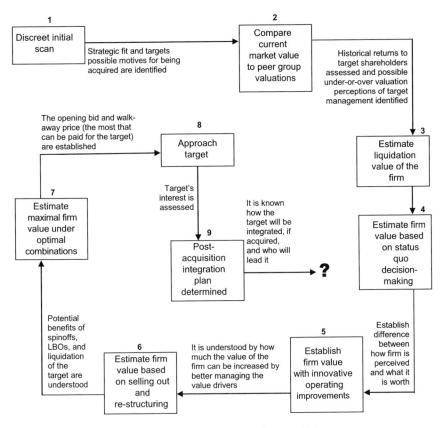

Fig. 19.1. Bob's nine-step approach to acquisitions.

- Mickey's had significant growth opportunities, both domestically and abroad.
- Mickey's was severely capital-constrained. The company was unlikely to be able to borrow more without significant new covenant restrictions from the banks. And the family was unwilling to commit any more equity capital to the business.

When Bob put these facts together, he realized that Mickey might be quite amenable to an offer if the price was right. In particular, Mickey might accept an offer that paid him, in part, for the growth options that he could not exploit himself. Perhaps not. But at least there was an opening. It was worth a try.

2. **Compare current market value to peer group and determine a valuation based on multiples:** There were valuations of Mickey's — which is

privately owned — done by Jerry's investment banker when Jerry's went public. Bob called up the investment banker again and got the valuation updated. When he looked over the valuation, as well as Mickey's historical performance over the last five years, he discovered the following:

- Based on the investment banker's valuation, Mickey's P/E ratio had hovered around 7 the last five years, well below the market P/E ratio of between 25 and 32.
- Mickey's P/E was also lower than those of comparable firms, which averaged nine.
- The investment banker also estimated that the relationship between Mickey's cost of equity capital and total returns to shareholders was given by Fig. 19.2.

Bob looked at the different business units that comprised Mickey's to get a better understanding of what was going on. This is given in Fig. 19.3.

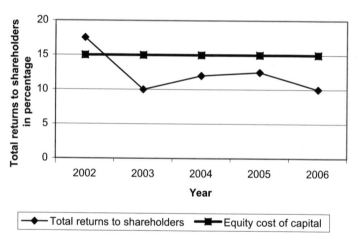

Fig. 19.2.   Mickey's historical shareholder value performance.

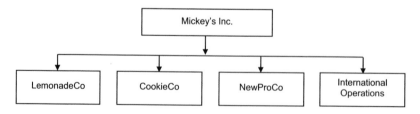

Fig. 19.3.   Mickey's businesses.

LemonadeCo is the division that supplies the basic lemonade products to the stores. The stores are also part of this division. It is the original unit with which the company started.

CookieCo is the cookie division. It supplies cookies and other variants of snacks to the stores.

NewProCo is the new product division. It makes new drinks — non-lemonade drinks — that are alternatives to the lemonade products. These are sold not only through the usual stores but also offered through selected retail outlets not owned by Mickey's.

International Operations is the smallest and newest of the four units. It is the unit that sells Mickey's products in Canada and Mexico. The Canadian stores are owned by the International Operations division, whereas the Mexican sales are through multiproduct retail outlets owned by others.

Figure 19.4 shows the economic profit breakdown by division for Mickey's.

As Bob looked over the numbers in Fig. 19.4, he realized that Mickey's core business had not been doing that well. The LemonadeCo division's price competitiveness vis-à-vis Jerry's had succeeded in taking market share away from Jerry's, but this success had come at the expense of Mickey's shareholder value.

Bob was reminded of the strategy employed by Japanese and Korean firms in the 1980s and 1990s. The strategy was simple. Cut margins to the bone to grab market share! But what about shareholder value? Apparently, it was not as important as market share. The consequences? Disaster for many Japanese and Korean firms, despite high labor productivity and excellent product quality. In the end, it contributed to the economic crises in both countries in the late 1990's. Japan is still trying to dig out from their malaise.

	Free cash flow in millions $	**Economic profit* in millions $**
LemonadeCo	$33	($20)
CookieCo	$15	($3)
NewProCo	$12	$9
International operations	$10	$4
Corporate center	($10)	—
Total corporation	$60	($10)

*For calculating economic profit, the corporate center expenses are allocated to the other divisions.

Fig. 19.4.   Divisional performance for Mickey's for 2006.

Returning to the task at hand, Bob could also see that there was probably untapped growth potential in NewProCo and International. Both had positive Economic Profits. Perhaps Mickey had recognized this potential. But if he couldn't raise the capital he needed, the recognition was not going to do him much good.

Bob's overall conclusion was that Mickey was at a crossroads. He probably thought that analysts would not share his upbeat assessment of the future and that, based on the company's mediocre past performance, it would be undervalued if he went public or tried to sell it. On the other hand, raising additional capital to exploit growth opportunities would require additional equity input, which Mickey seemed reluctant to do.

Jerry then looked at the valuation based on multiples that the investment banker had provided him. Mickey's valuation is $52/share, slightly above its book value of $50/share. It recorded net income (equity earnings) of $74.29 million in 2005. The investment banker had estimated an equity value of $668.61 million or a price/share of $66.9 based on an industry multiples approach to valuing Mickey's. Details are provided in the Addendum. Jerry's initial reaction was that this was a pretty hefty premium above the base valuation, based simply on the assumption that Mickey's deserved the same price/earnings multiple as the average firm within its peer group.

3. **Estimate liquidation value:** Bob had worked with the investment banker to determine a liquidation value for Mickey's. This did not mean that Jerry was planning to break up Mickey's after the acquisition. However, he did want to see how much Mickey's would be worth if broken up, so that he could determine if that was worth doing.

The approach Bob and the investment banker had taken was as follows. They first determined the book value of Mickey's equity, which was $500 million. They then assumed that its inventories could be liquidated at 50% of their book value of $100 million, which meant a loss of $50 million relative to book value. Similarly, they assumed that receivables could be sold at 80% of their book value of $50 million, yielding a loss relative to book value of $10 million. The investment banker had advised Bob that, excluding working capital, LemonadeCo could be sold for $2 million above its book value. The excess of liquidation over book value for each of the other divisions is given in Fig. 19.5.

Bob and the investment banker were than able to add up all the differences between market (liquidation) value and book value and add the sum to the book value of Mickey's equity to obtain an estimated liquidation value. As explained in

Division	Market value-book value
LemonadeCo	$2 million
CookieCo	$25 million
New ProCo	$178 million
International operations	$125 million

Fig. 19.5.   Excess of anticipated market value over liquidation value, excluding working capital.

the Addendum, this value has been estimated to be $780 million, or $78/share. Jerry wondered how Mickey could tolerate a valuation of $52/share when his company's break-up value was $78/share. Apparently, the experts think the company is worth more dead than alive!

4. Bob Examines Estimated Firm Value Based on Status Quo Decision-Making

Based on historical performance, Mickey's market share and projected industry dynamics, Bob extrapolated Mickey's performance out into the future. He estimated Mickey's FCF to grow from its current $60 million in 2006 to $120 million by 2011 and then remain constant thereafter. The pattern of forecasted cash flows is given in Fig. 19.6.

With these projections, Bob calculated the total enterprise value of Mickey's to be $1,067.80 million. Subtracting the $500 million in debt Mickey has, Bob calculated an economic value for Mickey's to be $567.8 million, or $56.78/share. Details are provided in the Addendum. Jerry was again struck by the fact that this number was not only lower than Mickey's liquidation value, but was also significantly lower than the $66.9/share value derived from a multiples valuation. Just goes to show you how unreliable multiples can be, thought Jerry. A recipe for overpaying, if you are not careful!

Year	FCF in $ millions
2007	$65
2008	$75
2009	$80
2010	$100
2011 and beyond	$120

Fig. 19.6.   Projected FCF for Mickey's with status quo decision-making.

Bob reached several conclusions based on his analysis. First, the LemonadeCo division was likely to be worth less than the capital invested in it unless its performance was improved a lot. This division was a major source of value evaporation.

Second, CookieCo was likely to just break even on Economic Profit terms, assuming that margins and volumes in the successful cookie brands could be maintained and the volume in the most successful cookie brand could be ramped up, as most industry observers expected it to be. Third, NewProCo accounted for a lot of the value created in the business.

5. Bob Analyzes the Potential Value of Mickey's

Having looked at what the business was worth based on the status quo, Bob now began to think about how much potential value it had under alternative strategies. That is, it was time to consider step 5 of the process.

• Firm value with innovative operating strategies

Bob began his exercise by examining his knowledge of the industry and what his earlier analysis had indicated. His value driver analysis yielded Fig. 19.7.

This figure shows how much the MVA of the division would change if a particular value driver changed by 1%.

Although much of what the analysis told Bob was what he expected, there were some new things he learned. First, Bob was not surprised that growth would be detrimental to the value of LemonadeCo, since its economic profits were negative. But he was a bit surprised that operating margin had such a large impact relative to the asset turnover ratio. When he thought about it, though, it made sense. The real problem with the LemonadeCo division was that the market would not support higher prices, so those operating margins were squeezed. The asset turnover ratio

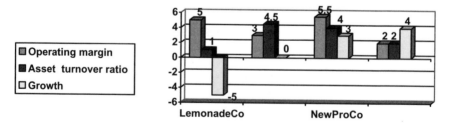

Fig. 19.7.   Impact of 1% change in key value driver on percentage change in MVA of division.

was pretty good the way it was, and further increases in it were not likely to impact value as much.[179]

Second, in the case of CookieCo, both operating margin and asset turnover are important drivers of value. What surprised Bob was that growth had no impact. Upon some reflection, Bob saw what was going on. Since this division had a slightly negative MVA under the status quo decisionmaking, with roughly zero economic profits projected out into the future, growth was not going to have much of an impact on value. In a sense, this exposes a specific aspect of the value-driver sensitivity analysis, namely that each value driver is varied, holding all the others fixed. Thus, in the case of CookieCo, if the asset turnover ratio or operating margin were to be increased, growth would not have zero-value consequences.

Third, it was clear that the most exciting growth prospects existed for New-ProCo. Even if none of the other value drivers were changed, growth would enhance value. Moreover, it was evident that if either the operating margin or the asset turnover ratio were increased, growth would create even more value. This division was clearly one that should be targeted for future growth.

Finally, the International Operations division was very similar in its prospects to NewProCo, although the value sensitivities were not as great. One reason for the lower sensitivities was that both asset turnover and operating margins were already higher for International Operations.

Based on this analysis and his memory of the Prosperity Diamond (recall Chapter 10), Bob concluded that the following actions could be taken:

- The investment in LemonadeCo could be cut, since it did not seem to significantly increase either the operating margin or the asset turnover ratio at current sales volume and capital commitment levels. The smaller size would be achieved by eliminating most of the money-losing lemonade products. This would leave the division with products that would not destroy as much value as the current product mix appears to be doing.
- The major problem in CookieCo was the product mix. Some of the fast-moving but low-margin (negative to zero economic profit) products were dragging down the division by tying up valuable capital and human resources that could otherwise be freed up for the higher-margin, positive-economic-profit products. Bob suspected that the low-margin products were viewed within Mickey's as "loss leaders" that were essential to "carry" the rest of the product line. But he was not sure that the underlying assumptions had been critically analyzed. If an

---

[179] In Bob's value-driver analysis, the relationships are concave, so the impact of a change in a value driver on value is smaller the higher its status quo impact.

alternative set of assumptions made more sense — as Bob suspected they would — the product mix could be changed in a value-enhancing way. The division would actually shrink in terms of total capital due to the elimination of some products. But some products would grow in volume, and overall value would be higher.

- The centerpiece of an altered strategy would be NewProCo. This division excited Bob. He figured that they could simultaneously increase all of the key value driver variables. His estimate was that they could increase the capital commitment to this business and increase value at the same time.
- Bob thought that they could easily integrate Mickey's International Operations into their own and make it a single business unit. That would facilitate both growth and an increase in margins, since Jerry's had a better-established international presence and distribution network, with minimal overlap in the territories.

Based on all this, Bob estimated the FCF projections to be those given in Fig. 19.8. When Bob ran his valuation calculation in this case, he found that innovative operating strategies would lead to a perpetual growth rate of 1% per year in free cash flows beyond year 2011, generating a total value of $1,480.51 million for the business, or $980.51 million for the equity value. This was a substantial increase over the status-quo decision-making case. The details of these calculations are given in the Addendum. These calculations are based on all of the changes in Bob's conclusions being implemented.

6. Estimated Firm Value Based on Restructuring

Bob was encouraged by his value-driver analysis. There was clearly potential in Mickey's business that had not yet been tapped. He was anxious to see if one could do better by spinning off some of the businesses and restructuring the firm, or by

Year	FCF in $ millions
2007	$75
2008	$85
2009	$105
2010	$130
2011	$155
FCFs beyond 2011	Expected to grow perpetually at 1% per year beyond 2011.

Fig. 19.8.   projected FCF for Mickey's with innovative operating strategies.

doing an LBO. In other words, what could a corporate raider like Carl Icahn or KKR do to Mickey's? Essentially, the value under restructuring would be some variant of the liquidation value, with some additional value possibly added in to account for the added debt tax shield under a leveraged buyout (LBO).

Bob concluded rather quickly that an LBO was probably not a great idea. There were a couple of reasons. First, an LBO would shift the firm's focus almost exclusively to generating cash flow. No harm in that per se. But Bob felt it would sacrifice long-term-growth-oriented initiatives. An exclusive cash-flow focus could jeopardize committing new capital to businesses like NewProCo and International Operations, which are the stars of the company. Second, there was virtually nothing an LBO could achieve that could not be achieved without an LBO after the acquisition.

After careful consideration, Bob determined that the LemonadeCo division could be sold off for $432 million. This was based on a valuation estimate given to him by his investment bank and was, of course, conditional on finding a willing buyer.

7. Maximal Firm Value Under Optimal Combination of Initiatives

Bob looked at the numbers for a long time. He wanted to know what would maximize the value of the business. He decided that there was not anybody out there who could do better than Jerry's in managing the value creation in CookieCo, NewProCo and International Operations. These divisions were not just competitors/substitutors to Jerry's. They complemented Jerry's nicely.

However, LemonadeCo was a different story. The best that Jerry's could hope for with this division was to bring it to zero Economic Profit, and it was more likely Economic Profits in the future would be negative. But the market was apparently willing to pay more than the adjusted book value for it. So selling the division off would fetch $432 million, which was $2 million more than its book value. Of course, this division was responsible for the leasing of all the stores. Bob thought that the simplest way to run the numbers on this was to suppose that Jerry's could assume all the contracts. This way they could keep the stores and sell just the lemonade products.

The leases had all been recently renewed. Bob viewed them as essentially zero-NPV investments. Keeping the stores would therefore not affect the purchase price a buyer would be willing to pay for LemonadeCo.

Why would someone be willing to pay more for LemonadeCo than it was worth to Jerry's?

For one thing, there were a lot of redundancies across that division and Jerry's. They sold very similar, competing products. And often in the same malls, a few feet apart. Taking these stores and selling something other than lemonade would make more sense.

Second, another buyer would take the lemonade products and would not be constrained by existing locations in deciding where to sell. So, rather than taking Jerry's head-on, this buyer could offer these products in areas where no Jerry's stores existed. Typically, these would be lower-volume market segments. But they might also be higher-margin segments. Eventually, they might decide to compete directly with Jerry's.

Bob thus concluded that if they acquired Mickey's, they should sell the brand names and products that LemonadeCo owned, and keep the stores as well as the rest of the divisions. Operating improvements would be made in these divisions along the lines of the earlier analysis.

Bob concluded that selling LemonadeCo would reduce the present value of free cash flows with innovative operating strategies from $1,469.93 million to $1,069.93 million. Adding to this the $432 million proceeds from selling LemonadeCo would yield a total firm value of $1,069.93 + $432 = $1,501.93 million, or an equity value of $1,501.93–$500 million (debt) = $1,001.93 million. This yields a maximum price per share of $100.2.

8. Bob Meets with Jerry to Approach the Target

Bob Meets Jerry

Having done his analysis, Bob called Jerry for a meeting. At the meeting they first decided that Jerry would call Mickey personally to set up a lunch meeting, at which he would raise the issue. No numbers would be mentioned at this meeting. Rather, they would talk about what the merger would do for the two companies and what each offered the other. The idea was merely to see if there was any interest.

If Mickey showed interest, then a negotiating team consisting of Jerry, Bob and Jerry's Chief Legal Counsel would meet with a negotiating team from Mickey's. Bob and Jerry agreed that their opening bid for 100% of Mickey's equity would be $600 million or $60 per share, which was below the liquidation value of Mickey's but 20% higher than the book value of its equity and a premium of 15% above Mickey's current stock valuation. Their walkaway offer would be $900 million. Jerry was uninterested in going above $90 per share even though the highest valuation Bob had come up with was about $100 per share. After all, Jerry's shareholders had to profit from the deal as well. Besides, a $90/share price would represent also a significant increase over Mickey's liquidation value and a rather astounding 92% premium over Mickey's pre-acquisition valuation. Not an offer to be turned down.

The Prelude and the Meeting

Soon after Jerry met with Bob, he contacted Mickey and set up a meeting for the following week. In preparation for the meeting he decided to meet with some of his key executives to get their views. Everything was still confidential, of course. But he felt he needed to get some more people involved in the discussion.

For the most part, the meeting with the key executives went as planned. They expressed surprise and doubted the deal could be done. But they felt that it was a good idea if it could be done with the right set of terms. All except Doug Harris, who expressed the strongest reservations. He felt that they should ". . . try and bury Mickey's instead of acquiring it." He did not feel that it was the kind of organization that should be brought into the fold.

Jerry was more than a bit surprised. Not at the fact that Doug spoke his mind. He always did. And Jerry expected nothing less from an old friend. But Doug had no access to Bob's analysis. It was not like him to express such a strong opinion based on what Jerry viewed as very little fact. Anyway, it didn't seem terribly important at the time. Jerry put it out of his mind and thought ahead to his meeting with Mickey.

The meeting with Mickey turned out to be anticlimactic. Given the nearly hostile relations between the two companies, Jerry had expected emotional roadblocks to any sensible business discussion. He was surprised. Mickey was every bit the businessman Jerry was. Jerry realized that the hostility was almost cultivated. Mickey did what he did for purely business reasons. There was nothing personal.

This made Jerry's overtures easier to make. The two men talked at length about their visions of the future and what it might be like to combine their resources. At one point, Mickey turned to Jerry and asked him point blank, "I think I know how this usually goes, so let me get this out of the way right now. I don't know if this whole thing will go through or not, but if it does, what will my role be?"

Jerry paused. He had thought about this. "I'm not sure about that, Mickey. But I do know this. I don't have any preconceived notions about your role. All I do know is I don't think you can run a company effectively with two CEOs. By the same token, my goal is to make this the best company we can. So I'll rely on you to tell me how you could help us after the merger. If you and I agree, then I don't see why we couldn't combine our knowledge and experience and work together.

I know this sounds a bit vague. So if defining this more clearly is a precondition to our doing business, let me know. I'm sure we could fill in the details when the time is right."

Mickey said that was fair enough and that he appreciated Jerry's honesty. The two men parted company with a date set for the next event.

The Due Diligence Reveals a Surprise

A couple of weeks after Jerry and Mickey met, a Due Diligence team from Jerry's visited Mickey's to collect the necessary information and analyze it. The team was headed by Bob.

There were not that many surprises in the Due Diligence. Bob was able to go back and refine his valuation estimates with the better access to the financial and operating data that he now had. But the numbers did not change dramatically. Bob had almost finished going over all the papers when a computer printout fell to the floor. He picked it up. It was an e-mail message printed out by a member of Mickey's Strategic Planning staff.

Bob was about to file it away with the rest of the papers when something caught his eye and made him look again. The message described some of the new products that Jerry had planned to introduce! Bob was stunned. This was amazing competitive intelligence. He looked up at the sender's name. It was Doug Harris!

Bob sat slumped in his chair for a few minutes before he got up and walked over to Jerry's office. He told Jerry about it but had no advice about what to do. All he could say was, "Jerry, are you sure you want to do business with people like this?"

Jerry thought it over for a while before speaking:

"Let's not overreact. You are assuming this was Mickey's idea. But we don't know. Maybe this does not go any higher in the organization than this guy who was getting information from Doug."

Bob nodded and asked, "Are you going to confront Mickey with this?"

Jerry looked at Bob and spoke almost in a whisper, "Not yet. It's too early. It could make Mickey defensive and poison the waters. Let's complete the Due Diligence, and go through the negotiations. When the deal is close to being signed, I'll raise the issue privately with Mickey. If I feel he gave the order, the deal won't go through. But if he didn't know, I'll ask his advice about what to do about his guy. His response will tell me a lot. As for Doug, don't say a word now. I'll deal with him after the acquisition is finalized."

9. The Final Deal

When the deal was close to being signed, Jerry asked Mickey about the espionage. Mickey expressed great surprise. He was either a great actor or he really did not know.

Mickey did say that he'd been slightly suspicious once or twice when he thought about how this guy had consistently been the most innovative new-product ideas generator in the company over the last two or three years, and about how his product ideas seemed to so accurately anticipate the competition!

"No wonder. Now I know how," said Mickey.

"What should we do with him?" asked Jerry.

Mickey looked slightly surprised by the question, "Fire him, of course. Let's do it together. That way he won't think of it as vendetta on your part."

That clinched it for Jerry. They agreed that Mickey would take over as President of Overseas Operations, a new division created to include the non-U.S. businesses of the two companies, with an aggressive plan for global expansion.

Along with his friend at Mickey's, Doug was fired too.

The acquisition was completed at a price of $805 million for 100% of the equity in Mickey's. The purchase was financed with a combination of cash, Jerry's Lemonade stock and additional debt. To Jerry's delight, the price of Jerry's stock moved up from $28 per share to $30.58 when the acquisition announcement was made. Bob made it a point to emphasize to Jerry that this "endorsement" of the acquisition by the stock market was not commonplace. Many acquirers find their stock prices decline a bit when they announce acquisitions.

Main Lessons

- Companies that do not create shareholder value, because they are motivated by other goals like market share or an exclusive focus on sales revenue growth, often become targets for takeovers.
- Growth targets should be set in MVA terms. In particular, one goal could be to capture an increasing share of the total MVA in your industry. This reinforces the shareholder value focus.
- Divisions/assets that generate negative economic profits and show no prospect of generating positive economic profits in the future should be divested or the assets devoted to other uses.
- Periodically value your own company on a liquidation value basis to determine the restructuring and value-enhancement opportunities that a potential acquirer would see. If the firm itself exploits these opportunities, the potential acquirer would have less of a reason to make a bid.
- A careful valuation of any potential acquisition should involve at least a status quo valuation and a maximal value estimation. To create potential value for the acquiring firm's shareholders, the acquirer should set the "walkaway price"

below the maximal value. The negotiating should be disciplined enough so the acquirer never agrees to anything more than the walkaway price unless there are positive-value revelations during the negotiations. Done this way, acquisitions can be an important part of the Strategy component of the Value Sphere.

• Companies that do many small acquisitions over time, and have their processes, generally prepare better than companies that do large, infrequent acquisitions.

End-of-Chapter Exercises

1. What is the driving force behind growth in your company? How do you set your growth targets and what are the metrics by which you measure your growth? Are these metrics aligned with shareholder value?

2. Perform a segment-by-segment liquidation valuation of your company based on your internal forecasts of future cash flows. What are the restructuring and value-enhancement opportunities that emerge from this analysis?

3. Post-audit your previous acquisitions. Which of them have created value for your company and why? Which have destroyed your shareholder value and why?

4. Can you identify three targets your company could acquire? Do a valuation of them and determine the premium over market price you would be willing to offer for each.

Practice Problems

1. Consider the Omicron Corporation. It has 4 business units: applications, business systems, circuits, and direct sales. The data on these business units are given below.

	($ Millions)				
Business unit	Applications	Business systems	Circuits	Direct sales	Firm
EBIT	$20	$60	$30	$10	
NOPAT valuation multiples of comparable traded companies (i.e., the market values of equity of comparable traded companies are these multiples of their NOPATs)	5	4	6	8	
Book value of equity	$48	$130	$85	$10	$313

The tax rate is 40%. The current stock price of the firm is $46 per share and there are 10 million shares outstanding.

(1) What is the market value of this firm's equity?
(2) What is the liquidation value of this firm's equity?
(3) What is the dollar value of this firm's (portfolio) strategy as assessed by the market?
(4) Would you break this firm up? Why or why not?

2. A. Brown Engines, Inc. is a Michigan-based company whose stock is actively traded on the NYSE. Its weighted average cost of capital is 16%. Its debt is risk-less and has a yield of 10%. In market value terms, Brown Engines' (long-term) debt constitutes 50% of its total assets in the company's optimal capital structure. The risk premium return on the market portfolio is 7%. Assume an effective tax rate of 40%.

   i. What should be the equity beta of Brown Engines?
   ii. What would its equity beta if it was unlevered?
   iii. What is the premium for financial risk attached to Brown Engines' equity, given its current leverage?

   B. Suppose the following data are given to you for Brown Engines (assume this is December 31, 2005).

	Year-end ($ millions)		
	2005 ($)	2006 ($)	2007 ($)
Operating profit	—	$150	$200
Current assets	$60	$70	$75
Net fixed assets	$100	$105	$115
Bank debt	$30	$35	$35
Accrued expenses and payables	$20	$25	$30

3. Calculate the total market value of Brown Engines assuming that its FCF (free cash flow) beyond 2005 will grow perpetually at 2% per year.
4. If Brown currently has $370 million in interest-bearing debt outstanding, what is the market value of its equity?

Addendum–Chapter 19

A. BASIC DATA RELATED TO MICKEY'S

Book value of equity = $500 million
Book value of debt = $500 million
P/E ratio = 7
Peer group average P/E ratio = 9
Number of shares outstanding = 10 million
Book value/share = $50
Current valuation = $52
2006 Earnings (net income) = $74.29 million
EPS = $7.429.

B. MULTIPLES VALUATION

Formula is: Mickey's estimated equity value

= [Peer group average 2006 P/E ratio] × [Mickey's 2006 earnings]

= 9 × $74.29 = $668.6 million.

On a per-share basis, this is $668.6 million = $66.9/share.

C. LIQUIDATION VALUE

The formula for computing liquidation value is as follows:

Liquidation value of the whole firm

$$= LV$$

$$= \text{Book value of equity for the whole firm}$$

$$+ (LV_1 - BV_1) + (LV_2 - BV_2) + \cdots + (LV_n - BV_n)$$

$$= BV + \sum_{i=1}^{n} (LV_i - BV_i)$$

where BV = book value of the whole firm
BV_i = book value of asset i within the firm
LV_i = liquidation value of asset i within the firm.

Applying this to Mickey's, we get book value of Mickey's equity = $500 million.

Increments of Liquidation Value Over Book Value ($LV_i - BV_i$)

Inventories	−$50 million
Accounts receivables	−$10 million
LemonadeCo	+$2 million
CookieCo	+$25 million
NewProCo	+$188 million
International operations	+$125 million
Total	**$780 million**

D. VALUE BASED ON STATUS QUO DECISION-MAKING

The formula for the value of the firm based on the present value of future FCFs is:

Enterprise value (EV)

$$= \frac{FCF_1}{1 + k_w} + \frac{FCF_2}{(1 + k_w)^2} + \frac{FCF_3}{(1 + k_w)^3} + \cdots + \frac{FCF_n}{(1 + k_w)^n} + \frac{TV_n}{(1 + k_w)^n}$$

$$= \sum_{t=1}^{n} \frac{FCF_t}{(1 + k_w)^n} + \frac{TV_n}{(1 + k_w)^n}$$

where FCF_t = FCF in year t; k_w = weighted average cost of capital (WACC) applicable to FCFs of the target (this should be a WACC that reflects the risk in the target's FCFs; it should *not* be the acquirer's WACC)

$$TV_N = \text{terminal value in year } N = \frac{FCF_n[1 + g]}{k_w - g}$$

where g = perpetual growth rate in FCFs beyond year N

$$FCF_N = \text{FCF in year } N.$$

Bob has calculated that the appropriate k_w = 10% or 0.10.
Applying this to Mickey's status quo FCFs in Fig. 19.2, we obtain:

$$EV = \frac{\$65}{1.1} + \frac{\$75}{(1.1)^2} + \frac{\$80}{(1.1)^3} + \frac{\$100}{(1.1)^4} + \frac{\$120}{(1.1)^5} + \frac{TV_5}{(1.1)^5}$$

where $TV_5 = \$120/(1.1)^5$ since $g = 0$.
Thus, $EV = \$1,067.80$.

This implies that economic value of equity = EV − Debt

$$= \$1,067.80 - \$500$$

$$= \$567.80 \text{ million}$$

or

$$\frac{\$567.8}{\$10 \text{ million}} = \$56.78/\text{share}.$$

E. VALUE BASED ON INNOVATIVE OPERATING STRATEGIES

Based on the formula given above and the data provided in Fig. 19.8, we have:

$$EV = \frac{\$75}{1.1} + \frac{\$85}{(1.1)^2} + \frac{\$105}{(1.1)^3} + \frac{\$130}{(1.1)^4} + \frac{\$155}{(1.1)^5} + \frac{TV_5}{(1.1)^5}$$

where

$$TV_5 = \frac{\$155[1 + 0.10]}{0.10 - 0.01} \quad \text{since } g = 1\% \text{ or } 0.01.$$

Thus,

$$EV = \$1,480.51 \text{ million},$$

which implies economic value of equity $= \$1,480.51$ million $- \$500$ million

$$= \$980.51 \text{ million}$$

or \$98.05/share.

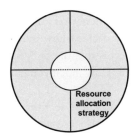

Chapter 20

RESOURCE ALLOCATION
FOR NON-TRADITIONAL
PROJECTS

1. Can we put some Science Behind Our Expense Budgets?

The decision to fire Doug Harris had been painful for Jerry. He had known Doug since high school. Almost as long as he had known Bob Butterfield. But what was even more painful was the realization that Doug had betrayed him. He had always thought of Bob and Doug as old friends who were partners with him in shaping the business. How could Doug sell out to a major competitor?

After a few minutes, Jerry tried to refocus on his work. But all the effort he made to get Doug Harris out of his mind could not keep his mind from wandering back to that sordid episode. Things like that took a lot of the joy out of running the business. If it was more money that Doug wanted, why didn't he just say so? Or was it something that Jerry had inadvertently done to sour their personal relationship? He'd never been able to ferret that out of either Doug or anyone else. And to think that he might never have found out had the acquisition of Mickey's business not gone through!

Jerry began to get annoyed with himself. It was not like him to wallow in depression or self pity for long. There was work to be done, especially with all of the post-acquisition integration activities involved in absorbing Mickey's business.

That realization jolted Jerry back to business. Just in time to remember that he had a meeting with Bob and Barb Sidwell in a few minutes. He had barely begun thinking about it when there was a knock on the door. Bob and Barb were there for the meeting.

Bob began the conversation as he and Barb sat down. "Jerry, we have finished our analysis of Mickey's business. We took an internal perspective this time, as opposed to the external perspective that was part of our Due Diligence before the acquisition. And I must say we have a lot of work to do," said Bob.

Barb joined in, "That's right, Jerry. They have spent a lot of money on HR and other functions, but we can not figure out exactly how they decided how much to allocate and where. To the best of our knowledge, it seems that the budget-setting process for Staff Support functions was pretty political. How much you got depended on who you were."

Bob followed up with, "And to make matters worse, they had all sorts of "unbudgeted" projects that came up from time to time that also received funds."

Jerry turned to Bob, "What's wrong with that? Don't we also do that?"

"Not for 40% of our total capital allocation, Jerry," replied Bob.

"OK, so let's start at the top," said Jerry. "Tell me what the major integration issues are and what we need to do."

Bob began. "Well, there are four things that we think are critically important. First, we need to implement the head-count reduction that was part of the cost savings we estimated in computing the price we were willing to pay in this acquisition. Second, we need to revamp their capital allocation and expense budgeting systems so they are consistent with ours. Third, we need to redesign their performance appraisal and compensation systems so they are what we want. And finally, we need to make some key personnel decisions."

Barb interjected. "Yeah, they have some good people that I'd like to see us retain. I know the headhunters have already approached some of them. Also, I'd like to add one more item to Bob's list. We need to figure out ways to reduce SG&A expenses that go beyond just reducing the head count."

Bob nodded his agreement and looked at Jerry for his reaction.

Jerry looked out his window at the summer sky. Barb and Bob had succeeded in taking his mind off Doug. He focused on the points Barb and Bob had raised. Finally, he spoke.

"Guys, tell me something. Do we have an expense budgeting system as part of our Resource Allocation system? I know we have a capital budgeting system, but what's the difference between capital and expenses? After all, a dollar is a dollar. What I am wondering is how we expect to make good decisions about the issues you have raised without some sort of a system."

Barb shifted uncomfortably in her seat, reaching for her lemonade so her hand would have something to do besides tapping on the table in front of her. Bob knew Jerry had a point. But he wasn't quite sure what.

"Jerry, let me see if I understand you. Are you saying we need a new expense budgeting system? Don't you think we're doing a good job of determining our budgets?" questioned Bob.

Jerry was a little amused by the fact that Barb probably had the same reaction Bob had. But she did not push back the way Bob did. Why? Probably because she did not feel as comfortable in her relationship with Jerry as Bob did. Jerry made a mental note to himself to do something to make his executives more comfortable in voicing their real thoughts. He did not need all this high-priced talent if they did not challenge him.

Jerry turned to Bob and said, "I do think we're doing a pretty good job of determining our expenses, Bob. But that's because we spend a lot of time going over the plans submitted by our staff support functions. That's pretty labor intensive. It works because we haven't been that big so far. Also because we know each other so well. But now we've almost doubled our size with this acquisition. We're going to be dealing with a lot of people we don't know too well, people who are used to different policies and procedures. I think we need a system now. Otherwise, we will have a flawed resource allocation process and a Value Sphere that isn't quite synchronized."

Bob smiled. He knew Jerry was right. He looked at Barb. She nodded in agreement as well, before speaking up. "Jerry, what exactly would this system be designed to do for us?"

Jerry looked at the ceiling. "I'm not sure, Barb. I think we all need to give that some thought. For a start, I would like us to think about a system that enables us to decide how much to spend on marketing initiatives, how much to spend on advertising, how to decide on head-count reductions, and how to determine how much we should spend on employee training and education.

"Correct me if I'm wrong, Bob, but aren't these decisions similar to our capital allocation decisions?"

Bob nodded. "You're right, Jerry. Money is money. From our shareholders' perspective, there's no difference between an expense and a capital outlay. The problem is we have no examples of other companies doing anything about this. There's a lot of science behind capital budgeting, but precious little on how to determine expense budgets."

"Then let's not call them expense budgets," countered Jerry. "Why not just treat everything as a project subject to the capital budgeting process?"

Bob smiled wryly. "Sure we could do that. I'm just not sure how."

"Well, then we know what we need to do, don't we, Bob? Its time to come up with a new framework," said Jerry. "I'm sure if you and Barb put your heads to it, along with a few other people, you could come up with something really good."

Bob and Barb knew the meeting was over. They had their marching orders. Neither wanted to ask Jerry what kind of time frame he had in mind for the new framework. They were going to be starting from scratch. And they had little idea how long this was going to take.

2. How do we Allocate Capital for Non-Traditional Projects?

After having discussed it briefly with Barb, Bob decided to have a retreat with his staff, Barb's HR people, and some of the key Marketing managers. There was a nice golf resort just outside town where they decided to meet for a day.

The retreat was a great success. What Bob wanted were some ideas about how the HR and Marketing functions would view the application of capital budgeting to the allocation of funds to their initiatives. Moreover, he also wanted to know how they felt about their roles on cross-functional teams that would be responsible for capital budgeting analyses of these projects.

He found great receptiveness among the retreat participants. Many of them felt that proper analyses of their projects would make it more likely they would obtain the funds they needed for their projects. They liked this better than the current budget setting process.

Bob decided to try out the principles discussed at the retreat. The idea was to ask HR and marketing to each identify a major spending project that would be analyzed by a cross-functional team. The group would reconvene for another retreat a month later to analyze the two reports, summarize the main learning points, and then prepare final versions for submission to Jerry.

The principles that were to be deployed in these analyses were as follows:

- Both marketing and HR would need to quantify estimates of future benefits from their projects. This is not something they normally did. The recommended process for making these estimates is summarized in Fig. 20.1.

The basic idea behind this approach is simple. If one can break up costs and benefits into the smallest possible components, and settle on a value for each component that minimizes the likelihood that the assigned value is unreasonable, then the eventual cash flow estimates are unlikely to be challenged. By going around the room and asking each member of the cross-functional project team to challenge each of the tiniest components of cash flows, one exposes most of the relevant assumptions that underlie the cash flow estimates. This brings to bear an important

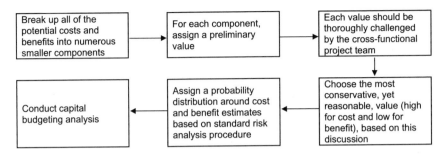

Fig. 20.1.   Cash flow estimation.

discipline on the process that is particularly important when one is dealing with "soft" (intangible) benefits that are often hard to quantify.

- Carefully analyze the number of time periods over which benefits are expected to accrue. Most HR and marketing projects involve investments that are expected to yield payoffs that accrue over long time periods in the future. While this is true for most projects, marketing or HR projects are "special," in that the investments in them are usually expensed, so it is all too easy to focus on the current expense implications and ignore the (nonquantified) future benefits.
- View the expense outlays as capital investments and assess a capital charge at the firm's weighted average cost of capital.
- Carefully establish all future outlays that will be required to implement the project.
- Establish a spending threshold so only projects involving outlays above that limit are subjected to this analysis.

3. The HR Project

Barb Sidwell selected a training program as the HR project to be analyzed. Jerry had asked her to consider the development of a program to train about 150 of the company's managers, directors and executives in business analysis. Jerry had been very pleased with the resource allocation training. He now wanted something similar done in the area of business analysis.

By business analysis, what Jerry had in mind was the routine analysis of the ongoing business with a view to monitoring developments continuously. The goal was to make decisions in a timely manner. Included in this would be things like analysis of the macroeconomic environment, competitive actions, environmental risks, and so on. Root cause and variance analysis would also be included.

Jerry felt that such training was needed because his business was getting more complex and he was concerned that value would migrate away from the firm in an undetected manner.[179]

When Jerry first talked to Bob about the training program, Bob agreed it was an outstanding idea. However, he said he had no idea how to conduct the training internally. He did not know of any course offered in any of the business schools he was familiar with that dealt with the issues Jerry was concerned about.

Jerry then decided to let Barb work on it. Barb sent out requests for proposal (RFPs) to external vendors for developing this training course. The vendor selected for the task was a consulting firm that relied largely on leading business school faculty to help it develop and offer executive training programs.

The vendor was told that the focus of the program should be on the Value Sphere. All of the company's internal literature on the Value Sphere was delivered to the vendor.

The Analysis: The vendor quoted the following:

- $100,000 for developing the course and writing a company manual;
- $100,000 for each week-long training program, conditional on the company running four programs or less, with this amount falling to $90,000 for each program if the company purchased five programs or more;
- At the end of each program, there would be teams of participants who would each leave with a well-defined project to work on that would result in improving some aspect of business analysis in the company;
- Each program would consist of no fewer than 15 participants and no more than 30 participants.

Based on the case studies that were expected to be developed for the course, as well as the specific business analysis situations that the course would cover, the training specialists in HR had identified seven distinct areas in which the course would improve performance. This was not difficult to do, since the design of the course was based on performance-based training principles. Barb had done some benchmarking with companies like Whirlpool and Motorola, which had considerable experience with performance-based training for their people.

The basic idea behind performance-based training was simple. First, identify the areas in which you want excellence in on-the-job performance. Then identify the set of skills needed to perform excellently in those areas. Third, take stock of

---

[179]Jerry had read Adrian Slywotzky's book, *Value Migration*, Harvard Business School Press, Boston, 1996.

the existing skills of those in the target population. Where are the skill gaps, given the skills required for excellent performance? Finally, design a training program to eliminate the identified skill deficiencies.

The HR training specialists thus delineated seven areas of desired enhanced performance. They labeled these areas A1 through A7. Under each area, the specific functions within the company that would be affected were identified, and a cross-functional team consisting of a representative from each function was put together for that area.

Each team was thus assigned one specific area in which the training program was expected to enhance performance. Each of the seven teams was then asked what projects/opportunities were likely to come up during a typical year that would permit a display of enhanced performance as a direct result of the training program? The principles outlined in Fig. 20.1 were used here to eliminate opportunities that were deemed to be unlikely (low probability) events, or those that the training program would not address.

In the next round of brainstorming, each group was asked to estimate an increase in revenue or a saving in cost associated with each of the opportunities identified in the previous step. Again, the principles outlined in Fig. 20.1 were used. Each opportunity was broken down into smaller components, and the most conservative estimate of cash flow benefit was chosen for each component.

For example, one area (A2) was the company's financial reporting system. The A2 group agreed that this system had become somewhat counterproductive. It took too long to generate the numbers in the report, thereby leaving the so-called financial analysts with little time for analysis. If even modest improvements were made here, the reporting cycle time could be significantly improved. The benefits of this would be twofold. First, senior executives would get reports faster, leading to better decisions. Second, analysts would have more time for analysis, leading to an earlier spotting and correction of potential problems.

The group then reflected on the events of the past two years and determined there were dozens of areas in which better decisions could have been made if the reporting system was more efficient. Out of these, they selected one that was judged as average. It was an example of inadequate root-cause analysis due to insufficient time spent on it. This inadequacy resulted in the company learning about material cost increases too late to make the appropriate manufacturing and marketing adjustments. A post-audit of this situation revealed that the warning signs were evident in the numbers contained in the financial reports long before the problem actually hit the company. It is just that nobody had the time to analyze the numbers. The group estimated the company could have saved $75,000 that year with a timely analysis of the root causes of these problems.

Each group thus came up with one opportunity for improvement in the area assigned to it. In each case, this was just one of the many opportunities they identified. All the groups then met together to make sure there were no overlaps in the identified projects, i.e., no double counting. An interesting aspect of the opportunities identified by the groups was that each group felt strongly that the cash flow benefits they had estimated could reasonably be expected to be perpetual. Barb thought this was a bit optimistic, but relented, because in each case the chosen opportunity was but one of many, so the likelihood of overestimating the total benefits was remote.

The final outcome of the exercise is summarized in the table below.

The total present value of benefits, conservatively estimated in Fig. 20.2, are thus $3.3 million. What about the costs of the training? The direct cost of training 150 people will be $100,000 (development cost) + $540,000 (cost of six programs) = $640,000 paid to the vendor. In addition to this, on an average, each program participant would lose two weeks of time "on the job." One week spent in the program and one spent on the project. On an average, each of the people in the target audience earned $150,000 annually in salaries and benefits and worked 45 weeks per year. So the opportunity cost of training these people and having them work on projects would be:

$$\frac{2 \text{ weeks}}{45 \text{ weeks}} \times \$150,000 \times 150 \text{ participants} = \$1 \text{ million.}$$

Area	Single-year net cash flows	Duration of benefit	Present value at 10% weighted average cost of capital
A1: Relating expense budgets to capital budgets	$40,000	Perpetual	$400,000
A2: Financial reporting	$75,000	Perpetual	$750,000
A3: Variance analysis	$100,000	Perpetual	$1,000,000
A4: Competitive analysis	$25,000	Perpetual	$250,000
A5: Application of statistical process control techniques to business analysis	$35,000	Perpetual	$350,000
A6: Analysis of macroeconomic trends and market conditions	$40,000	Perpetual	$400,000
A7: Improved consulting (process-partner) skills among analysts	$15,000	Perpetual	$150,000

Fig. 20.2. Training program cash flow benefit estimates.

Thus, the NPV of the training program is:

$3.3 million − $640,000 − $1 million = $1.66 million.

Even without a full-blown risk analysis, one can see that this is an excellent project. The actual NPV of this project is likely to be much higher than $1.66 million since this analysis accounts for only *one* opportunity in each area, when no one disputes that there are multiple opportunities in each area.

4. The Marketing Project

The Marketing group, under Bruce Acito, Senior Vice President of Marketing, took a unique approach. They first examined an existing "project." This was the decision to spend an additional $500,000 in advertising, compared to last year. This was approved by the Executive Committee as part of the approval for the overall advertising budget for the year. The $500,000 represented a planned increase in the advertising dollars spent by the company, and it was based on the goal of increasing market share by 1%. It was estimated that a 1% growth in market share would add about $2.17 million to pre-tax revenue the coming year, and that this benefit would decline to $1 million the following year, then vanish altogether.

A quick NPV analysis was done as follows. At a 40% tax rate, the $2.17 million increase in pre-tax revenue translates into a $1.3 million increase in NOPAT. The year after that, the $1 million increase represents a $600,000 increase in NOPAT. Thus, the NPV of this proposed $500,000 increase is:

$$= \$1.18 \text{ million} + 0.5 \text{ million} - \$0.5 \text{ million}$$
$$= \$1.18 \text{ million}.$$

Thus, even though this decision had not been subjected to capital budgeting analysis, it appeared to be justified on a two-year NPV basis.

However, the project team soon realized it had not fully accounted for all the costs. Even though supporting the higher sales volume associated with the 1% growth in market share would not require the purchase of any new equipment, it would result in additional inventory and the leasing of a few more machines. At a 10% weighted average cost of capital, the capital charge for these previously ignored items would be $660,000 the first year and $363,000 the second year. Thus, the revised NPV is:

$$\frac{\$1.3 \text{ million} - \$0.66 \text{ million}}{1.1} + \frac{\$600,000 - \$363,000}{(1.1)^2} - \$500,000 = \$280,000.$$

It was still a good idea to invest the additional advertising dollars. But the idea did not look quite as good as it did before.

The project team now asked itself whether this was the best use of the $500,000 outlay. The answer was obviously yes if there were no other ideas to compete with this one.

But the project team soon came up with another idea. A national upscale department store chain had made a proposal to join hands with Jerry's Lemonade. The idea was that, for every $100 spent at the department store, the customer would get a $5 coupon toward the purchase of anything at Jerry's Lemonade. The cost of this $5 coupon would be split equally between the department store and Jerry's Lemonade. This was a relatively recent proposal that was generating serious discussion in Marketing.

When the project team ran the numbers on this proposal they discovered that over 75% of this department store's customers were currently not customers of Jerry's Lemonade. The amount of new advertising Jerry's Lemonade would have to do the first year to support this initiative would be $300,000. After this, "maintenance advertising" would be done by the department store, and Jerry's Lemonade would bear only a modest $20,000 cost per year in printing and distributing promotional leaflets at its own retail outlets.

A careful analysis revealed that the annual increment to cash flows as a consequence of this promotional initiative would be $200,000, and this would account for the $2.50 per-coupon cost, the $20,000 ongoing cost of promotional leaflets, and the capital charge associated with increases in working capital, etc. The team also estimated that this relationship would fruitfully last — no pun intended — for at least 10 years.

Thus, its NPV analysis was as follows:

$$= \$928,913.$$

This clearly exceeds the NPV from investing $500,000 more in advertising.

Of course, in a perfect world, the team would like to do both projects. But they do not believe that, given the company's permanently value-consistent growth projections, it would be advisable to do both (see Chapter 16). They must therefore choose, and their clear choice is the promotional initiative with the department store.

Such a choice represented a small cultural revolution in marketing. Opting for the $300,000 initiative rather than the $500,000 initiative meant "returning" $200,000 of funds to Corporate that had already been approved! However, Bruce stressed to his team that it would not only be in the shareholders' best interest, but also in their best interest to provide to senior management such tangible examples that the Marketing group was no longer thinking parochially. Credibility with senior management is valuable in any organization.

5. Jerry Reads the Report

The report containing the HR and marketing studies reached Jerry's desk about six weeks after his meeting with Bob and Barb. Jerry had not set a specific time-table for the reports or for the training program he had asked Barb to investigate. He knew everybody was busy and that he had effectively communicated to his executives the importance of the initiatives. They would figure out the optimal time-table.

Jerry decided to read the Marketing study as soon as he had finished reading the overall recommendations. Marketing had been a lot on Jerry's mind lately. He had recently studied the decline of Levi Strauss & Co. The world-famous maker of blue jeans — often referred to generically as Levi's — had seen its US market share plummet from 30.9% in 1990 to a mere 18.7% by end 1997. On November 3, 1997, Levi Strauss had announced that it would close 11 of its US plants and lay off about a third of its North American workforce. This came on the heels of its announcement in February 1997 that it would lay off 1,000 salaried employees.

How did Levi Strauss, a $7 billion company, get hit with such value evaporation? According to Robert D. Haas, Levi Strauss Chairman and CEO at the time, it was because the company took its eye off the customer.[180] On July 31, 1997, the company learned the outcome of a year-long market research study which showed that the company's products had lost their "coolness" appeal with those in the 15–19 year-old age group.

The problems were twofold. First, the company discovered its marketing was not sharply focused on the things that appealed to teens. The company addressed this in part by running new ad campaigns. One of these featured a young man driving through a car wash with the windows down, something that elicited positive reactions from Levi's target group. But this exposed the second problem. When kids responded to the ads by visiting Levi Strauss stores, they were greeted mostly with traditional styles. No new sales!

Jerry was determined not to let this happen to his company. His suggestion to examine the possibility of setting up a capital budgeting system for marketing outlays was partly to force careful attention on marketing issues. The more you analyze things, the more you focus attention on hidden assumptions, and the better your chances of not missing shifts in customer preferences.

---

[180]See Linda Himelstein, "Levi's is Hiking Up Its Pants," *Business Week*, 12-1-1997, pp. 70–75.

As he read the Marketing study, he was pleased on two counts. First, the will-ingness of the group to "give up" $200,000 that had already been approved indi-cated a serious awareness of what mattered most to shareholders. No more corporate games, thought Jerry. That's great!

Second, he had an intuitive feeling that linking up with an upscale department store with a national scope was going to be very good for the brand image of his products. The study verified his intuition.

Jerry could not help but think of the marketing trends in the healthcare industry. He'd read an article[181] that Evanston Hospital and the upscale retailer Nordstrom had entered a partnership whereby customers would get discounts for purchasing medical services at Evanston Hospital through Nordstrom. For example, a cus-tomer purchased a mammogram at Nordstrom and received $40 off the $139 test at Evanston Hospital, plus a free facial at Nordstrom. Part of the appeal of the package was the atmosphere at Nordstrom, which eased the customer's mind. This was just one example of the increasingly aggressive promotional initiatives in the healthcare industry. For example, Target Corporation now offers walk-in clinics in some of their discount stores.

Eventually, Jerry got to the HR report. He was fascinated by it. He had never seen such a thorough analysis of an issue as "fuzzy" as executive training. He made a mental note to personally congratulate Barb.

What appealed to Jerry about the study was that it had great potential to be applied to the headcount reduction and SG&A expenses rationalization they were contemplating after the acquisition of Mickey's. He was not quite sure how it could be done, but he was confident Bob could figure it out. They would not lay off people or slash SG&A expenses just to cut costs in the short run. The decision would be made after considering all the factors that affected shareholder value, so the Value Sphere would be kept synchronized.

Main Lessons

- To the shareholder, there is no difference between an expense and a capital outlay. Both are equally important elements of the Value Sphere.
- It is foolish to exclude "nontraditional" projects from rigorous capital budgeting analysis, even though quantifying the benefits from projects in areas such as marketing and human resources may be challenging. A business case is needed for all major spending, regardless of whether it is treated as a capital expenses or

---

[181]Peter Galuszka, Gail DeGeorge, A. T. Palmer, and Jessica McCann, "See the Doctor, Get a Toaster," *Business Week*, December 8, 1997.

not. Recall, this is why a rigorous analysis of leasing expenditures is required (see Chapter 9).

- To maximize value retention, one should use a systematic approach to quantifying the benefits and estimating the costs of nontraditional projects. The costs should be capitalized, and the project cash flows should then be "charged" for these costs at the weighted average cost of capital.

End-of-Chapter Exercises

1. What are the differences in the processes by which your company does its expense and capital budgeting? Are your expense budgets linked in a meaningful way to your capital budgets?
2. How do you determine how much to spend on "nontraditional" projects like executive education, employee training, advertising, and significant marketing outlays? Are these expenses subject to the same rigorous process as your capital expenditures?
3. How do you post-audit the effectiveness of your capital and expense budgets? How are the potential benefits quantified and tracked?
4. In your company, is next year's expense budget based on how much was spent this year? If so, what sort of value evaporation behavior does this generate?
5. Do you reward your employees for underspending their expense and/or capital budgets?

Practice Problems

1. What is the difference between expense dollars and capital dollars from the shareholders' standpoint?
2. What difference does it make within a firm whether something is classified as an expense or a capital outlay?
3. Can you think of a capital budgeting approach for HR and marketing outlays that improves on the approach developed here? How would you approach it conceptually?

Chapter 21

POST-ACQUISITION INTEGRATION ISSUES

1. Now Comes the Hard Part: The Morning after the Merger

Leaning back in his chair, Bob looked at his appointments for the day. The first person he was going to meet was George Hausch, who was the Controller at Mickey's before Jerry's purchased the business. Bob had reassured George that there would be a place for him in the new organization, but he had not been specific. Bob guessed this appointment was probably to clarify that issue.

Bob was ambivalent about Hausch. While the man possessed good technical accounting skills, he was far too narrow a specialist to be an effective strategic partner with the line executives who ran the business. Bob was not sure whether this was because George simply did not know enough about the business or because he was an introvert. But it was clear he did not possess the leadership skills Bob was looking for.

On the other hand, he could be useful for his accounting skills. Besides he knew Mickey's organization well. No point in pushing him out the door.

There was a brief knock on the door. Hausch had arrived for the meeting. After exchanging pleasantries, he got straight to the point. "Bob, I'm here to submit my resignation."

Bob was shocked! He did not view Hausch as a highly "marketable" person with a lot of job mobility. Besides, he had been with Mickey's forever. Why would he want to leave?

When Bob asked him to explain, it was apparent Hausch was unwilling to elaborate on his plans. Bob could sense the bitterness in the man as he spoke. "I just don't feel like there is going to be a meaningful role for me in this organization. It's now been eight weeks since the acquisition, and I still don't know what I'm going to be doing in the long run. There are decisions coming down that I'd have made myself in the past. Now I'm not even involved in them. I used to be so busy I had no time to relax. Now I have a couple of hours a day with nothing to do."

Bob spoke carefully, "George, I know this must be hard on you. But I want to assure you that no one is ignoring you. We've all been so tied up with the post-acquisition integration issues that some of the interpersonal issues have probably been ignored. I've been meaning to talk to you about your new role. But I didn't want to make a unilateral decision about it. I though we might discuss it together."

"I'm afraid it's a bit late for that, Bob. I have already accepted a job as CFO of Java Hutt Pizza Stores. It's a smaller outfit than this, but they have ambitious growth plans," replied Hausch.

Bob was bemused and slightly annoyed. Hausch had not had the professional courtesy to talk to Bob before making his decision. This was not a meeting to discuss anything. It was merely to communicate a decision.

Bob also wondered how long Hausch had been in negotiations with Java Hutt Pizza. These sorts of things often take weeks, not days, to finalize. That means the conversation may have begun well before the acquisition was completed. Perhaps even when they first began discussions with Mickey's. In that case, this had little to do with how Hausch thought he was treated after the acquisition and more to do with his perception of what things would be like after the acquisition.

Bob stood up and said, "George, I'm truly sorry to hear that. No organization can afford to lose good people. But it looks like you've already made up your mind. I wish you every success in your new job. If there's anything I can do to help, please don't hesitate to call. Incidentally, you may want to schedule an exit interview with Jerry soon. Perhaps you can give him pointers on how best to integrate Mickey's business into ours."

Hausch nodded in agreement, shook Bob's hand and walked out.

2. Butterfield's Epiphany

The rest of the day was a blur for Bob. But he had time to think about the morning's events as he drove home. His initial annoyance with Hausch had given way to the conclusion that his departure had little to do with anything that happened after the acquisition. However, during the drive home he began to question that conclusion. Why would Hausch wait eight weeks if he had decided he was leaving anyway? Why was he so bitter? He should have been ecstatic at having been appointed CFO.

Perhaps the truth was a combination of the two possibilities. It was likely that the new job was no more than a form of insurance for Hausch. He had probably determined that he would make a final decision only after seeing how things progressed after the acquisition. In this case, the post-acquisition events probably had a lot to do with his decision. Why am I thinking about this so much? I did not even like the guy. It is not a big loss, Bob thought to himself.

And then it struck him like a thundering revelation. It was not Hausch's departure that bothered him. Rather, it was the vague feeling that the perceptions Hausch had were widely shared by others in that organization. What if there were mass departures? That would be a disaster. You could just toss out the window all those financial projections that supported the acquisition price they paid. The value evaporation would be enormous. Had they really botched this whole thing? The thought sent shivers down his spine.

The next day, Bob walked over to Barb Sidwell's office. He wanted to find out whether HR had encountered employee turnover problems at lower levels than Hausch's.

What Barb said surprised Bob. "We've already lost about half the people we were planning to lay off, although I'm not sure all the departures are the right people. I was initially happy because voluntary departures cost a lot less than layoffs. But now I'm concerned. Many of those who've left are actually people we wanted to keep. Not surprising really. They have the most mobility.

"But there's another issue that bothers me. All of Mickey's people want to know what our vision is for the future. I keep pointing them to the Vision Statement that is now on almost every wall in their buildings. But I get the impression that's not what they're looking for. It's like they don't understand what we're about, and there's nothing I can do that helps them."

Bob quietly absorbed what Barb had just said. His mind wandered to a book he had read on leadership.[182] It claimed that people's thirst for vision increases with uncertainty. It makes a lot of sense. A vision statement is a sort of map of the future because it tells us where we want to go. As uncertainty increases, the future becomes harder to visualize with any clarity. A sharply-defined vision statement helps to clarify things.

And what could add more uncertainty to an organization than to be taken over? The standard takeover script is well known to them all. When a company is taken over, the acquirer installs its own people in charge, alters policies and procedures, and generally reconfigures the organization. The acquirer's managers are supremely

---

[182]See Robert Quinn, *Deep Change: Discovering the Leader Within*, Jossey-Bass Publishers, San Francisco, 1996.

confident in their belief that they can run the company better. So out go the senior decision makers in the target company. A good case in point is the Swedish appliance company, Electrolux, whose global growth strategy has long been predicated on acquiring financially troubled companies and replacing their senior managers with their own.

Moreover, the premium paid in a typical acquisition depends on plans to cut costs. And that usually means headcount reductions. More uncertainty for employees of the target firm. But this time it affects people at all levels, not just senior managers in the target. A good example is the Bank of America acquisition of Security Pacific Bank. More than 10,000 people were laid off after the acquisition.

In such turbulent times, people want to see a clear course of action, a vision for the future that helps them define their new roles. Is not this what Hausch wanted? Suddenly, Bob realized there was a lot they should have done that had not been done.

He decided to call a friend of his at the business school who had extensive consulting experience with acquisitions. He would hire him on a brief consulting assignment to help them with this post-acquisition integration.

3. The Integration Plan: Overview

After spending some time with his consultant friend, Bob had a good idea of what needed to be done. An unexpected payoff from the exercise was that he now also had a blueprint of what to do in the next acquisition. It was time to meet Jerry.

In preparation for his meeting with Jerry, Bob sent him a copy of his post-acquisition integration report. It was essentially a plan of action. Moreover it outlined what the company should do in future acquisitions.[183]

Post-Acquisition Integration Plan

Short-Term Actions: We need to immediately (within the next three to four weeks) attend to the following matters:

- Finalize immediately (in less than a week) the list of key individuals from Mickey's who are expected to play an important role in the future, and hold individual meetings with them to explain their roles in the new organization. Their concerns

---

[183]The plan was based in part on a model developed by GE Capital that is described in Ashkenas, Ronald N., Lawrence J. DeMonaco, and Suzanne C. Francis, "Making the Deal Real: How GE Capital Integrates Acquisitions," *Harvard Business Review*, January-February, 1998, pp. 165-178.

should be heard as well, and every effort should be made to ensure that none of these people leave.

- Hold a series of "town hall" style meetings in which senior executives (including Jerry Wyman, Bob Butterfield, and Barb Sidwell) meet with groups of employees from Mickey's business and explain to them clearly:

  o the new organizational vision for them
  o the strategy that will support this vision
  o the headcount reductions and other restructuring that will take place and when
  o outplacement support for departing employees
  o the new organization structure that will emerge, along with the new reporting relationships and responsibilities

It would be advisable to start at the top of the organization and work down. That way, the existing leaders can explain things to their own people even before the town-hall meetings take place.

- Train those of our new employees who need training about financial and other reporting systems in our company.

Long-Term Actions (Next Three to Four Months)

- Appoint a group of HR professionals to conduct a quick "cultural diagnostic," to determine the key aspects of the corporate culture at Mickey's. After this, we should identify the differences between their culture and ours, and make sure all our new employees understand the new culture in which they will be operating, and why. For example, at Mickey's the focus was largely on short-term business results in assessing performance. By contrast, we also reward our people on how they train and develop those who report to them.
- Reengineer the information technology, capital budgeting, and financial analysis systems at Mickey's and completely integrate them with ours.
- Train the appropriate subset of our new employees in our approach to financial analysis.
- Identify a portfolio of relatively short-term projects across different parts of the company and appoint teams consisting of our most experienced people, as well as those from Mickey's, to attack these projects. This will ensure the appropriate sharing of best practices, cross-fertilization of ideas, and absorption of our new colleagues into our organization.

Bob had also provided details that describe a systematic procedure that the company should follow in its post-acquisition in the future.

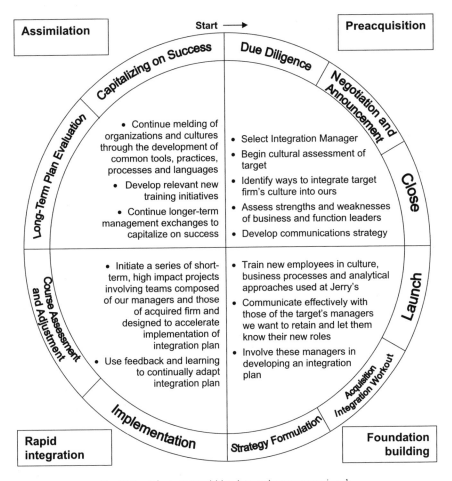

Fig. 21.1.   The post-acquisition integration process at Jerry's.

4. The Integration Plan: Details

This addendum is based in part on the approach used by GE Capital.[184] An adapted version of that approach is presented in Fig. 21.1.

Phase 1: Preacquisition Activities

The basic lesson we have learned from this acquisition is that we did not start our planning early enough. This did not help us properly manage the people and

---

[184]Reported in the earlier-mentioned article by Ashkenas, *et al.* (1998). See page 23, Brav, *et al.*, op.cit.

organization culture segment of our Value Sphere. We cannot start thinking about post-acquisition integration after the documents are signed. Rather, we need to begin our integration planning when we initiate due diligence, and it should run through the ongoing management of the acquired firm. There are four key steps in this first phase.

Select Integration Manager: As GE Capital has recognized, acquisition integration is an ongoing process, so someone is needed to manage it. The reason is that the key players involved in an acquisition — the due diligence team including representatives from finance, tax, business, development, human resources and technology, the negotiating team of the acquiring firm, and the negotiating team of the target — are not those who end up focusing on integration.

Our due diligence team in the acquisition of Mickey's probably developed the deepest knowledge of that company. They thus probably had the best insight into what was needed to integrate it after the deal closed. Unfortunately, we have already disbanded this team. Clearly, the members of this team should be candidates for the new job of integration manager.

Integration managers manage the integration process, not the business. To do so, they:

1. Facilitate and manage integration activities by:

   - working closely with the managers of the acquired company to make its practices consistent with Jerry's requirements and standards
   - creating strategies to quickly communicate important information about the integration effort to employees
   - helping the new company add value-enhancing processes and practices that may not have existed before, such as risk-based capital analysis

2. Help the acquired business understand our business by:

   - assisting managers of the newly acquired company as they navigate through our system, e.g., what analysis is involved in a lease-vs.-buy analysis in our company
   - educating the new management team about our business cycle, HR performance reviews, and such other processes as strategic planning, budgeting, and human resource procedures and the company's benefit plan
   - translating and explaining our various acronyms
   - helping managers of the acquired company understand our culture and business customs
   - helping managers of the acquired company understand both the fundamental and minor changes in their jobs, e.g., a treasury person used to being judged

for helping business profitability should understand that our focus on the Value Sphere might imply a different risk management strategy

- introducing our business practices to the new company, including the Value Sphere and leadership training

3. Help our people understand the acquired business by:

- making sure managers of the newly acquired company are not swamped with requests for information from us, e.g., we could insist that all requests for information go through them so that they can sort through the important ones and allow the other managers to stay focused on the business
- briefing our executives about the newly acquired company to help them understand why it works the way it does

If we pursue a strategy of growth in acquisitions, our objective should be for the integration manager to be a permanent position, and to have a small team dedicated to the integration task. The team should provide continuity by being involved in the integration of all our future acquisitions.

Cultural Assessment of Target and Cultural Integration: We should assess the corporate culture of the target carefully prior to the acquisition. We should use this cultural audit to examine the areas in which the target's culture is significantly different from ours, so the integration manager can begin to work with our HR staff on plans to meld the two cultures. In some cases, this may involve a change in our culture, not theirs.

Assess Strengths and Weaknesses of Business Function Leaders: We should conduct a careful assessment of the leadership attributes of senior executives in the target. This would allow us to begin to think about the roles these people would play after the acquisition.

Develop Communication Strategy: Prior to every acquisition, we should develop a strategy for both internal and external communication. Our internal communication strategy should focus on:

- informing our employees about the value of the acquisition to us and the changes it will entail for them
- deciding what we would like to tell the managers of the target company about our vision, strategy and business processes

Our external communication strategy should focus on:

- informing the financial markets about our motives for the acquisition
- informing our vendors and customers about the implications of the acquisition

Phase 2: Foundation Building

This phase, which begins after we have signed the documents, involves three main activities.

Train New Employees: We must design training programs for our new employees that focus on making them very familiar with our business processes. For example, they should understand how we:

- do strategic analysis
- do our risk-based capital analysis
- apply our Value Sphere principles
- manage our human resources
- develop our leaders
- construct a model of our customers and view our relationship with them

Communication with Target Managers: To prevent some of the mishaps we have had with managers in Mickey's, we should communicate with our new managers what roles we have proposed for them in the new organization. It is important to keep the following points in mind:

- Tell the managers we want to retain and those we want to remove what we intend to do.
- Be completely honest.
- Make sure that we do not carve in stone the roles we want people to play before we talk to them. We should let them participate in defining their roles in the new enterprise.

Involve Target Managers in Integration Plan Development: Once we have identified the managers we want to retain, we should work with them to refine the integration plan developed prior to the acquisition.

Phase 3: Rapid Integration

In this phase, we should focus on rapidly integrating the acquired firm. There are two key activities.

Initiate high-impact projects: We should identify numerous high-impact projects that satisfy the following conditions:

- They should be relatively short term so that the results become visible in the near future.
- They should involve many of our business processes so that our new managers can learn our processes quickly.

- They should also include some of our more experienced managers so they can play the role of teachers. These managers should be drawn from both organizations.

Use Feedback for Integration Plan Adaptation: We should use these short-term projects as well as other feedback mechanisms to learn from the acquired firm's managers.

Phase 4: Assimilation
The last phase is complete assimilation of the acquired firm. There are three steps.

Continue Melding Organizations and Cultures: We should put in place a process whereby we do not just force the acquired firm to accept our culture. Rather, we should choose what is best in both corporate cultures and meld them together, so we have the best set of common tools, practices, processes, and languages.

Develop Relevant New Training Initiatives: As we begin to assimilate the acquired firm, we should also examine what new training initiatives can be put in place to upgrade our human capital. Moreover, we should stress to our new executives that we expect them to be active participants in our training programs as teachers and mentors.

Continue Longer-Term Management Exchanges: We should ensure that we eventually dissolve any real or imagined boundaries between the acquired entity and ourselves. We can do this by exchanging managers, placing our experienced managers to run the acquired business and placing theirs to run our older businesses.

5. The Integration Plan Reaches Jerry

As Jerry finished reading the integration plan that Bob had sent to him, he was pleased. He had felt strongly that the post-acquisition integration issues transcended the capital and expense allocation problems discussed in his last meeting with Bob and Barb (see Chapter 20). It was good to see that Bob had recognized it too.

Even though he had known Bob for a long time, Jerry could not help but be impressed with his latest initiative in developing a systematic approach to post-acquisition integration. He had not only taken steps to solve the problems created by this latest acquisition, but had actually used it as an *opportunity* to develop a world-class process. He had surpassed himself.

What also impressed Jerry was that Bob was *not* just playing the traditional reporting, controlling and financing role of a CFO. He had evolved into a true strategic partner for the business executives of the company. And a leader too. Jerry realized it would not be easy to hire someone to replace him. He made a mental note to recommend to the Executive Compensation Committee of the Board of Directors to give Bob a special raise as well as congratulations. He then recalled something he had read in *CFO Magazine* in connection with the "CFO Awards," a set of awards for CFOs who had displayed outstanding strategic partnership: ". . . the growing recognition that leveraging financial acumen throughout an organization can be a very effective competitive weapon." He would nominate Bob immediately.

Main Lessons

- Post-acquisition integration is a deliberate process. If left to chance, it could end up being a bad accident. The potential for value evaporation is enormous.
- If the acquirer does not follow a well-defined post-acquisition integration process, many of the assumptions about cost reductions and synergy benefits made in the pre-acquisition valuation analysis could become suspect. The actual results could make the acquisition a negative NPV project for the acquirer.
- The planning for post-acquisition integration activities should begin prior to the acquisition. This is the best way to manage the people and organization culture segment of the Value Sphere for the new enterprise.
- After an acquisition, the acquirer should move quickly to diminish uncertainty for the acquired firm's employees by clearly articulating the new vision and strategy, and also by discussing with employees the new roles they will be expected to play.

End-of-Chapter Exercises

1. Compare the post-acquisition integration process at your company with that designed at Jerry's Lemonade. Can you rationalize, on shareholder-wealth-maximization grounds, why your process differs from Jerry's? It may be helpful to use the following table for this purpose.

The Post-Acquisition Process at your Company

Phase	Name of phase	Key activities that should be performed	What we do	Gaps	Reasons
1.	Preacquisition activities	• Select integration manager • Cultural assessment of target and cultural integration • Assess strengths and weaknesses of business function leaders • Develop communication strategy			
2.	Foundation building	• Train new employees • Communicate with target managers • Involve target management in integration plan development			
3.	Rapid integration	• Initiate high-impact projects • Use feedback for integration plan adaptation			
4.	Assimilation	• Continue melding organization and cultures • Develop relevant new training initiatives • Continue longer-term management exchanges			

Practice Problems

1. Why is post-merger acquisition difficult and how can it both facilitate and interfere with the realization of anticipated merger synergies?
2. Discuss and evaluate the post-acquisition integration process developed in this chapter and analyze its pros and cons.
3. Can you think of two major mergers that failed because they did *not* follow the basic principles outlined here? Write a brief essay on each.

Chapter 22

JERRY WRESTLES WITH
CORPORATE GOVERNANCE

1. Introduction

Jerry had just finished his last glass of lemonade for the morning — he was not much of a coffee drinker — when Bob stopped by for a chat.

"Jerry, how are you doing?" said Bob in his most pleasant voice. "I need to talk with you about something important."

"It's always important to you, Bob." Jerry shot back, a little perturbed that Bob had interrupted his reading of the morning newspaper. Jerry always tried to read the local paper and *The Wall Street Journal* each morning. That habit kept him informed of all the key local and business news.

"Well Jerry, I hate to tell you this, but we need to start an initiative right away to ensure compliance with the Sarbanes–Oxley legislation. There are a lot of provisions in the new law, now affectionately known as SarbOx, that require action on our part. You know the government, Jerry. If we fail to comply there are very stiff penalties. I am afraid we have no choice but to put a task force together immediately." Bob waited for along time to hear Jerry's response.

"Bob, why does the government keep meddling in my business? The last thing I need is a bunch of new rules and regulations that accomplish nothing but added expense for me. All of these regulations amount to nothing more than a full employment act for accountants and attorneys!" Bob could see that Jerry was getting worked up over this issue.

"You know, Jerry, the government is trying to clean up the mess created by the corporate scandals of the late 1990s–early 2000 period. I am sure you recall

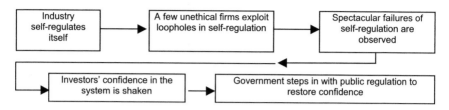

Fig. 22.1.   From self-regulation to public regulation.

reading about the stock price crashes and fraud at WorldCom, Global Crossing, and others. Congress responded with the Sarbanes–Oxley Act ("SarbOx") of 2002 to restore confidence in the securities markets because the market failed to appropriately govern these companies. Evidentially, congress believes corporate governance should be determined by government regulation."

"Yes, Bob, I read about the companies you mentioned. I know they committed fraud and pulled other shenanigans. But why should we penalize all companies because of a small number of bad actions in other corporations? It is not fair."

"I agree Jerry, but this is typical of the way regulation works. The government initially lets private institutions and markets regulate themselves. But if self-regulation fails, the government often steps in. It is like this picture I always used to show my students." Bob proceeded to sketch Fig. 22.1 on a flip chart. "In any case, whether we like it or not, SarbOx is now the law of the land. We must comply."

"Okay, Bob, why don't you summarize the key elements of the new regulations and then we can get together to talk about."

"You'd better give me a week, Jerry. The regulations are very complex."

2. Sarbanes–Oxley Act of 2002

As Bob started to put his report together he noticed that much has been written about SarbOx and even the Internet was overflowing with sites dedicated to SarbOx. Of course many of these sites were maintained by accountants, lawyers, and consultants who see a fee bonanza in the making. He was particularly struck by a quote from Larry Ribstein, a law professor at the University of Illinois, who stated "This Act is the most sweeping federal law concerning corporate governance since the adoption of the initial federal securities laws in 1933 and 1934."[186]

---

[186]L.E. Ribstein, "Market vs. Regulatory Responses to Corporate Fraud: A Critique of the Sarbanes–Oxley Act of 2002," *Illinois Law and Economics Working Paper Series*, No. LE02-008.LE02-008, University

As we discussed earlier (in Chapter 4), agency problems arise in corporations because of the separation of ownership in control. These problems can be mitigated by:

- The threat of a takeover.
- The monitoring of corporate directors, institutional shareholders, debt rating agencies, security analysts, law firms, and accounting firms to ensure that managers perform their legal duty to shareholders. These are the so-called "gate keepers" of the corporation.
- The appropriate incentive compensation for management (the subject of the following chapter).

In the cases of WorldCom, Tyco, and the others these mechanisms failed and the regulators stepped in.

An overview of the Sarbanes–Oxley Act provided by the AICPA is contained in the addendum to this chapter. The most chilling feature of the Act is its breadth, covering many corporate relationships. The Act creates a public company oversight Board to register public accounting firms, adopt standards, conduct investigations of public accounting firms and impose sanctions.

Thousands of companies face the task of ensuring their accounting operations are in compliance with the Sarbanes–Oxley Act. Auditing departments typically first have a comprehensive external audit by a Sarbanes–Oxley compliance specialist performed to identify areas of risk. Next, specialized software is installed that provides the "electronic paper trails" necessary to ensure Sarbanes–Oxley compliance.

The summary highlights of the most important Sarbanes–Oxley sections for compliance are listed below. Note that certification and specific public actions are now required by companies to remain in SOX compliance. The key provisions of the Act are summarized by the Sarbanes–Oxley–101.com website.

SOX Section 302–Corporate Responsibility for Financial Reports

a. CEO and CFO must review all financial reports.
b. Financial report does not contain any misrepresentations.
c. Information in the financial report is "fairly presented".
d. CEO and CFO are responsible for the internal accounting controls.
e. CEO and CFO must report any deficiencies in internal accounting controls, or any fraud involving the management of the audit committee.

---

of Illinois, September 2002. This paper is an excellent summary of the Act and helped to shape this chapter.

f. CEO and CFO must indicate any material changes in internal accounting controls.

SOX Section 404: Management Assessment of Internal Controls

All annual financial reports must include an internal control report stating that management is responsible for an "adequate" internal control structure, and an assessment by management of the effectiveness of the control structure. Any shortcomings in these controls must also be reported. In addition, registered external auditors must attest to the accuracy of the company management's assertion that internal accounting controls are in place, operational, and effective.

SOX Section 409–Real Time Issuer Disclosures

Companies are required to disclose on a almost real-time basis information concerning material changes in its financial condition or operations.

SOX Section 902–Attempts and Conspiracies to Commit Fraud Offenses

It is a crime for any person to corruptly alter, destroy, mutilate, or conceal any document with the intent to impair the object's integrity or availability for use in an official proceeding.[187]

These provisions require an immediate response by Jerry's Lemonade. Of particular interest is that both the CEO and CFO must accept responsibility for financial reports and the requirement under Section 404 that internal contacts are adequate and effective as verified by external auditors.

I propose the following action agenda for the SarbOx task force at Jerry's Lemonade.

- We must immediately canvass the current board of directors with the following issues in mind:
  - All members of the board audit committee must be "independent" (Section 301)
  - At last one member of the audit committee must be a "financial expert" (Section 407)
  - The SEC may prohibit any officer or director who has committed security fraud (Section 1105)
  - All directors must be made to understand that they now face increased personal liability for their actions.[188]

---

[187]Source, Sarbanes–Oxley-101.com website. This site has a wealth of information concerning SarbOx.
[188]In the WorldCom settlement, directors had to pay substantial penalties out of their own pockets.

- o The insurance policy for directors and officers liability must be reviewed and updated.
- All hedging and speculative activities and all off-balance sheet transactions of the company must be reviewed in light of the increased liability risk (Section 401).
- The relationship with our audit firm must be investigated:
  - o The audit firm cannot provide non-audit services (Section 201).
  - o The lead auditor must rotate every five years (Section 203).
  - o The auditor must report to the audit committee (Section 204).
  - o C-level officers cannot have been employed the company's audit firm one year prior (Section 206). We have a potential problem here since we recently hired Terry from our audit firm to be our new controller.
  - o The fees for audit work will likely increase as a result of SarbOx. Some people expect audit fees to double.
- The code of ethics for senior financial officers must be updated and disclosed (Section 406).
- The policy for retention of audit work papers, records in Federal investigations and bankruptcy must be reviewed in light of the substantial penalties which could be imposed (Section 802). To limit exposure corporate email records will also have to be retained. A substantial increase in record keeping and information technology costs is expected.[189]
- The company has to establish a whistle blower hotline for employees to report unethical or unlawful behavior (Section 806).
- One of the biggest concerns in my opinion is the provision in Section 404, which pertain to the adequacy and effectiveness of internal controls.
  - o Each annual report must contain an internal control report.
  - o Information controls not only relate to financial applications but also data storage, software, networks, security, transaction processing systems, and desktops.[190]
  - o Before signing off on financial statements the auditor must assess the risks of controls, processes, and reporting procedures. Detailed mapping of processes and controls that flow into financial statements is needed.
  - o Given the magnitude of assuring all of the controls we should hire a consultant to help us ASAP with Section 404 compliance.

---

[189] Internetneus, C. Boulton, "Taking the SarbOx Challenge," May 27, 2005 reports that IT compliance in onerous because "Public companies must establish a disputed accounting framework that can generate reports that are verifiable with source data. Source data must remain intact and any revisions must be documented as to what changed, who changed it, why and when."

[190] Ibid.

Bob marveled at the magnitude of the task force's agenda. However, he was sure that he didn't cover all the corporate governance implications of the SarbOx legislation. He was sure Jerry would not be happy with his report especially since he was upset initially.

3. Jerry and Bob Have a Heated Sarbox Discussion

Bob walked slowly into Jerry's office and knew from the look on Jerry's face that this meeting would be a tough one. Bob could see the veins in Jerry's neck.

"Bob, this is just what I thought," Jerry began in frustrated tone of voice. "Task-force, consultants, record keeping, IT investments — this SarbOx is a nightmare. It is much worse than I expected!"

"It is a very comprehensive piece of legislation that has the potential to affect all aspects of our Value Sphere". Bob responded. "Perhaps we should look at this as an opportunity."

"How do you figure that, Bob? In no way do I see anything good coming out of this," said a somewhat exasperated Jerry.

"Well," Bob interjected, "these SarbOx initiatives may help us perform better. Good documentation will enable us to keep better track of the drivers of revenue growth and expenses. We are all concerned about expense control at our company. In particular, there should be some real opportunities in procurement if we can consolidate all the data from our various locations. A review and enhancement of our processes could yield substantial benefits just like when we redid our capital allocation process. I think you would agree that effort generated huge results. There is also some evidence that good governance goes hand in hand with an increase in shareholder value.[191] This SarbOx stuff doesn't have to be all bad. It will not necessarily solve some of the small problems related to the career concerns of our directors and so on.[192] It is by no means a panacea, but it may improve on some things."

Jerry looked out the window as he spoke, "You may be right, Bob. But these initiatives are going to cost us a bundle. Do you know how much?"

Bob was quick to respond: "The way I see it, Jerry, we'll have to hire a director of internal audit, pay higher audit fees, hire outside consultants, and hire more internal people. I'd estimate the first year costs to be $1 million. Of course, compliance will

---

[191] Roberto Newell and Gregory Wilson, "A Premium for Good Governance," *The McKinsey Quarterly*, 2002, Number 3.

[192] These issues are explored theoretically in Fenghua Song and Anjan Thakor, "Information Control, Career Concerns and Corporate Governance," *Journal of Finance*, 61(4), August 2006, pp. 1845–1896.

	Cost to companies with revenues less than $1 billion	Cost to companies with revenues over $1 billion
D&O Insurance	$850,000	$2.2 million
Accounting	$825,000	$1.2 million
Legal	$468,000	$841,000
Board compensation	$313,000	$247000
Lost productivity	$160,000	$2.5 million
Other Sarbanes–Oxley-related costs	$100,000	$246,000
Governance set-up costs	$147,000	$174,000
Total	$2.86 million	$7.41 million

Fig. 22.2.   Costs of public ownership in 2003.
Source: Foley & Lardner LLP, Accounting Costs Based on Standard & Poor's Database. Originally appeared in the September 2004 issue of *Business Finance*.

require an on-going annual budgeted expenditure of about $600,000. These are only estimates. It could cost more. A breakdown of the costs of public ownership is shown in Fig. 22.2."

"Wow! Is there any way to opt out of these regulations? The hassle and expenses are going to kill us, Bob," Jerry said with some frustration.

Bob looked pensive as he replied, "Actually there is a way out, but it is quite drastic. Some US companies and foreign firms are delisting and deregistering, thereby avoiding the SarbOx regulations. The standards are tough though. If you are already registered with the SEC, you can only withdraw the registration if you have fewer than 300 US shareholders. Since many shareholders keep stock in bro-kerage street name accounts, it may be easier to meet the 300 test than you think. For example, Fidelity Brokerage could be a single record holder for thousands of investors."[193]

"Is this a viable alternative for us, Bob?," asked Jerry.

"I don't think so!" said Bob authoritatively.

"SarbOx notwithstanding, public ownership is an important aspect of a well-synchronized Value Sphere for us. Public ownership has numerous advantages for us. It provides us ready access to the public equity market, as our IPO demonstrated. This affects our resource allocation process and helps us execute our growth strategy. It also means that our shareholders' ownership is liquid and they do not demand the same liquidity premium in the cost of capital that they would with private ownership. Thus, a lower cost of capital for us. Moreover, I doubt that we'll meet

---

[193]Ilan Mochari, "Go Ahead, Delist Me!," *CFO Magazine*, April 2004.

the fewer-than-300-shareholders test of the SEC. Delisting is easy. Deregistering is not," continued Bob.

"I suppose a lower cost of capital is an advantage not to be overlooked," said Jerry in agreement.

"Absolutely," said Bob, "Our cost of capital also affects our valuation. We would not have the same valuation for our company if we were private. It is not unusual for private companies to have *half* the multiples-based valuations of comparable public companies."

Jerry nodded his head, "I guess we are stuck, Bob. Before we go off with our task force and hire consultants, I have a question that has been nagging me ever since I read your report. How do we even know things are under control?"

Bob smiled. "I'm glad you asked that question, Jerry. I had the same concern. Fortunately, I have come across a chart that answers that question. See Fig. 22.3. All of the auditors seem to be using this Treadway Commission framework."

Everyone will have a different opinion when it comes to what constitutes "under control," it is a very subjective judgment. The SEC requires that the control environment must be analyzed according to an integrated framework — and there is only one in widespread use. It was developed by the Committee of Sponsoring Organizations (COSO) of the Treadway Commission in the United States and recognizes controls as consisting of five interrelated components:

- **Control Environment**

  The "tone at the top", i.e.: the integrity and ethical values of the company, including its code of conduct, involvement of the Board of Directors and other actions that set the tone of the organization.

- **Risk assessment**

  Management's process of identifying potential risk that could result in misstated financial statements and developing actions to address those risks.

- **Control activities**

  These are the activities usually thought of as "the internal controls". They include such things as segregation of duties, account reconciliations and information processing controls that are designed to safeguard assets and enable an organization to prepare reliable financial statements on a timely basis.

- **Information and communication**

  The internal and external reporting process and includes an assessment of the technology environment.

- **Monitoring**

  Assessing the quality of a company's internal controls over time and taking actions as necessary to ensure it continues to address the risks of the organization.

Fig. 22.3.   What is best practice?

"As you can see, Jerry, the concept of under control is not an easy concept to grasp," continued Bob.

Jerry shook his head, "No wonder the costs of compliance are so high. I am shocked at the costs of being a public company as shown in Fig. 22.2. If I would have known this before, I am not sure I would have gone public with the IPO."

"Yes, Jerry, the costs are high. But don't forget, we needed the IPO money to grow the business. We could not have done that with our own resources," pointed out Bob.

Jerry wondered loud, "Do you think shareholders are benefiting from all the SarbOx oversight?"

Bob shrugged as he spoke, "It may be too early to tell, Jerry, but some initial studies suggest that shareholders have not benefited yet. A recent study by Zhang reports a \$1.4 trillion cumulative loss for shareholders of public companies attributable to the adoption of Sarbanes–Oxley.[194] Furthermore, studies show that companies perceived to have weak corporate governance prior to passage of the Act lost more value than others. This is consistent with the hypothesis that the market sees little benefit and significant costs from the legislation. In the light of these findings, it is difficult to suggest shareholders have benefited. Of course, the flip side is that in the absence of SarbOx one does not know the value losses that may have resulted from unchecked agency problems and value evaporation at some companies."

"Bob, can we expect to be rated on the effectiveness of our corporate governance and board independence?", asked Jerry.

"Of course, Jerry," responded Bob, "A market will be filled by rating services purporting to calibrate the corporate governance effectiveness of public companies. Already we have seen Institutional Shareholder Services, Board Analysts and Morningstar's Stewardship enter the market. Unfortunately, there is no consistency amongst the rating systems. For example, Fidelity National Financial, and title insurance and financial processing provider, achieved an a rating from Morningstar but the Board Analyst rated the company F, indicating major governance-related difficulties.[195] Such divergent rankings make one question their value."

"Is there anything else I need to consider about this SarbOx legislation?" Jerry asked Bob in an expectant voice.

---

[194] I.X. Zhang, "Economic Consequences of the Sarbanes–Oxley Act of 2002," working paper, William E. Simon Graduate School of Business Administration, University of Rochester, February 2005.

[195] Report by Joe Rauch, "Institutional Investors often Consider Grades," *The Business Journal of Jacksonville*, June 12, 2005.

Bob nodded, "I am sure we will uncover more issues when we get into the SarbOx requirements in more detail. However, one issue caught my eye in writing the report. That is, we need to consider SarbOx compliance when we investigate potential acquisition candidates to implement our growth strategy. Poor SarbOx compliance could be a deal breaker."

4. Jerry Moves Forward with the SarbOx Task Force

Jerry stood up as he spoke, "Let's move forward with the SarbOx task force, Bob. It appears we have no choice and maybe if we start early enough, we can reduce our costs. My objective is to have the best overall corporate governance possible. However, I still think the market does a better job of monitoring and enforcing good governance without a host of regulations.[196] In fact, I suspect Jerry's Lemonade will engage in some takeovers to resurrect poorly performing companies with inadequate governance. Nothing beats market discipline!"

Bob smiled, "That's the spirit, Jerry. Don't forget, however, a well-designed compensation system contributes to good corporate governance as well. And I think we have one."

Main Lessons

- The spectacular failures of Tyco, WorldCom, and others convinced the US Congress to pass the Sarbanes–Oxley Act of 2002, the most important financial legislation in over 50 years.
- Market mechanisms can be effective in overcoming the agency problems arising from the separation of management and ownership in corporations.
- The numerous provisions of the SarbOx regulations are meant to step in where the market mechanisms failed and to restore trust and confidence in the US securities markets.
- The costs to comply with the SarbOx regulations are great, especially for relatively small firms like Jerry's Lemonade.
- Good corporate governance is beneficial to companies, but it is difficult to measure and it is unclear that the regulatory approach, represented by SarbOx, is superior to market mechanisms. In fact, given the high costs of compliance it is likely to be inferior.

---

[196]Ribstein, op.cit., endorses this view as well.

End-of-Chapter Exercises

1. How has Sarbanes-Oxley charged corporate governance at your company? Which specific provisions had the most effect?
2. Did the adoption of changes due to SarbOx help your company reduce value evaporation in any form? Be specific.

Practice Problems

1. What are the market mechanisms that lead to good corporate governance? Why do they fail in the case of some companies?
2. List the costs to comply with the SarbOx regulations. Be sure to include the indirect costs, which are likely to be substantial, as well as the direct costs.
3. In light of the SarbOx regulations, would you recommend that a small company go public? What are the pros and cons of private versus public ownership?
4. Why is it so difficult to rate effective corporate governance? Do you think the companies that provide such ratings are helpful to investors?
5. What are the potential economic benefits of SarbOx in terms of reducing value evaporation?

Addendum

Summary of Sarbanes–Oxley Act of 2002

From The American Institute of Certified Public Accountants (AICPA) Website

---

Section 3: Commission Rulesand Enforcement

A violation of Rules of the Public Company Accounting Oversight Board ("Board") is treated as a violation of the '34 Act, giving rise to the same penalties that may be imposed for violations of that Act.

Section 101: Establishment; Board Membership

The Board will have five financially-literate members, appointed for five-year terms. Two of the members must be or have been certified public accountants, and the remaining three must not be and cannot have been CPAs. The Chair may be held by one of the CPA members, provided that he or she has not been engaged as a practicing CPA for five years.

The Board's members will serve on a full-time basis.

No member may, concurrent with service on the Board, "share in any of the profits of, or receive payments from, a public accounting firm," other than "fixed continuing payments," such as retirement payments.

(Continued)

(*Continued*)

Members of the Board are appointed by the Commission, "after consultation with" the Chairman of the Federal Reserve Board and the Secretary of the Treasury.

Members may be removed by the Commission "for good cause."

Section 101: Establishment; Duties of the Board
Section 103: Auditing, Quality Control, and Independence Standards and Rules

The Board shall:

1. register public accounting firms;
2. establish, or adopt, by rule, "auditing, quality control, ethics, independence, and other standards relating to the preparation of audit reports for issuers;"
3. conduct inspections of accounting firms;
4. conduct investigations and disciplinary proceedings, and impose appropriate sanctions;
5. perform such other duties or functions as necessary or appropriate;
6. enforce compliance with the Act, the rules of the Board, professional standards, and the securities laws relating to the preparation and issuance of audit reports and the obligations and liabilities of accountants with respect thereto;
7. set the budget and manage the operations of the Board and the staff of the Board.

Auditing standards. The Board would be required to "cooperate on an on-going basis" with designated professional groups of accountants and any advisory groups convened in connection with standard-setting, and although the Board can "to the extent that it determines appropriate" adopt standards proposed by those groups, the Board will have authority to amend, modify, repeal, and reject any standards suggested by the groups. The Board must report on its standard-setting activity to the Commission on an annual basis.

The Board must require registered public accounting firms to "prepare, and maintain for a period of not less than 7 years, audit work papers, and other information related to any audit report, in sufficient detail to support the conclusions reached in such report."

The Board must require a 2nd partner review and approval of audit reports registered accounting firms must adopt quality control standards.

The Board must adopt an audit standard to implement the internal control review required by Section 404(b). This standard must require the auditor evaluate whether the internal control structure and procedures include records that accurately and fairly reflect the transactions of the issuer, provide reasonable assurance that the transactions are recorded in a manner that will permit the preparation of financial statements in accordance with GAAP, and a description of any material weaknesses in the internal controls.

Section 102(a): Mandatory Registration
Section 102(f): Registration and Annual Fees
Section 109(d): Funding; Annual Accounting Support Fee for the Board

In order to audit a public company, a public accounting firm must register with the Board. The Board shall collect "a registration fee" and "an annual fee" from each registered public accounting firm, in amounts that are "sufficient" to recover the costs of processing and reviewing applications and annual reports.

(*Continued*)

(Continued)

The Board shall also establish by rule a reasonable "annual accounting support fee" as may be necessary or appropriate to maintain the Board. This fee will be assessed on issuers only.

Section 104: Inspections of Registered Public Accounting Firms

Annual quality reviews (inspections) must be conducted for firms that audit more than 100 issues, all others must be conducted every 3 years. The SEC and/or the Board may order a special inspection of any firm at any time.

Section 105(b)(5): Investigation and Disciplinary Proceedings; Investigations; Use of Documents

Section 105(c)(2): Investigations and Disciplinary Proceedings; Disciplinary Procedures; Public Hearings

Section 105(c)(4): Investigations and Disciplinary Proceedings; Sanctions

Section 105(d): Investigations And Disciplinary Proceedings; Reporting of Sanctions

All documents and information prepared or received by the Board shall be "confidential and privileged as an evidentiary matter (and shall not be subject to civil discovery other legal process) in any proceeding in any Federal or State court or administrative agency, … unless and until presented in connection with a public proceeding or [otherwise] released" in connection with a disciplinary action. However, all such documents and information can be made available to the SEC, the US Attorney General, and other federal and appropriate state agencies.

Disciplinary hearings will be closed unless the Board orders that they be public, for good cause, and with the consent of the parties.

Sanctions can be imposed by the Board of a firm if it fails to reasonably supervise any associated person with regard to auditing or quality control standards, or otherwise.

No sanctions report will be made available to the public unless and until stays pending appeal have been lifted.

Section 106: Foreign Public Accounting Firms

The bill would subject foreign accounting firms who audit a US company to registrations with the Board. This would include foreign firms that perform some audit work, such as in a foreign subsidiary of a US company, that is relied on by the primary auditor.

Section 107(a): Commission Oversight of the Board; General Oversight Responsibility

Section 107(b): Rules of the Board

Section 107(d): Censure of the Board and Other Sanctions

The SEC shall have "oversight and enforcement authority over the Board." The SEC can, by rule or order, give the Board additional responsibilities. The SEC may require the Board to keep certain records, and it has the power to inspect the Board itself, in the same manner as it can with regard to SROs such as the NASD.

The Board, in its rulemaking process, is to be treated "as if the Board were a 'registered securities association'"-that is, a self-regulatory organization. The Board is required to file proposed rules and proposed rule changes with the SEC. The SEC may approve, reject, or amend such rules.

(Continued)

(Continued)

The Board must notify the SEC of pending investigations involving potential violations of the securities laws, and coordinate its investigation with the SEC Division of Enforcement as necessary to protect an ongoing SEC investigation.

The SEC may, by order, "censure or impose limitations upon the activities, functions, and operations of the Board" if it finds that the Board has violated the Act or the securities laws, or if the Board has failed to ensure the compliance of accounting firms with applicable rules without reasonable justification.

Section 107(c): Commission Review of Disciplinary Action Taken by the Board

The Board must notify the SEC when it imposes "any final sanction" on any accounting firm or associated person. The Board's findings and sanctions are subject to review by the SEC.

The SEC may enhance, modify, cancel, reduce, or require remission of such sanction.

Section 108: Accounting Standards

The SEC is authorized to "recognize, as 'generally accepted'... any accounting principles" that are established by a standard-setting body that meets the bill's criteria, which include requirements that the body:

1. be a private entity;
2. be governed by a board of trustees (or equivalent body), the majority of whom are not or have not been associated persons with a public accounting firm for the past 2 years;
3. be funded in a manner similar to the Board;
4. have adopted procedures to ensure prompt consideration of changes to accounting principles by a majority vote;
5. consider, when adopting standards, the need to keep them current and the extent to which international convergence of standards is necessary or appropriate.

Section 201: Services Outside the Scope of Practice of Auditors; Prohibited Activities

It shall be "unlawful" for a registered public accounting firm to provide any non-audit service to an issuer contemporaneously with the audit, including: (1) bookkeeping or other services related to the accounting records or financial statements of the audit client; (2) financial information systems design and implementation; (3) appraisal or valuation services, fairness opinions, or contribution-in-kind reports; (4) actuarial services; (5) internal audit outsourcing services; (6) management functions or human resources; (7) broker or dealer, investment adviser, or investment banking services; (8) legal services and expert services unrelated to the audit; (9) any other service that the Board determines, by regulation, is impermissible. The Board may, on a case-by-case basis, exempt from these prohibitions any person, issuer, public accounting firm, or transaction, subject to review by the Commission.

It will not be unlawful to provide other non-audit services if they are pre-approved by the audit committee in the following manner. The bill allows an accounting firm to "engage in any non-audit service, including tax services," that is not listed above, only if

(Continued)

(*Continued*)

the activity is pre-approved by the audit committee of the issuer. The audit committee will disclose to investors in periodic reports its decision to pre-approve non-audit services. Statutory insurance company regulatory audits are treated as an audit service, and thus do not require pre-approval.

The pre-approval requirement is waived with respect to the provision of non-audit services for an issuer if the aggregate amount of all such non-audit services provided to the issuer constitutes less than 5% of the total amount of revenues paid by the issuer to its auditor (calculated on the basis of revenues paid by the issuer during the fiscal year when the non-audit services are performed), such services were not recognized by the issuer at the time of the engagement to be non-audit services; and such services are promptly brought to the attention of the audit committee and approved prior to completion of the audit.

The authority to pre-approve services can be delegated to 1 or more members of the audit committee, but any decision by the delegate must be presented to the full audit committee.

Section 203: Audit Partner Rotation

The lead audit or coordinating partner and the reviewing partner must rotate off of the audit every 5 years.

Section 204: Auditor Reports to Audit Committees

The accounting firm must report to the audit committee all "critical accounting policies and practices to be used all alternative treatments of financial information within [GAAP] that have been discussed with management ramifications of the use of such alternative disclosures and treatments, and the treatment preferred" by the firm.

Section 206: Conflicts of Interest

The CEO, Controller, CFO, Chief Accounting Officer or person in an equivalent position cannot have been employed by the company's audit firm during the 1-year period preceding the audit.

Section 207: Study of Mandatory Rotation of Registered Public Accountants

The GAO will do a study on the potential effects of requiring the mandatory rotation of audit firms.

Section 209: Consideration by Appropriate State Regulatory Authorities

State regulators are directed to make an independent determination as to whether the Boards standards shall be applied to small and mid-size non-registered accounting firms.

Section 301: Public Company Audit Committees

Each member of the audit committee shall be a member of the board of directors of the issuer, and shall otherwise be independent.

"Independent" is defined as not receiving, other than for service on the board, any consulting, advisory, or other compensatory fee from the issuer, and as not being an affiliated person of the issuer, or any subsidiary thereof.

The SEC may make exemptions for certain individuals on a case-by-case basis.

(*Continued*)

(*Continued*)

The audit committee of an issuer shall be directly responsible for the appointment, compensation, and oversight of the work of any registered public accounting firm employed by that issuer.

The audit committee shall establish procedures for the "receipt, retention, and treatment of complaints" received by the issuer regarding accounting, internal controls, and auditing.

Each audit committee shall have the authority to engage independent counsel or other advisors, as it determines necessary to carry out its duties.

Each issuer shall provide appropriate funding to the audit committee.

Section 302: Corporate Responsibility for Financial Reports

The CEO and CFO of each issuer shall prepare a statement to accompany the audit report to certify the "appropriateness of the financial statements and disclosures contained in the periodic report, and that those financial statements and disclosures fairly present, in all material respects, the operations and financial condition of the issuer." A violation of this section must be knowing and intentional to give rise to liability.

Section 303: Improper Influence on Conduct of Audits

It shall be unlawful for any officer or director of an issuer to take any action to fraudulently influence, coerce, manipulate, or mislead any auditor engaged in the performance of an audit for the purpose of rendering the financial statements materially misleading.

Section 304: Forfeiture of Certain Bonuses and Profits
Section 305: Officer and Director Bars and Penalties; Equitable Relief

If an issuer is required to prepare a restatement due to "material noncompliance" with financial reporting requirements, the chief executive officer and the chief financial officer shall "reimburse the issuer for any bonus or other incentive-based or equity-based compensation received" during the twelve months following the issuance or filing of the non-compliant document and "any profits realized from the sale of securities of the issuer" during that period.

In any action brought by the SEC for violation of the securities laws, federal courts are authorized to "grant any equitable relief that may be appropriate or necessary for the benefit of investors."

Section 305: Officer and Director Bars and Penalties

The SEC may issue an order to prohibit, conditionally or unconditionally, permanently or temporarily, any person who has violated section 10(b) of the 1934 Act from acting as an officer or director of an issuer if the SEC has found that such person's conduct "demonstrates unfitness" to serve as an officer or director of any such issuer.

Section 306: Insider Trades During Pension Fund Black-Out Periods Prohibited

Prohibits the purchase or sale of stock by officers and directors and other insiders during blackout periods. Any profits resulting from sales in violation of this section "shall inure to and be recoverable by the issuer." If the issuer fails to bring suit or prosecute diligently, a suit to recover such profit may be instituted by "the owner of any security of the issuer."

(*Continued*)

(*Continued*)

Section 401(a): Disclosures in Periodic Reports; Disclosures Required

Each financial report that is required to be prepared in accordance with GAAP shall "reflect all material correcting adjustments... that have been identified by a registered accounting firm..."

"Each annual and quarterly financial report... shall disclose all material off-balance sheet transactions" and "other relationships" with "unconsolidated entities" that may have a material current or future effect on the financial condition of the issuer.

The SEC shall issue rules providing that pro forma financial information must be presented so as not to "contain an untrue statement" or omit to state a material fact necessary in order to make the pro forma financial information not misleading.

Section 401(c): Study and Report on Special Purpose Entities

SEC shall study off-balance sheet disclosures to determine a) extent of off-balance sheet transactions (including assets, liabilities, leases, losses and the use of special purpose entities); and b) whether generally accepted accounting rules result in financial statements of issuers reflecting the economics of such off-balance sheet transactions to investors in a transparent fashion and make a report containing recommendations to the Congress.

Section 402(a): Prohibition on Personal Loans to Executives

Generally, it will be unlawful for an issuer to extend credit to any director or executive officer. Consumer credit companies may make home improvement and consumer credit loans and issue credit cards to its directors and executive officers if it is done in the ordinary course of business on the same terms and conditions made to the general public.

Section 403: Disclosures of Transactions Involving Management and Principal Stockholders

Directors, officers, and 10% owner must report designated transactions by the end of the second business day following the day on which the transaction was executed.

Section 404: Management Assessment of Internal Controls

Requires each annual report of an issuer to contain an "internal control report", which shall:

1. state the responsibility of management for establishing and maintaining an adequate internal control structure and procedures for financial reporting; and
2. contain an assessment, as of the end of the issuer's fiscal year, of the effectiveness of the internal control structure and procedures of the issuer for financial reporting.

Each issuer's auditor shall attest to, and report on, the assessment made by the management of the issuer. An attestation made under this section shall be in accordance with standards for attestation engagements issued or adopted by the Board. An attestation engagement shall not be the subject of a separate engagement.

The language in the report of the Committee which accompanies the bill to explain the legislative intent states, "— the Committee does not intend that the auditor's evaluation be the subject of a separate engagement or the basis for increased charges or fees."

(*Continued*)

(Continued)

Directs the SEC to require each issuer to disclose whether it has adopted a code of ethics for its senior financial officers and the contents of that code.

Directs the SEC to revise its regulations concerning prompt disclosure on Form 8-K to require immediate disclosure "of any change in, or waiver of," an issuer's code of ethics.

Section 407: Disclosure of Audit Committee Financial Expert

The SEC shall issue rules to require issuers to disclose whether at least 1 member of its audit committee is a "financial expert."

Section 409: Real Time Disclosure

Issuers must disclose information on material changes in the financial condition or operations of the issuer on a rapid and current basis.

Section 501: Treatment of Securities Analysts by Registered Securities Associations

National Securities Exchanges and registered securities associations must adopt conflict of interest rules for research analysts who recommend equities in research reports.

Section 601: SEC Resources and Authority

SEC appropriations for 2003 are increased to $776,000,000. $98 million of the funds shall be used to hire an additional 200 employees to provide enhanced oversight of auditors and audit services required by the Federal securities laws.

Section 602(a): Appearance and Practice Before the Commission

The SEC may censure any person, or temporarily bar or deny any person the right to appear or practice before the SEC if the person does not possess the requisite qualifications to represent others, lacks character or integrity, or has willfully violated Federal securities laws.

Section 602(c): Study and Report

SEC is to conduct a study of "securities professionals" (public accountants, public accounting firms, investment bankers, investment advisors, brokers, dealers, attorneys) who have been found to have aided and abetted a violation of Federal securities laws.

Section 602(d): Rules of Professional Responsibility for Attorneys

The SEC shall establish rules setting minimum standards for professional conduct for attorneys practicing before it.

Section 701: GAO Study and Report Regarding Consolidation of Public Accounting Firms

The GAO shall conduct a study regarding the consolidation of public accounting firms since 1989, including the present and future impact of the consolidation, and the solutions to any problems discovered.

(Continued)

(*Continued*)

Title VIII: Corporate and Criminal Fraud Accountability Act of 2002

It is a felony to "knowingly" destroy or create documents to "impede, obstruct or influence" any existing or contemplated federal investigation.

Auditors are required to maintain "all audit or review work papers" for five years.

The statute of limitations on securities fraud claims is extended to the earlier of five years from the fraud, or two years after the fraud was discovered, from three years and one year, respectively.

Employees of issuers and accounting firms are extended "whistleblower protection" that would prohibit the employer from taking certain actions against employees who lawfully disclose private employer information to, among others, parties in a judicial proceeding involving a fraud claim. Whistle blowers are also granted a remedy of special damages and attorney's fees.

A new crime for securities fraud that has penalties of fines and up to 10 years imprisonment.

Title IX: White Collar Crime Penalty Enhancements

Maximum penalty for mail and wire fraud increased from 5 to 10 years.

Creates a crime for tampering with a record or otherwise impeding any official proceeding.

SEC given authority to seek court freeze of extraordinary payments to directors, offices, partners, controlling persons, agents of employees.

US Sentencing Commission to review sentencing guidelines for securities and accounting fraud.

SEC may prohibit anyone convicted of securities fraud from being an officer or director of any publicly traded company.

Financial Statements filed with the SEC must be certified by the CEO and CFO. The certification must state that the financial statements and disclosures fully comply with provisions of the Securities Exchange Act and that they fairly present, in all material respects, the operations and financial condition of the issuer. Maximum penalties for willful and knowing violations of this section are a fine of not more than $500,000 and/or imprisonment of up to 5 years.

Section 1001: Sense of Congress Regarding Corporate Tax Returns

It is the sense of Congress that the Federal income tax return of a corporation should be signed by the chief executive officer of such corporation.

Section 1102: Tampering With a Record or Otherwise Impeding an Official Proceeding

Makes it a crime for any person to corruptly alter, destroy, mutilate, or conceal any document with the intent to impair the object's integrity or availability for use in an official proceeding or to otherwise obstruct, influence or impede any official proceeding is liable for up to 20 years in prison and a fine.

(*Continued*)

(Continued)

Section 1103: Temporary Freeze Authority

The SEC is authorized to freeze the payment of an extraordinary payment to any director, officer, partner, controlling person, agent, or employee of a company during an investigation of possible violations of securities laws.

Section 1105: SEC Authority to Prohibit Persons from Serving as Officers or Directors

The SEC may prohibit a person from serving as an officer or director of a public company if the person has committed securities fraud.

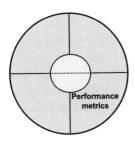

Chapter 23

JERRY RECONSIDERS EXECUTIVE COMPENSATION

1. Introduction

Bob was relaxing in his office, pleased at the way the SarbOx-related changes had been implemented. After his initial irritation, Jerry had actually embraced the changes quite enthusiastically. His quiet reflection was interrupted by his secretary announcing that Jerry wanted to see him. As Bob got up to go to Jerry's office, Jerry walked in and started, "Bob, sorry to bother you first thing in the morning, but it seems like our SarbOx-related work is not done yet. Now the Board's compensation committee wants us to prepare a report on the compensation for our top executives. We need to discuss this."

"Sure, Jerry", responded Bob, "what specifically do they have in mind?"

"I wrote it all down. Here." said Jerry as he handed Bob a sheet of paper.

On the heels of the debate regarding corporate governance reform, and ultimately the Sarbanes–Oxley legislation, Bob was not terribly surprised at this request. Apparently, the Board had enlisted the help of a large compensation consulting firm, but wanted to hear Bob's thoughts on the topic, given his experience as an academic researcher and consultant.

Some of the questions they posed were as follows. What do firms typically offer to top executives? How should compensation be structured? How has compensation practice changed over time? And so on.

Bob put this request at the top of the pile, and settled in to read up on it immediately. Below is the report he prepared in its entirety.

2. Bob's Report on Executive Compensation

Having an effective corporate governance system should be one of every publicly-traded company's top goals. Its effectiveness certainly shapes the behavior of the firm and its ultimate performance for shareholders. How a company's top executives are compensated is a critical component of any corporate governance system. Executive compensation has the primary goal of motivating, rewarding, and retaining key players on the Executive Committee. Although it is commonly believed that managerial pay packages can be a powerful tool for aligning the interests of executives with those of shareholders, it is probably this facet of corporate governance that sparks the most heated debates.

Theoretically, tying a manager's pay to the firm's stock price (or other measure of firm performance, such as earnings per share or economic profit), either through bonus plans, direct shareholdings in the firm or stock option grants, implies that the executive will only profit if his shareholders do (recall the discussion in Chapter 12). Thus, one would expect that an executive with high-powered incentives in the compensation contract (i.e., one that is heavily tied to performance) is more likely to take actions that maximize the wealth of the shareholders.

The immediate question is: Are these facts borne out in the data? That is, do firms in which executives have more high-powered incentives in their compensation do better for their shareholders? In general, the answer is yes. For example, Professor Hamid Mehran empirically documents that in the United States, firms whose executives were offered remuneration packages with high-powered incentives — including both stock and stock option holdings — were more likely to have better performance than firms that offered lower-powered incentives.[197] Thus, if increased share price performance is the goal of the board, a stock-based incentive plan appears to work quite well.

2.1. *Do High-Powered Incentives Have a Downside?*

These findings notwithstanding, outside of academic research, there has been an active debate over whether popular compensation plans — especially those that heavily utilize the granting of stock options — are necessary or desirable to accomplish the goal of value maximization. One of the most common criticisms made

---

[197] See Hamid Mehran, "Executive Compensation Structure, Ownership, and Firm Performance," *Journal of Financial Economics*, 38, 1995, pp. 163–184. See also Kevin J. Murphy "Executive Compensation," in Handbook of Labor Economics, Orley Ashenfelter and David Card (eds.), Vol. 3, 1999, North Holland, for a discussion of other evidence that is suggestive of the positive effects of performance-based compensation plans on firm performance.

by the camp that views high-powered incentives with skepticism is that top management pay has simply risen out of control, even when firms' stock prices have stagnated, and that the bulk of this rise has come from the granting of stock options. In fact, the average level of CEO pay at S&P 500 firms has grown significantly. For the years 1993 through 2003, the average level of total CEO pay in these large firms has increased from $2.7 million in 1993, to $8.5 million in 2003, translating to an average growth rate each year of over 13%.

2.2. Executive Compensation Trends: The Hard Data

Data on executive compensation are abundant, and help us to further dissect the facts to understand important trends in executive compensation, including the rise in the level of compensation referred to above. Firms are required to disclose the total dollar value and details of the firm's top five executives' compensation plans at the end of each year. In these disclosures, we observe what these executives earned in the form of fixed salary, payouts from yearly bonus plans, payouts from long-term bonus plans, and any monetary gains earned from exercising stock options that were granted in previous years. We also observe the value of newly-issued stock options and restricted stock grants. These common elements of executive pay packages are summarized and defined in Fig. 23.1.

Over time, the composition of top executive pay has changed dramatically. In Fig. 23.2, I have graphed the median yearly levels of total compensation, along with the median values of salary, bonus, stock option grants, and other pay for the S&P 1500 firms over the years 1992–2003.[198] As can be seen there, the median level of pay grew from $1.7 million in 1992 to $3.2 million in 2003. Salary levels grew more modestly over this time period, but observe that the dollar values of stock options grew dramatically.

To highlight the evolution of executive pay practices over time, in Fig. 23.3, I have graphed the percentage of total compensation given by salary, bonus, stock option grants and other pay, respectively. Such a picture highlights the declining relevance of salary, and the increasing relevance of variable pay components such as stock options.

2.3. Key Questions About Why Executive Pay is Designed the Way It Is

In the remainder of this report, I first provide a summary of the theoretical foundations of executive pay, and summarize the lessons learned from this literature

---

[198]The S&P 1500 contains the large firms of the S&P 500, the medium-sized firms of the Mid-Cap 350, and the smaller firms in the Small–Cap 650.

Pay component	Definition
Salary	The base salary earned by the executive. This component of pay is *not* directly sensitive to firm performance in the given year. Note, however, that on a year-by-year basis, salary levels could clearly be revised upwards or downwards based on historical performance.
Bonus	Yearly payouts that occur *only* when certain performance criterion are met, typically those relating to operating performance, such as net income. For example, an executive could receive a percentage of net income earned during the year. This component of executive pay is clearly performance-sensitive, where the performance is most often measured in accounting terms.
Stock option grants	These are claims given to executives that give them the right, but not the obligation to buy shares of stock in the firm at a pre-specified price (also known as the *exercise price* or *strike price*). The executive will only exercise the options when they are *in-the-money* (i.e., the market price of the firm's stock is greater than the exercise price). Stock option grants usually have *vesting* periods during which the executive cannot exercise the options until this period has passed.
Restricted stock grants	Shares that are awarded to executives, but carry restrictions in the sense that the executive cannot access the shares to sell for a pre-specified period of time (i.e., the vesting period). Restricted stock grants are analogous to stock options where the exercise price has been set at zero.
Stock option gains from exercise	The dollar value earned when the executive exercises her stock options. This is calculated by multiplying the number of options exercised times the difference between the current market price and the exercise price.
Total direct compensation	This represents the sum of an executive's salary, bonus, the value of stock options grants, the value of restricted stock grants, and any other miscellaneous compensation items.

Fig. 23.1.   The components of executive compensation.

with regard to the types of compensation we should observe across different types of firms. With the theory in hand, I provide a discussion of the existing empirical evidence. To this end, the report addresses the following questions:

- Why do we need compensation?
- What is pay-for-performance and what purpose does it serve?

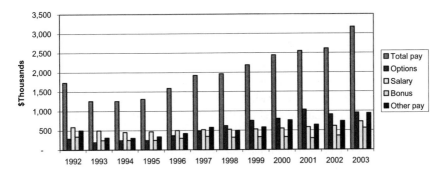

Fig. 23.2.   Median levels of CEO pay from 1992–2003 (S&P 1500 FIRMS).

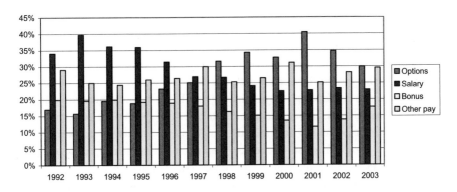

Fig. 23.3.   Decomposition of CEO pay from 1992–2003 (S&P 1500 FIRMS).

- How do various firm and managerial characteristics affect the need for pay-for-performance?
- Are management stock options the best vehicle for providing pay-for-performance? What are their costs?
- How does pay-for-performance vary empirically with firm and management characteristics?

2.4.   *The Basic Theory Underlying the Design of Executive Compensation*

The theoretical study of executive compensation has spanned many academic disciplines, including human resources, economics, finance, and accounting. However, there is a simple economic rule that crystallizes why we need compensation: everyone should receive something that is positively linked to that person's *value-added* as compensation for the person's efforts. That is, managers should receive some fraction of the value they produce, i.e., the marginal product of their effort. Economists argue that this is necessary to provide the appropriate participation incentives, and that the principle applies to all individuals employed by the firm, from the assembly-line worker to the CEO.

Arguably, the marginal value-added by an individual varies tremendously depending on the nature of the tasks being performed, and theory states that compensation should naturally vary along this dimension. This "value-added" calculation then determines the minimum amount of pay a firm could offer to insure the retention of a particular employee. An alternative way to think about the minimum compensation that could be offered is that it represents the employee's "reservation wage", i.e., what the employee could obtain in an alternative (next best) employment opportunity. Just as we select among projects by requiring that a selected project deliver an expected return at least equal to that which our next best investment opportunity would give us, a manager's reservation wage is determined by the value of the manger's next best employment opportunity.

Beyond the issue of determining the level of compensation, the more subtle question is: what *kind* of compensation do we need? Naturally, if the type of pay did not matter, firms could simply pay all managers a base salary and not worry about any other components. In practice, firms ultimately use a variety of instruments to compensate management. These include straight salary (otherwise known as base or fixed pay), short-term bonus schemes often tied to performance, stock options, and other long-term incentive plans, including restricted stock plans.

The inclusion of any of these items besides straight salary, such as a bonus scheme based on earnings per share or management stock options, represents *pay-for-performance*. That is, ideally the manager only gets paid a bonus if her performance is good. In the case of the earnings-per-share-based bonus plan, the manager would only receive her bonus if say, earnings per share were above some predetermined target. The next subsection explores some of the pioneering research on pay-for-performance contracts and what drives the variation in compensation that we observe in practice.

2.5. *Why do we Need Pay-for-Performance?*

The issue of why economists think managers need "pay-for-performance" dates back to some research carried out in the 1970s.[199] The implications of this research

---

[199] See Steven Ross, "The Economic Theory of Agency: The Principal's Problem," *American Economic Review*, 63, 1973, pp. 134–139, James Mirrlees, "The Optimal Structure of Incentives and Authority Within an Organization," *Bell Journal of Economics*, 7, 1976, pp. 105–131, and Bengt Holmstrom, "Moral Hazard and Observability," *The Bell Journal of Economics*, 10, 1979, pp. 74–91.

are so important and fundamental that they have carried through to even the most recent studies of management compensation. The model proposed in this collection of research papers is called a "hidden action" model and relates to a *principal* who hires an *agent* to run the firm on his behalf.[200] The principal can be thought of as the owner of the firm (i.e., the shareholder or group of shareholders), or even a representative thereof (such as the board of directors). The agent is the manager hired to run the firm. This creates an *agency problem*. (Recall our discussion of this in Chapter 4).

The manager (or agent) takes an action that affects the value of the output owned by the principal. The strict interpretation of this particular action is the manager's "effort" level. The basic idea is simple. The harder the manager works, the greater will be the output. In essence, this "effort choice" is really a metaphor for how the manager runs the firm, including the types of projects accepted, the strategic plans implemented, which businesses are divested and which are acquired, and so on. If we are thinking about the CEO as being the agent, then the measure of output could be the firm's cash flow in a given year, or the firm's stock price, or even earnings.

There are two critical assumptions in these "hidden action" models. First, the manager's action choice is assumed to be unobservable by the shareholders (i.e., the principal). Naturally, if the action choice is in fact the manager's effort, it is understandably difficult to know exactly how hard a manager is working. For instance, an individual may be in the office 70 hours a week, but how hard she is working and thinking about the best courses of action for the firm is certainly hard to quantify. Alternatively, if the "action" is not effort, but instead the strategy employed by the manager, some may question whether this is observable or not. While at first blush this may seem like an unreasonable assumption. In reality what is unobservable is the amount of thought and investigation of what the best course of action really was. Thus, these models, although stylized, are still quite useful for thinking about the CEO's actions.

The second key assumption is that the manager finds it costly to provide increased levels of the action. For example, if the action is in fact the level of effort put forth, the idea is that the manager finds it personally costly to provide each additional hour of labor, as she may prefer to spend that extra time on some leisure activity. This assumption is reasonable in that it implies that harder work takes the manager's time away from more enjoyable things like relaxing, playing golf, spending time with the family, going on vacation and so on.

---

[200] Hence, the model employed in this collection of research projects is often referred to as a Principal-Agent model.

With these two assumptions that output-relevant managerial effort is both unobservable to the shareholders and personally costly to the manager, the search is on for the optimal compensation contract that will motivate the manager to put forth the desired level of effort. Observe that if the manager's effort choice were observable, the compensation contract would be a simple one. One could just pay the manager a wage that matches her next best outside opportunity if the desired effort was indeed expended, and pay nothing otherwise. In the case of the CEO, if it was obvious to the Board of Directors knew *exactly* what the CEO should do to maximize firm value, they would just tell the CEO what to do and provide compensation only when this was done.[201]

In the more realistic case in which the manager's effort choice is unobservable, shareholders must try to infer this choice from the firm's ultimate performance (the output). Since output is positively affected by increases in managerial effort, observing a high output makes it *more likely* that the manager put forth a high level of effort. Therefore, one way to motivate the manager is to share part of the output with the manager. Not surprisingly, this type of contract is called a "sharing rule." Having a sharing rule of any kind in the manager's compensation contract represents "pay-for-performance."

Ultimately, there are several ways to make managers "share" in the gains and losses of the firm as means of motivating them to take appropriate actions. Choosing the type and the degree of pay-for-performance they want to impose on the manager depends on what outcomes the board is trying to motivate. If they were interested in earnings per share, a bonus that pays for increasing earnings per share would make sense. If they were interested in an increased stock price over the long run, a long-term stock option plan seems to be the obvious candidate. However, there are several factors that affect the optimal design of any pay-for-performance plan. These factors are the manager's risk aversion (which is discussed in more detail in the next section), the variability of the observed output, the manager's reservation wage, and how much of the manager's wealth is tied up in the firm.

To illustrate the effects of these four parameters on how big the sharing rule can be, let us consider an example. Suppose that a firm's cash flow at the end of the period was given by

$$Y = a + \varepsilon$$

where a is the manager's effort in this current period and can take the value of zero or one, with effort levels of zero and one considered as "low effort" and "high

---

[201] Another interpretation of these models is that shareholders (or more accurately, the board) simply are not in a position to know exactly what the optimal managerial action is for the firm. Thus, they hire a manager to not only take a desirable action, but to also uncover what is indeed optimal.

effort", respectively. The ε term represents random noise that can take the values of -1, 0, or $+1$, and could be interpreted as market movements that are outside of the control of the manager. As described above, assume that the effort is not observable to shareholders and that the manager finds it more costly to provide effort of one than to provide effort zero.

The important question is then straightforward: How should shareholders design a wage contract to elicit the high level of managerial effort?

According to the discussion above, they can look at the actual cash flow at the end of the period and try to infer how hard the manager worked. Observe that there are only four possible outcomes here: cash flow (Y) can either be -1, 0, $+1$, or $+2$. If cash flow is -1 or $+2$, shareholders know *for sure* what action the manager took. Only a combination of no effort and a random noise realization of -1 could produce cash flow of -1. Similarly, only a combination of high effort and a random noise realization of $+1$ could produce a cash flow of $+2$. These cases are straightforward, and the manager could be penalized (in the case of $Y = -1$) or rewarded (in the case of $Y = +2$), accordingly.

However, the inference is not so simple for intermediate levels of performance. Observe that if the cash flow turns out to be either zero or one, there are two possible combinations for each. If cash flow is zero, the manager may have worked hard (expended high effort) and simply had bad luck with the realization of the noise term turning out to be -1; alternatively, the manager may have put forth low effort and the noise term may have turned out to be zero. Two combinations of effort and noise are also possible when the cash flow turns out to be 1.

So what can shareholders do? If they choose to pay a fixed wage in all circumstances, under the assumption of managers attaching a high personal cost to putting in the "high effort," the manager will would choose to put in no effort and claim that bad luck hurt the cash flow when it turns out to be zero. The manager obviously cannot say this if cash flow is negative one, but since the manager is paid a fixed salary in this hypothetical contract no matter what the cash flow outcome, there is nothing to lose anyway.

Alternatively, the firm could promise to only pay for the good cash flow realization of 2, but this imposes a heavy risk on a risk-averse manager, who will only receive compensation in one of the four possible outcomes.[202]

---

[202]To say that an individual is "risk averse" implies that she strictly prefers *certainty* to *uncertainty*. For example, a risk-neutral individual (i.e., one that is neutral to the effects of risk) strictly prefers to receive \$1 million for sure instead of receiving a claim to a cash flow that pays off \$2 million one half of the time and \$0 the other half of the time. While the expected (or average) value of this risky claim is $1/2 \times \$2$ million $+ 1/2 \times \$0 = \$1$ million, the individual attaches a greater "cost" to the zero payoff

As it turns out, the optimal solution to this problem is to offer the manager a *fixed wage along with a bonus scheme* that pays her more the higher is the observed cash flow. The fixed wage insures the manager against the bad state of nature when the random noise term turns out to be −1. The bonus schedule is then designed to motivate the manager to exert the high effort by allowing the manager to share in the good outcome. Thus, a possible bonus scheme would pay the manager no bonus if cash flow was zero or negative one, and pay her a moderate bonus if cash flow was one and a bigger bonus if cash flow was two. How the two components of fixed salary and bonus are weighted in the total wage package depends on how risk averse the manager is. As the manager's risk aversion increases, either more weight must be placed on the fixed wage component or the bonus must be increased significantly to outweigh the risk the manager faces.

The simple compensation scheme from above can be written algebraically as follows:

$$\text{Total compensation} = \text{Fixed wage} + b \times \max\{Y, 0\},$$

where b represents how much of the output (Y) the manager gets and the $\max\{Y, 0\}$ term means that the manager gets a share of Y (the cash flow) only when it is positive, receiving nothing when the cash flow is negative. Naturally, the percentage of the cash flow paid out to the manager should be between 0% and 100% as the shareholders certainly want to keep some of the output! This expression is presented graphically in Fig. 23.4.

How steep this line is (i.e., its slope as given by b) determines the magnitude of the sharing rule, or more generally, the amount of *pay-for-performance* shareholders offer to the manager. Here, performance is the output Y, and a manager will receive

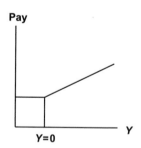

Fig. 23.4.   Pay-for-performance.

---

than the "benefit" of the $2 million payoff. Thus, she perceives that the value of the risky claim is less than $1 million. The more risk averse the individual is, the less value she will attach to risky payoffs.

the amount of b × Y in the form of a bonus. Solving for just the right amount of pay-for-performance to offer is the critical task. Next, we turn to a discussion of the key factors that helps us resolve this task.

2.6. *What Determines Pay-for-Performance?*

As it turns out, our simple example from above allows us to say lot about the determinants of pay-for-performance (i.e., the "b"). In fact, the amount of pay-for-performance shareholders should offer to a manager is decreasing in:

- the manager's risk aversion,
- the amount of wealth this executive has tied up in the firm, and
- the amount of noise (or variability) in the firm's output.

The reasons for the first two results are straightforward. If the manager is more risk averse, being subjected to a risky pay scheme is less desirable than receiving straight salary, and thus less weight must be put on performance in the compensation package. Similarly, a manager that has a disproportionate percentage of his/her own personal wealth invested in the firm that employs him/her is highly undiversified. This makes "risky pay" even more costly to him/her, and we would expect the pay-for-performance in this manager's compensation contract to be lower.

Lastly, as the firm's output becomes more variable (i.e., the range of possible values it can take becomes wider), more risk is imposed on the manager. Again, theory would suggest that less weight should be attached to performance. To see the intuition here, recall that in our simple example, the manager faces a risk of working very hard and still getting a negative shock from the market, resulting in a cash flow of zero. Suppose that this market shock term (i.e., the random noise term) could now take on any whole number between negative 10 and positive 10. The firm's ultimate output can now range from negative 10 to positive 11. However, there are still only two (of the now 22) outcomes in which the shareholders know for sure what the manager did (these are the outputs of −10 and +11). Each possible output value between negative nine and positive 10 can occur from either the combination of high effort and bad luck, or low effort and good luck. Thus, more volatility in the output puts a greater risk on the manager and the sharing rule (pay-for-performance) must be reduced.[203]

---

[203]To the extent that the manager can manipulate the observed output (such as through accounting choices), pay-for-performance would have to be reduced as managerial manipulation also adds noise to the inference process.

Observe that our example above refers to a very generic measure of firm performance, denoted by Y. In practice, when someone speaks to the "pay-for-performance sensitivity" of one compensation plan relative to another, they are usually characterizing how sensitive one manager's pay is to the stock price of the firm that employs her relative to another manager's sensitivity to her own firm. As we will discuss later, the actual pay-for-performance sensitivities of CEOs' compensation packages in practice vary greatly. To make sense of these disparities, we first describe a few more key results from theory about what drives the optimal sensitivity of CEO pay to her firm's stock price.

Much theoretical research has been done on management compensation since the 1970s. A large number of these studies have sought to determine how firm characteristics affect the prescribed degree of pay-for-performance in compensation contracts. Such characteristics include the firm's financial leverage, the magnitude of the firm's growth opportunities, the degree of product market competition, the diversity of the firm's operations, and firm size.

Professor Michael Jensen argued that the *amount of leverage* used to finance a firm's assets can have an important effect on managerial decision making.[204] In fact, he claims that a high amount of debt in a firm's capital structure can partially substitute for compensation contracts with high pay-for-performance. The intuition is that if the firm is heavily leveraged with debt, the manager is already compelled to manage the business in an efficient way given the potential risk of bankruptcy if things go awry. Thus, as long as the manager attaches some personal benefit to being in control of the firm, incentives to maximize firm value may already be quite strong and less pay-for-performance is necessary.

Another firm-related variable that affects pay-for-performance relates to the *nature of the firm's assets*. That is, we can think of the total value of the firm as the sum of the assets in place and the NPV of current and *future* investment opportunities. Here, the proportion of each of these components of value varies greatly across firms. For example, research-intensive firms have a significant portion of their value today given by the expected value of future growth opportunities. The effect of current managerial decisions on the value of these long-term projects is quite difficult to infer with traditional performance measures such as earnings per share. However, in an efficient financial market, stock prices can be thought of as a reliable guide to the future profitability of the firm. Thus, we would expect to see stronger pay-for-stock-performance in firms with lots of growth opportunities as the firm's stock price is the only true forward-looking measure of performance.

---

[204]See Michael Jensen, "Eclipse of the Public Corporation," *Harvard Business Review*, 1989.

Interestingly, the contributing factors behind a firm's value can also dictate the *type* of stock-related pay we might expect to see. In situations where value creation is primarily expected to occur in the long run, we are more likely to see the use of restricted stock (stock given to managers with restrictions on their ability to sell that stock) and stock options that only *vest* after several years. The use of such long-term incentives should motivate the manager to remain with the firm to manage its projects until they reach fruition.[205]

Similar to the amount of firm leverage, the extent of *competition in the firm's product market* is predicted by theory to be negatively related to the use of incentive pay. That is, competition in the product market can (at least partially) substitute for the explicit use of compensation incentives. Intense product-market competition places direct pressure on the manager to take better decisions on behalf of the shareholders of the firm; otherwise, the firm will fail in its ability to compete effectively. For example, if the firm operates in a highly-competitive industry (such as a public utility company), we would expect pay-for-performance to be lower.

Another driving force in the direct use of stock-based pay-for-performance relates to the *diversity of the firms' operations*. When a firm operates in very diverse business segments, directly inferring whether the CEO is managing one particular division well at the expense of another is quite difficult. In these cases, using a market-derived measure such as the stock price that aggregates the performance of all the divisions in a firm might be desirable. Thus, we would expect to find pay-for-performance sensitivities to be greater in firms with more diverse operations.

The *size of the firm* also has implications for the optimal amount of pay-for-performance. Observe that *firm size* typically increases as the number of business activities under one corporate umbrella becomes greater. Based on the argument above, this would suggest that pay-for-performance would be increasing in firm size. However, there is a countervailing force at work here. Observe that the size of the compensation plan that must be offered in a larger firm to generate an equivalent pay-for-performance sensitivity (i.e., to award the same "b") in a smaller firm is enormous! For example, offering pay-for-performance of 10% in a $10 million firm implies that the manager's share of the company is worth $1 million. However, to offer the same pay-for-performance in a firm worth $1 billion implies that the manager's share must be worth $100 million. All else equal, pay-for-performance as measured by the manager's "share" in the firm is thereby decreasing in firm size.

---

[205] Most restricted stock and stock option grants have *vesting* periods of several years. During the initial years when these grants have not vested, the manager does *not* have the ability to cash them out.

2.7. *Pay-for-Performance in Practice: The Empirical Evidence*

With the discussion of the economic theory underlying management compensation in hand, I now turn to the existing empirical evidence. In this section, I summarize how well the data on compensation practices within firms fit this theory.

The most fundamental insight from the discussion summarized above is that CEOs, as the top "agents" in their firms, should receive compensation that exhibits positive pay-for-performance. Specifically, the prediction that one would want to take to the data is that *CEO pay should vary positively with changes in shareholder wealth.* Professors Michael Jensen and Kevin Murphy offered one of the earliest and most important analyses of this prediction.[206] They collected compensation data for the 800 American firms listed in the Forbes 500, spanning the years 1974 through 1987. To be included in the Forbes 500, a firm must have been among the top 500 for sales, market value, or total assets.

For each CEO in these 800 firms, the data during this 1974–1987 time period included a CEO's salary and bonus, other cash compensation that included long-term bonus payouts, and the realized gains from exercising stock options.[207] Jensen and Murphy also collected an estimate of the percentage of the employing firm's stock held by the CEOs, but did not have access to this number for every CEO in their sample.

They went on to empirically estimate the average pay-for-performance sensitivity, measured as the correlation between changes in each CEO's pay and changes in shareholder wealth. They found that the average CEO enjoyed an increase in pay of $3.25 for each $1,000 increase in shareholders' wealth. Thus, given this positive association between pay and performance, the natural conclusion is that there is in fact pay-for-performance in practice, which is consistent with the theoretical prediction.

This conclusion may come as little surprise today. However, in 1990, compensation disclosure was more moderate and the answer was unknown. Since 1990, available CEO compensation data have become much richer, and it appears that the theory is more strongly supported than originally documented by Professors Jensen and Murphy.[208] More recent undertakings of this test have uncovered a significantly

---

[206]See Michael Jensen and Kevin Murphy, "Performance Pay and Top-Management Incentives," *Journal of Political Economy*, 98, 1990, pp. 225–262 and Michael Jensen and Kevin Murphy, "CEO Incentives — It's Not How Much You Pay, But How," *Journal of Applied Corporate Finance*, 1999, pp. 36–49.

[207]The realized gain on exercising stock options would be calculated as the difference between the firm's stock price at the time the options were exercised and the exercise price, multiplied by the total number of options held.

[208]All of the large firm US data noted in this report is drawn from Compustat's ExecuComp database. This database covers 1,500 of the largest, publicly-traded US companies and spans the years 1992–2003.

higher average pay-for-performance sensitivity for US CEOs in the 1990s. For example, a more recent study estimated that the average pay-for-performance sensitivity of American CEOs was approximately $20 per $1,000 change in shareholder value.[209]

To put this number in perspective, suppose that a firm had a market value of $1 billion. A 10% total shareholder return over the year would lead to an increase in shareholder wealth of $100 million. If the Jensen–Murphy estimate of a $3.25 change in CEO wealth per $1,000 increase in shareholder wealth still held, then the CEO's wealth would increase by $325,000. Using the more recent estimate of $20 per $1,000 increase in shareholder wealth, the CEO would enjoy an increase in wealth of $2 million. Thus, it is a commonly-held belief that the pay-for-performance sensitivities of US CEOs has increased dramatically over the 1990s, primarily due to the explosion of stock option grants.

While some may argue that the average pay-for-performance sensitivity observed in US CEOs' pay packages is too high and others may argue that it is too low, it is critical to note that there is a large variance in the actual company-specific pay-for-performance sensitivities. These values range from approximately $0 to as high as $350 per $1,000 increase in shareholder value. Above, we listed several firm and management characteristics that were suggested as being related to the theoretically optimal pay-for-performance sensitivity. Many academics have sought to bring those predictions to the data. Below, I summarize the main findings of these empirical studies.

For instance, one determinant of pay-for-performance sensitivities was given by the variability of the firm's performance. Recall that the more variable the performance measure is, the more difficult it is to infer a manager's contribution from realized performance. A recent research paper tests this hypothesis.[210] First, the authors calculated the total volatility (i.e., the variance) of each firm's stock returns. Next, they created 100 separate subsamples based on these estimates of total variability of firm performance. Essentially, this placed each firm in one of a hundred "risk buckets." The first portfolio represented firms with the lowest stock return volatility and the 100th portfolio contained firms with the highest stock return volatility. They then re-ran the Jensen–Murphy regression to estimate how pay-for-performance sensitivities vary, if at all, across these "risk-based" profiles.

What they found again confirmed the theory. They documented that pay-for-performance in the highest-risk portfolio was approximately $20 lower than the

---

[209]See Todd Milbourn, "Reputation and the Heterogeneity of Stock-Based CEO Compensation," *Journal of Financial Economics*, 68(2), 2003, pp. 233–262.

[210]See Rajesh Aggarwal and Andrew Samwick, "The Other Side of the Trade-off: The Impact of Risk on Executive Compensation," *Journal of Political Economy*, 107(1), 1999, pp. 65–105.

portfolio with the lowest risk. Therefore, it appears that firms do adjust a CEO's pay-for-performance sensitivity to risk factors, relying more heavily on stock-based pay (which is implicit in these estimates of pay-for-performance) when stock prices are less noisy, and thereby more informative of the CEO's actions.

Utilizing a similar methodology, another study examined the effect of firm size on pay-for-performance.[211] This study found that the largest firm in the sample offers a CEO compensation package with a pay-for-performance sensitivity of $24 per $1,000 change in shareholder wealth *less* than the CEO pay package offered in the smallest firm. Again, the theory is well supported. The empirical findings for firm risk and firm size, as well as the remaining pay-for-performance control variables delineated earlier are summarized in Fig. 23.5.[212]

In summary, the empirical observations from the United States are highly consistent with management compensation theory. Specifically, it appears that in practice firms adjust the management compensation contracts they offer in a theoretically optimal manner. These findings are also consistent with the simpler hypothesis that compensation contracts are custom designed for each firm and each manager.

Empirical control variable	Predicted effect on pay-for-performance	Supported by the data (yes/no/untested/ untestable)
Variability of stock returns	↓	Yes
Firm size	↓	Yes
Firm leverage	↓	Yes
Proportion of value contributed by growth opportunities	↑	Yes
Diversity of firm operations	↑	Untested
Degree of product market competition	↓	Yes
Managerial risk aversion	↓	Untestable
Percentage of managerial wealth invested in the Firm	↓	Untestable[213]

Fig. 23.5. Summary of factors determining pay-for-performance sensitivities.

---

[211] See Milbourn, ibid.

[212] For an excellent review of the papers underlying these empirical results, see Kevin Murphy, "Executive Compensation," in *Handbook of Labor Economics*, Orley Ashenfelter and David Card (eds.), Vol. 3, 1999, North Holland.

[213] Given the absence of data on managerial private investment holdings, this prediction is not directly testable.

2.8. *How do Management Stock Options Affect Firm Value?*

There is no question that the granting of stock options to top management dramatically increased in the United States across the 1990s and in the early parts of the 21st century.[214] Recall the evidence contained in Fig. 23.3 There we saw that not only did total compensation rise for the average executive, but the lion's share of this growth stemmed from stock option grants.

On the upside, there is no question that observed pay-for-performance sensitivities rose as a consequence. However, many have argued that such options impose real costs on the organizations that grant them. One cost is known as "stock option overhang," which is the potential *dilution* imposed on shareholders when executives within a firm exercise their options and the firm is forced to issue new shares. Estimates of stock option overhang vary by firm, and one study estimates that the average amount of overhang in firms is approximately 10.5% for US companies spanning the years 1992–2000, and range from 0% to over 1,000%![215]

Clearly, employee stock options represent a significant potential source of dilution for shareholders in many firms. It is also well known that reported earnings tended to understate their associated costs as the value of employee stock option grants were *not* expensed in the calculation of a firm's net income prior to mid-year in 2004. That said, an efficient stock market should show no such bias and one would expect that a firm's stock price would incorporate the potential dilution of the shareholders' claim stemming from stock option exercises. However, if stock prices *do* underestimate the future costs implied by stock option grants, option exercises will produce negative abnormal returns.

The Garvey and Milbourn study designs and implements a stock-picking rule based on predictions of stock-option exercise using widely-available data. Surprisingly, the simple stock-picking rule identifies stocks that subsequently suffer significant *negative abnormal returns* (i.e., the returns were less than were expected given market movements).[216] According to their point estimates, if the cost of employee stock options as a fraction of market capitalization is 10%, the stock will subsequently exhibit a *negative* abnormal return of between 3% and 5%. Therefore, it appears that

---

[214]Interestingly, stock options have become increasingly important for the rest of American workers over this time period as well. According to Professors Brian Hall and Kevin Murphy, 45% of salaried employees in 1998 received stock options, and 10% of hourly employees also received them. See Brian Hall and Kevin Murphy, "Optimal Exercise Prices for Executive Stock Options," *American Economic Review*, 90(2), 2000, pp. 653–691.

[215]See Gerald Garvey and Todd Milbourn, "Do Stock Prices Incorporate the Potential Dilution of Employee Stock Options?," Washington University in St. Louis working paper, 2008.

[216]More formally, the authors measure abnormal returns using either a CAPM or three-factor Fama-French benchmark.

dilution caused by the granting of management stock options is a serious matter and should be considered by the board and its shareholders.

Based on the evidence from above and the desire for greater transparency in financial reporting, in 2004, FASB put forth a proposal mandating that Net Income be calculated *after* deducting for the cost of employee stock options. Only time will tell whether such a measure affects the stock market's ability to better assess the costs of employee stock options.

2.9. *Recent Innovations in Management Stock Options*

In recent years, some practitioners have argued that stock options should be "indexed" to the performance of the stock market or an industry portfolio. An indexed stock option is such that the exercise price*moves up or down* as the stock market or industry group's price level rises or falls. The intuition behind such a scheme is to avoid rewarding an individual manager for simply holding stock options when there is a bull market. Another stock option variant with a similar theme is one that involves a fixed exercise price, but only vests if the firm (or individual manager) has satisfied some prearranged hurdle of performance. These are sometimes referred to as *conditional stock options.*[217]

Conditional stock option plans received a lot of publicity in the United Kingdom on the heels of the famous 1995 Greenbury report which called for the replacement of "plain vanilla" stock options with conditional stock options. In response to this report, the UK government tightened existing restrictions on the amount of "plain vanilla" stock options that could be awarded. Moreover, institutional investors suggested that the value of management options should not exceed an amount of four times the manager's salary.

Based on some compensation data collected for a proprietary research project, a study found that in 1997, nearly one-third of the FTSE-100 companies had already implemented conditional stock option plans. Interestingly, the overwhelming majority of these plans set one singular performance hurdle as the criteria for vesting. This hurdle was that "EPS growth must exceed inflation plus 2% annually over three consecutive years" for the options to vest.[218]

---

[217] These options should be distinguished from plain vanilla stock options that simply do not vest for three years, or perhaps only 25% of the total option grant vests each year, as are most often issued in the United States. The term "conditional" here implies that vesting requirements are two fold. First, a certain amount of time from the grant date must pass, such as a period of time of three years. Second, a performance hurdle must be satisfied sometime between the vesting date and the expiration date.

[218] A cynical interpretation of these data would be that since EPS-based hurdles were offered by Sir Greenbury as one candidate example of how performance might be additionally measured, many firms might have adopted them without hesitation in an attempt to avoid further criticism.

One message, however, is clear. At a minimum, setting custom-designed performance measures as the performance hurdle is economically rational. It is highly unlikely that maximizing EPS should be the overarching goal of every firm. For capital-intensive firms, a measure like economic profit that accounts for the actual cost of capital employed by the business might be a more efficient hurdle. For research-intensive firms, non-financial measures like the number of new initiatives (products) might be appropriate. If firms were to explicitly identify what drives firm-value maximization and tie these measures to conditional stock option plans, efficiency gains might be earned.

In the United States, indexed and conditional stock option plans are virtually nonexistent as of the end of 2003. Most have argued that prevailing accounting and tax standards play a key role in explaining their absence. Stock options have tended to receive favorable treatment in the United States on both of these dimensions. In terms of their tax treatment, stock options are not considered a taxable event at the time of the grant. Thus, they are truly a form of deferred compensation for tax purposes. They are only taxable to the individual manager at the time they are exercised, and it is at this time that the company "incurs" a tax-deductible expense.

In terms of accounting treatment, the details of stock option grants to top executives have been fully disclosed in the financial statements since the Compensation Disclosure Act of 1993. However, through the early part of 2004, such detail was relegated to the footnotes of the financial statements. As noted above, a firm's net income was not affected by stock option grants as long as they were issued *at-the-money* or *out-of-the-money*.[219] That is, they were considered "free" from an accounting standpoint. While such accounting treatment explains why discount stock options might be discouraged (i.e., those options with an exercise price *below* the current market price, or more simply put, options that are *in-the-money*), it does not explain why premium stock option plans (i.e., those where the exercise price is *above* the firm's current market price) are not used more regularly. Such a puzzle remains unanswered.

2.10. *The Future: Will Executive Compensation Keep Rising?*

Management compensation has the objective of attracting, retaining, and motivating managers. However, the dynamics of the market for managerial talent have arguably changed dramatically in the last couple of decades. It is now a rarity for a manager to spend her entire career in one firm, whereas historically this was quite common.

---

[219] A stock option is at-the-money if the exercise price equals the current market price of the firm's stock, and an option that is out-of-the-money is one where the exercise price currently *exceeds* the current market price.

Firms no longer restrict themselves to insiders to succeed outgoing CEOs. In fact, many CEO appointments are made across industries. In discussing just such a change, *The Wall Street Journal Europe* in 1991 noted that a "banker-turned-utility executive runs Delta Air Lines [and] a former finance professor and cereal executive runs Times Mirror Co." Simply put, firms are now seeking out the best in managerial talent, and not necessarily searching for the "best man in the industry."

Why does this matter? These top executives carry with them a very high reservation wage owing to their reputations. These higher reservation wages then map into spectacular compensation packages designed to lure them to any given firm. Certainly the evidence over 1992–2003 is consistent with this hypothesis.

Apparently, this phenomenon of the "winners" receiving a larger prize in recent years reaches far beyond corporate America. Frank and Cook (1995) claim[220]:

> "These high stakes have created a new class of unknown celebrities: those pivotal players who spell the difference between corporate success and failure. Because their performance is crucial, and because modern information technology has helped build consensus about who they are, rival organizations must compete furiously to hire and retain them.
>
> The widening gap is apparently not new ... Alfred Marshal wrote over a century ago, '... the relative fall in the incomes to be earned by those of moderate ability, however carefully trained, is accentuated by the rise in those that are obtained by many men of extraordinary ability'."

A continuance of this trend suggests that top executive pay will continue to rise for the foreseeable future in America's companies. That said, innovations in the underlying design of executive pay packages will surely continue to evolve. In particular, an important venue for future research will be to characterize the affect of the new stock-option expensing rule on both the willingness of corporations to grant options and the types of options that will be granted.

3. Jerry Digests the Report

Jerry spent some time studying Bob's report and then set up a time to talk with him.

"This is an excellent report, Bob," complimented Jerry.

---

[220]See Robert H. Frank and Philip J. Cook, *The Winner-Take-All Society*, The Free Press, New York, 1995.

Bob smiled. He had put a lot of work into it. He cleared his throat and said, "Thanks, Jerry. I suppose your next question will be: what do we do now?"

"Exactly," beamed Jerry.

"Well," Bob began, "From the standpoint of the Board, we should provide this report, but I suspect what they really want to know is whether the amounts we are paying our senior executives are in line with what other companies of similar characteristics (size, for example) are paying their senior executives. That is, our salary levels have to be justifiable in the shareholders' eyes. The best way to do this would be to encourage the Compensation committee to go ahead and hire the Executive Compensation consulting firm they have been in touch with, and ask them to provide a benchmarking report. The last time I had done this, the information we obtained was very helpful in determining compensation design in our company."

"You are right, Bob," said Jerry, "What else do you think they will want?"

"Well," responded Bob, "I think they will want to know if our compensation packages are sufficiently sensitive to shareholder value. We have worked hard to make sure they are as you know. We have tied our executives' compensation to economic profit (see Chapter 10) and also given them restricted stock and options as part of their compensation. But it may not be a bad idea to wait until we receive the consultant's report to see if there are ways to sensibly increase our pay-for-performance sensitivity, based on what other firms may be doing that we may have missed. And finally, we need to make sure that we are not criticized for designing executive compensation in such a way that we get more compensation regardless of how our stock price does. Sort of like 'heads we win, tails the shareholders lose!' Some of the criticism of high executive compensation I referred to in my report has been due to the perception that this is how some executives have been paid."

"I agree. As a shareholder, I could not agree more. Waiting for the consultant's report and then having another discussion with the Board sounds like a good plan," said Jerry, as he concluded the meeting.

Main Lessons

- The design of top management compensation is a critical component of a firm's corporate governance system. It serves the role of attracting, motivating, and retaining key managers within the firm.
- The necessary degree of pay-for-performance in management compensation depends on many firm-related characteristics, such as firm size, its capital structure, and the intensity of competition in its product markets.

- In practice, there is a rich diversity of pay-for-performance among corporate CEO's.

End of Chapter Exercises

1. Characterize the differences in compensation packages (e.g., fixed versus performance-based pay mix) at various levels of your organization. Are the variations that you identify consistent with the lessons of this chapter?
2. How important is compensation at your company vis-à-vis the other corporate governance mechanisms that were discussed in Chapter 22?
3. Has Sarbanes–Oxley had any tangible effects on compensation practice? If so, would you characterize these as positive or negative effects?

Practice Problems

1. Given the discussion of designing stock-based managerial compensation contracts, why might a divestment of one division from a multi-divisional firm be value-creating?
2. As firms become increasingly global, what changes do you foresee for top management compensation?
3. How might a firm manage the dilution of its ownership owing to managerial stock option plans?
4. What identifiable trade-offs emerge if a firm puts forth a charge to unilaterally increase performance-based pay at all levels of the organization?

Chapter 24

MANAGING IN TOUGH TIMES VERSUS INNOVATING

With the acquisition of Mickey's and the post-acquisition process behind him, Jerry began to think about building a sustainable organization. He had read so many conflicting things. Should his company focus on being efficient? Or should it focus on innovation? Or both? He decided to call Bob.

1. How do you Manage in Tough Times?

"I believe you're asking a deep and fundamental question, Jerry. Focusing on efficiency is something that is required during tough times. Recessions, market downturns and so on. So, the broader question is: how do we develop the competence to manage this company well during tough economic times?" began Bob.

Jerry looked at the soft snow flakes falling outside his office window. He loved the snow and the rare tranquility it provided. He looked out the window as he spoke, "Ok, Bob. I agree. That is a better question. So, what do we do now?"

Bob cleared his throat, "Well, Jerry, this is something I have been thinking about for a while. I've studied a lot of firms that successfully navigated through tough times. I believe there are some valuable lessons to be learned from their experiences."

"What lessons?" asked Jerry.

Bob went over to a flip chart in Jerry's office and began to write:

- Focus on improving cash flows.
- Focus on cost productivity and asset productivity.

- Keep your eye on operating margin.
- Make heroes out of employees who find ways to save money.
- Develop an organization culture where rules are followed and successes are celebrated, but then people begin to think about new challenges.
- Focus on business process innovation that improves efficiency, rather than product innovation.

Jerry looked over Bob's list and asked: "This all seems reasonable, but I suppose having an organization focused on this requires deliberate planning and considerable effort. Plus some hard choices, I presume."

Bob nodded in agreement: "Yes, Jerry. I don't think you can turn the faucet off and on when it comes to developing an efficiency-focused organization that is "hard-wired" to run smoothly during tough times. And these prescriptions involve plenty of hard choices. To, see this, consider focusing on improving cash flows. How do you do that? Well, one way is to increase sales. But this may be difficult in an economic downturn. So then we are left with balance-sheet maneuvers to increase cash flows. There are three ways to do this:

a. speed up the conversation of receivables into cash, stretch out payables as much as possible, and work hard at minimizing inventories — recall the cash conversion cycle we discussed earlier (Chapter 5);
b. cut back on new investments; and
c. liquidate marginally productive assets.

"Are all of these equally desirable?" asked Jerry.

Bob shook his head, "No, not at all. My preference would be to focus on (a) first, so that our balance sheet is as light on net working capital as possible. As you know, Dell and Wal-Mart are considered masters at this. Their business designs have focused very effectively on minimizing net working capital. This is something we should do anyway. It's good for us in tough times as well as good times."

"Well," said Bob, "I would resort to (b) and (c) only out of necessity. Cutting back on new investments can choke off good growth. Not something we want to do, unless our survival is at stake. Ditto for liquidating marginally productive assets. If these assets are not generating RONAs exceeding our cost of capital, then they should be liquidated. But *not* otherwise, unless, of course, we need the cash flow to survive or some other company offers us a huge price for the assets. In fact, using (c) as a cash-flow-enhancement tool is called "liquidating the balance sheet." Analysts pay attention to it and do not view it as sustainable. This means improvements in cash flow obtained this way are unlikely to be rewarded as much by the stock market as cash flow improvements due to higher profits. In fact, savvy analysts keep track of the difference between cash flow from operations and operating income, a difference referred to as "excess cash margin."[221] If this difference either goes up or down significantly, analysts become suspicious. And if they find that cash flow has grown relative to earnings due to asset sales, they view it as a non-sustainable cash flow growth."

Jerry rubbed his hand on his cheek and said, "Well, let's hope we never have to resort to that."

"Right," said Bob, "Now let's talk about the second and third bullet points on this flip chart — focusing on cost and asset productivity and operating margin. Cost productivity improvements and improved asset turnover are both going to improve our cash flows without having the resort to asset liquidations. And if we do these things well, our operating margin will stay at a healthy lend. In fact, I believe a key to Dell's success has been that CEO Michael Dell has been very concerned with operating margin. Dell does not view racking up profits or growing the top line or market share as enough. Executives are expected to price products low enough to induce customers to buy, but not so low that cut unacceptably into profits. When Dell's senior executives in Europe did not meet profit targets in 1999 because they didn't cut costs fast enough, they were replaced."[222]

"Wow!" marveled Jerry, "that's a pretty tough organizational culture."

Bob smiled, "Yes. And one that produces results! Let us now turn to the next two bullet points: making heroes out of employees who save money and develop an organization culture where rules are followed and successes are celebrated before the next challenge is contemplated. Again, I think Dell provides the best example of this that I can think of. There are some organizations where people are heroes if they invent a new product. Being a hero at Dell means saving money. This philosophy pervades the entire organization from Michael Dell all the way down. Michael Dell's own ego-less demeanor permeates the entire company. No stars. Everyone is expected to subordinate their own interests to the interests of the business. That means following rules and no free lancing. This makes sense because the company has such good internal processes that adherence to these processes is what produces results. The company also often pairs up executives to run an important business. They call this approach "two-in-a-box." This way they work collaboratively together and offset each others' weaknesses. And they share the responsibility if something goes wrong."

"Admirable," conceded Jerry, "I think these are ideas worth adopting."

---

[221] See Ronald Fink, "Mind the Gap," *CFO*, December 2003.

[222] Bob was basing his comments here and later in this chapter on an article by Peter Burrows and Andrew Park, "What You Don't Know About Dell," *Business Week*, November 3, 2003.

"I agree," said Bob, "and that brings me to my last point — focusing on business process innovation that improves efficiency, rather than product innovation. If one develops a penny-pinching organization culture that is constantly focused on efficiency, it is very difficult for the organization to also excel at product innovation. Penny-pinching and innovation are competing values in an organization,[223] and it is extremely difficult to accommodate both.

Dell provides a good example. It invests far less in product development and future technologies compared to other technology companies. In 2002, IBM spent $4.75 billion (5.9% of its revenues) on R&D, HP spent $3.3 billion (5.8% of its revenues), whereas Dell spent only $455 million (1.3% of its revenue)."

Jerry scratched his head, "How can they hope to be competitive then?"

"Precisely my point," said Bob, "They are planning to compete not on product innovation but rather on their strength as a super efficient manufacturer and distributor. That means their focus is on *business process innovation*. The company has won 550 business-process patents. These include ideas like using wireless networks in factories and configuring manufacturing stations four times as productive as a standard assembly line."

Jerry nodded, "Aha! I see their strategy. Focus on what you are good at and don't worry about competitors outdoing you on a dimension that is not a part of your game plan. I recall our earlier discussion that strategy is what we choose to do and what we choose *not* to do."

"Correct," said Bob, "but the important point is that it's very difficult to have your cake and eat it too. If you are going to be super efficient and champion at managing in tough times, you're unlikely to lead the pack in product innovation."

2. The Innovation Dilemma

"Hmm," mused Jerry, "so it's difficult to do both. So, tell me, what kind of organization would we use if we wanted to be innovation champions?"

"That may be even more difficult than developing a super efficient organization," replied Bob.

"Why? I thought being super efficient was hard enough."

Bob went back to the flip chart and began, "well, wait till I list the things we'd need to do to be successful at innovation."

Here's what Bob wrote on the flip chart:

• Separate the "innovation budget" from the rest of the capital budget and figure out strategically how large you want the innovation budget to be.

---

[223]See Anjan Thakor, *Becoming a Better Value Creator*, Jossey-Bass Publishers, 2000.

- Establish the role of the CFO as an internal venture capitalist (VC).
- Do not expect to fund positive-NPV projects from the innovation budget. In fact, a criterion we may want to adopt for projects that "qualify" for this budget may be that they have negative NPV and high option value.
- Expect no returns from the projects funded by the innovation budget when it comes to making either internal or external earnings and cash flow forecasts. That is, we should bake into our EPS forecasts the assumption that the innovation projects will pay nothing and may even consume additional cash.
- Hold those whose innovation projects are funded accountable for results. However, accountability should be based not on the success or failure of a single project, but rather on the total payoff from the portfolio of funded projects.
- Develop an innovation culture.

Jerry looked at the list for what seemed like a long time before he spoke, "Bob, this looks interesting. Why don't you walk me through each bullet point?"

"Ok," said Bob, "Let's take the first four bullet points because they're closely related. For our normal capital budget, I believe we have to adopt all of the principles we've already gone over and adopted. Projects must have sufficiently low risk, attractive economic profits and positive NPVs. However, these rules are not appropriate for innovative projects. A truly innovative project is typically going to be very risky, may promise a long string of negative economic profits initially and may even have a negative NPV. But the payoff from the project, if it succeeds, is so high that it's worth considering the project. This is similar to the Brake I and Brake II analysis we discussed earlier in the context of real options. So ..."

"Hold on," interrupted Jerry, "this real option stuff is still a bit confusing to me. Tell me again why we should invest in negative–NPV projects."

"Well," responded Bob, "think of it as follows. Suppose our people come to us with a thousand innovative projects, each of which has an NPV of −\$1, based on all the objective information that is available. So, if we funded all of them, we would have a portfolio NPV of −\$1,000. However, we know that there is a 0.01 probability that one of these projects will pay off \$1 million. We don't know *which* of the thousand projects this gem happens to be. But our business sense is that it is one of them. So, the expected value of that pay off is $0.01 \times \$1$ million $= \$10,000$. This obviously exceeds the negative–portfolio NPV, so that we would want to fund all ten projects for a *net* NPV of \$9,000."

"Hmm," mused Jerry, "there's a little bit of trickery here, one suspects. You could have simply started by saying that there's a one in thousand chance for each project of having a 0.01 probability of a \$1 million payoff, so that the correct NPV for each project would be $= \$1 + [0.01 \times 1 \times \$1$ million$]$ which is \$9 per project, or \$9,000 for the portfolio. So that way I'm not funding negative–NPV projects."

Bob threw his hands up in mock surrender, "Alright, Jerry, you got me! You are correct from a strictly mathematical standpoint. And this is also not exactly what we talked about in the context of real options. But the point I was making is that this example is a somewhat simplified version of the investment decision a VC faces. You fund a thousand projects. Each one, evaluated strictly on its own merits, has a negative NPV. Only one has a small chance of paying off really big. But you don't know which one. Moreover, you may have to invest in all of them to find out which project is the gem, and to be able to transfer the learning from failed projects that have to be terminated to other projects that have a chance to succeed. The 1,000 projects give you a lot of opportunity to terminate projects in mid-stream that don't look promising, learn from those failures, and then apply that knowledge to the remaining projects, until you find one that pays off big. *Were it not for the knowledge you gathered from the failed projects, you may not know enough to recognize the gem in your portfolio.* That is, if you had invested in only one out of the thousand projects and had been lucky enough to pick the gem, you may still have terminated it prematurely because you lacked the knowledge to recognize it as a gem."

"Aha," said Jerry, "a bit like Columbus sailing with three ships to find the spice-trade route to India, and coming back with only one ship that inadvertently found the "New World", rather than what he set out to find."

"I suppose so," responded Bob, "in the sense that you have to diversify your bets across a lot of different projects in order to learn and find the one that pays off. Ex post, we may find that each and every one of the thousand projects was a dud with a negative NPV. In fact, the odds are that we will. We knew up front that 999 were going to be duds. So that's not a surprise. And the gem also had only a one in hundred chance of succeeding. So the probability was 0.99 that it too would turn out ex post to be a dud. This is the mindset VCs have. Only one in ten projects may pay off. But that payoff is so big that the portfolio return is over 30%."

"Alright," said Jerry, "so what does this mean for us?"

"Well," responded Bob, "it means that I have to be like an internal VC when it comes to the innovation budget. We will have to determine how large this budget can be, given that *most* projects we fund will pay nothing, and that we will have to bake this into our EPS forecasts. The projects we will fund will have negative individual NPVs based on objective data and reasonable forecasts. However, we realize that they will pay off really big if they succeed. That is, these will be high-option-value projects, and we will evaluate them as real options. And this brings me to my fifth bullet point. We will hold our people accountable for these projects, but the accountability will be for portfolios rather than individual projects. The point to remember when it comes to dealing with innovative projects is simple. A project may have negative NPV as a stand-alone project and hence not be worthy of funding. But it may produce spillover benefits — such as learning — that may have value in a portfolio context and hence the project may be worth funding as part of a portfolio."

"Ok," nodded Jerry in agreement, "so that brings us to your last bullet about culture."

"Yes," said Bob, "and that is the most important one. An innovation culture has two key dimensions: *capital budgeting dimension* and a *people dimension*. We have talked quite a bit about the capital budgeting dimension in our discussions up to this point. But there's one thing I would add. And that is our attitude toward cannibalization. An innovation culture does *not* punish new product ideas for cannibalizing existing products. Rather, it takes the *EMC* approach of *encouraging cannibalization*. *EMC*, famous for its data storage equipment, has been highly successful at product innovation because it has actively sought to replace existing products with new ones even when the existing products have been at the height of their sales cycle and have promise of significant future sales.[224] It is an approach that keeps me-too copy-cat competitors at bay."

"Makes sense," said Jerry, "although not easy to do in practice, I suppose."

"Yes," agreed Bob, "and that brings me to the people dimension. An innovation culture has four "people dimensions." First, people are allowed to commit resources and work on ideas of their own choosing for a certain percentage of their total work time, without being questioned. This is practiced at leading innovators like 3M, the maker of the famous post-it notes, and W.L. Gore, a $1.5 billion privately-held company that makes Gore-Tex fabric and various other specialty products.

Second, people whose skills are of no obvious use to the organization are hired. Innovation requires a diversity of viewpoints, and this can only be achieved by hiring people with ideas very different from those of the rest of the work force. Companies that specialized in innovation, like IKEA, have made this an integral part of their hiring practices.

Third, let people break your own rules while innovating. There is no sure-fire formula for innovation. When someone in our organization comes up with an innovative idea, it is very likely that that person's boss will think the idea is a dog and will order that the idea be abandoned. If our people always follow orders, we will not have an innovation culture. Some of the most spectacular product innovations at HP and 3M began as ideas that were ordered to be abandoned. The only reason why these products saw the light of day is because orders were disobeyed.

Finally, when it comes to innovation, punish people for *inaction*, not for failure. Successful innovation is often a consequence of the *number* of ideas explored, many

---

[224]See Anjan V. Thakor, *Becoming a Better Value Creator*, Jossey-Bass, 2000, for more details.

of which fail, rather than a solitary flash of insight. Famous innovators like Leonardo da Vinci did not have a higher success rate than their peers. They just produced more!"

3. Putting It All Together

"Wow," exclaimed Jerry, "that's pretty radical stuff. I don't know how one could manage such an organization."

Bob nodded, "Well, you see now my point about the virtual impossibility of being super efficient and innovative at the same time."

"Yes, I do," responded Jerry, "and we haven't even discussed the financial policy ramifications of the choice."

"No, we haven't," agreed Bob. "If we choose to be super efficient, we would have more predictable cash flows and steady growth. I'd choose to pay out relatively high dividends and have a moderate amount of debt in our capital structure. By contrast, if we were going to be focused on innovation, our cash flows would be more volatile and our growth less predictable, albeit expected to be high. I'd favor a much lower dividend payout and a much lower debt-to-total-assets ratio. This may be a good time to put all our ideas together on a single chart."

Bob proceeded to produce Fig. 24.1.

As Jerry looked at the chart, he was lost in thought. Bob interrupted his musings with, "Well, Jerry, what do you think?"

"I see your point, Bob," responded Jerry, "There are so many conflicts between being super efficient and being innovative that it is hard to visualize being both. But my gut tells me we will have to get good at each of these. Let's think about how we can marry these seemingly opposite ideas. It seems to me that if we are going to be an innovative company, we need to seriously consider adopting at least the first four best practices for innovation you have listed. And possibly #7 as well. But I don't want to become less cost efficient either. Let me work on it and prepare a proposal."

"Ok," said Bob, "that's an inspiring challenge."

The meeting then concluded.

Main Lessons

- Managing in tough times requires a firm to develop the competence of being super efficient. This requires a focus on cash flow, operating margins, and business process innovation as opposed to product innovation. It also requires a culture where people follow rules.

Best practices for super efficiency	Best practices for innovation
(1) Focus on improving cash flows by reducing net working capital, cutting back on new investments, and possibly liquidating assets	(1) Separate the "innovation budget" from the rest of the capital budget
(2) Focus on cost productivity and asset productivity	(2) Establish the role of the CFO as an internal VC to allocate funds from the innovation budget
(3) Maintain acceptable operating margins	(3) Fund innovative projects that have negative–NPV as stand-alone projects, but high option values and portfolio spillover benefits
(4) Make heroes out of employees who save money	(4) Bake into your EPS forecasts the assumption that the innovation projects will make no contribution to earnings
(5) Develop an organization culture where rules are followed and successes are celebrated but then people begin to think about new challenges	(5) Hold the innovators accountable for portfolios of projects rather than stand-alone projects
(6) Focus on business process innovation that improves efficiency, rather than product innovation	(6) Develop an innovation culture:
	— do not punish new products for cannibalizing existing products;
(7) Have a relatively high dividend payout ratio and a moderate debt-to-total-assets ratio	— allow employees to spend a certain percentage of their time on ideas of their own choosing;
	— hire people whose skills are not apparently needed for the routine business;
	— let people disobey orders;
	— punish people for inaction, not failure
	(7) Have a low dividend payout ratio and a low debt-to-total-assets ratio

Fig. 24.1. Managing in tough times (super efficiency) versus innovating.

- Being a highly innovative organization requires the opposite competencies. It requires a venture capital mindset of funding portfolios of projects, each of which may have negative NPV as a stand-alone project. It requires a culture where people can "free-lance" and break the rules. The focus is on product innovation rather than business process innovation.
- Few, if any, organizations are successful at both. The innovators are usually not super efficient, and the super efficient are usually not great product innovators.

End-of-Chapter Exercises

1. Do an assessment of your organization using the criteria specified in Fig. 24.1 and determine where you would place your organization in the grid below.
2. Now choose some innovation metric (e.g., number of patents or percentage of sales from new products) and an efficiency metric (e.g., operating margin) and benchmark your organization against others within your industry and similar industries. Compute a percentile rank for your organization on each metric and determine where your organization would belong in the grid above.
3. Summarize key learnings and action steps from this exercise.

Practice Problems

1. What are key principles of success for being super efficient and managing in tough times? Why do these principles make sense?
2. Identify three companies you believe are super efficient and compare their key financial ratios that measure operating efficiency with those of others in their industries. What do you learn?
3. What are the key principles of being innovative? Why do these principles make sense?
4. Why is it difficult for a company to simultaneously excel at efficiency and innovation?
5. Identify three companies you believe are effective innovators and compare their key financial ratios to others in their industries. What do you learn?

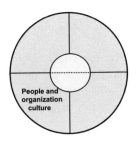

People and
organization
culture

Chapter 25

CORPORATE CULTURE: BRINGING
EVERYTHING TOGETHER

1. Marketing and Finance Clash

A few weeks after the post-acquisition Plan had been approved, an integration manager was appointed. Jerry could now turn his attention to other matters.

One issue he was particularly concerned about was a matter that had just come to his attention. Bruce Acito, his Senior Vice President of Marketing, had expressed a strong desire to increase the amount of money they were spending on new product development and other innovation initiatives. He also wanted to increase the value of the free coupons customers could collect when they were dissatisfied with a product they bought from Jerry's. Was not that consistent with the customer-focused philosophy embedded in the company's Value Sphere?

Bob disagreed. He thought they were spending enough money on marketing initiatives and it was not a good idea to spend any more.

Jerry decided to have a meeting with both of them. He was reminded of his earlier discussions with Bob about the choice between super efficiency and innovation. Was this dispute simply a resurfacing of that question?

2. The Meeting

Bruce and Bob arrived promptly for the meeting. Each executive stated his case. When Jerry responded only by sipping further on his orange-flavored lemonade, Bruce spoke up:

"You know I believe in shareholder value just as much as anybody. But we should also remember what being customer-focused really means. When L. L. Bean was starting out and customers began to complain about hunting boots whose leather uppers separated from their soles in water, the company replaced all their customers' boots for free. Nearly put the company out of business. But it profoundly impacted how the company would look at customers in the future."

Bob smiled and said, "That's a great story, Bruce. But for every L. L. Bean, there are dozens of companies out there that went bankrupt trying to please the customer. Walt Disney was one of the world's most customer-focused companies in 1984. But they didn't serve the shareholder, and it cost the CEO, Ron Miller, his job."

That was a little sneaky, thought Jerry, reflecting on Bob's reference to a CEO losing his job. No harm in spooking this CEO a bit to make your point!

Jerry decided he was not going to be able to decide this right away. There was a lot of money involved. And he did not just want this to be an ad hoc decision. Since he wanted more serious reflection, he concluded the meeting with a promise to get back to his executives. As Bruce left the room, Bob stayed behind.

"Jerry, there's another issue. I've been getting a lot of feedback from my people that they're having a hard time training the finance folks we've acquired in this acquisition. The main problem they are having is explaining our strategy in simple terms."

Jerry replied, "That's bothersome. Why do you think they're having trouble?"

Bob looked puzzled. "I don't know. Perhaps it's because our own people don't understand our strategy well. Perhaps it's because Mickey's people are befuddled by the newness of it all."

Jerry concluded the meeting by telling Bob he'd think about the matter as well.

3. An Integrated View Emerges

Jerry decided to call Charlie K. Peters, a professor and strategy consultant, for some advice. He told him about the two recent incidents.

"I don't want specific advice on how to handle just these two problems, C. K. But I think they are representative of broader issues on which I'd like to know if there's a good cognitive framework I can use to make decisions," was the mandate Jerry gave to Peters.

A month or so later, Peters met with Jerry. He handed him his report and also explained it. The meeting and the report cleared up a lot of things for Jerry.

A major theme of the Peters report was that there were a variety of tensions that every firm must resolve in managing its Value Sphere. And most of these tensions were related to balancing the short run and the long run, or, more generally, the conflicting interests of the company through time. Jerry was reminded of a quote from the movie, "Star Trek: Generations":

"Time is the fire in which we all burn."

3.1. The Peters Report

Every company has to internalize the fact that there are three types of focus a company can have in optimizing the management of its Value Sphere, as shown in Fig. 25.1.

The *Manufacturing Focus* phase can be best described as one involving an intense focus on the efficiency of manufacturing and technological innovation that leads to product design changes. This was the age of "Total Quantity." Firms like General Motors, U. S. Steel, and other behemoths exploited economics of scale in high-volume manufacturing to lower per–unit costs. The key to competitive survival was your manufacturing focus. Engineers were kings.

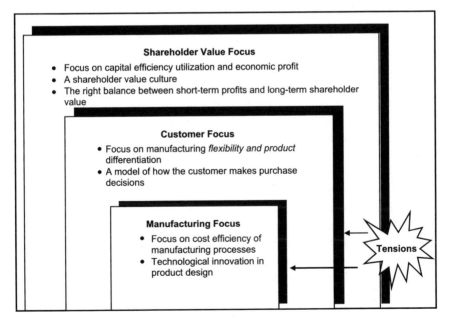

Fig. 25.1. The three faces of focus.

Then came "Total Quality Management." The focus shifted to the customer. Companies could no longer afford the Henry Ford motto, "The customer can have any color he wants, as long as it is black." *Customer focus* means having a model of how the customer makes purchase decisions. Understanding the customer and *anticipating* customer needs drive product design decisions. This calls for *flexible* manufacturing that is responsive to changes in product design.

For example, Wabash National, the world's largest manufacturer of customized and standard truck trailers, has an extremely flexible manufacturing facility. It can be reconfigured rather easily to handle a relatively large range of product design changes.

Achieving the appropriate customer focus is one of the hardest things for companies because they lack a good model of the customer. All that they do is keep copying each other's products. Not surprisingly, this leads to hypercompetition.

A *Shareholder Value Focus* is the highest focus. The focus is now on the *entire* value chain. The company must now attend to capital utilization efficiency and economic profit. It cannot, of course, ignore the cost and efficiency of manufacturing either. Furthermore, it is often impossible to create shareholder value if one does not understand the customer.

So, what we have is a box inside a box inside a box. A manufacturing focus is necessary for a customer focus. If you do not make a high-quality product, customers are not going to buy it. Look at any company that has a "dominant customer franchise." You will see high-quality and excellent product reliability. Examples are BMW and Lexus cars, iPod music players, and Louis Vuitton handbags.

But a manufacturing focus is *not sufficient* for a customer focus. You can make products with great utility and reliability that no one wants to buy at a price that will allow you to earn profits. Thus, the manufacturing focus box is entirely inside the customer focus box and smaller than it.

This means a shareholder value focus requires the company to have a manufacturing focus as well as a customer focus. But these two are not sufficient to be shareholder-value-focused.

What is important to note is that at the edges of boxes are unavoidable *tensions*. That is, there is a tension between being manufacturing-focused and being customer-focused. Manufacturing-focused firms tend to be dominated by their engineers and other manufacturing and technology (M and T) people. Their interest is to be given sufficient resources to make great products. It is up to the marketing people to figure out how to sell them.

On the other hand, in customer-focused firms, it is usually the marketing people who dominate. Their view is that they are the keepers of information about what the customer wants. The job of the M and T staff is to manufacture what they tell them to.

The tension between these two groups must be effectively resolved if the company is to synchronize its Value Sphere and create shareholder value. If the M and T people are allowed to dominate, there is a risk of churning out products that will not sell at sufficiently high margins. If the marketing people are allowed to dominate, there is danger that there will be uneconomically high product variety. The resulting stock keeping unit (SKU) complexity could drive up manufacturing costs to unacceptable levels.

There is also a tension between a customer focus and a shareholder-value focus. For example, Federal Express is a company commonly cited as being highly customer-focused. In fact, it is commonly benchmarked for its great customer focus. Yet, during 1987–94 it experienced a negative economic profit every single year! During that eight-year period, there was only one year (1988) that its economic profit was not worse than negative $100 million, when it was around negative $50 million. Even for those who believe in the long run, this would be disappointing shareholder value performance.

You have just seen an example of it in your company — the clash between your CFO and Senior Marketing VP.

Here the key is to understand that both finance and marketing are right. If you had no short-term concerns, then you may be well-advised to go with the recommendation of your marketing VP. Investing in things that will improve your appeal to your customers is obviously going to benefit you in the long run. But it is going to be costly. Your short-term financial results are likely to be adversely affected. This is what your CFO is worrying about.

Thus, the tension here is between the short run and the long run. It is a mistake to view short-term profits as being synonymous with shareholder value. In my opinion, shareholder value has two dimensions: a short-term dimension and a long-term dimension. To attend to shareholder value effectively, you must find the right balance along this time dimension of shareholder value.

How do you go about developing a shareholder value culture? As shown in the next diagram, you have to attend to the following.

All of these elements must harmoniously hold together and be driven by a single-minded focus on long-term shareholder value. All employees in your company should be able to describe what shareholder value means in terms of their activities.

From our conversations it appears you have already spent considerable time on your organization structure, information systems, the resource allocation system, and compensation system. You also have a clearly-defined vision. Your Value Sphere construct is very similar to my Fig. 25.2.

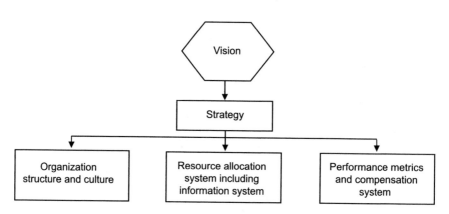

Fig. 25.2.   The elements of a shareholder value culture.

However, I do not believe your strategy is as clearly defined as it could be. I have prepared a strategy diagnostic instrument (Fig. 25.3) for you to use to refine your strategy.

To help Jerry understand the strategy diagnostic instrument better, Peters provided examples of companies that he thought had clearly-articulated strategies that were tied to the value drivers in their businesses — Executive Jet Aviation, Enterprise Car Rental, and Progressive Insurance. These are summarized in Fig. 25.4.

4. Jerry Reflects on the Report

Jerry liked the report. He would schedule a one-day retreat with the Executive Committee to conduct the strategy diagnostic instrument Peters had provided. Perhaps he would invite Peters as a facilitator. He realized that embedded in all this was the fundamental choice between super efficiency and innovation that he had not made yet. Perhaps the retreat would help make the choice.

Once that was over, other such diagnostic sessions could be cascaded down the rest of the organization. This should help to refine the strategy, clarify it to everybody, and get the desired buy-in.

Clearly, there was work to do. There always would be. But there was also a feeling of achievement and joy. It had been a long journey, and one that had been traveled well. Jerry had learned a lot from the experience — about business and about life.

He was glad to have people like Bob Butterfield on board. He had learned what shareholder value really meant. He now knew how to create it and how

To see if your strategy passes the test, subject it to the following questions:

1. How simple is the strategy statement?
2. What are the three most important activities it focuses your attention on?
3. Could everybody in the company remember what these three things are without having to refer to a manual?
4. Could you capture the essence of the strategy in a one-minute sound bite for a TV news reporter or an hourly employee?
5. What are the three most important activities that the company would have engaged in without the strategy statement that the strategy now *precludes*?
6. How much consensus is there in the company that a strategy is "right" for the company and will create significant shareholder value?

   Below the managerial level _____
   At the managerial level _____
   At the level of directors _____
   At the Vice-President level _____
   At the Executive Committee level _____

7. How effectively do you believe the strategy has been communicated to various levels in the organization?
8. How effectively has the strategy been linked to performance measures and rewards?
9. Are your business processes and resource allocation consistent with your strategy? If not, where do the gaps exist?
10. How effectively have you put in place mechanisms for supplying strategic feedback at various levels in the organization and for facilitating strategy review and learning?
11. How *different* is your company's strategy from the strategies of your major competitors?

Fig. 25.3. Does your strategy pass the test?

to minimize its evaporation. Most of all, he had learned that the key to share-holder value creation and managing the Value Sphere was people. Having the right people and creating an organization culture in which they feel empowered to give their best were essential. Every employee should feel like an owner, not an employee.

He had recently come across a book that claimed that a publicly-traded company could improve its market value as much as 30% with exactly the same strategy and external operating environment as before if it improved its management of the rest of

Company	Industry	Value driver	Strategy
(1) Executive Jet Aviation	Airlines	Cost of capital savings for corporate customers through flying-time consolidation	TO PROVIDE COMPANIES (CUSTOMERS) CORPORATE JET OWNERSHIP WITHOUT THE BURDEN OF OWNING AN ENTIRE JET. Customers are allowed "fractional ownerships" of corporate jets whereby a company buys a quarter or an eighth of an aircraft for a certain number of flying hours per day.
(2) Enterprise Car Rental	Automobile rental	Unmet consumer demand arising from auto repair shops not catering to customers' temporary transportation needs.	RENT CARS TO PEOPLE WHO REQUIRE A CAR TO REPLACE THE ONE THEY OWN WHILE IT IS BEING REPAIRED, OR SOME OTHER TEMPORARY SITUATION. Major auto car rental companies (e.g., Avis and Hertz) fight tooth and nail for market share in the business of renting cars to travelers at airports all over the world. But value being created for these companies' shareholders is limited. Enterprise addresses a different need. It recruits fresh college grads (unlike others' focus on hiring low-paid service employees) and rewards them highly to build profitable locations. Cars are delivered to customers' homes and picked up at the end of the rental.
(3) Progressive Insurance	Automobile insurance	Unmet market demand arising from a lack of recognition by the insurance industry that speeding tickets, per se, are not predictors of future accidents, but that *one* accident is a good predictor of future accidents.	PROVIDE AFFORDABLE CAR INSURANCE TO "NONSTANDARD" DRIVER (PERSON WITH THREE OR MORE SPEEDING TICKETS IN FIVE YEARS).

Fig. 25.4. Value drives and strategies of selected companies.

the Value Sphere.[225] Clearly, synchronizing the Value Sphere for Jerry's Lemonade and putting into practice the lessons he had learned could help the company grow and create more value than many other comparable companies, mused Jerry. All that was needed was the discipline to implement the key concepts and stay the course.

Main Lessons

- A company can have one of three different types of focus in managing its Value Sphere: manufacturing focus, customer focus, and shareholder value focus. A manufacturing focus is necessary for a customer focus but is not sufficient. That is, a customer focus requires a manufacturing focus and more. Similarly, a customer focus is necessary for a shareholder value focus but is not sufficient.
- Being manufacturing-focused requires excellence in low-cost, high-quality manufacturing processes. That is, operational excellence is central to a manufacturing focus.
- Being customer-focused requires a model of how the customer makes purchase decisions and what matters to the customer. That is, a "market awareness" is central to a customer focus.
- Being shareholder-value focused requires effectively resolving the tension between what is good for shareholders in the short run and what is good for them in the long run. That is, it requires a deep understanding of the entire Value Sphere and its evolution through time.
- The most critical requirement for long-term shareholder value creation is to have the right people who are properly trained, empowered, and incented.

End-of-Chapter Exercises

1. Which of the three phases of focus (see Fig. 25.1) do you believe your company is in?
2. Can you identify the specific tensions that exist in your organization at the intersections of the different types of focus? What organizational initiatives do you have to deal with these tensions?
3. Administer the strategy test outlined in Fig. 25.3 to various groups (at different levels) in your company. Then compare the responses to see the differences. What do these differences indicate? What do you need to do?

---

[225]See Anjan V. Thakor, *Becoming a Better Value Creator: Improving Your Company's Bottom Line and Your Own*; Jossey-Bass Publishers, July 2000.

Practice Problems

1. Describe manufacturing focus, customer focus, and shareholder focus and explain how these are related and how they differ.
2. Can you identify at least one company that fits each of the three foci identified above? Write an essay on the operating philosophy and culture of each company and what you learn from it.
3. What is the relationship between the concepts of super efficiency and innovation on the one hand and manufacturing, customer and shareholder focus on the other?

Index